Detraditionalization

Detraditionalization

Critical Reflections on Authority and Identity

Edited by
Paul Heelas
Scott Lash
and
Paul Morris

Centre for the Study of Cultural Values at
Lancaster University

Copyright © Blackwell Publishers Ltd 1996, except for the following:
chapter 6 copyright © John B. Thompson 1996; chapter 10 copyright © Richard Sennett
1996; chapter 14 copyright © Mark Poster 1996.

First published 1996
2 4 6 8 10 9 7 5 3 1

Blackwell Publishers Inc.
238 Main Street
Cambridge, Massachusetts 02142, USA

Blackwell Publishers Ltd
108 Cowley Road
Oxford OX4 1JF
UK

Library of Congress Cataloging-in-Publication Data

De-traditionalization : critical reflections on authority and identity
  at a time of uncertainty / edited by Paul Heelas, Scott Lash, and
  Paul Morris.
    p. cm.
  Papers from a 1993 conference organized by the Centre for the
Study of Cultural Values at Lancaster University.
  Includes bibliographical references and index.
  ISBN 1-55786-554-X. — ISBN 1-55786-555-8 (pbk.)
    1. Social values—Congresses. 2. Group identity—Congresses.
3. Acculturation—Congresses. 4. Civilization, Modern—20th
century—Congresses. 5. Postmodernism—Social aspects—Congresses.
I. Heelas, Paul. II. Lash, Scott. III. Morris, Paul (Paul M.)
IV. Lancaster University. Centre for the Study of Cultural Values.
HM73. D45   1996
303.4—dc20   95–14818
                                     CIP

British Library Cataloguing in Publication Data

A CIP catalogue record for this book is available from the
British Library.

Typeset in 10^1/$_2$ on 12 pt Garamond 3
by Graphicraft Typesetters Ltd., Hong Kong
Printed in Great Britain by T.J. Press Limited, Padstow, Cornwall

This book is printed on acid-free paper

Contents

Preface

The papers presented in this volume largely derive from an international conference held in 1993. The conference, 'Detraditionalization: Authority and Self in an Age of Cultural Uncertainty,' was organized by the Centre for the Study of Cultural Values at Lancaster University. Founded in 1988, the Centre initially addressed the values of the enterprise culture. Having moved on to a related topic – contemporary forms of consumption, in particular the 'authority' of the consumer – it then decided to turn to a different research theme. However, this theme – to do with the role played by tradition in identity provision – soon evolved so as to incorporate earlier concern with individualized renderings of cultural values. The outcome thus has to do with both individualized and traditionalized modes of authority and identity.

Unfortunately, it is not possible to acknowledge all those who have contributed to the events – the 1993 conference (with some 110 speakers), public lectures, workshops, and other Centre activities – which have addressed traditions and detraditionalization. Especial thanks, though, are due to the multidisciplinary team with whom we worked to organize the conference: Sara Barnes, Deirdre Boden, Mick Dillon, Suzette Heald and Nigel Whiteley, Even more gratitude must be paid to the Assistant to the Centre, Eileen Martin, for all her efforts in administering the conference and helping prepare this volume.

We would also like to acknowledge the support afforded by the Economic and Social Research Council, the Goethe Institut of Manchester, Lancaster University's Committee for Research and the University's Departments of Religious Studies, Sociology and Visual Arts.

List of Contributors

THE EDITORS

Paul Heelas, Reader in Religion and Modernity, Department of Religious Studies, Lancaster University, UK.

Scott Lash, Professor of Sociology, Department of Sociology, Lancaster University, UK.

Paul Morris, Senior Lecturer, Department of Religious Studies, Lancaster University, UK; Professor in Religious Studies and Head of Department of Religious Studies, University of Victoria at Wellington, New Zealand.

The editors are all members of the Management Committee of the Centre for the Study of Cultural Values at Lancaster University. Paul Heelas is also Director of the Centre.

LIST OF CONTRIBUTORS

Barbara Adam, School of Social and Administrative Studies, University of Wales, UK.

Zygmunt Bauman, Emeritus Professor, University of Leeds, UK.

Ulrich Beck, Institute for Sociology, Munich University, Germany.

Elisabeth Beck-Gernsheim, Institute for Sociology, Hamburg University, Germany.

Colin Campbell, Department of Sociology, University of York, UK.

Paul Heelas, Department of Religious Studies, Lancaster University, UK.

Scott Lash, Department of Sociology, Lancaster University, UK.

Thomas Luckmann, Department of Sociology, Konstanz University, Germany.

Niklas Luhmann, Faculty of Sociology, Bielefeld University, Germany.

Timothy W. Luke, Department of Political Science, Virginia Polytechnic Institute and State University, USA.

Paul Morris, Department of Religious Studies, Lancaster University, UK; Department of Religious Studies, University of Victoria at Wellington, New Zealand.

Mark Poster, Department of History, University of California, Irvine, USA.

Nikolas Rose, Department of Sociology, Goldsmiths College, University of London, UK.

Richard Sennett, Department of History, New York University, USA.

John B. Thompson, Jesus College, Cambridge, UK.

1

Introduction: Detraditionalization and its Rivals

Paul Heelas

The heart wants what the heart wants.

Woody Allen

Writing of the earlier seventeenth century, Christopher Hill notes that the Church 'guided all the movements of men from baptism to the burial service . . . the Church controlled men's feelings and told them what to believe . . . this is why men took notes at sermons' (1959, pp. 10–11). Our times are clearly very different. All those politicians, public commentators and academics who announce the demise of tradition surely have good grounds for doing so. They can point to the loss of faith in once familiar landmarks, in long-standing values, more specifically in religion (less than 10 per cent now go to church on Sunday), in the family (single people now make up a quarter of all British households), in the monarchy and in the political system (over 40 per cent of people under the age of 25 did not vote in 1992). However, although it cannot be denied that detraditionalization has taken place, it is nevertheless possible to argue that claims that we have lurched – or are lurching – into a post-traditional age are highly contestable. The worldwide resurgence of nationalism and ethnic conflict, together with the development of divisive forms of multiculturalism or politics of cultural difference, are among the factors which count heavily against those who see the individual *qua* individual ruling our times. So, too, is the consideration that great swathes of the populace would appear to have quite distinctive and enclosed ways of life.

This volume is designed to contribute to the growing debate concerning the extent to which our age has moved beyond tradition. Claims that we have entered a post-traditional or post-modern period have not lost momentum. Nevertheless, they are increasingly being subjected to criticism, revision or qualification. The volume thus attends to a number of specific questions. Have traditions, and all they stand for, indeed been left behind? If so, what does the post-traditional world look like? if not, what roles – perhaps modified – do traditions continue to play? Should processes of detraditionalization be explained in connection with other processes serving to encourage traditional forms of life, or is the task simplified by having to explain detraditionalization as an all-conquering development?

A DEFINITION AND TWO SCENARIOS

As a working definition, detraditionalization involves a shift of authority: from 'without' to 'within'. It entails the decline of the belief in pre-given or natural orders of things. Individual subjects are themselves called upon to exercise authority in the face of the disorder and contingency which is thereby generated. 'Voice' is displaced from established sources, coming to rest with the self.

Theorizing which accords a *pre-eminent* role to this shift can be distinguished from theorizing which sees detraditionalization taking its place *alongside*, or *together with*, tradition-maintenance, re-traditionalization and the construction of new traditions. The first of these options – henceforth called *the radical thesis* – is well-formulated by (critically-minded) John Thompson. As he puts it, 'One of the most powerful legacies of classical social thought is the idea that, with the development of modern societies, tradition gradually declines in significance and eventually ceases to play a meaningful role in the lives of most individuals' (below, chapter 6). Given this powerful legacy (owing much to Enlightenment optimism concerning the engineering of detraditionalization), and given the popularity of claims attending to the post-modern condition (itself seen as comprehensively detraditionalized), it is not surprising that many still think in terms of the radical, end-of-tradition thesis. Paul Piccone, for example, shows no hesitation in introducing a recent issue of *Telos* (1993–4) with the claim, 'Clearly, today traditions are so eroded that they seem to pose no obstacle to anything', and indeed writes of their 'demise' (p. 3); and Anthony Giddens asserts that 'the radical turn from tradition intrinsic to modernity's reflexivity makes a break . . . with preceding eras' (1991, pp. 175–6).

Somewhat to our surprise, however, many of the contributors to the conference on which this volume is based have decided to argue against such a 'triumphalist' version of detraditionalization. They advocate versions of what shall henceforth be called *the coexistence thesis*. (The term is drawn from

Timothy Luke (chapter 7) and Barbara Adam (chapter 8).) Detraditionalization might indeed have taken place. But rather than being envisaged as leading to across-the-board eradication of all traditions, it is seen as competing, interpenetrating or interplaying with processes to do with tradition-maintenance, rejuvenation and tradition-construction. And from this point of view, those *periodizing* contrasts (of the modernity v. late modernity/post-modernity variety), associated with radical before-and-after theorizing, are seen as unable to handle the multivocal complexities of our times.

THE RADICAL THESIS

The difference, then, is between radical and coexistence theorizing. Concentrating for the moment on the first, advocates think in terms of oppositions: closed (cold, repetitive, ritualized) v. open (hot, experimental, revisable); fate (or the pre-ordained) v. choice (or reflexivity); necessity v. contingency; certainty v. uncertainty; security v. risk; differentiated (or organized) culture v. the de-differentiated (or disorganized); the embedded (situated or socio-centric) self v. the disembedded (de-situated or autonomous); self under control v. self in control; and virtues v. preferences (with values coming in between). With each opposition informed by a basic 'past to present/future' dynamic, detraditionalization involves the *replacement* of the closed (etc.) with the open (etc.). And as the importance attached to replacement serves to indicate, the characteristics of the past and the present tend to be conceived in a mutually exclusive fashion. That is to say, traditional cultures are seen as dominated by fate or the embedded, largely – if not entirely – excluding choice or the disembedded. And the converse applies to conditions designated as high modernity or post-modernity.[1]

Looking at this somewhat more closely, key points derive from the claim that traditional societies are informed by belief in established, timeless orders. Such overarching orders, rooted in past events – or simply 'the past' – and legitimated by such association, are highly authoritative. Existing over-and-above the individual, they are 'sacred' in the Durkheimian sense of the term. That is, serving to convey the wisdom of the timeless, they cannot be questioned. Inviolate, they cannot be modified or revised in the light of utilitarian or any other version of self-informed calculation. Accordingly, selves are embedded in pre-given orders of things. Persons think in terms of 'external' (supra-individual) voices of authority, control, and destiny. Living the good life, solving problems, seeking advancement or obtaining salvation are matters of obeying over-and-above the self, loci of duty, obligation, obedience and entitlement. Constituted as the person is by position in the order of things, there is little (or no) scope and incentive to exercise autonomy or freedom of expression.

Given that thought is directed in terms of others – divine or socio-cultural vehicles of membership – this *order of the self* is by definition collectivistic or communal. It is other-informed or socio-centric rather than self-informed or individualistic. As Durkheim, for example, makes the point, 'the individual personality is lost in the depths of the social mass' (1992, p. 56). And claims of this variety lead on to a related point, namely that traditional formations are generally (although not always) held to be exclusivist. With the self *belonging* to (as informed or constituted by) a particular and true order, what does not belong (namely selves belonging to alien or different orders) is not accorded equivalent dignity. 'Our way is the right way; you are excluded, rendered inferior, because you do not follow our immemorial path.'

Generally speaking, then, the tradition-informed way of life is hierarchically differentiated: both within particular traditions, and with regard to how other ways of life are evaluated. Little or no validity is accorded to those who might attempt to speak with their own, out-of-place voice. Identities are inscribed, rather than being at stake for discursive controversy. Indeed, the authorial taken-for-grantedness of identities precludes the necessity of questioning those discourses which serve to legitimate the order of things.

Detraditionalization, the argument continues, cannot occur when people think of themselves as belonging to the whole. For detraditionalization entails that people have acquired the opportunity to stand back from, critically reflect upon, and lose their faith in what the traditional has to offer. They have to arrive at a position where they can have *their own* say. But why should this shift of authority take place? Without going too deeply into this complicated matter, an important set of considerations has to do with processes which undermine the authoritative or 'sacred' properties of cultural metanarratives. One such process concerns technology, to do with the speeding up of communication. With components from different cultures becoming more and more available in any particular cultural setting, the cultural realm becomes more pluralistic. Cultures come to contain a fragmented, variegated range of beliefs and values. Faced with diversity, it is then suggested, people lose faith in what has been traditionally sustained by way of socialization within a closed environment. The choices afforded by multivocal culture serve to confuse. Differentiation serves to undermine the exclusivistic claims and credibility of what was previously homogeneous and therefore unquestioned. In sum, 'plausibility structures' lose their credibility – even collapse.

Another process – now concerning the marketing technologies of capitalism

– is also widely seen as contributing to the devalidation of external voices of authority. 'The cultural logic of late capitalism', to use Fredric Jameson's (1991) phrase, refers to the ways in which capitalistic producers seek to increase sales. Crucially, for present purposes, this has involved the construction of mass consumer culture: one in which the consumer has the right, or authority, to purchase commodified forms of cultural items. And to cater for the consumer, high culture becomes trivialized; becomes sanitized; is rendered undemanding. The auratic disappears. Religion, which once served to regulate human passion, increasingly becomes a way of pleasuring the self, and one which can on occasion be purchased. The Gulf War is 'sold' as a media spectacle. Universities lose many of their 'professional' humanistic standards in face of demand for vocationally-effective degrees. In short, to the extent that the cultural realm is adjusted to accommodate and titillate the consumer, it loses much of its challenging, ethically or aesthetically demanding qualities. There is less to have faith in; less to challenge self-interest.[2]

So for these reasons and others, organized culture – sustained voices of moral and aesthetic authority serving to differentiate values, to distinguish between what is important and what is not, to facilitate coherent, purposeful, identities, life-plans or habits of the heart – has disintegrated. (Witness an entry in the *Daily Telegraph*, announcing the deaths of Frank Zappa and the Earl of Bessborough and placing the latter – a high bastion of the establishment – on the lower half of the page.) The fact that culture has become increasingly disorganized and weakened, it can then be argued, means that people have to turn to their own resources to decide what they value, to organize their priorities and to make sense of their lives. That is to say, the weakening of traditional bonds to cultural values, social positions, religion, marriage and so on, means that people find themselves in the position where they have to select from those packaged options or styles to which the cultural realm has been reduced in order to construct their own ways of life.

But this process of individualization, it can also be argued, is not simply due to the self being 'thrown back' upon itself; being forced to take refuge in its own subjectivity. Attention is also directed to the role played by those practices which have contributed to the perceived *value* of being an autonomous and self-responsible agent. Historically, one might think of the role ascribed to the Reformation, the Enlightenment, the Romantic movement, individualistic capitalism, the liberal ethic and democracy. More recently, one might think of the construction of the 'sovereign' consumer, the 'enterprising' individual, and the 'therapeutic' self. Whatever their differences – and there are many – such developments have encouraged detraditionalization by cultivating the capacities or authority of the individual: the right to elect governments rather than remaining dutiful to historical orders; the view that values are (largely) a matter of individual choice rather than being pre-determined; the belief that one should be true to oneself rather than simply heeding others; the freedom to move in and out of marriages – or religions – rather than having to remain faithful; the assumption that consumer choice can fashion individual identity rather than consumption being regulated by socio-culturally provided modes of identity provision.

Finally, by way of introducing the radical thesis, it remains to spell out some of the main ways in which our (supposedly) detraditionalized age is portrayed. One stance – vividly seen in Francis Fukuyama's *The End of History* (1992) – is couched in terms of the Enlightenment project. Rational selves come to agree that life is best led in terms of a liberal ethic: clearly quite detraditionalized, although taken to be substantive enough to ensure the smooth functioning of social and individual affairs. A related but different stance – seen, for example, in Allan Bloom's *The Closing of the American Mind* (1987) – is that egalitarian ('respect the other') values have ensured that the liberal ethic has virtually ceased to have any substantive content. Having become arch-relativists – bar the basic value of respecting the other – we no longer know what to believe in; we no longer know how to discriminate between the different ways in which cultures conceive the good and bad in life.

Or one might approach the matter by way of the distinction – found, for example, in Robert Bellah et al.'s *Habits of the Heart* (1985) – between utilitarian and expressive individualism. Both these modes are detraditionalized in that what matters is heeding those voices which come from the self: respectively, the desires associated with 'self-interest' and the feelings or intuitions associated with 'authenticity'. In both cases, traditional formations – with their attempts to regulate selves in ways which might well not correspond with the demands of voices from within – are regarded with suspicion if not contempt. And, as many researchers have claimed, both modes are rampant: utilitarian individualism is central to portrayals of con-sumer culture and 'the culture of contentment' (Galbraith, 1992); expressivist individualism is central to what Ronald Inglehart (1990) calls 'postmaterialist' culture; and utilitarian-cum-expressive individualism is central to Alasdair MacIntyre's (1985) 'emotivist culture' or Christopher Lasch's (1980) 'narcis-sistic' rendering.[3]

There are many quite different ways of characterizing the detraditionalized morality and selfhood. Indeed, not all accord much – if any – identity and authority to the individual. One might think of Peter Berger et al.'s (1974) portrayal of the confused and inchoate 'homeless mind'. Somewhat more radically, one might consider those theorists who introduce the term 'post-modern' to highlight the fact that the 'self' has ceased to exist. (Jameson, for example, writes of 'the "death" of the subject itself – the end of the autonomous bourgeois monad or ego or individual' (1991, p. 15).) As already noted, taken to its egalitarian – and therefore relativistic – extreme, the liberal ethic ceases to provide any determinate sense of moral identity: a feature called post-modern by Ernest Gellner (1992), for example. It can also be argued that the intensification of consumer culture has resulted in the disintegration of whatever sense of identity the utilitarian self might have been able to achieve. The idea here is that that collection of desires, wishes, needs and ambitions – which comprise the utilitarian self – become yet more fragmented and dispersed as the 'subject' is invaded, taken over, by a whole range of variegated consumer-seductions. In short, whatever the role which the shift to the self might have played in detraditionalization, theorists of post-modernity typically see detraditionalization leading to a world where the person ceases to be able to act as a coherent or determinate moral subject; where the person dissolves into whatever consumer delights are on offer.[4]

THE COEXISTENCE THESIS

The best way to emphasize detraditionalization is to posit a comprehensively tradition-dominated past, a comprehensively post-traditional present/future, and to attend solely to those processes which serve to detraditionalize. In contrast, the best way to criticize the (radical) loss-of-tradition thesis is to argue that 'the traditional' (serving to gauge what has been lost) is not as tradition-dominated as might be supposed, that 'the modern/post-modern' is not as detraditionalized as might be claimed, and that detraditionalizing processes do not occur in isolation from other processes, namely those to do with tradition-maintenance and the construction – or reconstruction – of traditional forms of life.

Most comprehensively formulated, coexistence theory holds that people – whether 'pre-modern'/'traditional', 'modern' or even 'post-modern'/'post-traditional' – *always* live in terms of those typically conflicting demands associated, on the one hand, with voices of authority emanating from realms transcending the self *qua* self, and, on the other, with those voices emanating from the desires, expectations, and competitive or idiosyncratic aspirations of the individual. As advocates of coexistence might ask: is it really reasonable to suppose that 'traditional' societies can swallow up the person to the extent of muting or denying the exercise of autonomous voices, or to suppose that dwellers in 'modern' or 'post-modern' societies are content, let alone able, to live with little or no guidance from determinate orders?

Concentrating as it does on the contemporary world, this volume does not provide the occasion for systematically exploring coexistence claims as they bear on 'traditional' or 'pre-modern' settings. However, the matter cannot be ignored entirely. For if indeed such societies are less tradition-dominated than they have often been portrayed, one has to question the extent to which detraditionalization has taken place.

Timothy Luke (chapter 7) argues that 'Traditions are no more than traces of practices, signs of belief, and images of continuity revealed in human thought and action, which are continuously sent and chaotically received throughout all the generations.' The point is that traditions are never simply received as pre-given verities. Traditions are always open to human agency. The 'inviolates' of traditions are always subject to some degree of questioning or revision. Thus, as anthropologists have come to emphasize, small-scale, supposedly isolated or closed societies are far from being 'islands'. Such societies are pluralistic, at least in the sense of knowing about alternative ways of life (most obviously those followed by their neighbours). It follows that participants cannot be entirely unreflexive about their own beliefs. More significantly, however, anthropologists are also increasingly emphasizing the fact that small-scale societies are internally pluralistic. Approaching 'the traditional' from different points of view – from their own individual, political or socially-defined positions – participants do not see things in the same way. Accordingly, 'the traditional' is interpreted in different ways. In the words of Renato Rosaldo (who is specifically referring to the Ilongot of northern Luzon), life is 'more actively constructed than passively received' (1980, p. 22).[5]

Historians, too, are at work deconstructing the essentialist 'past *as* traditional' viewpoint. A considerable amount of evidence now counts against the claim that the cultural history of the West can be periodized in terms of a clear-cut break with '*the* traditional'. The classic formulation of such a rupture, involving the liberation of individual agency and reflexivity, was provided by Jacob Burckhardt. In a famous passage, we read that during the Middle Ages 'Man was conscious of himself only as a member of a race, people, party, family, or corporation – only through some general category' (1890, p. 129). Although historians today might well agree that Italy saw the development of certain aspects of individualism, few are now happy with the Burckhardtian portrayal of the Mediaeval self as other-dominated and embedded. As Alan Macfarlane, perhaps controversially, argues, 'individualism in economic and social life is much older than [the Renaissance] in

England. In fact within the recorded period [from the thirteenth century] covered by our documents, it is not possible to find a time when an Englishman did not stand alone . . . in the centre of his world' (1978, p. 196).[6]

Evidence of individualizing – and therefore detraditionalizing – tendencies in the past (or in small-scale societies) helps ground the coexistence thesis as a whole. But the crux of the matter, so far as the focus of this volume is concerned, clearly has to do with ascertaining whether or not traditionalizing processes remain important today. The converse of the coexistence claim that people are never *simply* tradition-informed is that neither are people *simply* autonomous. Ideologies of the autonomous self might be important today, but the fact remains that we are socio-cultural beings. Our voices of authority might appear to come from within ourselves, but have been acquired in terms of established values and practices. We can, of course, speak as individuals. What we cannot do is speak as individuals without being informed by all those sustained voices of external authority which – alone – can give enough 'shape' to our lives to enable us to act as identifiable *subjects*.

Together with providing theoretical objections – of the variety just introduced – to the notion that societies can become radically detraditionalized or post-traditional, coexistence theorists also seek empirical evidence to support their cause. Without denying that detraditionalization has taken place, the argument is that this has not resulted in the systematic collapse of authoritative cultural voices. Evidence pertaining to the operation of 'cultural contradictions' (Daniel Bell, 1976), different 'moral sources' (Charles Taylor, 1989), the 'wars' of cultural identity politics (John Fiske, 1993), the 'competing moral visions' seen in controversies over such matters as abortion (James Hunter, 1994) or 'tribal' identities (Michael Maffesoli, 1994) can be drawn upon to argue that culturally *differentiated* or *fragmented* responses to pluralism must be considered alongside claims to do with the de-differentiated or relativized collapse of established values. For evidence of this kind surely indicates that differentiated components confront each other with the kind of authority which can only come from the operation – however 'invented' – of the tradition-authenticated.

Another line of argument is to draw attention to what might be called *quasi-traditions*. One of the great advantages of thinking in terms of the *process* of 'detraditionalization' is that attention can be focused on that which might be relatively detraditionalized but which nevertheless serves to provide sustained voices of established authority. In practice – and despite the language of autonomy and choice – we are controlled by routines, rules, procedures, regulations, laws, duties, schedules, diaries, timetables and customs. Companies have their own ways of doing things.[7] Universities operate with a sacrosanct order of values – specifically those spelling out what counts as success – which, together with the timetable, serve to dominate the lives of students and staff. Consumer activities show distinct signs of being profoundly routinized and regulated. The great majority of tourists like to follow each other; year after year, Coronation Street remains the most popular TV programme, helping fix the evening schedule for some fifteen million viewers. (With particular attention to consumption, George Ritzer (1993) argues that society is becoming 'McDonaldized'. Drawing on Max Weber's analysis of modernity as an 'iron cage', an important feature of this process has to do with control and the closure of choice.) Then it might be argued that 'experts', apparently functioning to inform choice, actually serve to perpetuate specific values and beliefs. For example, rather than facilitating expressivist or personal authenticity in their clientele, the claim is that therapists (etc.) serve to encourage the transmission of a well-established body of truth. The 'reflexive projects' and 'freedoms' of the expressivist are thereby routinized. 'Choice' ceases to be choice in any significant sense of the term. (Cf. Strathern, 1992.) In addition, there is the argument that the very faith in the value of individual autonomy is tradition-informed. This point is surely implied by Bellah et al.'s characterization of contemporary culture, namely: that 'We believe in the dignity, indeed the *sacredness* of the individual. Anything that would violate our right to think for ourselves, judge for ourselves, make our own decisions, live our lives as we see fit, is not only morally wrong, it is *sacrilegious*' (1985, p. 142, my emphases).

Briefly turning to how an age of coexistence can be portrayed by reference to what it means for the person, there are at least three responses to culturally diverse modes of being. In contrast to the picture painted by radical detraditionalization theorists, the scenario here is of people having to handle a range of alternatives. The person might live a contradictory if not schizophrenic life, oscillating, for example, between the contextualized demands of public life – which are relatively traditionalized – and the relatively detraditionalized freedoms of the private realm. (Prince Charles would appear to provide a good illustration of (hybridized) oscillation, on the one hand shooting foxes in accord with his upbringing, and on the other talking to trees in accord with that spirituality which lies beyond particular religious traditions.) Alternatively, the person might synthesize or amalgamate what would appear to be mutually-exclusive cultural components. Yuppies, at least during the 1980s, might drink champagne and practice yoga. But the yoga has been detraditionalized. That is to say, it has become a simple matter of combatting stress. And thirdly, consider the person who has affiliated to a particular mode of being. Fundamentalist Christians, for instance, attempt

– with varying degrees of success – to reject the alternatives which face them in everyday life.

Overall, the coexistence approach builds on the work of all those theorists – including Bell, Bellah and Taylor – who see our times as a mixture of various trajectories, from the more tradition-informed to the more individualized. The working assumption of the approach – namely that investigation reveals the universal operation of a variety of processes – is backed up by theoretical claims concerning the impossibility of purely tradition-informed and purely autonomous modes of being. Attention is thereby shifted from attempting to characterize or periodize societies as 'traditional' or 'post-traditional', dominated by 'fate' or by 'choice'. Such designations are seen as being unable to handle the complexity of states of affairs and processes in particular settings. This shift of attention, however, does not rule out the possibility of arguing that certain peoples, for example, have more elaborated ideologies of autonomy than others, or have more opportunities to exercise choice in such matters as as religion, marriage or consumption. And in such specific regards, it is surely possible to refer to them as being *relatively* detraditionalized.

THE CONTRIBUTIONS

The volume is divided into four parts. The reader is asked to bear in mind that allocation to these sections is only designed to emphasize the main thrust of chapters. Contributors also make points which intersect, complement (or contradict) those made by others.

Part I – 'Losing the Traditional' – dwells on radical, and therefore periodizable change. Ulrich Beck and Elisabeth Beck-Gernsheim (chapter 2) theorize change in terms of 'individualization', an important aspect of which concerns the disintegration of previously existing social forms, even routines. 'What is historically new', they write, 'is that something that was earlier expected of a few – to lead a life of their own – is now being demanded of more and more people.' In particular, they dwell on marriage, charting the fact that 'whereas marriage was earlier first and foremost an institution *sui generis* raised above the individual, today it is becoming more and more a product and construct of the individuals forming it'. Zygmunt Bauman (chapter 3), thinking along much the same lines, arguably presents a bleaker portrayal. The untying or disencumbering of identities, the crumbling of belief in foundational morality, as well as other factors, are associated with the development of the age contingency, an age which has seen the rise to prominence of the 'vagabond' and the 'tourist'. (At the same time, however, Bauman closes on an optimistic note, referring to a post-modern ethic stemming from 'the moral capacity of the self'.) Like Bauman, Niklas Luhmann (chapter 4) draws attention to the significance today of contingency and preference. These characteristics are theorized in terms of a break which is held to have taken place – especially during the latter half of the eighteenth century – from society differentiated according to the principle of stratification to society differentiated according to the principle of function. A key point is that 'functional differentiation makes possible greater complexity than does stratification'. The 'contingency' which is thereby generated, it is then suggested, means that 'a need arises for new "inviolate levels"'; a 'need that the semantics of value satisfy, and which in turn pronounces them unavoidable today'. Finally, Thomas Luckmann's (chapter 5) basic contention – resonating with themes discussed in this part of the volume – is that functional specialization has meant that 'the eminently social reality of morals and religion [have] found their location in the most singular "institution", the individual person'. Among other considerations this means that an ethics of 'motive and subjective disposition' has (largely) replaced 'a traditional or dogmatized ethics of responsibility and accountability'.

Although these four contributions are arguing for what we are calling the radical thesis, it is not without significance that aspects of the coexistence approach are also introduced. The Becks, for example, criticize the notion of 'unfettered' autonomy, drawing attention to the 'institutional reference points marking out the horizon within which modern thinking, planning and action must take place'; and Luhmann refers to 'new "inviolate levels"'. Such considerations lead to the next section of the volume, where the coexistence thesis is more systematically addressed and advocated.

Part II – 'Detraditionalization and Traditions Today' – follows on from the first in that contributors accept that detraditionalization has taken place. However, none sees detraditionalization as a process leading to the eradication of what is informed by the past. Instead, all refer to various ways in which traditions continue to operate. Accordingly, there is a strong tendency for contributors to be unhappy with a periodized contrast between tradition and modernity.

John Thompson (chapter 6) considers some of the ways in which the role of tradition has 'been refashioned by the expansion of mediated forms of communication'. Although he is not happy with the term 'detraditionalization' – associating it with claims concerning post-traditional society – it is apparent that the process is accepted. However, the decline of certain functions of tradition goes together with increased reliance on others: 'the decline of traditional authority and the traditional grounding of action does not spell the demise of tradition but rather signals a shift in its nature and role, as individuals come to rely more and more on mediated and de-localized traditions as a means of making sense of the world and of creating a sense of belonging'. Like Thompson, Timothy Luke (chapter 7) is highly critical of what he describes as the 'enduring' idea that there is a continuous struggle between 'the powers of tradition' and 'the forces of modernity'. One criticism is that traditions require reflexive subjects and *vice versa*. A related criticism is that it is possible to find ample evidence of 'tradition-in-modernity' or 'modernity-as-tradition'. Indeed, one should not overlook 'how "traditional" modernity has become'. At the same time, however, Luke explores how the 'destabilization' of spatially-specific and spatially-defined 'sites' serves to 'detraditionalize practices by collapsing the settings and accelerating the meter of human action'. (Interesting comparisons might be made with Thompson in this regard.) Barbara Adam's contribution (chapter 8) is another sustained critique of the oppositional, 'once there was and now there is' formulation of detraditionalization. Arguing, like Luke, that all societies have traditions and that 'reflexivity is ontological to all of humanity', Adam replaces the 'either-or' with the 'and'. Because there is 'a multitude of modernities', including those traditions which are 'central' to the complex and those features which are associated with reflexivity, theorizing should concentrate on 'coexistence' and 'interpenetration' rather than on 'replacement'. Finally, although Colin Campbell (chapter 9), who closes this section, accepts that (quite radical) detraditionalization has taken place, his contribution is included here because he also rejects any clear-cut distinction between the past and the present. In particular, 'habit' belongs to both the traditional past and the present of modernity. When other features of the traditional pass away, habit serves to perpetuate aspects (or quasi-aspects) of what it is to be tradition-informed. Accordingly, 'not only is the modernist dream of a completely reflexive actor an impossibility, but so too is the idea of a personal and social world without traditions'.

Part III – 'Detraditionalization, Human Values and Solidarity' – has much in common with that which precedes it. What is distinctive, however, is that detraditionalization and traditionalization are examined with specific focus on new(ish) traditions – as well as on the role which tradition should play – to do with ways of relating to others. The section is thus more normative – and increasingly more philosophical – contributors dwelling on the value of particular forms of relationship.

Richard Sennett (chapter 10) explores 'a fundamental conflict in our civilization', 'between the truth-claims of place and beginnings versus the truths

to be discovered in becoming a foreigner'. He traces the development of a
new form of nationalism, one which 'began to find its voice in the [French]
Revolution of 1848' and which 'marks a distinct version of collective identity
in our civilization'. This powerfully traditionalized mode of belonging, it is
argued, has contributed to the difficulties of being a foreigner. Modern nationalism has 'made those who leave their nations seem like surgical patients
who have suffered an amputation'. At the same time, however, Sennett
emphasizes the virtues – 'the positive moral value' – which can ensue when
people are 'displaced' from their 'roots'. Of particular note, the experience of
being a foreigner is seen as playing a crucial role in combating 'pluralistic
self-enclosure in ethnicity' with all its associated threats to 'liberty'. The
foreigner, asserting that 'one has rights as a political animal, a *zoon politikon*,
wherever one lives' counters that modern ground-rule of identity which
'threatens constantly to restrict personal freedom to cultural practice'. Accordingly, the foreigner can help 'defeat the segregating game of pluralism';
can 'force the dominant society to acknowledge that there is . . . a public
sphere beyond the borders of [communitarian] anthropology'; indeed, is 'the
only way to survive being personally imprisoned in a Balkanized, unequal
city of differences'. In a number of regards, then, Sennett's contribution is an
attack on the ('illiberal') features of what has come to be known as the
politics of cultural difference. 'Experiencing *difference*' – 'at the expense of
community' – the foreigner re-envisages 'others and oneself as concrete,
particular human beings rather than as cultural types'. And the foreigner
thus stands for liberal, co-operative or socialist values.

Paul Heelas (chapter 11) discusses similar, if not identical values. Drawing
on Durkheim's analysis, he argues that detraditionalization has played an
important role in ensuring that 'the ethic of humanity' has become a powerful, if not the dominant tradition of our times. Having developed at the
expense of traditionalized communities and their specific ethics of identity,
the universalized ethic of humanity nevertheless serves as a kind of community. Adherents belong to a cultural formation (or 'type' in Sennett's usage)
constituted by that which is taken 'to be human'. Sense of identity is significantly influenced by the sense of belonging to – being bound up with –
humanity as a whole. And, it is claimed, the authority of humanity serves as
an important bulwark against processes which encourage relativized moral
collapse or stimulate exclusivistic forms of communal identity. In contrast
to Heelas, Paul Morris (chapter 12) rejects a unitary understanding of
universalistic community, instead arguing for the need to recognize that
there are (and should be) different forms of community. In contrast to other
contributors, the notion of re-traditionalization is here used to refer to the

development of 'tradition' itself, so that paradoxically, 'traditional' communities are 'communities beyond tradition'. Rejecting communitarian traditionalist accounts of community (especially that provided by Charles Taylor) and building on the work of Jean-Luc Nancy, a heuristic distinction is forged between communities of assent and those of descent, in the attempt to rethink community in the context of detraditionalization. Scott Lash (chapter 13), in somewhat different fashion – 'solidarity' is now emphasized – also draws attention to the importance of having traditions today. His argument is even more philosophical, directed at establishing what radical political culture should look like. The argument is developed by a sustained critique of much contemporary theorizing, in particular by those who advocate a version of identity politics 'whose core assumptions are deconstruction and difference'. Heidegger, Levinas and Derrida are seen as informing such advocacy. And 'the problem is that none of their versions of deconstruction gives space for intersubjectivity . . . their notions of difference lack tradition and exclude the possibility of solidarity'.

Part IV – 'Dissolving Detraditionalization' – stands in stark contrast with the first, and the emphasis there placed on the collapse of the traditional. Arguments of the kind found in the second and third parts, countering the periodized version of the detraditionalization thesis, are taken further. For whereas such arguments generally refer to detraditionalization – albeit in connection with coexistence claims – those presented in the fourth adopt a predominantly Foucault-inspired way of considering matters. And this approach serves to undermine the very notion of the detraditionalized.

Mark Poster (chapter 13) notes that Foucault strove to 'construct a theory of discourse that . . . reveals the way discourse functions as power and spotlights the constitution of the subject'. Denial of the existence of the 'sovereign, founding subject' goes hand in glove with the claim that discourse has 'a power effect on the subject even in moments of "liberation"'. The subject, in other words, is always subjected to 'structures of domination', which 'then act upon him or her'. More exactly, the universal operation of these structures ('rules, styles, inventions to be found in the cultural environment', as Foucault is cited) ensures that there is no such thing as a detraditionalized self. The autonomous self, apparently central to the idea and process of detraditionalization, is itself as much constructed as the supposedly traditionalized self. Furthermore, Poster goes on to argue, the current operation of the 'super-panopticon' – to do with the development of databases – serves to 'refute the hegemonic principle of the subject as centred, rational and autonomous'; that is, serves to 'constitute subjects decentred from their ideologically determined unity'. The 'new era' in which we live is one in which 'the culture of modernity' – with its ideology of the autonomous self – 'enjoys less and less verisimilitude'. To the extent that people come to experience the super-panopticon, it might be concluded, the days of the notion that the self enjoys detraditionalized autonomy are numbered.

Nikolas Rose (chapter 14) adopts a broader frame of reference than Poster, arguing against those who find evidence of 'general and unidirectional changes in forms of selfhood across history'. A key argument, very much in line with Poster's view of the universal operation of discourses as power-over-'self', is that 'the notion of a "detraditionalized" self is of very little use because it fails to engage with the ways in which different localized practices . . . presuppose, represent and act upon human beings as if they were persons of certain sorts'. Rather than opposing the traditional (e.g. allegiance to the community) and the modern (e.g. involving individualization), a specific claim, accordingly, is that 'managing persons as individuals always entails identifying subjects in relation to the norms of particular collectivities'. From this point of view, 'we have not seen the "detraditionalization of the self" in our present, but a modification in the complex of authorities which govern the relations that different sectors of the population, in different practices, are urged to establish with themselves, and a modification in our relations with these authorities of subjectification'. Furthermore, as reference to 'different practices' serves to indicate, Rose is also arguing that practices bearing on the individual are always heterogeneous. Together with evidence that the supposedly new can be found in the past – making it 'absurd' to hold that our times are 'late, new or post' – the volume clearly ends with a position far removed from the periodized version of detraditionalization with which it commences.

This is not the place to engage in sustained critique of different arguments and approaches concerning the study of detraditionalization. Clearly, the complexity of the issues and material under consideration ensure that there are no easy answers. Contributors recognize this, often drawing attention to lines of inquiry which go beyond the viewpoints which they are primarily advancing. However, it can be noted that there is quite widespread consensus that we live at a time when many consider themselves to be self-directed and reflexive. Detraditionalized authority and selfhood is *culturally* significant. Nevertheless, it is surely mistaken to concentrate exclusively on the ideology of autonomy, as though it were entirely dominant. Other forms of authority are surely operative: a consideration which lends considerable weight to those who want to de-periodize detraditionalization by drawing attention to the coexistence of those processes lending complexity to our world. Indeed it is precisely because of this complexity that we live at a time of uncertainty.

There are too many options as to what to value, leaving us unclear, for example, about the respective virtues of living an autonomous life of change or a life of belonging and commitment.

THREE REPLIES TO DETRADITIONALIZATION AND ITS CONSEQUENCES

Assuming – as we surely must – that detraditionalization is an important aspect of our times, it remains to highlight three of the more important normative responses to the process.

First, one can endorse the increasing reflexivity of modernity, thereby denying that it is unhappy. The argument in this regard is that detraditionalization has positively opened up wide ranges of possibilities in the quality of life. Private life, for example, has been transformed in that women especially have begun to accumulate the material and cultural resources to throw traditional family conventions into question, and have become more free to construct their own narratives of identity. In the sphere of work a number of labour processes are becoming increasingly flexible, progressively more information-intensive, and assume more devolution of risk and responsibility-taking. In environmental matters, an increasingly ecologically cognizant public has come to challenge and monitor the excesses of the authority of science.

Secondly, one can criticize the order-giving reflexive self, instead embracing flux, contingency, ambivalence and the Nietzschean *amor fati*. Reflexive modernity is seen here as discursively normalizing, and excluding its 'other' as woman, homosexual, Black or Jew. As opposed to the discursive ordering of the reflexive self, cultural theorists have endorsed 'complexity', 'contradiction', 'difference' and 'allegory'. The assumption is that detraditionalization has not gone far enough in casting our times adrift from foundations, including the authority of the coherent self.

And thirdly, one can argue that the problem is not that detraditionalization has not gone far enough, but instead that it has gone too far. The process has become too unsettling. This response underlies, for example, the return to vernacular architecture; to 'guild' methods of building; to the ethos of Heideggerian anti-discursive *bauen, wohnen und denken*. It also forms the 'unthought' of intellectual involvement with new forms of community. This response, in ideal-typical form, involves a rejection of reflexivity, not in favour of contingency and complexity but in favour of simplicity, of habits and habitus. It is in favour of pre-understandings, of harmonic relations with nature. It advocates organically-inscribed practices and the perception of order as once again natural: whether as pre-given 'social nature', revaluated 'outer nature' or reconstituted 'inner nature' on the basis of collective memory.

The uncertainty of our times, it might well be concluded, is exacerbated by the fact that detraditionalization opens the way for both the good and the bad. Liberation from the restraints, differentiations and exclusivities of tradition might be valuable. But the life of freedom has its own perils.

NOTES

This introduction owes a great deal to ideas which have been shared and contested during the activities of the Centre for the Study of Cultural Values. Thanks are due to Steve Pumfrey and Linda Woodhead for having provided detailed points of revision.

1 One of the clearest statements of the radical thesis is provided by Peter Berger (1979), especial attention being paid to the 'movement from fate to choice' (p. 11). (Berger himself is especially indebted to Arnold Gehlen's (1949/1980) thesis of 'deinstitutionalization', namely the process whereby stable and well-defined patterns of conduct lose their taken-for-granted plausibility.) Others who have developed contrasts which lend themselves to radical theorizing include Karl Popper, who has written of 'the transition from the tribal or "closed society", with its submission to magical forces, to the "open society" which sets free the critical powers of man' (1945, p. 1), and Claude Lévi-Strauss, with the distinction between 'cold' and 'hot' peoples (1966, pp. 233–4).

2 On the consumerization of religion, see Reginald Bibby (1990); on the Gulf War, see Christopher Norris (1992); for more general discussion of 'the authority of the consumer' see Russell Keat et al. (1994).

3 The anti-traditional stance of such forms of individualism, with particular reference to the more expressivistic guise, is well-formulated by Edward Shils. Writing of the 'metaphysical dread of being encumbered by something alien to oneself, he continues: 'There is a belief, corresponding to a feeling, that within each human being there is an individuality, lying in potentiality, which seeks an occasion for realization but is held in the toils of the rules, beliefs, roles which society imposes. In a more popular, or vulgar, recent form, the concern to "establish one's identity", to "discover oneself", or to "find out who one really is" has come to be regarded as a first obligation of the individual' (1981, pp. 10–11). It can also be noted that emotions are quite widely supposed to have intrinsic validity. This view of emotions as inner states, deserving expression and informing decisions, stands in contrast with traditionalized emotions, which serve as institutionalized codes of conduct. (Cf. Niklas Luhmann, 1986.)

4 Douglas Kellner (1992) provides a useful discussion of the impact of consumer culture on identity.

5   For a critical examination of those 'island metaphors' which have underlain so
    much anthropological study, see Thomas Eriksen and the importance attached
    to 'fluctuating systems of signification' rather than 'stable social units' (1993,
    p. 133); see also Lila Abu-Lughod (1986) on 'contradictory discourses' among the
    Awlad Ali Bedouin; Ann Caplan (1975) on the significance of choice in a Swahili
    community; Suzette Heald on the 'forceful individualism', together with the
    associated absence of 'coercive authorities', of Gisu culture (1989, p. 200); Ian
    Keen (1994) on the claim that Yolngu (North East Arnhem Land) do not receive
    their religion without interpreting it as they decide; and Charles Stewart and
    Rosalind Shaw (ed.) (1994) on the significance of syncretism in 'traditional' set-
    tings.
6   Among other historians who might be cited, John Benton draws attention to the
    'striking' sense of 'self-awareness' found in the twelfth century (1982, p. 285).
7   A good example of the collective values of 'The Organization' – and how these
    clash with the discourse of individualism – is provided by William Whyte (1956).

REFERENCES

Abu-Lughod, Lila 1986: *Veiled Sentiments*. London: University of California Press.
Bell, Daniel 1976: *The Cultural Contradictions of Capitalism*. London: Heinemann.
Bellah, Robert et al. 1985: *Habits of the Heart*. London: University of California Press.
Benton, John 1982: Consciousness of Self and Perceptions of Individuality. In R.
    Benson and G. Constable (eds), *Renaissance and Renewal in the Twelfth Century*,
    Oxford: Clarendon Press, pp. 263–95.
Berger, Peter 1979: *The Heretical Imperative*. New York: Anchor Press/Doubleday.
Berger, Peter et al. 1974: *The Homeless Mind*. Harmondsworth: Penguin.
Bibby, Reginald 1990: *Fragmented Gods*. Toronto: Stoddart.
Bloom, Alan 1987: *The Closing of the American Mind*. New York: Simon and Schuster.
Burckhardt, Jacob 1890: *The Civilization of the Renaissance in Italy*. London: George
    Allen & Unwin.
Caplan, Ann 1975: *Choice and Constraint in a Swahili Community*. Oxford: Oxford
    University Press.
Durkheim, Emile 1992: *Professional Ethics and Civic Morals*. London: Routledge.
Eriksen, Thomas 1993: In Which Sense do Cultural Islands Exist? *Social Anthropology*,
    vol. 1, Part B, pp. 133–47.
Fiske, John 1993: *Power Plays, Power Works*. London: Verso.
Fukuyama, Francis 1992: *The End of History and the Last Man*. Harmondsworth:
    Penguin.
Galbraith, John Kenneth 1992: *The Culture of Contentment*. London: Houghton Mifflin.
Gehlen, Arnold 1980: *Man in the Age of Technology*. New York: Columbia University
    Press.
Gellner, Ernest 1992: *Postmodernism, Reason and Religion*. London: Routledge.
Giddens, Anthony 1991: *The Consequences of Modernity*. Cambridge: Polity.
Heald, Suzette 1989: *Controlling Anger*. Manchester: Manchester University Press.

Hill, Christopher 1959: *The English Revolution, 1640*. London: Lawrence & Wishart.
Hunter, James 1994: *Before the Shooting Begins. Searching for Democracy in America's Culture War*. Oxford: Maxwell Macmillan International.
Inglehart, Ronald 1990: *Cultural Shift in Advanced Industrial Society*. Princeton: Princeton University Press.
Jameson, Fredric 1991: *Postmodernism*. New York: Verso.
Keat, Russell et al. (eds) 1994: *The Authority of the Consumer*. London: Routledge.
Keen, Ian 1994: *Knowledge and Secrecy in an Aboriginal Religion*. Oxford: Clarendon.
Kellner, Douglas 1992: Popular Culture and the Construction of Postmodern Identities. In Scott Lash and Jonathan Friedman (eds), *Modernity and Identity*. Oxford: Blackwell, pp. 141–77.
Lévi-Strauss, Claude 1966: *The Savage Mind*. London: Weidenfeld and Nicolson.
Lasch, Christopher 1980: *The Culture of Narcissism*. London: Abacus.
Luhmann, Niklas 1986: *Love as Passion*. Cambridge: Polity.
Macfarlane, Alan 1978: *The Origins of English Individualism*. Oxford: Basil Blackwell.
MacIntyre, Alasdair 1985: *After Virtue*. London: Duckworth.
Maffesoli, Michael 1994: *The Time of the Tribes. The Decline of Individualism in Mass Societies*. London: Sage.
Norris, Christopher 1992: *Uncritical Theory. Postmodernism, Intellectuals and the Gulf War*. London: Lawrence & Wishart.
Popper, Karl 1945: *The Open Society and its Enemies* (vol. 1). London: Routledge.
Ritzer, George 1993: *The McDonaldization of Society*. London: Pine Forge Press.
Rosaldo, Renato 1980: *Ilongot Headhunting 1883–1974*. Stanford: Stanford University Press.
Shils, Edward 1981: *Tradition*. London: Faber and Faber.
Stewart, Charles and Shaw, Rosalind (eds) 1994: *Syncretism/Anti-Syncretism*. London: Routledge.
Strathern, Marilyn 1992: Enterprising Kinship: Consumer Choice and the New Reproductive Technologies. In Paul Heelas and Paul Morris (eds) *The Values of the Enterprise Culture*, London: Routledge, pp. 165–78.
Taylor, Charles 1989: *Sources of the Self*. Cambridge: Cambridge University Press.
Whyte, William 1956: *The Organization Man*. New York: Simon & Schuster.

Part I

Losing the Traditional

2

Individualization and 'Precarious Freedoms': Perspectives and Controversies of a Subject-orientated Sociology

Ulrich Beck and Elisabeth Beck-Gernsheim

Dedicated to our teacher Karl Martin Bolte, in gratitude.

WHAT DOES 'INDIVIDUALIZATION OF LIFESTYLES' MEAN?

'Only the day before yesterday, only four years ago, a grand experiment for humanity, that had lasted forty years, came to an end here.' These words were spoken in Luther's town of Wittenberg by Friedrich Schorlemmer at the end of 1993.

> Seventeen million Germans lived in the walled province in enforced collectivization. A one-party state was seen as the highest form of freedom, individualization was damned as subjectivism. A risk-taking approach to the future was rejected in the name of 'scientific' optimism. The 'victors of history' were to set the norms and strive towards a unitary society (the socialist community). Human beings, understood as ceaselessly active communal creatures, were fed on the safe goal of communism, which was guaranteed by scientific laws. People were not allowed to decide anything because there was nothing left to decide, because history had already decided everything 'up there'. But they did not need to decide, either . . .
>
> Now, in freedom, they may and must decide for themselves; all the existing institutions have collapsed, all the old certainties are gone . . . The joy of freedom is at the same time a falling into a void. Now let everyone look after himself. What are the rules? Who's in charge? Those who have, and know how to increase what they have. Seventeen million people have reached this point, but the West's caravan moves on, calling to us: 'Come with us. We know the

way. We know the goal. We don't know any way. We don't know any goal. What is certain? That everything's uncertain, precarious. Enjoy our lack of ties as freedom.' (1993, p. 1)

The development in China is different, yet in many ways similar. There, too, the collective system that provided a guaranteed income, the 'iron rice-bowl', is breaking down. Earlier, people had hardly any scope for choice in private or professional life, but the minimal safety net of Communism offered them state-subsidized accommodation, training and health care. It is this state care from the cradle to the grave, tied to the work collective in the factory or on the land, that is now disintegrating. Its place is being taken by contracts linking income and job security to ability and performance. People are now expected to take their lives into their own hands and to pay a market price for services they receive. 'The constant refrain among urban Chinese is that they can no longer keep up with the quickened pace of life. They are confused by shifting values and outlooks on such fundamentals as careers, marriage and family relations' (Sun, 1993, p. 5).

Whatever we consider – God, nature, truth, science, technology, morality, love, marriage – modern life is turning them all into 'precarious freedoms'. All metaphysics and transcendence, all necessity and certainty is being replaced by artistry. In the most public and the most private ways we are becoming – helplessly – high-wire dancers in the circus tent. And many of us fall. Not only in the West, but in the countries that have abruptly opened their doors to Western ways of life. People in the former GDR, in Poland, Russia or China, are caught up in a dramatic 'plunge into modernity'.

Such examples, seemingly remote to citizens of the old Federal German Republic, point nevertheless to a dynamic that is familiar to us, too. Schorlemmer's address contains the catchword 'individualization'. This concept implies a group of social developments and experiences characterized, above all, by two meanings. In intellectual debate as in reality these meanings constantly intersect and overlap (which, hardly surprisingly, has given rise to a whole series of misunderstandings and controversies). On one hand, individualization means the *dis*integration of previously existing social forms – for example, the increasing fragility of such categories as class and social status, gender roles, family, neighbourhood, etc. Or, as in the case of the GDR and other states of the Eastern Bloc, it means the collapse of state-sanctioned normal biographies, frames of reference, role models. Wherever such tendencies towards disintegrations show themselves the question also arises: which new modes of life are coming into being where the old ones, ordained by religion, tradition or the state, are breaking down?

The answer points to the second aspect of individualization. It is, simply, that in modern societies new demands, controls and constraints are being imposed on individuals. Through the job market, the welfare state and institutions, people are tied into a network of regulations, conditions, provisos. From pension rights to insurance protection, from educational grants to tax rates: all these are institutional reference points marking out the horizon within which modern thinking, planning and action must take place.

Individualization in this sense, therefore, certainly does not mean an 'unfettered logic of action, juggling in a virtually empty space'; nor does it mean mere 'subjectivity', an attitude which refuses to see that 'beneath the surface of life is a highly efficient, densely-woven institutional society'.[1] On the contrary, the space in which modern subjects deploy their options is anything but a non-social sphere. The density of regulations informing modern society is well known, even notorious (from the MoT test and the tax return to the laws governing the sorting of refuse). In its overall effect it is a work of art of labyrinthine complexity, which accompanies us literally from the cradle to the grave.

The decisive feature of these modern regulations or guidelines is that, far more than earlier, individuals must, in part, supply them for themselves, import them into their biographies through their own actions. This has much to do with the fact that traditional guidelines often contained severe restrictions or even prohibitions on action (such as the ban on marriage, in pre-industrial societies, which prevented members of non-property-owning groups from marrying; or the travel restrictions and the recent obstructions to marriage in the Eastern Bloc states, which forbade contact with the 'class enemy'). By contrast, the institutional pressures in modern Western society tend rather to be offers of services or incentives to action – take, for example, the welfare state, with its unemployment benefit, student grants or mortgage relief. To simplify: one was born into traditional society and its preconditions (such as social estate and religion). For modern social advantages one has to *do* something, to make an active effort. One has to win, know how to assert oneself in the competition for limited resources – and not only once, but day after day.

The normal biography thus becomes the 'elective biography', the 'reflexive biography', the 'do-it-yourself biography'.[2] This does not necessarily happen by choice, nor does it necessarily succeed. The do-it-yourself biography is always a 'risk biography', indeed a 'tightrope biography', a state of permanent (partly overt, partly concealed) endangerment. The façade of prosperity, consumption, glitter can often mask the nearby precipice. The wrong choice of career or just the wrong field, compounded by the downward spiral of private misfortune, divorce, illness, the repossessed home – all this is called merely bad luck. Such cases bring into the open what was always secretly on the cards: the do-it-yourself biography can swiftly become the breakdown biography. The pre-ordained, unquestioned, often enforced ties of earlier times are replaced by the principle: 'until further notice'. As Zygmunt Bauman (1993) puts it,

> Nowadays everything seems to conspire against . . . lifelong projects, perma-nent bonds, eternal alliances, immutable identities. I cannot build for the long term on my job, my profession or even my abilities. I can bet on my job being cut, my profession changing out of all recognition, my skills being no longer in demand. Nor can a partnership or family provide a basis in the future. In the age of what Anthony Giddens has called 'confluent love', togetherness lasts no longer than the gratification of one of the partners, ties are from the outset only 'until further notice', today's intense attachment makes tomorrow's frus-tration only the more violent.

A kind of 'vagrant's morality' thus becomes a characteristic of the present. The vagrant

> does not know how long he will remain where he is, and it is not usually he who decides the length of his stay. He chooses his goals as he goes along, as they turn up and as he reads them off the signposts. But even then he does not know for sure whether he is going to take a rest at the next stopping-point, or for how long. He only knows that his stay is unlikely to be a long one. What drives him on is disappointment with the last place he stopped at, and the never-dying hope that the next, as yet unvisited place, or perhaps the one after that, will be free of the defects which have spoiled the ones up to now. (Bauman, 1993, p. 17; cf. this volume)

Are such portrayals, as some suspect, signs of egoism and hedonism, of an ego-fever rampant in the West? Looking more closely, we find that another feature of the guidelines of modernity is that they act against, rather than for, family cohesion. Most of the rights and entitlements to support by the welfare state are designed for individuals rather than for families. In many cases they presuppose employment (or, in the case of the unemployed, will-ingness to work). Employment in turn implies education, and both of these presuppose mobility or willingness to move. By all these requirements indi-viduals are not so much compelled as peremptorily invited to constitute themselves as individuals: to plan, understand, design themselves and act as individuals – or, should they 'fail', to lie as individuals on the bed they have made for themselves. The welfare state is in this sense an experimental apparatus for conditioning ego-related lifestyles. The common good may well be injected into people's hearts as a compulsory inoculation, but the litany of the lost sense of community that is just now being publicly intoned once more, continues to talk with a forked tongue, with a double moral standard, as long as the mechanism of individualization remains intact and no-one either wishes or is able to call it seriously into question.

Here, again, we find the same picture: decisions, possibly undecidable ones, within guidelines that lead into dilemmas – but decisions which place the individual, as an individual, at the centre and correspondingly penalize traditional lifestyles and behaviour.

Seen in this way, individualization is a social condition which is not arrived at by a free decision of individuals. To adapt Jean-Paul Sartre's phrase: people are condemned to individualization. Individualization is a compulsion, albeit a paradoxical one, to create, to stage-manage, not only one's own biography but the bonds and networks surrounding it, and to do this amid changing preferences and at successive stages of life, while constantly adapting to the conditions of the labour market, the education system, the welfare state, etc.

One of the decisive features of individualization processes, then, is that they not only permit, but demand, an active contribution by individuals. As the range of options widens and the necessity of deciding between them grows, so too does the need for individually performed actions, for adjustment, co-ordination, integration. If they are not to fail, individuals must be able to plan for the long term and adapt to change; they must organize and improvise, set goals, recognize obstacles, accept defeats and attempt new starts. They need initiative, tenacity, flexibility and tolerance of frustration.

Opportunities, dangers, biographical uncertainties that were earlier predefined within the family association, the village community, or by recourse to the rules of social estates or classes, must now be perceived, interpreted, decided and processed by individuals themselves. The consequences – opportunities and burdens alike – are shifted on to individuals who, naturally, in face of the complexity of social interconnections, are often unable to take the necessary decisions in a properly founded way, by considering interests, morality and consequences.

It is perhaps only by comparing generations that we can perceive how steeply the demands imposed on individuals have been rising. In a novel by Michael Cunningham (1991), a daughter asks her mother why she married her father:

'You knew that, of all the people in the world, he was the one you wanted to marry?' I asked. 'You never worried that you might be making some sort of extended mistake, like losing track of your real life and going off on, I don't know, a *tangent* you could never return from.'

But her mother 'waved the question away as if it were a sluggish but persistent fly . . . "We didn't ask such big questions then," she said. "Isn't it hard on you, to think and wonder and plan so much?"' (1991, pp. 189f)

In a novel by Scott Turow (1991), a meeting between father and daughter is described in similar terms:

Listening to Sonny, who was twisted about by impulse and emotion – beseeching, beleaguered, ironic, angry – it struck Stern that Clara [his wife] and he had had the benefit of a certain good fortune. In his time, the definitions were clearer. Men and women of middle-class upbringing anywhere in the Western world desired to marry, to bear and rear children. Et cetera. Everyone travelled along the same ruts in the road. But for Sonny, marrying late in life, in the New Era, everything was a matter of choice. She got up in the morning and started from scratch, wondering about relationships, marriage, men, the erratic fellow she'd chosen – who, from her description, still seemed to be half a boy. He was reminded of Marta, who often said she would find a male companion just as soon as she figured out what she needed one for. (p. 349)

To some, such examples sound familiar. To others they seem alien, tales from a distant world. It is clear that there is no such thing as 'the' individualized society. Unquestionably, the situation in cities like Munich or Berlin is different from that in Pomerania or East Friesland. Between urban and rural regions there are clear differences, which are empirically demonstrable with regard, for example, to lifestyle and family structure.[3] What has long been taken for granted in one as a part of normal life, seems odd, irritating, threatening in the other. Of course, lifestyles and attitudes from the town are spreading to the country – but refractedly, with a different gloss. Individualization means, implies, urbanization. But urbanization carries the role models of the world out there into the village living room – through the expansion of education, through tourism, and not least through advertising, the mass media and consumerism. Even where seemingly unaltered lifestyles and traditional certainties are chosen and put on show, they quite often represent decisions against new longings and aroused desires.

It is necessary, therefore, to check each group, milieu and region to determine how far individualization processes – overt or covert – have advanced within it. We do not maintain that this development has achieved blanket coverage of the whole population without differentiation. Rather, the catch-word 'individualization' should be seen as designating a trend. What is decisive is the systematic nature of the development linked to the advance of modernity. Martin Baethge (1991) writes: 'something which points to-wards tomorrow can hardly be representative of today' (p. 271). Individuali-zation has elements of both – it is an exemplary diagnosis of the present and the wave of the future.

What is heralded, ultimately, by this development is the end of fixed, pre-defined images of man. The human being becomes (in a radicalization of Sartre's meaning) a choice among possibilities, *homo optionis*. Life, death, gender, corporeality, identity, religion, marriage, parenthood, social ties – all are becoming decidable down to the small print; once fragmented into options, everything must be decided.[4] At best, this constellation reminds us of Baron Munchhausen, who reputedly solved what has now become a universal prob-lem: how to pull oneself out of the swamp of (im)possibilities by one's own pigtail. This artistic state of civilization has been summed up perhaps most clearly (with a pessimistic twist) by the poet Gottfried Benn (1979): 'In my view the history of man, of his endangerment, his tragedy, is only just beginning. Up to now the altars of saints and the wings of archangels have stood behind him; his weaknesses and wounds have been bathed from chal-ices and fonts. Now is beginning the series of his great, insoluble, self-inflicted dooms . . .' (pp. 150f).

ON THE IMPOSSIBILITY OF LIVING MODERN LIFE: THE DE-ROUTINIZATION OF THE MUNDANE

It is easily said: certainties have fragmented into questions which are now spinning around in people's heads. But it is more than that. Social action needs routines in which to be enacted. One can even say that our thoughts and actions are shaped, at the deepest level, by something of which we are hardly or not at all aware. There is an extensive literature which stresses the relief afforded in this way by internalized, pre-conscious or semi-conscious routines – or more precisely, the indispensable role they play in enabling people to lead their lives and discover their identities within their social co-ordinates. As Hartmann Tyrell (1986) shows, everyday life is concerned primarily with

the temporal order of doing . . . But it is not only the temporal order as such which matters, but the associated stratum of experiences repeated 'over and over again', the normal, the regular, the unsurprising. At the same time, daily life is a sphere of reduced attention, of routinised activity, of safe, easy availability, and thus of actions that can be repeated 'again and again' . . . It is about 'what is done here', sometimes in a decidedly particularist sense, in the family circle, the village, the region, etc. It is about the commonplace and familiar . . . what 'everyone does here'. (p. 255)

It is precisely this level of pre-conscious 'collective habitualizations', of matters taken for granted, that is breaking down into a cloud of possibilities to be thought about and negotiated. The deep layer of foreclosed decisions is being forced up into the level of decision-making. Hence the irritation, the endless chafing of the open wound – and the defensive–aggressive reaction. The questions and decisions rising up from the floor of existence can be neither escaped nor changed back into a silent ground on which life can be lived. At most, such pacification is achieved temporarily, provisionally; it is permeated with questions that can burst out again at any time. Think, calculate, plan, adjust, negotiate, define, revoke (with everything constantly starting again from the beginning): these are the imperatives of the 'precarious freedoms' that are taking hold of life as modernity advances. Even not deciding, the mercy of having to submit, is vanishing. Sometimes its place is taken by a hybrid, simulating what has been lost: the decision in favour of chance, of not deciding, an attempt to banish doubt which yet is pursued by doubt even in its interior dialogues.

> I thought I'd be pregnant soon. I'd stopped taking precautions. But I couldn't seem to tell anyone, not Bobby or Jonathan. I suppose I was ashamed of my own motives. I didn't like the idea of myself as calculating or underhanded. All I wanted, really, was to get pregnant by accident. The unexpected disadvantage of modern life is our victory over our own fates. We're called on to decide so much, almost everything . . . In another era I'd have had babies in my twenties, when I was married to Denny. I'd have become a mother without quite deciding to. Without weighing the consequences. (Cunningham, 1991, p. 203)

Life loses its self-evident quality; the social 'instinct substitute' which supports and guides it is caught up in the grinding mills of what needs to be thought out and decided. If it is correct that routines and institutions have an unburdening function which renders individuality and decision-making possible, it becomes clear what kind of encumbrance, exertion and stress is imposed by the destruction of routine. Ansgar Weymann (1989) points to the efforts the individual makes to escape this 'tyranny of possibilities'

– such as flight into magic, myth, metaphysics. The overtaxed individual 'seeks, finds and produces countless authorities intervening in social and psychic life, which, as his professional representatives, relieve him of the question: "Who am I and what do I want?" and thus reduce his fear of freedom' (1989, p. 3). This creates the market for the answer-factories, the psycho-boom, the advice literature – that mixture of the esoteric cult, the primal scream, mysticism, yoga and Freud which is supposed to drown out the tyranny of possibilities but in fact reinforces it with its changing fashions.

It is sometimes claimed that individualization means autonomy, emancipation, the freedom and self-liberation of humanity.[5] This calls to mind the proud subject postulated by the philosophy of the Enlightenment, which will acknowledge nothing but reason and its laws. But sometimes anomie rather than autonomy seems to prevail – a state unregulated to the point of lawlessness. (Emile Durkheim, in his classic study of anomie, sees it as the 'evil of missing boundaries', a time of overflowing wishes and desires, no longer disciplined by social barriers (1993, pp. 289, 311).) Any generalization that seeks to understand individualized society only in terms of one extreme or the other – autonomy or anomie – abbreviates and distorts the questions that confront us here. This society is characterized by hybrid forms, contradictions, ambivalences (dependent on political, economic and family conditions). It is also characterized, as we have said, by the 'do-it-yourself biography' which – depending on the economic situation, educational qualifications, stage of life, family situation, colleagues – can easily turn into a 'breakdown biography' (Hitzler, 1988; Beck and Beck-Gernsheim, 1993). Failure and inalienable freedom live in close proximity and perhaps intermingle (as in the 'chosen' lifestyle of 'singles').

At any rate, the topics that individuals wear themselves out on project into the most diverse spheres of life. They may be 'small' questions (such as the allocation of housework), but also include 'large' questions of life and death (from pre-natal diagnosis to intensive medical care). The abolition of routine thus releases questions of very different social and moral weight. But they all bear on the core of existence. One can even say that decisions about lifestyles are 'deified'. Questions that went out of use with God are re-emerging at the centre of life. Everyday life is being post-religiously 'theologized'.

A secular line can be drawn: God, nature, social system. Each of these categories and horizons of meaning to an extent replaces the previous one; each stands for a particular group of self-evident assumptions and provides a source of legitimation for social action, which can be seen as a sequence of secularized necessities. As the dams become permeable and are breached, what was once reserved for God or was given in advance by nature, is now transformed into questions and decisions which have their locus in the conduct of private life. (With the successes of reproductive medicine and human genetics the anthropology of the human species is even being drawn quite literally into the area of decision-making.) To this extent, from the viewpoint of cultural history, it can be said that modernity, which dawned with the subject's claim to self-empowerment, is redeeming its promise. As modernity gains ground, God, nature and the social system are being progressively replaced, in greater and lesser steps, by the individual — confused, astray, helpless and at a loss. With the abolition of the old co-ordinates a question arises that has been decried and acclaimed, derided, pronounced sacred, guilty and dead: the question of the individual.

WHAT IS NEW IN INDIVIDUALIZATION PROCESSES? THE EXAMPLE OF THE SOCIAL HISTORY OF MARRIAGE

In his book *The Civilization of the Renaissance in Italy*, published in 1860, Jakob Burckhardt writes that in the Middle Ages human consciousness lay

> dreaming or half awake, beneath a collective veil. The veil was woven of faith, illusion, and childish prepossession, through which the world and history were seen clad in strange hues. Man was conscious of himself only as a member of a race, people, party, family, corporation — only through some general category. In Italy, this veil first melted into air, an *objective* treatment and consideration of the state and of all the things of this world became possible. The *subjective* side at the same time asserted itself with corresponding emphasis; man became a spiritual *individual*, and recognised himself as such. (1987, p. 161)

Paradoxically, Burkhardt's description of the Renaissance has features of post-modernism. Everything is taken over by fashions; the politically indifferent private person comes into being; biographies and autobiographies are written and invented; women are educated according to masculine ideals. 'The highest praise which could then be given to the great Italian women was that they had the mind and the courage of men.' From the standpoint of the nineteenth century, Burckhardt notes, something emerged which 'our age would call immodesty' (1987, p. 428).

Anyone reading this and similar accounts will ask: what is new and specific in the individualization processes of the second half of the twentieth century?[6] To give a concise and direct answer, what is historically new is that something that was earlier expected of a few – to lead a life of their own – is now being demanded of more and more people and, in the limiting case, of all. The new element is, first, the democratization of individualization processes and, secondly (and closely connected), the fact that basic conditions in society favour or enforce individualization (the job market, the need for mobility and training, labour and social legislation, pension provisions, etc.).

This history of the spread to pre-eminence of individualizations can be illustrated by various social phenomena and formations. Such will now be done by means of an exemplary sketch of the social history of marriage. To state our thesis at the outset: whereas marriage was earlier first and foremost an institution *sui generis* raised above the individual, today it is becoming more and more a product and construct of the individuals forming it. Let us now trace this historical curve in more detail.

As late as the seventeenth and eighteenth centuries, marriage was to be understood not from below to above but from above to below, as a direct component of the social order. It was a socially binding mode of living and working which was largely inaccessible to individual intervention. It prescribed to men and women what they had to do and not to do even in the details of daily life, work, economic behaviour and sexuality. (Of course, not everyone complied. But the social mesh of the family and village community was tight, and possibilities of control were omnipresent. Anyone who infringed the prevailing norms therefore had to reckon with rigorous sanctions.) To overstate slightly: marriage was a kind of internalized 'natural law' which – hallowed by God and the authority of the church, secured by the material interests of those bound together within it – was, so to speak, 'executed' in marriage. This emerges clearly through what seems to be an example of the contrary, a hard-won divorce reported by Gisela Bock and Barbara Duden (1977):

> In the early 18th century, in the Seine/Marne region of France, two people appeared before the responsible church court: Jean Plicque, a vintner in Villenoy and Catherine Giradin, his wife. Seven months earlier she had with difficulty achieved a separation of bed and board on grounds of absolute incompatibility. Now they came back and declared that it would be not only better, but 'much more advantageous and useful for them to live together than to remain apart'. This couple's realisation is typical of all rural and urban households: husband and wife were dependent on each other because and as long as there was no possibility of earning a livelihood outside joint family work. (1977, p. 126)

This couple's realisation points up a situation that (despite all the diversity) seems to have been typical of pre-industrial society. Apart from church and monastery, there was no basis for material existence outside marriage. Marriage was not held together by the love, self-discovery or self-therapy of two wage-earners seeking each other and themselves, but was founded on religious obligation and materially anchored in the marital forms of work and life. Anyone who wishes to understand the meaning of this institution of marriage must leave aside the individuals and place at the centre the overarching whole of an order finally founded on God and the afterlife. Here marriage did not serve individual happiness, but was a means for achieving succession, hereditary family rule in the case of the nobility, and so on. The stability of the social order and hierarchy depended on it in a very tangible way.

With the beginning of the modern age the higher meanings superimposed on forms of social existence were loosened. The trend towards individuality – first in the middle-class 'market individual' founded on private capital – called into question the gravity of collective identities and action units, at least latently. With the separation of the family from the economic sphere, the working, economic unit of husband and wife was ruptured. Characteristically, the response to this dissolution of the material basis of the marriage community was a heightening of the moral and legal underpinnings of marriage. Here, again, marriage is justified 'deductively', that is from above to below, but now with a moral exclamation mark, as a cornerstone of the bourgeois–Christian world order. A draft of the German Civil Code, published in 1888, states: 'A German Civil Code, following the general Christian view among the people, will have to start from the assumption that in marital law it is not the principle of the individual freedom of the spouses that prevails, but that marriage should be seen as a moral and legal order independent of the will of the spouses' (cited by Blasius, 1992, pp. 130f).

'Not the principle of individual freedom', but an 'order independent of the will of the spouses': the threatening possibility resonates implicitly in the negation. However, the community is a one-sided one. The wife is expressly forbidden to use her own name. The surname thus becomes that of the husband. In exemplary fashion, the general element is equated with power – here, that of the husband. As late as 1956 we read in a judgement: 'Rather, Article 6 GG allows equal rights to come into play in family law only to the extent that our traditional concept of the family, as determined by Christianity, remains intact. All exaggerated individualistic tendencies are thereby denied an effect on marital law . . . This must also apply to marital law as it relates to names' (cited by Struck, 1992, p. 390). Here we already find the exorcising formulation about the 'exaggerated individualistic tendencies' that has lost nothing of its topicality. By it the Beelzebub of individualism was supposed to be sprinkled and driven out with the holy water of tradition.

Family registers are an unopened treasure trove of idealized family images proclaimed, as it were, *ex cathedra*. Two of them will be juxtaposed here: one from the time of National Socialism and one from the 1970s in the German Federal Republic. The contrast could hardly be more radical. The prefatory remarks make clear the individualistic conversion that has taken place in Germany – even officially – within three decades.

In the register from the early 1940s we read: 'Prefatory note: Marriage cannot be an end in itself, but must serve a greater goal, the increase and survival of the species and the race. Adolf Hitler.'[7] This sounds like a command and is no doubt intended as one. The racial doctrine of National Socialism is an extreme example of the 'counter-modernization' which stages a masquerade of the past in order to push back the 'decadent' tendencies of modernity (Beck, 1993, ch. 4). It aims – using every means – to establish the unquestioned world of a re-integrated blood community. Marriage thus becomes a branch office of the state, a miniature state, the 'germ-cell of the state'. It is the place where the 'German race' is reproduced.

The commentary in the family register from the 1970s seems expressly to countermand the one just quoted. Here we read that 'the task of marriage under private law is not to see itself primarily as serving other aims beyond it, but to find its main purpose in marriage itself.'[8] Today's marriage manual no longer talks about the 'Christian world order and its values' or of 'state goals', and still less of the 'survival of the race'. Instead, it makes explicit the switch that has taken place from a view directed at the whole to one focused on people. The state even seems to slap its own wrist in warning the spouses entrusted to it not to do what up until then had been state law and policy regarding marriage, namely to follow 'traditional models':

> Caution is advised in face of the dangerous temptation to accept traditional models of marriage and of the family without question as 'natural', causing them to become fossilised in law. The rapid development of our modern industrial society, the increasing number of working women, the expected further reduction of working hours, the changing character of professions, etc., compel the legal system to adopt an open-minded, unprejudiced attitude towards new embodiments of marriage and the family.'[9]

The voice of sociology is audible here. This may even be a case of the (legendary) 'trickling down', the 'disappearance' of sociology – here, in the family register – which indicates its successful effect.

However, the newly-weds also find the following 'blessing' quoted in their marriage manual in a chapter on 'The Dissolution of Marriage': 'Once their disputes have reached a certain stage, they (the spouses) seem to each other like two surgeons operating on each other without anaesthetic, who "get better and better at knowing what hurts".[10] This is witty and apt, and could hardly contrast more dramatically with the 'racial marriage' or the 'Christian marriage' still legally binding in the 1950s. Nor could it show more clearly the radical change from the interpretation of marriage as something beyond the individual to the exclusively individual interpretation. Here, not only does an official text mention the dissolution of marriage in the same breath as the contract; marriage is also institutionalized as an individualized programme. The why, what and how long of marriage are placed entirely in the hands and hearts of those joined in it. From now on there is just one maxim defining what marriage means: the script is the individualization of marriage. The individual code of marriage is, so to speak, legally ordained.

This makes two things clear. First, even the old forms of marriage, now that they have been bureaucratically disowned, must be chosen and lived at one's personal risk. Even the marriage guidance manual contains, in effect, the warning that marriage – like excessive speed on a winding road – is a risky personal undertaking for which no insurances are valid. And secondly, no-one now can say what goes on behind the oh-so-unchanging label 'marriage' – what is possible, permitted, required, tabooed or indispensable. The world order of marriage is from now on an individual order which must be questioned and reconstructed by individuals as they go along.

To forestall any misunderstanding: even the new, individual order of marriage is not a mere product of individualization and its wishes. Rather, it is bound to institutional edicts – for example those of the legal system, which are central. It depends on the requirements of the educational system, the labour market, old-age pensions (the latter today pre-supposing that both partners – and not just the husband, as earlier – have their own independent biographies, as earners, and their own financial security). Even with regard to the twosome, therefore – that seemingly completely private, intimate sphere – individualization does not by any means imply that the increased freedom of choice is the same thing as a breakdown of order.[11] Rather, what we see here, as elsewhere, is what Talcott Parsons has called 'institutionalised individualism' (1978, p. 321). Freely translated, this means that in modern life the individual is confronted on many levels with the following challenge: You may and you must lead your own independent life, outside the old bonds of family, tribe, religion, origin and class; and you must do this within the new guidelines and rules which the state, the job market, the bureaucracy, etc. lay down. In this sense marriage, too, in its modern version, is not merely an individual order but an 'individual situation dependent on institutions' (Beck, 1986, p. 210).

PERSPECTIVES AND CONTROVERSIES OF AN
INDIVIDUAL-ORIENTATED SOCIOLOGY

All sociology splits into two opposed views of the same thing. The social dimension can be regarded either from the standpoint of *individuals* or from that of the *whole* (society, state, the common good, class, group, organization, etc.). (Cf. Bolte, 1983.) Both standpoints are founded on the structure of social action, which can be analysed either in terms of the agents or in terms of the social structure. However, that both standpoints are equally possible, equally necessary or equally original does not mean that they are equally valuable or have equal rights; still less does it mean that they are identical. Rather, each of these viewpoints relativizes, criticizes the other (subtly, but with abundant consequences): anyone who analyses society from the standpoint of the individual does not accept its form at a particular time as a pre-ordained, unalterable datum, but calls it into question. Here, sociological thought is not far from the 'art of mistrust', to use a formulation of Peter Berger (1977, p. 40), adapted from Nietzsche. Indeed, it tends to 'destabilise' existing power relationships, as Zygmunt Bauman (1991, p. 17), for example, puts it. By contrast, where the so-called 'operational requirements' of society (or subdivisions of it) provide the framework of reference, they are often presented to the outside world simply as the inner happiness of the ego. To apply this happiness there are funnels – known as 'duties' – and institutions for pouring it through these funnels, for purposes of intimidation: schools, courts, marriages, organizations, etc.

The prevailing sociology has usually made things easy for itself by cutting off the questions that arise here with the strict injunction, backed up by thick volumes, that individuals can only be or become individuals within society. In this way they continually repress the idea: what would happen if these individuals wanted a different society, or even a different type of society?

The old sociology, still well-endowed with university chairs, is armed against this idea: the general interest, congealed as structure, is condensed and glorified as Parsonian 'functional pre-requisites'. From such pre-requisites – as from a cornucopia of secularized ethical duties – pour forth 'role patterns', 'functions', 'demands', 'subsystems', equally remote from God and the earth, divorced from action and yet its pre-condition, which are to be applied as a standard to the confusion and refractoriness of individuals, to yield judgements such as 'normal', 'deviant', 'erroneous' and 'absurd'.

Accordingly, the 'individualistic' perspective on society has up to now been usually dismissed as presumptuous and self-contradictory. There is talk – using an up-to-date idiom – of 'demand inflation' and the 'ego society'.

The decay of values is deplored, while it is forgotten that such decay is as old as Socrates. The GDR – up to now – has had exemplary experience of the inverse question and has foundered on it: what happens to institutions without individuals? What does it mean when individuals withdraw their assent from the institutional elite? The same question was urgently posed in Italy in 1993 (and in France, Sweden, Finland, Germany, the USA, etc.), and the answer was the same: the political systems tremble. Where the functionalist viewpoint, based on system theory, is dominant, a 'subject-orientated' sociology often appears not only deviant but subversive. For it can sometimes reveal that the party and institutional elites are riders without horses.

Nor is it true, of course, that both conceptions of the social order are incomplete in themselves and need to supplement each other. But before such a need for harmony smooths over a conflict which has not yet been fought out openly, it should be pointed out here that for some centuries the view of the totality has suppressed that of individuals. In view of this it is time to turn the tables and ask what kind of society comes into being *after* the demise of the great political camps and the party-political consensus.

In other words: the two points of view remain until further notice incompatible; they are even becoming, through a modernization which is setting individuals and their demands and dilemmas free, more and more irreconcilable, and are giving rise to antithetical explanations, methods, theories and intellectual traditions.

It will be objected that this is not a meaningful antithesis. Entities which presuppose each other analytically, individuals and society, cannot be described as a social conflict. Moreover, both viewpoints lay claim to both viewpoints. He who embraces the 'whole' (of society) – the functionality of social formations – in his field of vision, self-evidently claims to include the standpoint of individuals as well. If necessary, this is presented as the morally correct standpoint, that must be asserted against the false self-consciousness of individuals in their own well-understood interests. Whereas, conversely, every variant of subject- or individual-orientated sociology naturally also offers statements and explanations about the intrinsic reality of social formations and systems, their structure, stage-management, etc.

What was shown in the preceding section through the example of marriage applies generally: the antithesis between the individual- and system-based viewpoints should be understood as a historical development. If, in traditional, pre-industrial societies, we can still – perhaps – assume a fairly balanced relationship between the two frames of reference, this pre-stabilized harmony breaks down with the unfolding of modernity. This is the central theme of sociology in Emile Durkheim and Georg Simmel. But both still assume that it is possible to integrate individualized society, as it were transcendentally, through values. Such a possibility, however, became more unrealistic the more individuals were released from classical forms of integration in groups, including family and class. What is emerging today can be called, with Hans Magnus Enzensberger, 'the average exoticism of everyday life':

> It is most obvious in the provinces. Market towns in Lower Bavaria, villages in the Eifel Hills, small towns in Holstein are populated by figures no one could have dreamed of only thirty years ago. For example, golf-playing butchers, wives imported from Thailand, counter-intelligence agents with allotments, Turkish Mullahs, women chemists in Nicaragua committees, vagrants driving Mercedes, autonomists with organic gardens, weapons-collecting tax officials, peacock-breeding smallholders, militant lesbians, Tamil ice-cream sellers, classics scholars in commodity futures trading, mercenaries on home leave, extremist animal-rights activists, cocaine dealers with solariums, dominas with clients in top management, computer freaks commuting between Californian data banks and nature reserves in Hesse, carpenters who supply golden doors to Saudi Arabia, art forgers, Karl May researchers, bodyguards, jazz experts, euthanasists and porno producers. Into the shoes of the village idiots and the oddballs, of the eccentrics and the queer fish, has stepped the average deviationist, who no longer stands out at all from millions like him. (1992, p. 179)

Under such conditions, institutions are founded on antiquated images of individuals and their social situations. To avoid endangering their own power, the administrators of these institutions maintain the status quo at all costs (supported by a sociology operating with the old conceptual stereotypes). An amusing consequence of this is that the political class regards the individuals 'out there' as no less stupid and brazen than the society of individuals considers the political class. The question as to which of them is right can – in principle – be easily decided. The idea that only the party elite and the bureaucratic apparatus knows what is what and that everyone else is imbecilic is one that characterized the Soviet Union – until it collapsed.

'This society', Enzenberger writes of the German Federal Republic,

> is no longer capable of being disappointed. It registered very early, very quickly what's going on in Bonn. The way the parties present themselves also contributes to this cynical view. The politicians try to compensate for the loss of their authority, the erosion of power and trust, by a huge expenditure on advertising. But these wasteful battles are counter-productive. The message is tautologous and empty. They always say only one thing, which is, 'I am I' or 'We are we'. The zero statement is the preferred form of self-presentation.

That naturally confirms people's belief that no ideas can be expected from this caste ... When the posters say: 'It's Germany's future', then everyone knows that these are empty words, at most it's about the future of the milk subsidy to farmers, of the health insurance contributions or benefits ... The Federal Republic is relatively stable and relatively successful not because of, but despite being ruled by the people who grin down from the election posters. (1992, pp. 143, 138)

The theory of individualization takes sides in political debate in two ways: first, it elaborates a frame of reference which allows the subject area – the conflicts between individuals and society – to be analysed from the standpoint of individuals. Secondly, the theory shows how, as modern society develops further, it is becoming questionable to assume that collective units of meaning and action exist. System theories, which assume an existence and reproduction of the social independence of the actions and thoughts of individuals, are thereby losing reality content. To exaggerate slightly: system theory is turning into a system *metaphysics* which obstructs the view of the virulent social and political process whereby, in all spheres of activity, the content, goals, foundations and structures of the 'social' are having to be renegotiated, reinvented and reconstructed.[12]

A sociology which confronts the viewpoint serving the survival of institutions with the viewpoint of individuals is a largely undeveloped area of the discipline. Almost all sociology, through a 'congenital bias', is based on a negation of individuality and the individual. The social has almost always been conceived in terms of tribes, religions, classes, associations, and above all, recently, of social systems. The individuals were the interchangeable element, the product of circumstances, the character's masks, the subjective factor, the environment of the systems, in short: the indefinable. Sociology's credo, to which it owes its professional identity, states over and over again that the individual is the *illusion* of individuals who are denied insight into the social conditions and conditionality of their lives.

The works of world literature, the great narratives and dramas that have held the epochs in thrall, are variations of this doctrine of the higher reality and dignity of the general, social dimension, the indivisible unit of which – as the term *individere* itself implies – is the individual. But is a science of *individere* actually possible? Is not a 'sociology of the individual' (unless it contents itself with the social history of that concept, in the context of discourse theory) a self-contradiction, a pig with wings, a disguised appeal for sociology to abolish itself?

One does not need to go to the opposite extreme to see that many of the main concepts of sociology are on a war footing with the basic idea of individualization theory: that traditional contexts are being broken up, re-connected, recast; are becoming in all cases decidable, decision-dependent, in need of justification. Where this historical development is asserting itself, the viewpoints from 'above' and 'below', from the social whole and from the individual, are diverging. At the same time, the questions stirred up by system theory's perspective are still in force, and even take on increased importance as they become more unmanageable. Take, for example, the declining birthrate, which can only be deciphered if seen against the back-ground of the changed wishes, hopes and life-plans of men and women. On the level of society as a whole, it brings with it a whole string of secondary consequences and questions (education policy, labour market management, pensions, local planning, immigration policy, etc.). Individuals, their prefer-ences and aversions, are becoming the interference factor, that which is sim-ply incalculable, a constant source of irritation, because they upset all calculations – education quotas, study plans, pension calculations, etc. Among politicians and administrators, and the academic experts who prepare their texts, this heightens the suspicion of irrationality, since it keeps turning the current legal, administrative and computing formulae into waste-paper. Where hitherto-accepted assumptions are found wanting, the clamour about 'mood democracy' and the 'elbow society' begins. Norms and moral standards are set. But the tidal wave of new life-designs, of do-it-yourself and tightrope biographies, cannot be either held back or understood in this way. The scurrying of the individualized lifestyles, elaborated in the personal trial-and-error process (between training, retraining, unemployment and career, be-tween hopes of love, divorce, new dreams of happiness), is unamenable to the need for standardization of bureaucratized political science and sociology.

No-one denies that important matters are thought about and initiated by these disciplines, too. But what was previously regarded as background noise to be neglected, is now being seen, more and more undeniably, as the basic situation. The frame of reference of institutionalized state politics and administration on one hand, and that of individuals trying to hold together their biography fragments on the other, are breaking apart and then colliding antagonistically in opposed conceptions of 'public welfare', 'quality of life', 'future viability', 'justice', 'progress'. A rift is opening between the images of society prevalent in politics and institutions, and those arising from the situations of individuals struggling for viable ways of living.

In this tension-laden field, sociology must re-think its concepts and its research routines. In the face of Enzensberger's 'average exoticism of everyday life', together with what is now formulated with scholarly caution as the 'pluralization of lifestyles', old classifications and schemata are becoming as ideologically suspect as they are necessary to the institutional actors. Take, for example, the studies which 'prove' that the increasingly numerous non-marital partnerships are really pre-conjugal communities, and that post-conjugal communities are actually only a preliminary form of the next marriage, so that marriage can be proclaimed the transcendental victor throughout all this turbulence. Such consolations have their market and their grateful customers: the turmoils of individualization, their message runs, are a storm in surviving marriage's teacup.

This confirms the old adage that the echo coming back out of the wood is the same as the shout that went into it. Anyone who 'maritalizes' alternative ways of living should not be surprised if he sees marriages wherever he looks. But this is a prime example of blind empiricism. Even methodical brilliance, that is able to avoid calling its categorical framework into question, becomes a second-hand bookshop stocked with standard social groups, which only exist as an ideal: though as such they are very much alive.[13]

PROSPECT: HOW CAN HIGHLY INDIVIDUALIZED SOCIETIES BE INTEGRATED?

Individualization has a double face: 'precarious freedoms'. Expressed in the old, wrong terms, emancipation and anomie form together, through their political chemistry, an explosive mixture. The consequences and questions erupting in all parts of society are correspondingly deep-reaching and nerve-deadening; they increasingly alarm the public and preoccupy social scientists. To mention only a few: how do children grow up when there are fewer and fewer clear guidelines and responsibilities in families? Can connections be made with the growing tendency towards violence among young people? Is the age of mass products and mass consumption coming to an end with the pluralization of lifestyles, and must the economy and industry adapt themselves to products and product fashions that can be combined individually, with corresponding methods of production?

Is it possible, at all, for a society in the drifting sand of individualization to be registered statistically and analysed sociologically? Is there any remaining basic unit of the social, whether the household, the family, or the commune? How could such units be defined and made operational? How should the various political spheres – for example local politics, traffic policy, environmental policy, family policy, welfare policy – react to the diversification and transitoriness of needs and situations? How must social work (and its educational content) change when poverty is divided up and, as it were, distributed laterally among biographies? What architecture, what spatial planning, what educational planning does a society need under the pressure of individualization? Has the end come for the big parties and the big associations, or are they just starting a new stage of their history?

Behind all these irritating questions, a basic question is making itself more and more clearly heard: is it still at all possible to integrate highly individualized societies? As is shown by the rebirth of nationalism, of ethnic differences and conflicts in Europe, there is a strong temptation to react to these challenges with the classical instruments of encapsulation against 'aliens': which means turning back the wheels of social modernization. No doubt, the acceptance of violence against foreigners in the streets (for example) may indeed be explained in this way. In Germany as in other western European states an uprising against the 1970s and 1980s is in progress, a *Kulturkampf* of the two modernities. Old certainties, just now grown fragile, are again proclaimed – from everyday life to politics, from the family to the economy and the concept of progress. The highly individualized, find-out-for-yourself society is to be replaced by an inwardly heterogeneous society outwardly consolidated into a fortress – and the demarcation against 'foreigners' fits in with this calculation.

To put the matter ironically: since man can no longer, 'unfortunately', deny the right of women to vote; since women's desire for education can only with difficulty be held in check, since everything that might be useful in this regard proves awkward, a perhaps quite serviceable alternative route is being taken – not quite consciously but not quite unconsciously either. It involves achieving the same goals through the dramaturgy of violence and nationalism. Here the breach of the taboo on right-wing extremist violence has a reason little regarded up to now: the counter-revolt, pent up in the West too, against the individualization, feminization and ecologization of everyday life. Quite incidentally, violence reinstates the priorities of orthodox industrial society – economic growth, the faith in technology, the nuclear family, the gender hierarchy – banishing the tiresome spirits of permanent questioning; or seeming to do so.

But nailing down the status quo or even doing a backwards *salto mortale* cannot, at the end of the twentieth century, provide a basis of legitimacy. The same is true of the three ways of integrating highly industrialized societies that are mentioned again and again in the debate. They, too, are becoming uncertain, fragile, unable to function in the longer term.

The first is the possibility of what might be called a transcendental consensus, an integration through values, which was the driving force of classical sociology from Durkheim to Parsons. Opposing this today is the realization that the diversification of cultural perceptions and the connections people have to make for themselves eat away the very foundations on which value-communities can feed and constantly renew themselves.

Others, secondly, contrast to this integration through values an integration founded on joint material interests. If an avowal of common values (which, of course, always has a narrowing, repressive side) is no longer possible, it is replaced in highly developed society by the share in prosperity that is felt by broad sections of the population, binding them into the society. According to this theory, the cohesion of the old Federal Republic rested primarily on the growing 'economic cake', whereas the new, enlarged republic – where recession, shortage and poverty are starting to take control – faces severe tests. But even disregarding this topical development, the basic assumption is itself questionable. To hope that only material interests and institutional dependence (consumption, job market, welfare state, pensions) create cohesion, is to confuse the problem with the solution, making a virtue (desired by theory) out of the necessity of disintegrating groups and group-allegiances.

Thirdly, national consciousness, too, is no longer able to provide a basis for stable integration. This is not only shown by the polarizations generated by the 'national project'. It is also, René König wrote as early as 1979, 'much too abstract in relation to real and very tangible fissures' (p. 364); it is simply no longer able to reach and bind these splits. In other words, with the mobilization of ethnic identities, it is precisely national integration which breaks down:

> This can be called a 'relapse into the middle ages', and the disintegration of
> the existing large societies into separate, opposed local powers can be seen as
> the decay of the old 'nations' – a process which has been a reality in some parts
> of the old and new worlds for some time now. Here, the old path from
> alliances to empires is reversed; the great empires sometimes split up into
> federative formations, or the individual parts split off along lines determined
> by political, ethnic or other factors. (Ibid., pp. 364f)

So what is left? In conclusion, we would like, at least, to indicate the possibility of a different kind of integration and to put it forward for discussion. To summarize our basic idea: highly individualized societies can only be bound together – if at all – first, through a clear understanding of precisely this situation; and secondly, if people can be successfully mobilized and motivated for the challenges present at the centre of their lives (unemployment, destruction of nature, etc.). Where the old sociality is 'evaporating', society must be re-invented. Integration therefore becomes possible if no attempt is made to arrest and push back the break-out of individuals. It can happen if we make conscious use of this situation, and try to forge new, politically open, creative forms of bond and alliance. The question of whether we still have the strength, the imagination – and the time – for this 'invention of the political' (Beck, 1993) is, to be sure, a matter of life and death.

In one of his last major essays, König sketched a positively utopian role for sociology in this connection. He believed it could contribute to integration through enabling the highly complex society to reflect and observe itself creatively and methodically. He criticized the 'ruling class of today' in the strongest terms because it had 'lived entirely on a legitimacy borrowed from old elites and had added nothing of its own'. In this situation, König goes on, 'sociology could make this highly complex thematic context transparent . . . Admittedly, integration could not then be achieved on the institutional level' – either ethnically, socially, economically or through state nationalism. 'To an extent, it can only be implemented "in thought".' Therefore, it could be achieved 'only within the framework of a new philosophy, which no longer revolved around "being" and "becoming", but around the chances for human beings under the conditions that have been described' (pp. 367ff; cf. Peters, 1993).

What König proposes is in fact very topical – an integration to be attained 'in thought', in the struggle for new existential foundations for industrial civilization. Post-traditional societies threatening the cohesion of this civilization can only become integrable – if at all – through the experiment of their self-interpretation, self-observation, self-opening, self-discovery, indeed, their self-invention. Their future, their ability to have and shape a future, is the measure of their integration. Whether they can succeed in this is, of course, questionable. Perhaps it will turn out that individualization and integration are in fact mutually exclusive. And sociology – is it really able to make an intellectual contribution to pluralist societies? Or will it remain stuck in its routines, obliterating the big outlines of change and challenge with its minute calculations of developmental trends?

In his novel *The Man without Qualities* (1961), Robert Musil distinguishes between a sense for reality and a sense for possibility. He defines the latter as 'the capacity to think how everything could "just as easily" be, and to attach no more importance to what is than to what is not'. Someone who sees possible truths, Musil goes on, has, 'at least in the opinion of their devotees . . . something positively divine, a fiery, soaring quality, a constructive will . . . that does not shrink from reality but treats it, on the contrary,

as a mission and an invention . . . Since his ideas . . . are nothing else than as
yet unborn realities, he too of course has a sense of reality; but it is a sense
of possible reality . . .' (pp. 12f). Undoubtedly, sociology, too, ought to develop such a sense of possible reality – but that is another matter.

NOTES

1 Respectively, this is how Ostner and Roy (1991, p. 18) and Karl Ulrich Mayer
   (1991, pp. 88f) understand individualization; for a summary of the debate on
   individualization, see Beck (1994).
2 Ronald Hitzler (1988) writes about 'do-it-yourself biography' (*Bastelbiographie*);
   Anthony Giddens (1991) writes about 'reflexive biography'; Katrin Ley (1984)
   deals with 'elective biography' (*Wahlbiographie*).
3 Hans Bertram and Clemens Dannenbeck (1990); Hans Bertram, Hiltrud Bayer
   and Renate Bauereiss (1993); Günter Burkart and Martin Kohli (1992).
4 Peter Gross refers to the multi-options society. His book on the subject will be
   published in autumn 1994.
5 E.g. Günter Burkart (1993).
6 Cf., for example, Dumont (1991); Macfarlane (1979); Morris (1972); Foucault
   (1984).
7 *Familienstammbuch mit Ahnenpass*, Paul Albrechts Verlage, Stolp and Berlin, no
   date (*c*.1940), cf. p. 3; for the interrelations between individualization, family,
   sex roles and love, see Beck and Beck-Gernsheim (1994).
8 *Stammbuch*, published by Bundesverband der Deutschen Standesbeamten, e.V.,
   Verlag für Standesamtwesen, Berlin and Frankfurt, no date (*c*.1970), no page
   references.
9 Ibid.
10 Ibid.
11 Zapf (1992) expressly opposes this widespread misunderstanding. (Cf. pp. 190f).
12 Cf. the theory of reflexive modernization in Beck (1993), esp. ch. III; and Beck,
   Giddens and Lash (1994).
13 The pragmatic, *a priori* method of mass-data sociology is worth noting: quan-
   titative methods presuppose pre-formed categories and concepts (even if they are
   nominally de-activated). However, a society which is individualizing itself eludes
   these standardizations imposed by research method (which is already giving rise
   to unmanageable complications in the introduction of flexible working time and
   work contracts, for example). It is therefore difficult for a sociology proud of its
   technical virtuosity to jump over its own shadow and address questions of a self-
   individualizing society. But at the same time it becomes clear, here again, how
   woefully sociology has so far neglected the question of what kind of sociological
   empiricism, of scholarly and social self-observation, is appropriate to a society
   caught in the draught and sand-drift of individualization. Cf. Beck and
   Allmendinger (1993).

REFERENCES

Baethge, Martin 1991: Arbeit, Vergesellschaftung, Identität – zur zunehmenden normativen Subjectivierung der Arbeit. In W. Zapf (ed.), *Die Modernisierung moderner Gesellschaften*, Frankfurt/M.

Bauman, Zygmunt 1991: *Thinking Sociologically*. UK: Oxford: Blackwell; USA: Cambridge.

Bauman, Zygmunt 1993: Wir sind wie Landstreicher – Die Moral im Zeitalter der Beliebigkeit. *Süddeutsche Zeitung*, 16/17 November 1993.

Beck, Ulrich 1986: *Risikogesellschaft. Auf dem Weg in eine Andere Moderne*. Frankfurt/M: Suhrkamp; *Risk Society*. London: Sage, 1992.

Beck, Ulrich 1993: *Die Erfindung des Politischen*. Frankfurt: Suhrkamp; translation forthcoming: Polity Press.

Beck, Ulrich 1994: The Debate on the 'Individualization Theory' in Today's Sociology in Germany. In Bernhard Schäfers (ed.), *Sociology in Germany – Development, Institutionalization, Theoretical Disputes*, Opladen: Leske Verlag.

Beck, U. and Allmendinger, J. 1993: *Individualisierung und die Erhebung Sozialer Ungleichheit*. Munich: DFG research project.

Beck, Ulrich and Beck-Gernsheim, Elisabeth 1993: Nicht Autonomie, sondern Bastelbiographie. *Zeitschrift für Soziologie*, vol. 3, June, pp. 178–87.

Beck, U. and Beck-Gernsheim, E. 1994: *The Normal Chaos of Love*. Cambridge: Polity Press.

Beck, U., Giddens, A. and Lash, S. 1994: *Reflexive Modernization – Politics, Tradition and Aesthetics in the Modern Social Order*. Cambridge: Polity Press.

Benn, Gottfried 1979: *Essays und Reden*. Frankfurt/M.: Fischer.

Berger, Peter L. 1977: *Einladung zur Soziologie*. Munich: Deutsche Taschenbuch Verlag.

Bertram, Hans and Dannenbeck, Clemens 1990: Pluralisierung von Lebenslagen und Individualisierung von Lebensführungen. Zur Theorie und Empirie regionaler Disparitäten in der Bundesrepublik Deutschland. In Peter A. Berger and Stefan Bradil (eds), *Lebenslagen, Lebensläufe, Lebensstile*. Göttingen: Schwartz, pp. 207–29.

Bertram, Hans, Bayer, Hiltrud and Bauereiss, Renate 1993: *Familien-Atlas, Lebenslagen und Regionen in Deutschland*. Opladen: Leske und Budrich.

Blasius, Dirk 1992: *Ehescheidung in Deutschland im 19. und 20. Jahrhundert*. Frankfurt: Fischer Taschenbuch Verlag.

Bock, Gisela and Duden, Barbara 1977: Arbeit aus Liebe – Liebe als Arbeit. In *Frauen und Wissenschaft. Beiträge zur Berliner Sommeruniversität für Frauen, Juli 1986*. Berlin: Courage Verlag, pp. 18–99.

Bolte, Karl Martin 1983: Subjektorientierte Soziologie – Plädoyer für eine Forschungsperspektive. In Bolte and Treutner (eds), *Subjektorientierte Arbeits – und Berufssociologie*. Frankfurt/M: Campus, pp. 12–36.

Burckhardt, Jakob 1987: *Die Kultur der Renaissance in Italien*. Stuttgart.

Burkart, Günter 1993: Individualisierung und Elternschaft – das Beispiel USA. In *Zeitschrift für Soziologie*, vol. 3, June 1993, pp. 159–77.

Burkart, Günter and Kohli, Martin 1992: *Liebe, Ehe, Elternschaft*. Munich: Piper.
Cunningham, Michael 1991: *A Home at the End of the World*. Harmondsworth: Penguin Books.
Dumont, Louis 1991: *Individualismus – Zur Ideologie der Moderne*, Frankfurt/M: Campus.
Durkheim, Emile 1993: *Der Selbstmord*. Frankfurt: Suhrkamp.
Enzensberger, Hans Magnus 1992: *Mediocrity and Delusion. Collected Diversions*, trans. Martin Chalmers. London: Verso.
Foucault, Michel 1984: *Le Souci de Soi*. Paris: Gallimard.
Giddens, Anthony 1991: *Self Identity and Modernity*. London: Polity.
Hitzler, Ronald 1988: *Kleine Lebenswelten – Ein Bietrag zum Verstehen von Kultur*. Opladen: Westdeutscher Verlag.
König, René 1979: Gesellschaftliches Bewusstsein und Sociologie. In Günther Lüschen (ed.), *Deutsche Soziologie seit 1945*, special edition 21, 1979.
Ley, Katrin 1984: Von der Normal – zur Wahlbiographie. In Kohli and Robert (eds), *Biographie und Soziale Wirklichkeit*. Stuttgart: Metzler, pp. 239–60.
Macfarlane, Alan 1979: *The Origins of English Individualism. The Family, Property and Social Transition*. New York: Cambridge University Press.
Mayer, Karl Ulrich 1991: Soziale Ungleichheit und Lebensläufe. In Bern Giesen and Claus Leggewie (eds), *Experiment Vereinigung*, Berlin, pp. 87–99.
Morris, Colin 1972: *The Discovery of the Individual, 1050–1200*. Toronto: University of Toronto Press.
Musil, Robert 1961: *The Man without Qualities*. London: Secker and Warburg.
Ostner, Ilona and Roy, Peter 1991: Späte Heirat – Ergebnis Biographisch Unterschiedlicher Erfahrungen mit 'Cash' und 'Care'. Project proposal to Deutsche Forschungsgemeinschaft (DFG), Bremen.
Parsons, Talcott 1978: Religion in Postindustrial Society. In *Action, Theory and the Human Condition*, New York.
Peters, Bernhard 1993: *Die Integration moderner Gesellschaften*. Frankfurt/M: Suhrkamp.
Schorlemmer, Friedrich 1993: Der Befund ist nicht alles. Contribution to debate on *Bindungsverlust und Zukunftsangst in der Risikogesellschaft*, 30 October 1993, in Halle; manuscript.
Struck, Gerhard 1991: Die mühselige Geichberechtigung von Mann und Frau in Ehenamensrecht. In *Neue Justiz*, vol. 9, pp. 390–2.
Sun, Lena H. 1993: Freedom has a Price, Chinese Discover. *International Herald Tribune*, 14 June.
Turow, Scott 1991: *The Burden of Proof*. Harmondsworth: Penguin Books.
Tyrell, Hartmann 1986: Soziologische Anmerkungen zur Historischen Familienforschung. *Geschichte und Gesellschaft*, 12, pp. 254–73.
Weymann, Ansgar 1989: Handlungsspielräume im Lebenslauf, in Weymann (ed.), *Handlungsspielräume. Untersuchungen zur Individualisierung und Institutionalisierung von Lebensläufen in der Moderne*. Stuttgart: Enke.
Zapf, Wolfgang 1992: Entwicklung und Sozialstruktur moderner Gesellschaften. In Korte, Hermann and Schäfers, Bernhard (eds), *Einführung in Hauptbegriffe der Soziologie*, Opladen.

3

Morality in the Age of Contingency

Zygmunt Bauman

The paradox of tradition is that once it has been spoken the tradition is no more what its spokesmen claim it to be. Tradition is invoked for the authority of its silence: a silence that neither needs nor brooks argument and which renders all argument superfluous, pretentious and impotent. Yet in order to yield its authority (that is, to be of that use whose prospect had seduced the speaker in the first place), tradition needs to be argumentatively established: its silence must be broken. But once it has been broken, its authority becomes of a kind altogether different from the now lost, virginal, unthinking allure. It is now but an authority of choice and declared loyalty: of a choice among choices, a loyalty among loyalties. The noun 'tradition' moves now, verb-like, from the past to the future tense, from the rhetoric of the forever-given to the rhetoric of the perpetually-uncertain. It is no more the self-assured silence, but the anxious continuity of speech that makes tradition possible, though it is exactly the opposite which, when speaking of tradition, the speech speaks about. Tradition vanishes in the self-same discourse which purports to make its presence tangible.

The discourse itself is the sign of that dissolution. It is said that human conditions do not exist until they are named: but they are not named until they are noticed, and they are hardly ever noticed until their existence becomes a matter of concern, of active search and creative/defensive efforts. Orthodoxy does not know of itself until kicked into shape by heresy. To be seen, named and talked about, tradition must first be challenged by novelty. It is the novelty that conjures up the tradition as its *other*, as something it is not, something it is up against, or something it lacks and misses – as nostalgia for an old home rather than the longing for a home yet unbuilt. It has been said that the remarkable thing about community is that it always has been. Tradition lives only posthumously, in the experience of detraditional-ization. Tradition is the upstart novelty's dream of dignified sedateness, the vagabond's dream of abode, the unfounded life's dream of foundations, the unwarranted being's dream of credentials.

The insecurity of speakers is the true subject matter of the discourse whose ostensible topic is the security of tradition. That discourse is about absences and an unslaked thirst. It is about what is missing and missed. First and foremost – it is about absent totality. Totality in space: a framed composition that would allow every brush stroke to bask in the glory of meaningful design. And totality in time: an unbroken thread that would keep every bead in place, and in its *right* place, as it is strung on the thread of time just after the one before and before the one that will come after. Tradition is such a missing totality. Or, rather, that entity which would make a totality out of fragments scattered in space and time: of the episodes otherwise devoid of connection, orphaned by the past and heirless.

Tradition is the talk of the town in a city in which flickering images, calculated for maximum impact and instant obsolescence, replace durable objects; in which freedom means 'keeping your options open' and not being able to keep them otherwise than open; in which the fading of a durable public world intensifies the fear of separation at the same time that it weakens the psychological resources that make it possible to confront that fear realistically. In other words, postmodernity being the renowned slaughterhouse of totalities, tradition is the talk of the postmodern town.

You recognize any human condition by what it thinks it does not have but should have; by what it talks about obsessively since it desires it badly while being hopelessly short of the means of acquiring it. You could recognize the modern condition by its compulsive concern with order and transparency. You can recognize the postmodern one by its infatuation with community.

Or, for that matter, with *identity*; another missing totality – or perhaps the same missing totality, only projected on another screen, that of the self. Identity is what would connect the unconnected, make a process out of random happenings, a life-project out of drifting and short-lived concerns. Identity is what one would be able to build up, brick by brick and floor after floor, so that it would grow in solidity and stature, with each step more secure and reliable. Identity is what would allow one to deploy freedom of choice in the service of determination and certainty, to streamline the succession of desperate and inconclusive forays into the pilgrimage of self-creation.

Postmodernity is the point at which modern untying (dis-embedding, dis-encumbering) of tied (embedded, situated) identities reaches its completion: *it is now all too easy to choose identity, but no longer possible to hold it*. At the moment of its ultimate triumph, the liberation succeeds in annihilating its object. The freer the choice, the less it feels like a choice. It lacks weight and solidity, as it can be revoked at short notice or without notice – and so binds no-one, including the chooser; it leaves no lasting trace, as it bestows neither rights nor responsibilities and as its consequences may be discarded or disavowed at will once they start feeling awkward or cease to satisfy. Freedom rebounds as contingency; the famed 'enabling' for which it is praised has given the postmodern seekers of identity all the powers of a Sisyphus. Postmodernity is the condition of *contingency* which has come to be known as beyond repair. Nothing seems impossible, let alone unimaginable. Everything that 'is', is until further notice. Nothing that has been binds the present, while the present has but a feeble hold on the future.

Contingency need not be experienced as impotence. On the contrary, it may well be – and often is – savoured as omnipotence. All things that can be done can be undone . . . Contingency may be lived as a state of perpetual new beginning and fresh start. Defeat in yesterday's game does not diminish one's chances in the game that starts tomorrow, much as yesterday's successes do not guarantee today's victory. Thinking of grand life-long projects may be foolish, but daily tasks can be handled with growing ease. While busily applying foolproof recipes to resolve little emergencies and make little things happen, one can forget the worry of big crises – and play down the meagre chances of holding on to the things already made.

One can think of postmodern life as one lived in a city in which traffic is daily re-routed and street names are liable to be changed without notice. Available maps do not guarantee that the house one seeks will be there at the end of the walk, and that the route still leads in the direction one wanted to go. The resulting agony is baseless, though, since the constant drifting of urban attractions makes it unlikely that the allure of the destination will outlast the duration of the walk. In such a city one is well advised not to plan long and time-consuming journeys. The shorter the trip, the greater is the chance of completing it, and the less the threat of disappointment at the end. A sensible person will avoid long-term commitments and long-distance expeditions. A rational postmodern person would not wish to build her/his identity of steel and concrete, but instead would fight tooth and nail any attempt to have it fixed or otherwise 'defined'. To be rational in the *modern* world meant to be a pilgrim and to live one's life as a pilgrimage. To be rational in the *postmodern* world means to be a vagrant or a tourist, or to act as one.

Everything seems to conspire these days against distant goals, life-long projects, lasting commitments, eternal alliances, immutable identities. One cannot build long-term hopes around one's job, profession, skills even; one can bet that, before long, the job will vanish, the profession will change beyond recognition, the skills will cease to be in demand. Your students will soon find out that the demand for their skills does not last as long as the time required for mastering them. One cannot build the future around partnership or the family either: in the age of 'confluent love', togetherness lasts no longer than the satisfaction of one of the partners, commitment is from the start 'until further notice', and today's intense attachment may only intensify tomorrow's frustrations. Rampant inflation, stock exchange or exchange rate vagaries, the volatile fortunes of investments, combine to make every hour of life rainy, and shift 'control over the future' from the realm of calculation to that of gambling and magic. Styles coveted today by many and admired by all will fall into ridicule before the day is out, yesterday's dreams will tomorrow become nightmares, objects of intense desire will soon lose their seductive power, today's proud possessions will turn into rubbish long before they lose their use and glitter, safe havens will become seats of most fearsome dangers, hard learned techniques of good living will yield mortal threats, and guaranteed wisdom will be debunked as ignorance or prejudice.

It has been said that there is no such thing as a 'good organization' – that is, an organization good for all conditions and eventualities. A solid, cohesive, accident-proof and secure structure, dreamt of and painstakingly constructed in a stable environment, becomes a liability in a rapidly changing habitat and in the face of untried challenges. Were, say, our planet devoid of its protective atmospheric layer, so that the meteorites kept hitting the earth, the sole life form likely to survive and thrive would be a formless plasma, uncommitted to any shape or structure. It seems that we have entered a time in which formlessness is the fittest of forms.

Obviously, ours is not a good time for Puritan pilgrims, for life lived as pilgrimage. With shrines shifting by the day and with built-in instant obsolescence being carefully designed, or unexpected, but always a standard feature of vehicles, what sensible person would set the destination at the beginning of life's journey and then measure progress by the shrinking distance to the goal of yore? It is not the pilgrims, but vagabonds and tourists who seem to respond sensibly to the chances our times offer and the ambushes they hold.

Look at the vagabond first. He does not know how long he will stay where he is now, and more often than not it won't be up to him to decide when the stay comes to an end. Once on the move, he sets his destinations as he goes and as he reads the road signs, but even then he cannot be sure whether he will stop, and for how long, at the next staging post. What he does know is that, more likely than not, the stopover will be temporary. What keeps him on the move is disillusionment with the place of his last sojourn and the forever smouldering hope that the next place that he has not yet visited, or perhaps the place after next, may be free of the faults which repelled him in the places he has already come to know. Pulled forward by hope untested, pushed from behind by the hope frustrated – the vagabond journeys through an unstructured space; like a wanderer in the desert, who knows only such trails as are marked with his own footprints, and blown off again by the next gust of wind. The vagabond structures the space he happens to pass through, only to dismantle the structure again as he leaves. Each successive 'structuring' is local and temporary – episodic.

Look at the tourist now. Like the vagabond, the tourist knows that he won't stay for long at the place in which he has arrived. And as in the vagabond's case, he has only his own biographical time on which to string together the places he has visited; nothing else seems to order them or decide their succession. This habit rebounds as an experience of the utmost pliability of space: whatever the intrinsic meanings of the sites he visits, whatever their 'natural' location in the 'order of things' – meanings and locations may be pushed aside; they are allowed into the tourist's world solely at the tourist's discretion. It is the tourist's aesthetic capacity – his or her curiosity, need of amusement, will and ability to live through novel, pleasurable, and pleasurably novel experiences – which appears to possess a nearly total freedom to 'structure' the tourist's life-world; the kind of freedom which the vagabond, who depends on the rough realities of the visited places for his livelihood and who may only avoid displeasure by escaping, can only dream of. Tourists pay for their freedom: the right to disregard native concerns and feelings, the right to spin a web of meanings all of their own, they obtain in a commercial transaction. Freedom comes in a contractual deal, the volume of freedom depends solely on the ability to pay: once purchased, it becomes a right which the tourist can self-righteously demand, pursue through the courts of the land and expect to be duly gratified and protected. Like the vagabond, the tourist is extra-territorial; but unlike the vagabond, he lives his extra-territoriality as a privilege, as independence, as the right to be free, to be free to choose; as a licence to re-structure the world to fit his wishes and to quit the world that refuses to fit. What may be routine quotidianity for the natives, is for the tourist a collection of exotic thrills. Restaurants with their strangely smelling dishes, hotels with strangely dressed (or undressed) maids, strange looking memorials to somebody else's historical dramas, strange rituals of someone else's daily routines – all wait meekly for the tourist to cast an eye at, pay attention to, derive pleasure from. The world is the tourist's oyster. The world is there to be lived pleasurably – and is given meaning by this purpose. In most cases, the aesthetic meaning is the only meaning that world needs – and can bear.

The vagabond and the tourist both move *through* the spaces other people live *in*: those other people may be in control of the spacing – but the outcome of their labours has little grip on the vagabond, and virtually none on the tourist. With the locals, the vagabond and the tourist have but the briefest and most perfunctory of encounters. As in theatre, the most dramatic and impressive of contacts are securely encased in the space between the stage-wings and within the time spanning the rise and fall of the curtain – inside that chunk of time–space set aside for the 'suspension of disbelief' – and guaranteed not to leak or spill over (unless preserved, at the tourist's discretion, as private property – confined to the pleasingly un-safe keeping of that ultimate product and symbol of postmodernity, the eminently eraseable and re-usable videotape). Physically close to the 'locals', spiritually remote: this is the formula of both the vagabond's and the tourist's life.

The seductive charm of such a formula is that it holds a solemn promise that the physical closeness will not be allowed to get out of gear, let alone out of control, and slide into a *moral* proximity. Particularly in the case of the tourist, the guarantee is very nearly foolproof. Freedom from moral duty has been paid for in advance; the adventure-tour kit holds the preventive medicine against pangs of conscience, neatly packed next to the pills preventing air sickness.

One thing that the vagabond's and the tourist's lives are not designed to contain, and most often are excused from containing, is cumbersome, incapacitating, joy-killing, insomniogenic moral responsibility. The pleasures of the massage parlour come clean of sad thoughts of children sold into prostitution; the latter, like the rest of the bizarre ways the natives have chosen, is not the punter's responsibility, not his blame, not his deed – and there is nothing the punter can do (and thus nothing he *ought* to do) to repair it. Nowhere as much and as radically as in the tourist mode is the uniqueness of the actor – that condition *sine qua non* of all moral responsibility – disavowed, erased, blotted out. No-one but the tourist is so blatantly, conspicuously dissolved in numbers, interchangeable, depersonalized. 'They all do the same.' The wobbly tracks are well trodden, kneaded by countless feet; the sharp sights rounded by countless eyes; the rough textures sanded to gloss by countless palms. Moral proximity, responsibility and the uniqueness – irreplaceability – of the moral subject are triune; they won't survive (or, rather, wouldn't have been born) without each other. Moral responsibility vanishes when 'everybody does it', which, inevitably, means also that 'everybody can do it', or (which morally speaking amounts to much the same) that 'no-one does it'. The tourist is bad news for morality.

Vagabonds and tourists are not postmodern inventions. What is new is that in the postmodern world the vagabond and the tourist are no longer marginal people or marginal conditions. They turn into moulds destined to engulf and shape the totality of life and the whole of quotidianity; the patterns by which all practices are measured. They are glorified by the chorus of commercial exploiters and media flatterers. They set the standard of happiness and successful life in general. Tourism is no longer something one practises when on holiday. Normal life – if it is to be a good life – ought to be and had better be, a continuous holiday. (One is tempted to say that what has been described as 'carnival culture' – those cyclical fairs of public morality-breaching, meant to be therapeutic breaks in the routine, momentary suspensions of normality and reversals of normal roles to make the norm and the routine liveable – turns itself now into the norm and the routine. It is the well spaced and short-lived public rituals of collective empathy with other people's collective calamities, of the 'rock relief' or 'comic relief' kind, that have taken over the function of therapeutic 'norm reversal'.) Ideally, one should be a tourist everywhere and every day. To be everywhere in, but nowhere of. Aloof. Free – the exemption from all non-contractual duties having been paid for in advance and duly insured. And with the sport-spoiling moral conscience having been fed the latest brand of tranquillizers.

Politics faithfully records, follows, and reinvigorates the trend. Moral issues tend to be increasingly compressed into the idea of 'human rights' – folkloristically translated as the right to be left alone. The dismantling of the 'welfare state' – a prospect only a few years ago deemed to be out of the question by most perceptive of minds – is now taking place, slowly yet relentlessly, in the full glory of expert applause and with not much more than a token resistance by the moralists.

The welfare state used to institutionalize *commonality* of fate, since its provisions were meant for every participant (every citizen) in equal measure, thus balancing everybody's privations with everybody's gains. The slow retreat from that principle into the means-tested, 'focused' assistance for 'those who need it most' has institutionalized the *diversity* of fate, and thus made the unthinkable thinkable. It is now the taxpayer's privations that are to be balanced against someone else's – the benefit recipient's – gains. Altogether different principles are embodied in, say, a child benefit for every parent, and child benefit for indolent parents alone. The first makes tangible the bond between public and private – community and the individual – and casts the community as the pledge of the individual's security. The second sets the public and the private against each other, and casts the community as the individual's (now re-forged into the taxpayer's) burden and bane. The loss of the first would be resented by most, as only for a few is such a loss likely to be balanced by the gain from reduced taxation. The loss or curtailment of the second would be welcomed by all, except the few who bear the loss. In almost every chapter of the Welfare State the invisible dividing line between the first situation and the second has by now been passed, and what used to be a collective insurance against individual disasters has been replaced by a nation divided between premium payers and the benefit recipients.

In the new constellation, services for those who do not pay are bound to be resented by those who pay – and calls to reduce or abandon them would find an ever growing number of willing ears. If the installation of the welfare state was an attempt to mobilize economic interests in the service of moral responsibility – the dismantling of the welfare state deploys economic interest as a means to liberate political calculation from moral constraints. Moral responsibility is now once more something that 'needs to be paid for'. The Samaritan would not be good if he had no money. 'Sorry, no money', is all one needs say to stop worrying about not being a Good Samaritan.

The dismantling of the welfare state spells hard times not only for the poor and unfortunate who need a society of morally responsible people most, but also (and perhaps, in the long run, primarily) for moral responsibility as such. It re-casts the 'being for others', that cornerstone of all morality, as a matter of accounts and calculation, of value for money, of gains and costs, of luxury one can or cannot permit: and that the wise man needs to refuse. The process is self-propelling and self-accelerating: the new perspective leads inevitably to a relentless deterioration of collective services (the quality of the public health service, of public education, of whatever is left of public housing or transport), which prompts those who can to buy themselves out from collective provisions – an act which turns out to mean, sooner or later, buying themselves out of collective responsibility.

It is a '*your* value for *my* money' (your benefits for my taxes) situation: citizenship means less expense, the right to pay less into the public kitty, to worry less and to feel less shame. Responsibility does not come into it, either as the reason or as a purpose. The ideal for the citizen is a satisfied customer. Society is there for individuals to seek and find satisfaction for their individual wants. The social space is, primarily, a grazing ground, the aesthetic space is a playground. None allows, and both resent, a moral spacing. One can as well be a Lombardian who sees no reason why he should pay for the lazy and improvident Calabrians who claim to be his brethren . . . Written or unwritten, the citizen's charter of consumer society condemns the flawed consumer, the imperfect citizen, to the life of a vagabond, while underwriting the status of the fully-fledged citizen as a tourist. Tourist always, on holiday and in the daily routine. Tourist everywhere, abroad and at home.

Tourist in society, tourist in life — free to find his or her own aesthetic position and forgiven the forgetting of the moral one. Life as the tourist's haunt.

Postmodern politics translates ethical issues as the demand for scandal-proof politicians, and rejects the rest of moral demands as an alien body. The demise of the welfare state is but one manifestation of the process. There are others, no less awesome. The relentless pulverization of collective solidarity by evicting communal services beyond the bounds of political process, by massive deregulation of survival provisions, and politically sponsored insti-tutionalization of individual egoism as the last bulwark of social rationality, has eventually led to a veritable 'social Munich'. Thirty-six million Europe-ans without work and a place in society, as well as the security and protection of employment of hundreds of millions of other Europeans, have been by the common consent of governments sacrificed to the pocket-lining aims of the 'defence of currency', public expense cutting, the rise of competitiveness and profitability, and promotion of a free market. Drawing its criteria of decency from the supermarket and dressing itself in its fashion, the Republic has vacated the battlefield of collective identities, abandoning it to the mercy of tribal war-lords. Ethnic herding and confessional flocking together take over when the collective responsibility of the *polis* fizzles out. The dissipation of the social rebounds in the consolidation of the tribal. As identities go, pri-vatization means tribalization.

It is time to ask what are the ethical consequences of postmodernity. Is there a future left for morality in a world populated by vagabonds desperate for the cosiness of tribal camp-fires and by tourists amused by the display of entertaining tribal customs?

Some say that there is no future, rejoice in the news, and exhort us to join in the rejoicing, announcing the advent of *l'après-devoir*, an era burdened no more with duties, commandments and absolute obligations; the final demise of self-sacrifice and the final triumph of pragmatism over utopia. The 'after-duty' is a time of unadulterated individualism and search for the good life, leaving room but for the most vestigial and minimalistic morality.

Lipovetsky's enthusiasm is not universally shared, but his diagnosis is – or almost is. Many people bewail what such writers want us to see and acknow-ledge, but they seldom doubt the truthfulness of the picture painted. By well-nigh common consent, postmodernity means the end of morality as we know it . . .

Perhaps this is indeed the case: the end of morality as *we know it*. Or, more correctly, as we have all learned to see it. Ethical philosophy hand in hand with morality-promoting practice have long identified morality with the

externally installed and fixed super-ego; their school differences notwith-
standing, all have agreed that morality is an imposition, and that only divine, or rational, but always supra-individual principles, promoted by sacred,
or secular, but always supra-individual powers, can secure their grip on the
unruly and essentially immoral, anti-human drives of humans. No wonder
that the crumbling belief in universal principles and the weakening grip of
universal authorities is widely perceived as the end of morality. Having
convinced ourselves that moral conduct must be 'founded' and follow universal 'rules', we find it difficult to conceive of a morality without foundations
and a universally accepted code.

And yet, perhaps, one may view the moral consequences of postmodernity
in a somewhat different fashion. One may say that the trade mark of
postmodernity being the massacre of illusions, the power-assisted image of
an externally founded ethics, grounded in universal principles, was but one
of the many illusions given the quietus. Killed in the massacre was but a
certain power-assisted ethical theory and practice, not the moral reality they
strove to subsume and control. The latter may well have escaped unscathed;
perhaps even – who knows? – strengthened. At least it must now, by necessity, face its own irredeemable solitude and find out that the only grounding
it can reasonably hope for (and, despite the assurances to the contrary, the
only grounding it might have ever possessed) may be found only in the moral
impulses, skills and competences of men and women living with, and above
all *for*, each other. There is no guarantee that this grounding will prove to
be sound enough to sustain a moral community; but, again contrary to
promises, the power-assisted, legislated ethics has spectacularly failed to sustain
it either – and we know now that it is unlikely to deliver it in the future.
And so there is little else we can do, except to carry our hopes to where the
last chance of the moral community, evicted from bankrupt shelters and a
fugitive from treacherous ones, has recoiled: to the moral capacity of the self,
instead of to the legislating and policing capacities of supra-individual powers; to the wondrous aptitudes of sociation, rather than the coercive resource-
fulness of socialization. This could be a descent into hell, we are warned. But
it may also be the moral person's voyage of self-discovery.

4

Complexity, Structural Contingencies and Value Conflicts

Niklas Luhmann

Complex systems have to satisfy a number of formal conditions.[1] They can only exceed a certain minimum size if they can do without solid, continuous connections between all their elements, and are internally able to organize the resulting instability. This can be achieved by selecting allowable connections – which are then, from an evolutionary point of view, more or less improbable. Or the system can work with temporally unstable links, so that A is in contact first with B and then with K, releasing B for a contact with V which, in this case, must temporarily detach itself from its neighbour W. Complexity can, therefore, be temporalized with regard to the allowed connections, and seek to achieve order through controlled succession. In extreme cases of very great complexity not only the connections but the elements themselves are temporalized. Such systems are then in a state of permanent decay. They consist entirely of events which vanish as they occur, leaving hardly any trace within the system. The problem of the system's survival then involves a constant replacement of the transient events by others, so that one can speak of a system only to the extent that the selection of subsequent events is, on one hand, highly selective but, on the other, not arbitrary. Even in the brain, elementary units that are constantly being released must be impregnated over and over again – otherwise no memory is formed.[2]

Such highly temporalized systems need a memory; that is to say, they need an arrangement for the exceptional case when transient events do leave traces within the system – or, in other words, when a past event remains recognizable in the recurrent network formed by the generation of further events, and contributes as an identical element to the system's continuous monitoring of its own consistency. Systems of this kind cannot, of course, operate within their own past, any more than within their own future or their own environment. But they can compensate for this inability by compiling cross-references, and to this end they produce identities. Even neurophysiological systems, and certainly systems of consciousness and social systems, have to monitor their own cohesion continuously with the aid of such identities (which may be either anchored on a molecular level, or represented as objects, or re-used via language), to safeguard the selectivity of their systemic coherence. This is done by replacing vanished events by memory values, which are condensed into entities and re-used again and again in new situations, and thus are confirmed and generalized. An overload situation, which might easily result, is avoided by suspending re-use and by forgetting.

Social systems are systems of the type described above. In analysing them, therefore, one must distinguish between the operative level of successive events, and the semantic level of meanings worthy of retention. The operative level is generated by currently occurring communications. What actually takes place is decided on this level. Here, the system always operates currently, that is, always simultaneously with the rest of the world – never before and never afterwards. The semantics generated in this way control the selection of links between events by remembering and forgetting. Without this self-monitoring through meaning, such systems could not exist. Hence the evolution of language is an essential requirement in the emergence of social systems.

These very general considerations can be used as a basis for a correspondingly general theory of society. However, if we want to consider questions of social history and, in particular, the structural and semantic problems of modern society, we have to refine our approach with some additional assumptions. This will be done with the aid of the hypothesis that the structure of complex systems, and particularly of complex societies, requires system differentiation – that is, the formation of systems within systems – at the operative level.[3] System differentiation makes it possible to achieve the advantage of system formation by assuming a pre-formed system already delimited from the environment, and then, as it were, demoting it to the status of an environment of the new subsystem that is being formed.[4] In this way the complexity and evolutionary improbability of the total system can be enhanced – provided, always, that the formation of the system within the system is successful.

System differentiation affects the operative level – that is, it limits the possibility of extending actually occurring communications by other actually occurring communications.

The level of complexity a society can attain in the course of its evolution depends primarily on the prevailing form of system differentiation. The transition from a primarily stratified form of differentiation to one organized primarily around functions, raises a society to a much higher level of complexity within a few centuries. This is because it is no longer necessary to give precedence to questions of rank before all other questions in daily communication.[5] Nor would one be prepared today, except in fundamentalist circles, to divide up the world in terms of moral criteria.[6] Thereby, the form of differentiation modifies the pre-conditions for the formation of a semantics by means of which the social system observes its own operations, actualizes recurrent elements and monitors its own cohesion. And this hypothesis brings us to the subject of this chapter. The thesis being advanced here states that the modern orientation by virtue of 'values' is connected to the functional differentiation of modern society, whereas earlier societies, with a predominantly hierarchical stratification, reacted quite differently to the need for selection imposed by their own complexity.

In methodological terms, therefore, the thesis involves a *comparison* of *relationships* between social structure (system differentiation) and semantics, and does not merely assert a simple connection. For there are many connections in any society. But if, in the context of problems of complexity, *the same* connection takes on *different* forms in societies differentiated *in different ways*, and if this can be traced back in both cases to problems concerning the management of great complexity (or, as we shall see, to a refusal to recognize paradox), this is a highly theoretical argument. From it, empirical historical research could identify the matters to which it should pay particular attention. Then it would not need to lose itself in the immense complexity of its own possibilities, in its 'mouse-eaten' sources or in 'data' that can be generated at will.[7]

The old European society was always a noble society, whether it was based on urban or feudal foundations. It was able to generate a centre/periphery differentiation, but was from then on, except for a few periods of empire formation (which could only be attempted in the Middle Ages, but which foundered on opposition from the Church), a polycentric society. This gave a special weight to the nobility, with its extensive regional contacts. With some abbreviation, therefore, we can speak of a primacy of hierarchical stratification.[8]

Noble societies, despite the high mobility enforced by demography, allocate fixed places to their families and thus to their individuals. Inclusion and exclusion are regulated by stratification – with a larger or smaller statusless marginal population of slaves (in households) and vagrants (outside households).[9] Accordingly, its description of the world is based on strongholds that offer resting places to motion. Or motion is conceived as circular, so that it comes to rest within itself. Being is grouped under characteristic features or ideas, and the preference for order as against disorder finds expression in the form of a normative concept of Nature.

Within ancient European philosophy, which observes this society and its world, we find it clearly expressed that this order is understood ontologically, so that being and non-being have to be distinguished. The question of why the distinction between being and non-being is important cannot therefore be allowed. It can only be characterized as a paradox and thereby excluded. All the same, that this is happening can be clearly seen. Zeno's paradoxes provide a supporting argument for ontological metaphysics. They point to a frontier that must not be crossed. While they have traditionally been regarded as a kind of philosophical game and used as the basis of philosophy's bivalent logic, in other texts we are better able to see how an ontology that has to assign fixed places to a being within a fixed order is constituted. Two illustrations will be sufficient.

In Plato's *The Sophist* (253D) we read 'that the division of things by classes (Greek: *géne*) and the avoidance of the belief that the same class is another, or another the same, belongs to the science of the dialectic'.[10] This provides the foundation for the necessity of distinguishing between classes, the nature of which is then defined in terms of ideas. This *génos*-technique dominated European thought up to Kant, who, while regarding it as empirically unavoidable, was more interested in *how* such an order of classes and types is *possible*.

In Aristotle's *Politics* (1254 b 36–7) we read that Nature should be observed in its natural state and not in its corrupted forms.[11] According to this, Nature can take on perfect and corrupt states, can be realized either in conformity or in opposition to itself, and in those cases where Nature recognizes itself – that is, in the case of the human soul – the perfect and not the corrupt forms should be respected. This inherently paradoxical concept of nature, containing its own antithesis, is thus given a normative form. The preference for perfection over corruption is built into the concept of Nature itself, and then expressed as a natural norm, as a natural law. The educational theory of the nobility followed this model; and the metaphor of the mirror, much used in the Middle Ages (e.g. the mirror of princes), signifies that in a mirror reality is not seen double – instead, its successful form, its virtue, is revealed.

Although early European thought encounters its own paradoxical foundations, it turns away and tries to resolve the paradoxes in ways that suit the given social order: by classifications and norms. Formulated paradoxes are kept in reservations, where they no longer touch on the order of the world. These reservations are found, on one hand, in the unfathomable regions of religion, in the theological concept of God and in the reports of mystics, which are deemed incomprehensible; and on the other, in rhetoric, which is allowed to comment on itself, but in terms which lack seriousness.[12]

This overarching cosmological concept collapses in the second half of the eighteenth century. The order formed of classes and types becomes recognizable as a product of evolution. Natural law is first transformed into the law of reason and then entrenched as constitutional law. Art breaks with the principle of imitation and accepts 'realism' only as one style among others. Rhetoric disappears, and 'recent theology deals more with religion than with God', as Hegel notes.[13] Historians have clearly recognized this collapse of the old European semantics, but have never really explained it.[14] From a sociological viewpoint, it is hardly an accident (although this does not, of course, imply a causal explanation) that this upheaval in semantics came at the time when stratification was giving way irreversibly to function as the principle of differentiation. But these connections are not observed as such, explained as such, or established as such. They are accepted as part of history, and assimilated by reconstituting the concept of history. Historians talk of the era of the modern states, the modern age, modern society, but a discourse describing the features of this age is dismissed as ideological. Sociology therefore prefers, with Max Weber, to do without its own concept of society, rather than become involved in a debate dependent on ideological positions.

It might be all the more interesting, therefore, if it were possible to demonstrate connections between structural complexity, social structure, and semantics in the modern society of the nineteenth and twentieth centuries.

About the middle of the nineteenth century, the semantics of 'values' began its historical career. Previously there had been the noble semantics of *valor* with its class-specific connotations, and an economic use of language that distinguished between value and price in order to take account of fluctuations in the latter. From the eighteenth century the word 'value' (*Wert, valeur*) is used in a sense, not further defined, which expresses generally accepted preferences. During the mid-nineteenth century, however, the distinction between being and validity was added, a distinction which makes it possible to assign values to a sphere, a world, an *a priori* status of their own, obeying different criteria from those of the sphere of the sciences, which concerns itself with what actually exists. (The fact that in Germany the sciences, and especially the human sciences, were also talked of in relation to validity (*Geltung*) is an academic peculiarity that did not gain general currency.) Within this sphere of the valid, further distinctions were drawn in terms of different value-relationships (Rickert) or orders of life (Weber), that could not be traced back to a common denominator, a system-principle, but

were of interest only as *differences*. In these areas, it is not possible to tran-
scend differences of values or of *a priori* assumptions – even those which are
of a political, religious, aesthetic, erotic, capitalist or scientific kind. And if
these differences cannot be resolved, the question of a unity behind the
distinction between being and validity, of the unity of a world in which this
distinction takes on a categorical importance, cannot even be raised.

This philosophy of values may well be thought to have gone out of fashion, and philosophers do indeed seem rather at a loss when asked for advice
in practical contexts, as in the formulation of party programmes, for example.
What impresses the sociologist, however, is the fact that, whatever philosophers may think, the semantics of values has become ingrained in the linguistic usage of politics and law, and seems to be as indispensable in
formulating party programmes and political goals as it is in interpreting the
constitution and in the jurisdiction of the Federal Constitutional Court.
Nowadays, questions of principle of this kind are often to be found under the
heading of 'ethics'.

But if we ask how 'ethics' are to be understood, all we come back to is
values – and always in the plural. This euphoria about values seems to suit
our contemporaries particularly well, and the question that arises is whether
there is an explanation for it.

At this point it might be helpful to look back at the general problem of
heightened complexity. As complexity increases, we said, selectivity and the
instability of relations between the basic units of the system also increase.
This unavoidable link is reflected in the upheavals in the semantic tradition
since the end of the eighteenth century. The lexicon *Geschichtliche Grundbegriffe*
distinguishes the temporalization and politicization of terminology, and its
tendency to be ideologized, as results of these upheavals.[15] More formally,
one might say that all connections are now described as *contingent*. They are
temporally contingent in that they are no longer determined by the past, by
an immutable Nature, by social origin; they are *objectively* contingent in that
they could always be different; and they are *socially* contingent in that they
no longer depend on consensus (keyword: 'democracy'). But as contingency
increases, a need arises for new 'inviolate levels', and it is this need that the
semantics of value satisfy, which in turn pronounces them unavoidable
today.[16]

Anyone seeking more exact information is pointed in two different directions, one empirical, the other logical; and anyone who still goes in for
metaphors of vertical might, say that the semantics of value offer an upper
and a lower 'inviolate level' – while *keeping quiet about both of them*.

Empirically, one can observe how communication with values is practised on the operative level. It is striking that the communication is not *about* values. Rather, the validity of values is *assumed*. Values are treated as *tacit knowledge*.[17] This protects them from contradiction. To contradict them, one needs first to elicit an overt profession of a value, so that one can say, 'I do not agree.' For communication requires references clearly stated within the communication. Someone who states their values explicitly provokes contradiction. For all communication is set up in such a way that the information transmitted can be accepted or rejected.[18] The French Revolution formulated its values as principles. One therefore knew at once what and who was meant, and could contradict easily and with good reasons. The doctor advises you: 'Do plenty of walking, it will do you good.' You then have to extrapolate the value of 'health' in order to decide whether it justifies such a sacrifice.

Ironic communication is another case of implicit communication. It makes greater demands, for it reveals its meaning through paradox, as the explication of the implication, and can only be understood if that is understood. Value-based communication, by contrast, keeps this paradoxicality quiet; it leaves the fact implicit that implicit communication is going on. But a concealed paradox remains: that what is being communicated is not communicated. Here again, sociology will be able to ask whether it is an accident that ironic communication is a typically modern phenomenon[19] – as if it had been invented as a special form which at the same time provokes and protects value-charged communication; after all, you cannot command someone to communicate ironically. The adherents of values ward off this imputation by describing irony as cynicism – a description which again merely presupposes the value of values.

Only theory, which draws attention to the paradoxical nature of irony, is as complicated as this. In everyday practice, communication based on values is quite simple and unavoidable. Nor is such communication, like irony, an invention of the modern age. But what might well be regarded as typically modern is the fact that, and the way in which, an explicit semantics of values supports itself on this operative level of the communication of preferences, elevating its preferences in order to inflate them into norms.

This brings us to the second of the two directions in which we have been pointed: the question of the logical structure of value relationships. The problem here is that there are many values and that there are no (so-called transitive) relationships of precedence between them. Each value merely precludes its antithesis (and not always even that).[20] The resolution of collisions between values is thus unregulated.[21] But decisions are only needed in the case of value collisions.[22] From this it follows that values are not able to regulate decisions. They may demand a consideration of the relevant values, but a conclusion does not follow from this as to which values are decisive in cases of conflict and as to which are set aside. All values may count as *necessary*, but all decisions remain, nevertheless, and for that very reason, *contingent*. We therefore have before us the figure of necessary contingency, well-known from the theology of Creation. And that is nothing other than a logically unambiguous paradox; for contingency is defined by the negation of necessity and impossibility.

On this foundation two possibilities are currently being tried out. Economic theory and, as an extension of it, the theory of 'rational choice' leave the preferences of the actors unexplained; they only presuppose that preferences exist, and attempt on this basis to arrive at scientifically tenable results. The other possibility is to see in values normative guidelines, but to neutralize their normativity, their validity against opposing guidelines by keeping the resolution of value conflicts open. Both versions offer modern society very adequate means of resolving paradoxes – though they are only adequate and plausible as long as one refrains from confronting paradoxicality itself, the paradox of necessary contingency. Accordingly *both* kinds of communication exist, and one only needs to know which is appropriate under which circumstance: the one with *declared preferences* or the one with *implied value judgements*.

To conclude, let us come back once more to the question of structural complexity or, more precisely, to the forms of system differentiation that produce structural complexity. They do so by restricting complexity in system-specific areas, thus propagating it throughout society as a whole. Our starting-point was that functional differentiation makes possible greater complexity than does stratification. This hypothesis can also be pursued on a second, more concrete level. Stratified societies contained household and corporation, but neither families nor organizations in the present-day sense. The dominant structure of the household was held together by kinship relationships and by patron/client relationships.[23] Corporations, such as monasteries, universities, towns, guilds, and in some parts of Europe corporations of the estates (*Standschaften*), enclosed the lives of their members completely. Political society (*societas civilis*) was the contact area between heads of households, who knew each other directly or indirectly and thus found it easy to make contact with each other when necessary. Anyone who wanted to live according to his own whim (preference) was referred to, on precisely that account, as an *idiótes*, and ignored.

In modern, functionally-differentiated society different conditions prevail in all these respects, and the conditions are so very different that not even point-to-point cross-references are possible.[24] Our families and organizations have no predecessors, the former household and corporations no successors.

The only common ground is that in both cases neither the whole society nor its primary subsystems could or can be given the form of a single household, corporation or organization. This difference of levels was even then, and still is now, a correlative of the degree of complexity already reached.

Unlike the estates in old society, the function-systems of modern society are based on the principle of *inclusion* of the whole population. All people have legal status; all, provided they have money, can take part in economic life. Politically, there is universal and equal suffrage. All children have to attend school, etc. Unequal treatment arises only from the internal logic of the individual systems.[25] However, it is also true that modern organizations are based structurally on a principle of *exclusion*. Members are recruited in a highly selective way, and even their membership roles embrace only a fraction of their actual behaviour. Only on this condition can the decision-making processes of organizations be regulated in their smallest details. The structurally enforced inclusion of the whole population in the function-systems is therefore precluded by an equally indispensable exclusion of almost everyone from all concrete organizations. Who, of all existing people, is a doctor at a particular hospital or a member of a certain political party, a teacher at a particular school or a policeman? Whereas the corporations of the old world were institutions complementing the stratified household structures, modern organizations are parts of the function-systems, but with the inclusion/exclusion relationship inverted.

It is also this aspect of modern society (and not only the abstract degree of its complexity) which prohibits the ordering of groupings in terms of classes and types; in terms of their essential features and natures. The semantics that have taken the place of those categories are based on a structural *emancipation of contingencies*.[26] As a result, the allocation of individuals to social categories is no longer based on origin or on a protected legal position (property), nor even on secure employment, but on careers, that link positions arrived at contingently to positions to be arrived at contingently – on the way up, or down, or into the margins. Under these conditions individuals are encouraged to identify themselves with their own preferences, to assert them as rights to themselves; all that is expected of them is that they declare their identities and make them available by communication. An impressive example of this is when extremist right-wing youths or 'skinheads' in Germany are not embarrassed, under police interrogation, to give 'hostility towards foreigners' as the reason for their criminal actions – as if that were a presentable motive. On the other hand, communication is governed by imputed values that only in extreme cases become thematically explicit enough to make yes/no decisions necessary.

No logically secure conclusions about semantics can be drawn from social structures. Nor may we suppose that any connections between the two are exclusively correct. We have no guarantee that the semantics of preferences attributable to individuals and of apparently self-evident values define, once and for all, the forms – reproducible and deserving to be retained – by which modern society should orientate itself. For us it must be enough that it is possible, despite the unique complexity of modern society, to have found connections that cannot be varied at will. And if we are inclined to abandon the semantics of values, we should ask ourselves how, under existing conditions, the underlying paradoxes are to be resolved differently, how they can be reduced to other distinguishable identities.

NOTES

1   For a more detailed discussion see Niklas Luhmann (1992).
2   Cf. Heinz Förster (1948).
3   In earlier cybernetics, part-functions and ultrastability would have been referred to at this point. Cf. W. Ross Ashby (1954, pp. 98f, 153ff; and 1956, pp. 82ff).
4   For a more detailed discussion see Luhmann (1990).
5   Admittedly, the introduction of book-printing technology also plays an important part. But as is shown by a comparison between early-modern Europe and China or Korea, the spectacular success of book printing in Europe was dependent on its access to market opportunities, i.e. to a pre-existing functional differentiation. When that is the case, the church and the political bureaucracy can only defend themselves through 'censorship'.
6   As Jean Pierre Camus (1609) does with regard to Heaven and Hell, dividing the world into 'two large and general classes in one or the other of which are enrolled, without exception, the good and the wicked' (fol. 73).
7   'Mouse-eaten records' are referred to by Sir Philip Sidney (1595), quoted in 1970 edn, Lincoln, Nebraska, p. 15, to show the possibilities of poetry, as against history, in their proper light.
8   The abbreviation mainly concerns commerce and commercial capital, with its rapidly growing importance from the late Middle Ages. However, it can be seen from the religious, moral and political evaluation of money that commerce was treated as a second-rank concern long after land had become a necessary basis for credit and thus purchasable, and the prohibition on interest had had to be relaxed. The 'optimal' state of a community in *De optimo Republicae Statu, deque nova insula Utopia* (1516), is one which manages without money but must already be presented as a paradox, a place existing nowhere.
9   The slave/vagrant distinction in terms of attachment to households is important because it leads to the prediction that with the reduction in slavery (attachment to households or bondage to land), vagrancy will increase.

10   I quote from the English translation, 1952, p. 401.

11   Translated from the author's own translation.

12   'They are onely but exercises of wit', writes Anthony Mundy (1969) in the dedicatory preface, p. A3 – as if to apologize for his presumption in concerning himself with paradoxes.

13   Translated from 'Vorlesungen über die Philosophie der Religion I', in *Werke*, 1969, p. 102.

14   The lexicon *Geschichtliche Grundbegriffe: Historisches Lexikon zur politisch-sozialen Sprache in Deutschland*, 7 vols, Stuttgart, 1972–92, is based on this assumption, which it dates in the second half of the eighteenth century.

15   Ibid., vol. 1, Introduction, pp. XVIff.

16   In the terminology of Douglas R. Hofstadter (1979), pp. 686ff. Hofstadter explains this need by the loss of a fixed starting-point for self-referential loops. In terms of system theory, this can be applied especially easily to modern society, which admits hierarchies only on the level of its organization and can only order its complexity heterarchically, in the manner of a brain.

17   Perhaps in the sense used by Michael Polanyi (1966). The formulation in the text quotes his title.

18   Expressed in terms of systems theory: this open state of the yes/no bifurcation comprises the operative closing-point and at the same time the 'autopoiesis' of the communication system. The system can only propagate itself by communication; but how this happens remains open. And if necessary, further communication is needed to clarify how the communication is to be understood.

19   As is well known, Georg Lukács (1971) described the modern novel as ironic in terms of its form. Irony as a form has been explicitly cultivated since the early Romantics. (We do not overlook the fact that the term itself originated in antiquity and was handed down by rhetoric. But there it denotes only a trope by which the opposite of what is meant is said. The Latin translation is *simulatio* or *dissimulatio*, although this is a controversial point.) For the early modern history of the concept up to shortly before the inception of Romanticism, cf. Norman Knox (1961).

20   For example, when the value/opposite value distinction is re-imported into value, as when the war/peace distinction reinterprets peace as the just war; or when the freedom/unfreedom distinction turns into freedom as the exclusion by natural law of *licentia* (= unrestricted freedom out of freedom), etc.

21   Max Weber sees the matter differently and more trenchantly. At least with regard to supreme values, he assumes that each of them, through its meaning, demands *unconditional* respect and thus negates all others. Cf. Hartmann Tyrell (1993, pp. 121–38).

22   One could use the formulation of Heinz von Foerster: 'Only *those* questions that are in principle undecidable, *we* can decide' – in Heinz von Foerster (1992, pp. 9–19, 14).

23   There was no special term for the intersection of kinship network and household, that we would now call the 'family'. '*Familia*', '*oîkos*', 'house' was the

household that contained women and children, servants and maids, land and heavy livestock.

24   It is worth noting that in present-day China precisely this is being attempted: to replace old family associations by structurally equivalent modern work organizations, giving the political control media, law and money, few chances to impinge directly on individual behaviour. Cf. Li Hanlin (1991).

25   That the reality is different for a large part, perhaps the major part, of the world's population is readily seen – and not only in rural regions of underdeveloped countries, but also in Sao Paolo and Bombay. For on the one hand functional differentiation is, in evolutionary terms, a highly improbable formal principle, and on the other, reinforcing the same point, demographic processes (growth, migrations) have taken on proportions that are simply unmanageable.

26   'Emancipation of contingency' – a formulation of David Roberts (1991, pp. 150, 158). Not by accident, no doubt, is it modern art that holds up this mirror to society.

REFERENCES

Camus, Jean Pierre 1609: *Les Diversitez*. Paris, vol. 2.

Foerster, Heinz von 1992: *Ethics and Second-Order Cybernetics and Human Knowing, I*.

Förster, Heinz 1948: *Das Gedächtnis: Eine Quantenphysikalische Untersuchung*. Vienna.

Hanlin, Li 1991: *Die Grundstruktur der Chinesischen Gesellschaft: Vom Traditionellen Klansystem zur Modern Danwei-Organisation*. Opladen.

Hegel 1969: Vorlesungen über die Philosophie der Religion, I. In *Werke*, Frankfurt, vol. 16.

Hofstadter, Douglas R. 1979: *Gödel, Escher, Bach: An Eternal Golden Braid*. Hassocks, Sussex: Harvester Press.

Knox, Norman 1961: *The Word IRONY and its Context, 1500–1755*. Durham, NC.

Luhmann, Niklas 1990: The Paradox of System Differentiation and the Evolution of Society. In Jeffrey C. Alexander and Paul Colomy (eds), *Differentiation Theory and Social Change: Comparative and Historical Perspectives*, New York: Columbia University Press, pp. 409–40.

Luhmann, Niklas 1992: Societal Complexity. In György Széll (ed.), *Concise Encyclopedia of Participation and Co-management*, Berlin 1992, pp. 793–806. Translation of Complessità Sociale, in *Enciclopedia delle Scienze Sociali*, Rome, vol. II, pp. 126–34.

Lukács, Georg 1971: *The Theory of the Novel: a Historico-Philosophical Essay on the Form of Great Epic Literature*. London: Merlin Press.

Mundy, Anthony 1969: *The Defence of Contraries*. Amsterdam.

Plato, *The Sophist*. Harold North Fowler edition, 1952. London: Loeb Classical Library.

Polanyi, Michael 1966: *The Tacit Dimension*. New York: Garden City.

Roberts, David 1991: *Art and Enlightenment: Aesthetic Theory after Adorno*. Lincoln, Nebraska: University of Nebraska Press.

Ross Ashby, W. 1954: *Design for a Brain: The Origin of Adaptive Behaviour*. London, 2nd edn.
Ross Ashby, W. 1956: *An Introduction to Cybernetics*. New York.
Sidney, Philip 1595: *The Defense of Poesy*. Lincoln, Nebraska, 1970 edn.
Tyrell, Hartmann 1993: Max Weber: Wertkollision und christliche Werte, *Zeitschrift für Evangelische Ethik*, 37.

5

The Privatization of Religion and Morality

Thomas Luckmann

The thematic outline for the Lancaster conference on detraditionalization expresses remarkable theoretical ambitions. The fate of tradition in modernity is a problem which does not admit simple solutions. For my part, I do not know whether my own presentation will contribute much to the discussion of the larger issues. My aim is more modest. I intend to restrict my remarks to a limited, although perhaps not insignificant, part of the wider problem, the nature of contemporary moral communication. I shall begin by sketching its relevance for the general topic of the conference; I shall then venture some guesses about traditional and modern components of that communication; and finally, I will illustrate my point with some data on the moral aspects of communicative interactions between ordinary people.

Although I do not plan to approach the big theoretical questions head-on, I may be allowed to add that I share the interest in the larger issue. How were social structure, culture and the individual transformed in the modern world? It was interest in this question which many years ago led me to join the search for an explanation of the profound changes in the manifestations of religion in modern societies. I was helped in this search by the conceptual frame of a functionalist version of the social theory of religion. I had formulated that theory after becoming disenchanted with the approaches and investigations which were then prevalent in the field. I thought that it was necessary to return to the question asked about the nature of modern societies by Durkheim and Weber, even if one did not accept all their answers. Looking at the scattered evidence available at the time – significantly, little of it was to be found in the mainstream of research in the sociology of religion – I speculated about the causes which had led to the decline of institutionally specialized religion, historically a particularly important social form of religion which had been established in the Christian West and which was represented by churches, sects and denominations. It was marked by monopolies or oligopolies in the production, distribution and maintenance of sacralized, transcendent universes. It had been the dominant social form of religion in the Western world for many centuries.

But even thirty years ago it was obvious that its dominance and pervasive social reach had come to an end. The widespread view that this meant the end of religion seemed erroneous to me. Even in the heyday of secularization theories, there were signs that a new, institutionally less visible social form of religion was emerging, and that it was likely to become dominant at the expense of the older form. Churches and sects would henceforth have to exist in a radically transformed social structural and cultural context. The new, basically de-institutionalized, *privatized* social form of religion seemed to be relying primarily on an open market of diffuse, syncretistic packages of meaning, typically connected to low levels of transcendence and produced in a partly or fully commercialized cultic milieu. The new situation permitted, even encouraged, individual bricolage. Relying for its essential legitimations upon the modern myth of the autonomous individual, it had a pronounced elective affinity for the sacralization of subjectivisms. The brooks, fed by sources such as Rousseau's *Les Confessions* and Goethe's *Die Leiden des Jungen Werther* flowed into the mass-cultural sea of subjectivity-cults.

A NEW SOCIAL FORM OF RELIGION: PRIVATIZATION, INDIVIDUAL SYNCRETISM, AND MASS CULTURE

Looking somewhat more closely at this theme, the privatization of religion is part of the general privatization of individual life in modern societies.[1] The social condition most directly connected with privatization is, of course, the high degree of functional differentiation in the social structure.[2] The 'big' institutions exert considerable control over individual conduct by their functionally rational norms and by the mixture of rewards and punishments characteristic of the political economy of modern capitalistic nation-states. But the institutional segmentation of the meaning of actions left large spheres of life without institutionally predefined meaning-structures and without obligatory models of biographical coherence.[3] The life-space that is not directly touched by institutional control may be called 'the private sphere'. As individual consciousness − not individual conduct − is liberated from social structural constraints, a process typically accompanied by legal provisions for freedom of opinion, people gain a sense of individual autonomy. Totalitarian reactions having been unsuccessful, the individual is given the freedom to choose from a variety of sacred universes. These have sprung up as the cultural correlate of structural privatization.

Modern social constructions designed to cope with various levels of transcendence are extremely heterogeneous. For several generations, the traditional Christian sacred universe was no longer the only transcendent reality mediated in the social processes of specialized churches, and sects did not even retain their monopoly on specifically religious themes without challenge from secular ideologies. Collective representations originating in social constructions of the intermediate transcendences of nation, race, classlessness, and the like, successfully shaped important aspects of modern consciousness. In recent decades, concern with minimal transcendences symbolized by such notions as self-fulfilment has become widespread, if not dominant. The derivation of such notions from romanticism, certain branches of philosophic idealism, and the more recent depth-psychologies is obvious. But what were marginal bohemian, avant garde, and intellectualist phenomena at one time, now seem to have become characteristic of the orientations of broad strata of *embourgeoisé* populations.

The shift of intersubjective reconstructions and social constructions away from the great other-worldly transcendences to the intermediate and, more and more, minimal transcendences of modern solipsism cannot be said to have been directly determined by a structural privatization of individual life in modern society. However, an elective affinity does seem to obtain between the latter and the sacralization of subjectivity that is celebrated in much of modern mass culture. Evidently, the traditional religious orientations (at whose centre are social constructions of the great transendences) have not disappeared. But their social distribution has become narrower, and the institutionally specialized basis of these orientations (the churches, sects, and denominations) no longer represents the socially dominant form of religion.

The ascendant privatized social form of religion is characterized by a wider range of different actors on the social scene being involved in the social construction of various kinds of transcendence.[4] The basic structure of the process is that of a demonopolized market supplied by (i) the mass media; (ii) the churches and sects that are trying to reinsert themselves into the processes of modern social constructions of transcendence; (iii) the residual carriers of nineteenth-century secular ideologies; and (iv) subinstitutional, new religious communities formed around minor charismatics, commercialized enterprises in astrology, the consciousness-expanding line, and the like. This social form of religion is thus characterized by an immediate mass-cultural accessibility of the supply of representations referring to varied levels of transcendence.

However, this does not mean that no form of mediation exists between the market and potential consumers. Much of modern (Byronian or Baudelairean) consciousness is rooted in the cultivation of immediate sensations and emotions – which are notoriously unstable and offer considerable resistance to clear articulation in myths, symbols, and dogmas. None the less, a variety of secondary institutions – typically arising in subinstitutional movements around charismatics, entrepreneurs, and small-group revival attempts of older occult, spiritualist, and similar movements – have taken the challenge and turned it into a profitable business. These institutions address the problem of the verbalization of topics arising in the private sphere, of packaging the results in easily digestible portions, and of distributing the results to potential consumers. Inner-worldly analogies to traditional devotional literature range from treatises on positive thinking to *Playboy* articles on the expansion of consciousness by various (for example, sexual) techniques, pocketbooks on popular psychology – especially psychoanalysis – Eastern mystical literature, astrological advice columns, offerings on bioenergetics and meditation, and the like. The products convey a more or less systematically arranged set of meanings (and, occasionally, techniques) referring to minimal, to intermediate and, rarely, to great transcendences. The set can be bought and kept for a short or longer period. It can be individually combined with elements from other sets. The sets are, of course, not obligatory models characteristic of the older social forms of religion. They *can* be taken up by groups – typically on the periphery of modern society – and converted into a sectarian model, but the chances of success for such firm institutionalizations are not great.

This social form of religion can best be illustrated by recent syncretistic developments[5] such as the New Age movement, and the new occultism and its predecessors, such as spiritism. The New Age movement lays stress on the spiritual development of each individual. Sometimes it revives elements of older religious traditions that were canonized and that it interprets in unorthodox (often far-fetched) ways. It collects abundant psychological, therapeutic, magic, marginally scientific, and older esoteric materials,[6] repackages them, and offers them for individual consumption and further private syncretism. The New Age movement programmatically refuses organization in terms of big institutions; instead, it cultivates the notion of networks. This allows the formation of commercially exploitable cultic milieu, which are characterized by varied – generally weak – forms of institutionalization.[7] The New Age movement illustrates the social form of the invisible religion. It has no stable organization, canonized dogmas, recruitment system, or disciplining apparatus. This may be a structural precondition for the successful maintenance of its vague holistic approach, which meets – among other things – the rising demand for an overall hierarchy of meaning that overcomes the specialization of those cultural domains, such as science, religion, art, and the like, that had found reasonably firm institutional bases. Instead of segmentation, it offers integration – no matter how superficial this may seem to the outside observer. Thus, the New Age and similar representatives of a holistic, magical world view supply individual searchers with the bricks and some straw for further individual bricolage (Campbell, 1972).

The structural conditions leading to various privatized forms of religion characterized by the search for a new wholeness – intended to overcome the segmentation of meaning into specialized institutional spheres and cultural regions – also give rise to another holistic option that is diametrically opposed to bricolage, that is to fundamentalism. One must distinguish between the sociostructural conditions (the specialization of institutional domains, the pluralism of mass culture, and the development of a market of world views – all of which are prevalent in modern industrial societies) and the strains similar conditions produce, upon their emergence in modernizing societies. The relatively sudden loss of religious legitimations for everyday life seems to lead to anti-modernist reactions among substantial segments of the populations of modernizing countries.[8] But even in modern Western societies, Protestant and Catholic versions of fundamentalism have chosen traditional models of wholeness in reaction to modernity (institutional specialization, the immorality of economic and political life, the lack of obligatory controls for private life and pluralism and a lack of cognitive support for one's own world view, disorientation, and mass availability of immoral products and behaviour).[9] It seems unlikely, however, that these reactions, which range from the Catholic *Opus Dei* to Protestant moral majorities, will prove successful in the long run. The fit between this kind of world view and the social structural determinants of modern life is rather poor. It can be improved, however, in closed communities of various kinds. On the whole, privatized syncretism seems to have a better chance to become established as a (minimally) social form of religion.

MORALIZING COMMUNICATION: OBSERVATIONS ON SOME MODERN PROCEDURES

Turning to some related notions about the nature of moral communication today, I suggest that it is in the processes of moral communication rather than in specifically moral institutions that one is likely to encounter the most significant part of whatever morality – traditional or other – can be found in modern societies. I shall try to show why I think that this is so and how that assumption can be linked, both substantively and by analogy, to the results of an analysis of the privatized social form of religion. I will also try to show

how it bears upon the larger issue of tradition and modernity. But first I should like to note that the restriction of my remarks to moral communication also has a methodological advantage. The limited scope of the questions addressed permits, at least in principle, empirical answers. Even so, investigation of the moral aspect of communicative interactions presents a difficult task to empirical research.

I do not pretend that even the restricted questions about contemporary moral communication which are discussed here will be easily and conclusively answered by the kinds of materials my colleagues on a research project on moral genres of communication and I have gathered. But I do think that the procedure I am following has some advantage when compared with attempts to approach the grand issues of tradition and modernity in a direct way. In any case, what would be a direct way? Public opinion polls, depth interviews and life histories, analysis of personal documents and content analyses of the mass media? All these are certainly better in furthering our understanding of life in modern societies than free-floating speculation. So are — or could be, if they existed — sophisticated hermeneutics of modern cultural productions, literary as well as electronic, which inform us about the product although not the reception side of modern culture. I think that our attempt to analyse concrete communicative interactions in which, after all, traditions are actively maintained, transformed or abandoned has the advantage of looking at the matter in situated contexts.

A few words about the nature of these materials: they consist of hundreds of hours of recordings and transcriptions of family table talks from the south and east of Germany, religious and secular conversion stories, gossip in private and institutional settings, entry interviews in psychiatric wards, fire department alarm calls, anti-smoking campaigns, meetings of local ecology groups, religious programmes on television, radio call-in programmes, public debates, *in situ* and on television, for example on the Gulf War, genetic counselling as well as general family counselling, etc.

Rich and voluminous as these materials are, they are restricted with few exceptions to Germany, and the family table talks are from lower-middle and middle-class families. Only after many more years of concentrated research producing similarly detailed and concrete data from other modern societies could one say with any certainty what moral genres, and other less rigorously structured forms of communication serving moral functions, constitute the specifically modern moral repertoire in the overall communicative budget of a society.

My observations must therefore remain tentative until such further evidence becomes available. None the less, they may be worth presenting even at this early stage. They address a limited but important aspect of the general

topic under discussion in the Lancaster conference, the persistence, change
and, perhaps, dissolution of traditions in modern society. And moving from
these observations to concrete examples may help in linking theory to the
kind of evidence available in the everyday life of our contemporaries. Examples, of course, cannot prove general assertions, but in addition to illustrating
a point, they may also bolster the plausibility of an assertion. When we ask
about the condition of typical modern individuals, both liberated from, and
deprived of, obligatory traditional models of proper conduct and a good life,
we would be well advised to look closely at what ordinary people do in social
interaction and communication.

When our contemporaries complain about others, accuse them of misdeeds
or apologize for their own faults, when they become indignant and join – or
refuse to join – in moral outrage, when they quote proverbs, transmit maxims and provide bits of wisdom, when they seek or offer advice, when they
gossip, they demonstrate the *persistence* of traditional forms of moral evaluation. At the same time, their communicative interactions may also offer
useful hints about possible *shifts* in the nature of moral communication and,
indirectly, the moral order, in the contemporary Western world.

When I suggested, above, that the most significant parts of whatever
morality can be found in modern societies will be located in the concrete
processes of moral communication rather than in moral institutions, I already
anticipated the first of my general observations. The second one is somewhat
more specific. I think that although many traditional forms of moral communication can also be found in the communicative repertoires of modern
societies, a shift in the style that is gaining the upper hand in many kinds
of social interaction rests on indirectness and obliqueness.

My first observation – that modern morality is primarily located in communication – needs to be placed in a general context. With a certain degree
of simplification one may assume that in archaic societies religion, morals
and law had a common location in the social structure, that is that the
institutions serving these functions were characterized by what Robert Redfield
(1965) once called 'primitive fusion' or, at least, that they were very closely
co-ordinated. The traditional moral code was specific in its values as well as
in the correlated behavioural *do's* and *don'ts*. Moreover, the code was generally
obligatory for the members of a society. Breaches of the code could be clearly
defined. The overall meaning of the moral order was plausibly legitimated by
reference to a transcendent sacred universe.

It seems obvious that a moral order of this kind no longer integrates
modern societies. In the course of history – more precisely, in the course of
several human histories and, most significantly with respect to the emergence

of modern societies in Western history – religion and law were functionally specialized in separate institutions. The institutionalization of rules of conduct, enforceable by the apparatus of the public agents of an (increasingly secular) political system, legalized but potentially also de-moralized these rules ('norms'). The 'upper reaches' of morals, those which legitimated the meaning of the rules of conduct by reference to a transcendent universe, remained in close attachment to the sacred universes and mundane institutions of religion. In the long process of functional differentiation of the political, legal and economic functions of social life, religious institutions too were increasingly restricted to their special function – or, rather, to what was increasingly defined as their special function, the individual soul in its relation to a sacred level of reality. The social reach and influence of religious institutions began to shrink, and so did the social reach and influence of the legitimatory level of morals.

As a consequence of complex social structural transformations, the eminently social reality of morals and religion found their location in the most singular 'institution', the individual person. In the most general terms, these transformations were the processes of the institutional specialization of functions. More specifically, they consisted of the legal institutionalization of the behavioural level of morals and the religious institutionalization of the legitimatory-meaning level of morals. As the reach of religious institutions diminished, the obligatory social and intersubjectively compelling evaluation of human conduct by reference to a transcendent reality became weaker. Morals and religion, structurally privatized, took a definitive inner turn in the form of conscience and faith.

Just over a century ago Durkheim (1893/1984) was concerned about the slowness with which organic solidarity – which he thought was the necessary integrating force for societies with a complex division of labour – was replacing the moral system associated with a simpler division of labour. He remained convinced that a society without a moral core as the centre of its integration was unthinkable. Almost fifty years later, Théodor Geiger, too, suggested in his studies in the sociology of law that modern society was characterized by the dissolution of a generally obligatory moral code. In his view, this was a necessary condition for the evolution of a functionally differentiated, rationally organized complex society; and the retreat of morals from the social structure started a process which he called the 'spiritualization of morality' (1969, p. 121). Weber (1976) provided long before Geiger a more detailed account of the secularization and partialization of traditional Christian ethics on an inner-worldly work-ethic.

The view of Durkheim, Weber and Geiger – and many others who proceed from similar assumptions and observations – that modern societies no longer possess a generally obligatory moral order, must be accepted. There can be differences, however, about the meaning of this state of affairs and its social consequences. Durkheim may be wrong in postulating that no society, not even complex modern societies, can exist without the integrating force of a specific yet generally obligatory moral order. Geiger's view that the rational organization of institutions in complex societies could only be hindered by such a moral order, has some degree of plausibility. One may consider Geiger's metaphor essentially correct and say with him that morals have retreated from the social structure. One may also assume with him that the type of individual morality that would be compatible with this state of affairs would have to be marked by an ethics of motive and subjective disposition (a *Gesinnungsethik*) rather than by a traditional or dogmatized ethics of responsibility and accountability. But there is no reason to accept his notion that concrete morality has evaporated into the thin air of spirituality.

A different possibility seems more likely. Morality always also had a location in the face-to-face interactions of the members of a society. If, in addition, complex moral-meaning configurations were integrated into the institutional norms of a society or even developed a special basis in moral-religious or specifically moral institutions, that did not entail a disappearance of morals from what Erving Goffman (1967) has called the interaction order. How could it? It merely meant that the abstract levels of morals with their elevated rhetoric could in some way influence practical morals on the level of situated social interaction. If it is true that morality has retreated from the institutions of social structure, if it is true that traditional moral-meaning configurations have lost their social structural base, it also remains true that notions of good and bad are still relevant to the planning, execution and evaluation of actions in the interactional order. That is the case even if one plausibly assumes that a dogmatized hierarchy of values with canonic ideas of a good life is no longer as pervasive as it may have been in other societies; and if one proposes that in analogy to privatization as the newly dominant social form of religion, morality, too, is privatized, showing an elective affinity for the type of morality best designated as *Gesinnungsethik*.

Now I come to my second point. Assuming that these are valid observations – first, that a generally obligatory and specific moral code is absent and, secondly, that moral evaluation according to some trans-situational standards remains a necessary component of the interactional order – some consequences may be deduced. In general it may be difficult to imagine any social interaction which is morally entirely irrelevant. Some risk of moral dissensus is inherent in all social interaction. But it is likely that even in situations where the interacting individuals do not know each other, they perceive one another in terms of more or less anonymous social categories which carry, directly or indirectly, some information about the other's moral status and views. The risk of which I just spoke can therefore be minimized – or, alternatively, consciously accepted in confrontation with moral 'deviants'. But in a wide variety of situations typical of modern life the risk is increased. In societies with a generally obligatory moral code and in which interaction based on highly anonymous social roles is less pervasive, moral consensus could be assumed until evidence to the contrary appeared. In modern societies, one could say with some exaggeration, the situation is reversed. Moral consensus can be assumed only after evidence for that assumption becomes available. Among persons who are not reasonably certain about each other's moral attitudes and views, social interaction in general – and most specifically, explicit moralizing – becomes a risky intersubjective undertaking. Similarity of views on morally relevant issues in social interaction needs to be cautiously negotiated in specific communicative processes between the parties to a social encounter. Even then the scope for consensus over different areas of social life will be as open to question as its stability in time.

This does not imply that already established moral-ideological 'communities of the mind' (*Gesinnungsgemeinschaften*) have not survived, especially if they historically found an institutional base. Nor does it imply that new *Gesinnungsgemeinschaften* cannot become established. They do, and some achieve a certain stability. The moral entrepreneurship of old and new *Gesinnungsgemeinschaften* continues and their moralizing activities are often vociferous and politically influential – at least temporarily – on specific issues. But the old ones are in crisis and the new ones only rarely achieve stability. On the one hand, the old ones, in crisis, may respond by *aggiornamento* and *moral indirection* or they may respond by *moral fundamentalism*. Many of the new ones, on the other hand, are characterized by the peculiar fact that they do not present themselves as *moral* communities. Their moral entrepreneurship is typically carried out behind scientific, medical, practical-problem-solving, façades. This, too, may be considered a form of indirection and obliqueness.

However, my concern here is with moral indirection and obliqueness in ordinary communicative processes rather than in moral entrepreneurship of one kind or another. In the following I will present some examples.

A brief terminological remark may help to understand the examples. No doubt all social interaction involves moral aspects and all communication contains a moral dimension. But these may be minimal and normally imperceptible to the participants. I will disregard this underlying morality of all social life. I shall present examples of communicative processes in which moral aspects, although they need not be explicit – in fact, my purpose is to show examples of moral indirection – are demonstrably perceived by the participants in the process. Here, we may first distinguish between the *thematization* of morals and *moralizing*. *Thematization* communicatively presents moral aspects of social interaction, either on-going or past interaction. The method of thematization varies from the concretely exemplary to abstract formulations. *Moralizing* communicatively evaluates actions or actors. Again, moralizing may refer to on-going interaction or to reconstructed past actions; moralizing may be addressed to persons and refer to them or refer to absent third parties. The methods of moralizing may be linguistic in the narrower sense – e.g. semantic-lexical, rhetorical, prosodic – or paralinguistic, mimetic or a combination of these. Thematization of moral aspects may be relatively free of moral purpose or it may be used specifically for moralizing purposes. Conversely, moralizing may be direct, using various kinds of thematization (such as the use of maxims, moralizing proverbs), or it may be indirect and oblique.

The speculation is that the significant parts of whatever there is of morals in modern societies are to be found in the interaction order, and that the dominant style of moralizing in many kinds of typically modern social institutions will tend towards indirection and obliqueness. My examples begin with forms of direct moralizing and then illustrate the speculation by introducing some indirect and oblique forms.

EXAMPLES

1 Thematization of Morals

Thematization of morals frequently occurs, as it does in the instance below, in communication between persons who were brought up in different cultures. (Here, in a conversation between a Chinese and a German teaching at a Chinese university.) This thematization is not an immediate part of a positive or negative evaluation of the value of 'activity' versus 'passivity'. The transcript of the entire episode shows, however, that Bu (negatively) evaluates passivity as an element of the conformism of Chinese culture.

BU: h'yeah then, well I've learned in Western culture one should always be ACTIVE.
GERMAN: And eh I also AGREE to that.
BU: I find the activity of a person very important.

GERMAN:　Yeah, but HERE it is different, the MORE PASSIVE you are the better.

BU:　Yeah actually one doesn't say passive but QUIET, yes one has to remain QUIET

GERMAN:　NOT say anything, hm'be contented with own situation with life, one should not have any wishes,

BU:　but being QUIET—this is emphasized very much.

2　Direct Moralizing

In this case of direct moralizing, the complaint of a young man is countered by his sister. Rather than sympathizing with him, she blames him 'character-ologically' (accusing him of once again starting something without following it through).

YOUNG MAN:　I haven't got time anymore for gymnastics.

SISTER:　Puuh, you always only start things and then stop again.

3　Indirect Moralizing

(a) 'Why' Constructions

'Why' constructions are a frequent form of indirect moralizing. The blame hides, as it were, behind a 'question'. That the 'question' is not a question is well understood by the 'culprit', who hastens to apologize to the operator.

The Telephone Operator
S. calls information and asks for the phone number of a family called 'Weisser' in Constance.

OPERATOR:　I have no family WEISSER in Constance, only a family WEISS.

'CULPRIT':　Yes I think they live on the Reichenau and actually not directly in Constance.

OPERATOR:　(*brusquely*) WHY did you say CONSTANCE then?

CULPRIT:　I am sorry, I thought the Reichenau belongs to Constance.

OPERATOR:　Well then the number is . . .

(b) 'I don't Understand' Constructions

Another well-used form of indirect blaming consists of 'I don't understand' constructions. It is again a sister who indirectly admonishes her brother not to let things (arrangements for the continuation of his studies) slide.

Antje and Paul
ANTJE:　Ok good, but it doesn't get you anywhere if you . . .

PAUL:　It won't get me anywhere but . . .

ANTJE: If you think about now you just have to first of all see how you can
get your stuff put in order. I don't understand, I don't understand either
why you just don't call whatchamacallhim in Stuttgart and say that when
you do your practical semester now, that you then would like to – next
semester continue in Stuttgart again next semester. Tell him what's going
on.

PAUL: I'm not gonna get a practical semester position any more.

(c) Reconstructions (Direct/Indirect Example)

This illustrates a narrative reconstruction of a past indirect blaming of a
Chinese student by his party secretary. (The 'why' format is evidently not
limited to one culture.) The narrative (expectedly?) elicits indignation and
solidarity on the part of the listener.

STUDENT: Then the secretary of the party at that time confronted me. Other
people then, wanted to confront me, WHY don't I ACT like the others,
like your fellow students? WHY must you, do you always have to dress
up so fancy?

LISTENER: (*filled with indignation*) Oh yeah.

(d) Litotes

In a phone-in tc a radio programme on the behaviour of foreigners in Germany, a sympathy-getting attempt at 'fairness' is made. The behaviour of
German tourists is not characterized as downright bad; it is not 'always very
good'.

SPEAKER: We Germans! You have to look at it this way sometimes. We
don't always behave in just the right way: it's not always very good.

(e) Overall Indirectness Constructions

In German genetic counselling, the historic context of Nazi racist eugenics
is not forgotten. The code of proper counselling prescribes the giving of
scientific information, and proscribes direct advice. At the same time, clients
often want precisely that which the counsellor is not allowed to offer. The
passage illustrates one of the practical ways in which the general problem is
solved by indirection ('I see no reason that one would . . .'). In other instances
the format, 'Other parents in this situation have decided to . . .' is used to
convey advice (often over life and non-life).

CLIENT: We would like to have children ourselves. We actually like children. I like them, and so does my wife.

COUNSELLOR: I think, well. I would actually . . .

CLIENT: I think . . .
COUNSELLOR: . . . See no reason that one would for that reason . . .
CLIENT: Hm.
COUNSELLOR: . . . go without children.
CLIENT: . . . It was actually interesting that they . . .

Other forms of indirectness and obliqueness include: euphemisms ('Just a bit misplaced'; or with litotes, for example, 'Not quite diplomatic'); disinfluences (false starts and reformulations); jocular modulations; and prosodic devices (complaining or brusque tone).

NOTES

1   This section of the chapter is drawn from a previous article (Luckmann, 1991, pp. 176–9).
2   Previously multifunctional institutions, which regulated social interaction in archaic and also in traditional societies, slowly accented *one* function and lost most of the other functional components that originally constituted them. At the same time, institutions with similar functions coalesced into large specialized domains, such as the state and the economy. In contemporary industrial societies, institutions have become highly interdependent elements of social subsystems. These subsystems, however, are, rather, autonomous parts of the social structure. The norms of each subsystem are *comparatively* independent of the rules that govern action in other subsystems. Depending on the domain in which it is performed, institutionalized social interaction obeys rather heterogeneous norms. The connection of these norms – which have been described by Max Weber as functionally rational ones – to the 'logic' of a transcendent reality is severed.
3   In this connection, Parsons spoke of 'institutional interstices'.
4   See Needleman and Baker (eds) (1981), especially Robert Wuthnow, and Joseph Chinnici. Also James Beckford (1986) and Beckford and Luckmann (1989).
5   See Colin Campbell and Shirley McIver (1987).
6   For an early study, see Andrew Rigby and Bryan Turner (1972).
7   Not unlike what Troeltsch rather misleadingly called 'mysticism'. For 'cultic milieu' see Danny Jorgensen (1982); also Rodney Stark and William Bainbridge (1986).
8   See, for example, Bassam Tibi (1985).
9   See Frank Lechner (1985); Donald Heinz (1985).

REFERENCES

Beckford, James A. (ed.) 1986: *New Religious Movements and Rapid Social Change*. London: Sage.

Beckford, James A. and Luckmann, Thomas (eds) 1989: *The Changing Face of Religion*. London, Newbury Park, and New Delhi: Sage.

Campbell, Colin 1972: The Cult, the Cultic Milieu and Secularization. In *A Sociological Yearbook of Religion in Britain*, vol. 5. London: SCM Press, pp. 119–36.

Campbell, Colin and McIver, Shirley 1987: Cultural Sources of Support for Contemporary Occultism. In *Social Compass*, 34, pp. 41–60.

Chinnici, Joseph P. 1981: New Religious Movements and the Structure of Religious Sensibility. In J. Needleman and G. Baker (eds) *Understanding the New Religions*, pp. 26–33.

Durkheim, Emile 1984/1893: *The Division of Labour in Society*. London: Macmillan.

Geiger, Théodor 1969: *On Social Order and Mass Society. Selected Papers*, R. E. Peck (ed.). London: University of Chicago Press.

Goffman, Erving 1967: *Interaction Ritual*. New York: Anchor Books.

Heinz, Donald 1985: Clashing Symbols: The New Christian Right as Countermythology. In *Archives de Sciences Sociales des Religions*, 59, pp. 153–73.

Jorgensen, Danny L. 1982: The Esoteric Community: An Ethnographic Investigation of the Cultic Milieu. *Urban Life*, 4, pp. 383–407.

Lechner, Frank J. 1985: Fundamentalism and Sociocultural Revitalization in America: A Sociological Interpretation. In *Sociological Analysis*, 46, pp. 243–59.

Luckmann, Thomas 1991: The New and the Old in Religion. In Pierre Bordieu and James S. Coleman (eds), *Social Theory for a Changing Society*, Boulder, San Francisco, Oxford: Westview Press; New York: Russell Sage Foundation, pp. 167–82.

Needleman, Jacob and Baker, George (eds) 1981: *Understanding the New Religions*. New York: Seabury Press.

Redfield, Robert 1965: *The Primitive World and its Transformation*. New York: Cornell University Press.

Rigby, Andrew and Turner, Bryan S. 1972: Findhorn Community, Centre of Light: A Sociological Study of New Forms of Religion. In M. Hill (ed.), *A Sociological Yearbook of Religion in Britain*, vol. 5, London: SCM Press, pp. 72–86.

Stark, Rodney and Bainbridge, William S. 1986: *The Future of Religion: Secularization, Revival and Cult Formation*. Berkeley: University of California Press.

Tibi, Bassam 1985: *Der Islam und das Problem der Kulturellen Bewältigung Sozialen Wandels*. Frankfurt: Suhrkamp.

Weber, Max 1976: *The Protestant Ethic and the Spirit of Capitalism*. London: George Allen and Unwin.

Wuthnow, Robert 1981: Religious Movements and the Transition in the World Order. In J. Needleman and G. Baker (eds), *Understanding the New Religions*, pp. 63–79.

Part II

Detraditionalization and Traditions Today

Tradition and Self in a Mediated World

John B. Thompson

One of the most powerful legacies of classical social thought is the idea that, with the development of modern societies, tradition gradually declines in significance and eventually ceases to play a meaningful role in the lives of most individuals. Tradition, it is claimed, is a thing of the past (in more ways than one); and 'modern societies' are contrasted in a general way with the 'traditional societies' that preceded them. 'All that is solid melts into air', Marx famously remarked; and many other thinkers, whether they shared Marx's perspective or not, have generally concurred in the view that the development of modern societies is accompanied by an irreversible decline in the role of tradition.

In recent years this line of reflection has been renewed and imaginatively extended by Ulrich Beck and Anthony Giddens, among others.[1] They have used terms such as 'detraditionalization' and the emergence of 'post-traditional society' to describe what they see as an inescapable aspect of the formation of modernity. They argue that, in the early phases of modernization, many institutions depended crucially on traditions that were characteristic of pre-modern societies – in the way, for example, that many early modern productive organizations depended on the continuation of traditional forms of family life. But as the process of modernization enters a more advanced phase (what Beck calls 'reflexive modernization' and what Giddens calls 'high' or 'late' modernity), pre-existing traditions are increasingly undermined and most forms of social activity – both at the collective and at the individual level – take place in contexts which are increasingly stripped of traditional mechanisms of support.

At first glance, these new arguments may seem little different from the old and rather tired controversies about rationalization and secularization which have preoccupied sociologists and others for many years. Detraditionalization, it might seem, is merely new wine in old bottles. But there are some important differences; let me highlight two. In the first place, those who use the term 'detraditionalization' generally argue not that traditions have altogether disappeared from the modern world, but that their status has changed in certain ways: they have become less taken-for-granted and less secure, as they have become increasingly exposed to the corrosive impact of public scrutiny and debate.[2] As traditions are called upon to defend themselves, they lose their status as unquestioned truths. But they may survive in various forms – for example, by being transformed into a kind of fundamentalism which rejects the call for discursive justification and seeks, against a background of generalized doubt, to re-assert the inviolable character of tradition.

A second distinctive feature of the literature on detraditionalization is that it explores, in an interesting and innovative way, the relation between the changing status of tradition and the process of self-formation. As traditions lose their hold in many spheres of social life, individuals are obliged increasingly to fall back on their own resources to construct a coherent identity for themselves. Whereas traditions once provided – or so the argument goes – a relatively stable framework for the self and for the process of self-formation, today individuals must chart their own course through a world of bewildering complexity, a world in which our capacity to understand is constantly outstripped by the unintended and far-reaching consequences of our actions.

In these and other ways, the arguments concerning detraditionalization have moved beyond earlier debates concerning the alleged decline of tradition. Nevertheless, the new arguments retain some of the ambiguities of earlier debates and remain, in some respects, deeply unsatisfactory. The notion of tradition is generally left unexamined and is used, as a kind of blanket term, to refer to beliefs and practices which were allegedly widespread in the past. Moreover, since detraditionalization is viewed as a largely one-way process (modernity destroys tradition, not vice-versa), it is difficult to understand the persistence of traditional beliefs and practices in any terms other than those of regression or reaction. For the proponents of detraditionalization, the persistence and even resurgence of traditional beliefs and practices will seem like a return to the past, a refusal to give up something which is doomed to disappear. Tradition survives, on this account, as a refuge for individuals who are unable or unwilling to live in an age of radical uncertainty.

But it is difficult to believe that there is nothing more to it than that. To view the persistence and renewal of tradition as merely a defensive reaction to the process of modernization is to fail to see that there are certain aspects of tradition which are not eliminated by the development of modern societies, aspects which provide a foothold for the continued cultivation of traditional beliefs and practices in the modern world.

In this chapter I shall therefore put aside the language of detraditionalization and post-traditional society – a language which is not, in my view, particularly helpful – and I shall seek to develop a rather different account of the nature of tradition and its role in modern societies. I shall also touch upon the question of how, with the development of modern societies, the process of self-formation has changed, although I shall not pursue this question in detail within the confines of this chapter.[3] In developing this alternative account I shall introduce a theme which has remained largely absent from discussions about tradition and its alleged decline: I shall argue that, if we wish to understand the changing character of tradition and self-formation, we must pay close attention to the development of communication media and their impact. If we put aside the conventional contrast between tradition and modernity and focus instead on the ways in which, with the development of modern societies, the components of tradition have been refashioned by the expansion of mediated forms of communication (among other things), then we shall gain a different – and, perhaps, a more compelling – view of the changing character of tradition and its role in modern societies.

THE NATURE OF TRADITION

What is tradition? How should we understand its traits? With a few exceptions,[4] the notion of tradition has received little systematic attention in the literature of sociology and social theory. Edward Shils (1981) notes that, in its most general sense, 'tradition' means a *traditum* – that is, anything which is transmitted or handed down from the past (p. 12). However, if we wish to explore the changing character of tradition, we shall need a more rigorous account. It is helpful, I think, to distinguish between four aspects of tradition. I shall describe these as the 'hermeneutic aspect', the 'normative aspect', the 'legitimation aspect' and the 'identity aspect'. In practice these four elements often overlap or merge together. But by distinguishing them, we can get a clearer sense of what is involved in the existence of tradition.

Consider first the hermeneutic aspect. One way of understanding tradition is to view it as a set of background assumptions that are taken for granted by individuals in the conduct of their daily lives, and transmitted by them from one generation to the next. In this respect, tradition is an interpretative scheme, a framework for understanding the world. For, as hermeneutic philosophers such as Heidegger and Gadamer have emphasized, all understanding is based on presuppositions, on some set of assumptions which we take for granted and which form part of a tradition to which we belong.[5] No understanding can be entirely presuppositionless. Hence the Enlightenment critique of tradition must, in Gadamer's view, be qualified. In juxtaposing the notions of reason, scientific knowledge and emancipation to those of tradition, authority and myth, the Enlightenment thinkers were not dispensing with tradition as such but rather were articulating a set of assumptions and methods which formed the core of another tradition, that of the Enlightenment itself. In the hermeneutic sense of tradition, the Enlightenment is not the antithesis of tradition but is, on the contrary, one tradition (or cluster of traditions) among others – that is, a set of taken-for-granted assumptions which provide a framework for understanding the world.

Many traditions also have what we may describe as a normative aspect. What is meant by this is that sets of assumptions, forms of belief and patterns of action handed down from the past can serve as a normative guide for actions and beliefs in the present. We can distinguish two ways in which this may occur. On the one hand, material handed down from the past can serve as a normative guide in the sense that certain practices are *routinized* – that is, things are done as a matter of routine, with relatively little reflection on why they are being done in that way. Large parts of most people's everyday lives are routinized in this sense. On the other hand, material handed down from the past can serve as a normative guide in the sense that certain practices can be *traditionally grounded*, that is, grounded or justified by reference to tradition. This is a stronger sense of normativity precisely because the grounds for action are made explicit and raised to the level of self-reflective justification. The question of grounds can be raised by asking why one believes something or behaves in a certain way; and these beliefs or practices are traditionally grounded if one replies by saying 'That's what we've always believed' or 'That's what we've always done', or some variant thereof.

The third aspect of tradition is what one could call the legitimation aspect. What is meant by this is that tradition can, in certain circumstances, serve as a source of support for the exercise of power and authority. This aspect is brought out well by Max Weber (1978, pp. 212ff). According to Weber, there are three principal ways in which the legitimacy of a system of domination can be established. Claims to legitimacy can be based on rational grounds, involving a belief in the legality of enacted rules (what Weber calls 'legal authority'); they can be based on charismatic grounds, involving devotion to the sanctity or exceptional character of an individual ('charismatic authority'); or they can be based on traditional grounds, involving a belief in the sanctity of immemorial traditions ('traditional authority'). In the case of legal authority, individuals are obedient to an impersonal system of rules. In the case of traditional authority, by contrast, obedience is owed to the person who occupies the traditionally sanctioned position of authority and whose actions are bound by tradition. Weber's account of traditional authority is helpful because it highlights the fact that, in certain contexts, tradition may have an overtly political character: it may serve not only as a normative guide for action but also as a basis for exercising power over others and for securing obedience to commands. It is in this respect that traditions may become 'ideological': that is, they may be used to establish or sustain relations of power which are structured in systematically asymmetrical ways.[6]

Finally, let us consider the nature of tradition in relation to the formation of identity – what I called the identity aspect of tradition. There are two types of identity formation which are relevant here – what we may call 'self-identity' and 'collective identity'. Self-identity refers to the sense of oneself as an individual endowed with certain characteristics and potentialities, as an individual situated on a certain life-trajectory. Collective identity refers to the sense of oneself as a member of a social group or collectivity; it is a sense of belonging, a sense of being part of a social group which has a history of its own and a collective fate. What is the relevance of tradition to these two types of identity formation? As sets of assumptions, beliefs and patterns of behaviour handed down from the past, traditions provide some of the symbolic materials for the formation of identity both at the individual and at the collective level. The sense of oneself and the sense of belonging are both shaped – to varying degrees, depending on social context – by the values, beliefs and forms of behaviour which are transmitted from the past. The process of identity formation can never start from scratch; it always builds upon a pre-existing set of symbolic materials which form the bedrock of identity.

Having distinguished these various aspects of tradition, we are now in a position to consider the ways in which the role of tradition has changed with the development of modern societies. I shall put forward the following argument (although in this chapter I shall concentrate on some themes at the expense of others):

- With the development of modern societies, there is a gradual decline in the traditional grounding of action and in the role of traditional authority – that is, in the normative and the legitimation aspects of tradition.
- In other respects, however, tradition retains its significance in the modern world, particularly as a means of making sense of the world (the hermeneutic aspect) and as a way of creating a sense of belonging (the identity aspect).

- While tradition retains its significance, it has been transformed in a crucial way: the transmission of the symbolic materials which comprise traditions have become increasingly detached from social interaction in a shared locale. Traditions do not disappear but they lose their moorings in the shared locales of day-to-day life.
- The uprooting of traditions from the shared locales of everyday life does not imply that traditions float freely: on the contrary, traditions will be sustained over time only if they are continuously re-embedded in new contexts and re-moored to new kinds of territorial unit. The significance of nationalism can be partly understood in these terms: nationalism generally involves the re-mooring of tradition to the contiguous territory of an actual or potential nation-state, a territory that encompasses but exceeds the limits of shared locales.

But if tradition remains an important feature of the modern world, is not the broad contrast between 'traditional' and 'modern' societies somewhat misleading? No doubt it is, and I shall be concerned to show that the relation between tradition and modernity is more puzzling and paradoxical than a sharp opposition of this kind would suggest. We can understand the paradox of tradition and modernity by focusing on this consideration: the decline of traditional authority and the traditional grounding of action does not spell the demise of tradition but rather signals a shift in its nature and role, as individuals come to rely more and more on mediated and de-localized traditions as a means of making sense of the world and of creating a sense of belonging.

TRADITION AND THE MEDIA

I have suggested that there is a connection between the transformation of tradition and the development of communication media. But what exactly is the nature of this connection? How has the development of the media affected the nature and role of tradition? Questions of this kind are not entirely new. They have been addressed in some of the literature on communication and development – for example, by Daniel Lerner (1958) in his classic work *The Passing of Traditional Society*.[7] This work is a detailed empirical study of the process of modernization in the Middle East. Although the study was carried out in the 1950s and is therefore rather dated now, Lerner's work remains of interest partly because of the emphasis he placed on the transformative impact of communication media. Lerner saw – rightly, in my view – that the development of the media profoundly alters the practical life-conditions of individuals. Exposure to the media stimulates the faculty of imagination and enables individuals to distance themselves from their immediate social circumstances, inclining them to take an interest in matters that do not bear directly on their day-to-day lives.

While there are aspects of Lerner's work which retain their significance today, nevertheless, as a general account of the interrelations between tradition, modernity and the media, Lerner's work is deeply flawed. Lerner tended to assume that the passage from traditional to modern societies was largely a one-way track, a process in which individuals would gradually shed the encumbrances of a traditional way of life and acquire the psychological attributes to engage in what he called 'the participant society'. In Lerner's view, the persistence of traditional ways and the adoption of modern life-styles were mutually exclusive options, and the shift from the former to the latter was more-or-less inevitable: 'The symbols of race and ritual fade into irrelevance when they impede living desires for bread and enlightenment' (1958, p 405). But it seems clear that this way of presenting the issues is unsatisfactory. For many people, the option of maintaining traditional ways or adopting modern life-styles does not present itself as an 'either/or' choice. On the contrary, they are able to organize their day-to-day lives in such a way as to integrate elements of tradition with new styles of living. Tradition is not necessarily abandoned in the quest for 'bread and enlightenment' but is, on the contrary, reshaped, transformed and perhaps even strengthened through the encounter – partly through the media – with other ways of life. The resurgence of Islam and other religions in the 1970s and 1980s provides many instructive examples of this.[8]

If we wish to understand the relation between tradition and the media, we must put aside the view that exposure to the media will lead invariably to the abandonment of traditional ways of life and to the adoption of modern life-styles. Exposure to the media does not entail, in and by itself, any particular stance vis-à-vis tradition. But if the development of the media has not led to the demise of tradition, in what ways have traditional beliefs and practices been affected by the emergence and growth of mediated forms of communication? In order to answer this question properly, we would have to provide a more systematic analysis of the nature of mediated communication and its impact. I shall not offer such an analysis here; in developing the following account, however, I shall take for granted arguments elaborated elsewhere.[9]

Prior to the development of the media, most people's sense of the past and of the world beyond their immediate milieu was shaped primarily by the symbolic content exchanged in face-to-face interaction. For most people, the sense of the past, of the world beyond their immediate locales, and of the socially delimited communities to which they belonged, was constituted primarily by oral traditions that were produced and reproduced in the social contexts of everyday life. With the development of the media, however, individuals were able to experience events, observe others and, in general, learn about worlds – both real and imaginary – that extended well beyond the sphere of their day-to-day encounters. They were increasingly drawn into networks of communication and forms of interaction that were not face-to-face in character.

We can distinguish two forms or types of interaction which were (and remain) particularly important in this regard – what I describe as 'mediated interaction' and 'mediated quasi-interaction'. By 'mediated interaction' I mean forms of interaction such as letter-writing, telephone conversations and so on. By 'mediated quasi-interaction' I mean the kinds of social interaction created by the media of 'mass communication', such as books, newspapers, radio and television. Both mediated interaction and mediated quasi-interaction involve the use of a technical medium (paper, electrical wires, electromagnetic waves, etc.) which enables information or symbolic content to be transmitted to individuals who are remote in space, in time or in both. Unlike face-to-face interaction, which takes place in a particular spatial–temporal locale, mediated interaction and quasi-interaction are stretched across space and time, and they therefore establish social relations between individuals who do not share the same spatial–temporal context. But whereas mediated interaction is dialogical in character, in the sense that it generally involves a two-way flow of information and communication, mediated quasi-interaction is largely monological or one-way. The viewer of a television programme, for instance, is primarily the recipient of a symbolic form whose producer does not require (and generally does not receive) a direct and immediate response.

Before the early modern period in Europe, and until quite recently in some other parts of the world, the exchange of information and symbolic content was, for most people, a process that took place exclusively within the context of face-to-face interaction. Communication networks depended largely on nodal exchanges that were face-to-face in character. Forms of mediated interaction and quasi-interaction did exist, but they were restricted to a relatively small sector of the population. To participate in mediated interaction or quasi-interaction required special skills – such as the capacity to write or read – which were predominantly the preserve of political, commercial or ecclesiastical elites. But, with the rise of the printing industry in fifteenth- and sixteenth-century Europe and its subsequent development elsewhere, and with the emergence of various types of electronic media in the nineteenth and twentieth centuries, face-to-face interaction was increasingly supplemented by forms of mediated interaction and quasi-interaction. To an ever-increasing extent, the exchange of information and symbolic content took place through mediated forms of interaction, rather than in contexts of face-to-face interaction between individuals who shared a common locale.

Viewed from the perspective of the individual, the historical rise of mediated interaction had far-reaching consequences. As individuals gained access to media products, they were able to keep some distance from the symbolic content of face-to-face interaction and from the forms of authority which prevailed in the shared locales of everyday life. For the purposes of forming a sense of self and of the possibilities open to them, individuals came to rely less and less on symbolic materials transmitted through face-to-face interaction. Increasingly they gained access to what we may describe, in a loose fashion, as 'non-local knowledge'. They also acquired the capacity to experience phenomena which they were unlikely ever to encounter in the locales of their daily lives; with the development of the media (and especially television), the capacity to experience was increasingly disconnected from the activity of encountering. The process of self-formation became more reflexive and open-ended, as individuals were able to draw increasingly on symbolic materials transmitted through the media to inform and refashion the project of the self.

How did these developments affect the nature of tradition? They did not undermine tradition – indeed, in some respects, traditions were largely untouched. Orally transmitted traditions continued to play an important role in the daily lives of many individuals, for example. In other respects, however, traditions were gradually and fundamentally transformed, as the symbolic content of tradition was increasingly inscribed in forms of communication which were not face-to-face in character. This in turn had several consequences; let me emphasize three.

(1) Since many forms of mediated communication involve some degree of fixation of symbolic content in a material substratum, they endow this content with a temporal permanence which is generally lacking in the communicative exchanges of face-to-face interaction. In the absence of material fixation, the maintenance of tradition over time requires the continual re-enactment of its symbolic content in the activities of day-to-day life. Practical repetition is the only way of securing temporal continuity. But with the fixation of symbolic content in a material substratum of some kind, the maintenance of tradition over time can be separated to some extent from the need for practical and continual re-enactment. The cultivation of traditional values and beliefs becomes increasingly dependent on forms of interaction which involve media products; the fixing of symbolic content in media products

(books, films etc.) provides a form of temporal continuity which diminishes the need for re-enactment. Hence, the decline of some of the ritualized aspects of tradition (such as church attendance) should not necessarily be interpreted as the decline of tradition as such: it may simply express the fact that the maintenance of tradition over time has become less dependent on ritualized re-enactment. Tradition has, in effect, become increasingly *de-ritualized*.

The de-ritualization of tradition does not imply that *all* elements of ritual will be eliminated from tradition, nor does it imply that tradition will become entirely divorced from the face-to-face interaction which takes place in shared locales. While the symbolic content of tradition may become increasingly fixed in media products, many traditions remain closely tied to the practical encounters of daily life (for example, within the family, the school and other institutional settings). Moreover, media products are commonly appropriated within contexts of face-to-face interaction, and hence the renewal of tradition may involve a constantly changing mixture of face-to-face interaction and of mediated quasi-interaction. This is evident to parents and teachers, who come to rely more and more on books, films and television programmes to convey to children the main themes of a religious or other tradition, and who see their own role more in terms of elaboration and explication than in terms of the cultivation of tradition from scratch.

(2) To the extent that the transmission of tradition becomes dependent on mediated forms of communication, it also becomes detached from the individuals with whom one interacts in day-to-day life – that is, it becomes *de-personalized*. Once again, this process of de-personalization is never total, since the transmission of tradition remains interwoven with face-to-face interaction. But as mediated forms of communication acquire an increasing role, so the authority of tradition is gradually detached from the individuals with whom one interacts in the practical contexts of daily life. Tradition acquires a certain autonomy and an authority of its own, as a set of values, beliefs and assumptions which exist and persist independently of the individuals who may be involved in transmitting them from one generation to the next.

The de-personalization of tradition is not, however, a uniform and unambiguous process, and we can see that, with the development of electronic media and especially television, the conditions are created for a renewal of the link between the authority of tradition and the individuals who transmit it. But the nature of this link is new and unprecedented: it is a link which is established and sustained largely within the framework of mediated quasi-interaction. For most people, individuals such as Billy Graham and Oral Roberts are known only as TV personalities. They are individuals one can witness and observe, watch and listen to (credulously or not, as the case may be); but they are not individuals with whom one is ever likely to interact in day-to-day life. Hence, while such individuals may succeed in 're-personalizing' tradition, it is a quite distinctive kind of personalization: it lacks the reciprocity of face-to-face interaction and it is dissociated from the individuals encountered in the shared locales of everyday life. It is a form of what I would describe as 'non-reciprocal intimacy at a distance'.[10]

(3) As the transmission of tradition becomes increasingly linked to communication media, traditions are also increasingly detached from their moorings in particular locales. Prior to the development of the media, traditions had a certain rootedness: that is, they were rooted in the spatial locales within which individuals lived out their daily lives. Traditions were integral parts of communities of individuals who interacted – actually or potentially – with one another. But with the development of the media, traditions were gradually uprooted; the bond that tied traditions to specific locales of face-to-face interaction was gradually weakened. In other words, traditions were gradually and partially *de-localized*, as they became increasingly dependent on mediated forms of communication for their maintenance and transmission from one generation to the next.

The uprooting or 'de-localization' of tradition had far-reaching consequences, some of which I want to pursue in the remaining sections of this chapter. It enabled traditions to be detached from particular locales and freed from the constraints imposed by oral transmission in circumstances of face-to-face interaction. The reach of tradition – both in space and in time – was no longer restricted by the conditions of localized transmission. But the uprooting of traditions from particular locales did not lead them to wither away, nor did it destroy altogether the connection between traditions and spatial units. On the contrary, the uprooting of traditions was the condition for the re-embedding of traditions in new contexts and for the re-mooring of traditions to new kinds of territorial unit that exceeded the limits of shared locales. Traditions were de-localized but they were not de-territorialized: they were refashioned in ways that enabled them to be re-embedded in a multiplicity of locales and re-connected to territorial units that exceed the limits of face-to-face interaction.

THE UPROOTING AND RE-MOORING OF TRADITION

What is involved in the uprooting and re-mooring of tradition? How should we analyse the process by which traditions are dislodged from particular locales and re-embedded in the practical contexts of daily life, though now in ways that re-connect traditions to new kinds of spatial unit? We can gain some insight into this process by considering what is sometimes referred to as 'the invention of tradition'.[11] Much of the literature on the invention of tradition has been concerned to emphasize the degree of fabrication involved in the retrospective cultivation of traditional practices and beliefs. Not only are many traditions less ancient than they seem, but they are also replete with myths and half-truths whose origins are so obscure that they are no longer recognized as such. But this literature illustrates another theme which is less obvious and less frequently discussed: it highlights the role played by the media in the re-fashioning of tradition and in the re-mooring of traditions to territorial units of various kinds. An example will help to demonstrate this point.

Many of the traditions associated with the British monarchy are a good deal less ancient than they seem. Of course, royal rituals were a common feature of Tudor and Stuart courts, as they were of courtly life in other parts of Europe. But, as David Cannadine (1983) has shown, many of the ceremonial practices associated with the British monarchy today are, in fact, a creation of the late nineteenth and early twentieth centuries. Prior to the late nineteenth century, royal ceremonies were performed largely for the benefit of other members of the court and aristocracy; they were, by and large, group rites in which London-based elites reaffirmed their corporate solidarity. During the first three-quarters of the nineteenth century, the major ceremonies of the British monarchy were extensively reported in the metropolitan and the provincial press. But the attitude of the press was largely hostile, and the monarchy was a popular object of criticism and caricature. The ceremonies themselves were generally conducted in a dreadfully incompetent fashion. 'In 1817, at the funeral of Princess Charlotte, the daughter of the Prince Regent, the undertakers were drunk. When the duke of York died, ten years later, the Chapel at Windsor was so damp that most of the mourners caught cold, Canning contracted rheumatic fever and the bishop of London died' (1983, p. 117). The coronations of George IV, William IV and Victoria were poorly managed and unrehearsed, and were the subject of scathing criticism by royal commentators at the time.

From the late 1870s on, however, the royal rituals and public image of the British monarchy began to change. A great deal more effort was invested in the planning and organization of the major occasions of state, beginning with Queen Victoria's Golden Jubilee in 1887. Ceremonies that had previously been rather ungainly affairs were gradually transformed into pageants of unprecedented splendour, meticulously planned and carefully rehearsed.

Moreover, with the emergence in the late nineteenth century of the mass-circulation popular press, there was a significant shift in the public portrayal of the monarchy. The mocking caricatures and critical editorials of earlier decades were replaced by an increasingly respectful representation of the monarchy in the popular press, and the great royal ceremonies were described in a sentimental and reverential way. At a time when the real political power of the monarchy was declining significantly, the position of the monarch as head of state and symbol of national unity was enhanced through the renewal and elaboration of royal rituals and their celebration in the popular press. Traditions that previously had been restricted primarily to London-based elites were now reshaped and made available, via the printed media, to a much larger constituency.

These traditions were not only transformed, indeed invented, in certain fundamental respects: they were also disconnected from their historical embeddedness in courtly life and increasingly made available to the population as a whole. The traditions of royal ritual were re-embedded in the daily lives of ordinary individuals through the appropriation of media products; and they were re-connected to the territorial boundaries of the nation-state, the unity and integrity of which these rituals were designed increasingly to represent.

In the period after the First World War, the role of the monarchy as the politically impartial embodiment of national unity was extended further by the advent of broadcasting. John Reith, the first Director General of the BBC, was a devotee of the monarchy and quickly recognized the potential of radio as a means of conveying a sense of participation in the great ceremonial occasions of state (Cannadine, 1983, p. 142).[12] The major royal ceremonies were broadcast live on radio, beginning with the Duke of York's wedding in 1923. Great care was taken to position microphones in a way which would enable listeners to hear the sounds of bells, horses, carriages and cheering crowds. In an age of rapid social change, the anachronism of the ceremonies merely enhanced their grandeur. They took on a fairytale quality. With the development of television in the 1950s, the anachronistic grandeur of royal ceremonies was made available in all its splendour. Now it was possible for a substantial proportion of the population not only to hear but also to see the ceremonies as they occurred. The Coronation of Queen Elizabeth in 1953 was the first occasion on which the crowning of a British sovereign could be seen by the public at large.[13]

By considering the ways in which royal ceremonies have changed over time, we can get a sense not only of the invented character of many traditions but also of the extent to which their significance and scope have changed.

While royal rituals were once performed largely for the benefit of members of the elite who were physically present on the occasions of their performance, increasingly they have been detached from the face-to-face contexts of courtly life and made available, via the media, to an extended range of recipients. And in so doing, the meaning and purpose of these rituals have changed. Today they are no longer concerned with the reaffirmation of the corporate solidarity of metropolitan elites; rather, the great ceremonial occasions of the monarchy have become mediated celebrations of national identity which all citizens, wherever they may be, are able to witness and in which they are invited vicariously to take part.

It is not surprising that traditions which have become so dependent on the media should also be vulnerable to them. In an age of mediated visibility, the monarchy is in a precarious position. On the one hand, the appeal of the monarchy, and of the royal rituals associated with it, stems from its capacity to stand above the mundane world of party politics and to present itself as a body whose integrity and probity is beyond reproach, a body clothed in ancient costumes and governed by time-honoured customs which, when re-enacted before us all in the carefully managed ceremonies appearing on our television screens, endow the monarchy and its temporal representatives with an other-worldly glow. On the other hand, in an increasingly mediated world, it is difficult for the temporal representatives of the monarchy to avoid appearing as ordinary individuals, as men and women who are little different from other individuals apart from the accident of their birth, and who are prone to the same temptations, driven by the same desires and subject to the same weaknesses as ordinary mortals. It is this tension between the other-worldly and the mundane, between the aloofness of the monarchy and the all-too-ordinary lives of its representatives, which lies at the heart of the scandals that have shaken the monarchy in recent years and renewed the speculation about its future.

In this section I have explored some of the ways in which traditions have been taken up, reshaped and, to some extent, re-invented in the course of their enactment and elaboration over time. Now it might be argued that the example we have considered, precisely because of its 'invented' character, is an 'artificial tradition' that is imposed on people from above, in contrast to the 'authentic traditions' of the past which, it might be claimed, arose spontaneously from below. Unlike the latter, it might be argued, these 'pseudo-traditions' are not rooted in the day-to-day lives of individuals; they are not created and sustained by them through their practical activities but, instead, are imposed on them by political elites, entrepreneurs, promoters of the tourist industry and an odd assortment of self-proclaimed guardians of the past.[14]

While this line of argument is not without interest, it does not, in my view, press to the heart of the matter. By insisting on the distinction between authentic and artificial traditions (and relegating the former largely to the past), this line of argument fails to grasp the significance of the fact that traditions have become increasingly interwoven with mediated symbolic forms. When the symbolic content of tradition is articulated in media products, it is necessarily distanced to some extent from the practical contexts of daily life; the establishment and maintenance of traditions over time become increasingly dependent on forms of interaction which are not face-to-face in character. But traditions which rely heavily on mediated symbolic forms are not *ipso facto* less authentic than those which are transmitted exclusively through face-to-face interaction. In a world increasingly permeated by communication media, traditions have become increasingly dependent on mediated symbolic forms; they have become dislodged from particular locales and re-embedded in social life in new ways. But the uprooting and re-mooring of traditions does not necessarily render them inauthentic, nor does it necessarily spell their demise.

MIGRANT POPULATIONS, NOMADIC TRADITIONS: SOME SOURCES OF CULTURAL CONFLICT

The uprooting and re-mooring of traditions are interwoven in complex ways with other trends and developmental characteristics of modern societies. I cannot explore these connections in detail here. But I want to conclude by considering one characteristic which is particularly important in this regard: namely, the migration, dislocation and resettling of populations. As people move (or are forcibly moved) from one region or part of the world to another, they often carry with them the sets of values and beliefs that form part of traditions. These mobile, nomadic traditions may be sustained partly through ritualized re-enactment and the retelling of stories in contexts of face-to-face interaction. With the passage of time, nomadic traditions may gradually alter in character, as they become increasingly remote from their contexts of origin and increasingly interwoven with symbolic contents derived from the new circumstances in which they are re-enacted.

While nomadic traditions may be sustained partly through ritualized re-enactment, they may also become closely interwoven with mediated symbolic materials, precisely because communication media tend to uproot traditions from particular locales and endow their symbolic content with some degree of temporal permanence and spatial mobility. Communication media provide a way of sustaining cultural continuity despite spatial dislocation, a way of renewing tradition in new and diverse contexts through the appropriation of mediated symbolic forms. Hence communication media can play an important role in the maintenance and renewal of tradition among migrant or dislocated groups. This role is likely to be particularly significant when the groups are settled in countries where different languages are spoken, and where traditions and customs diverge from their own. This is well illustrated, for example, by the popularity of Hindi films among families of south-Asian origin which are settled in Britain and other parts of the world.[15]

The dispersion of traditions through the media and through the movements of migrant populations has created a cultural landscape in the modern world of enormous complexity and diversity. It has also given rise to forms of tension and conflict which are, in some respects, new. We can discern these forms of tension in different contexts and at different levels. Within the context of the family, for instance, parents and children of migrant populations may have divergent views of the merits of traditions which are linked to a distant place of origin. Parents may place greater value on these traditions and on the maintenance of some degree of cultural continuity with a distant past; children, who may be more assimilated to the communities in which they have settled, may be more likely to view these traditions with scepticism or even contempt. Hence the appropriation of media products – for example, the family viewing of a film on videocassette – may be a somewhat discordant occasion, as parents may see the activity of appropriation as a valuable opportunity to renew traditional ties, while children may regard it as little more than a disagreeable obligation.

This kind of inter-generational tension and conflict can also be experienced subjectively, by a particular individual, as sets of values and beliefs which pull in different directions. An individual may feel some attraction to, and some sympathy with, the traditions linked to a distant place of origin; and yet he or she may also feel that these traditions have little bearing on the actual circumstances of his or her life. Despite the ritualized re-enactment of traditions and the continual appropriation of media products, it may be difficult to re-embed these traditions in the practical contexts of daily life. The individual may feel torn between a set of values and beliefs which provides a link to a past which is distant both in space and in time, on the one hand, and a cluster of values and beliefs which seem to point towards the future, on the other.

From this point of view, we can gain some appreciation of the complexity and ambiguity of what might be described as 'the quest for roots'. As a kind of cultural project that may be expressed in particular media products and linked to their appropriation, the quest for roots bears a strong but ambivalent relation to migrant populations. The appeal of the quest is that it offers a way of recovering and, indeed, inventing traditions which re-connect individuals to (real or imaginary) places of origin. The greater the distance of these origins in time and space, the more appealing the quest for roots may be, for it may help one to refashion an aspect of self which has been suppressed, ignored or stigmatized in some way. And yet individuals may also feel deep ambivalence towards the project of recovering the traditions associated with an alleged place of origin. For they may feel that, whatever the facts of migration and dislocation may be, these traditions have little to do with the kind of life they want to build for themselves. 'Parents use . . . films to represent their culture to their children,' remarked one young Londoner of south-Asian descent, 'but that will not work because those are not my roots, that place [India] has nothing to do with me anymore.'[16]

There are other ways in which the maintenance and renewal of tradition among migrant or dislocated groups may be a source of tension and conflict. The traditions of different groups are increasingly brought into contact with one another, partly as a result of cultural migrations and partly through the globalization of media products. But the increasing contact between traditions is not necessarily accompanied by an increase of mutual comprehension on the part of the individuals who belong to different groups. On the contrary, the encounter of traditions may give rise to intense forms of conflict which are based on varying degrees of incomprehension and intolerance – conflicts which are all the more intense when they are linked to broader relations of power and inequality. The Salman Rushdie affair is a particularly vivid example of this kind of cultural conflict. As a media product circulating in a global domain, *The Satanic Verses* precipitated a violent clash of values that are rooted in different traditions; and while the spatial barriers between these traditions have been eroded by cultural migrations and communication flows, the gulf of understanding remains.

Contact between traditions can also give rise to intensified forms of boundary-defining activity. Attempts may be made to protect the integrity of traditions, and to re-assert forms of collective identity which are linked to traditions, by excluding others in one's midst. These boundary-defining activities can be both symbolic and territorial – symbolic in the sense that the primary concern may be to protect traditions from the incursion of extraneous symbolic content, territorial in the sense that the protection of traditions may be combined with an attempt to re-moor these traditions to particular regions or locales in a way that forcibly excludes others. A region becomes a 'homeland', which is seen by some as bearing a privileged relation to a group of people whose collective identity is shaped in part by an enduring set of traditions. And we know only too well how this kind of boundary-defining activity – especially when combined with the accumulated means of political and coercive power – can manifest itself in the most brutal forms of violence.

I have dwelt on some of the ways in which the intermingling of populations and traditions can be a source of tension and conflict. But it should be stressed that this process of intermingling is also a source of enormous cultural creativity and dynamism. In the sphere of literature or popular music, of art or cinema, the weaving together of themes drawn from different traditions – this continuous hybridization of culture – is the basis of some of the most original and exciting work. It creates a kind of cultural restlessness which is constantly shifting directions, assuming new forms and departing from established conventions in unexpected ways.[17] And it attests to the fact that, in a world increasingly traversed by cultural migrations and communication flows, traditions are less sheltered than ever before from the potentially invigorating consequences of encounters with the other.

NOTES

1　See especially Beck (1992); Giddens (1991); Beck, Giddens and Lash (1994).
2　See Giddens, 'Living in a Post-Traditional Society', in Beck, Giddens and Lash (1994).
3　These and other questions are examined in more detail in John Thompson (1995), upon which this chapter is based.
4　The most significant exception is probably the work of Edward Shils (1981). A more recent work – which expresses, however, many of the 'traditional ways of thinking about tradition – is David Gross (1992). Of course, the notion of tradition has been discussed more extensively by anthropologists; for a recent example, see Pascal Boyer (1990).
5　See Martin Heidegger (1962), especially ss. 31–3; and Hans-Georg Gadamer (1975), especially pp. 235–74.
6　For a fuller account of the notion of ideology assumed here, see Thompson (1990).
7　See also Wilbur Schramm (1964).
8　See especially Gilles Kepel (1994).
9　See Thompson (1994, 1995).
10　See Thompson (1995, ch. 7).
11　See Eric Hobsbawm and Terence Ranger (1983); and Roy Porter (1992).
12　See also J. C. W. Reith (1949); and Andrew Boyle (1972).
13　For a discussion of the Coronation as a mediated ritual, see David Chaney (1983); see also Daniel Dayan and Elihu Katz (1992).

14   For a recent version of this argument, see David Gross (1992, ch. 4).
15   See Marie Gillespie (1989); see also Arjun Appadurai (1990).
16   Quoted in Gillespie (1989, p. 238).
17   See Nestor García Canclini (1989); James Lull (1994).

REFERENCES

Appadurai, Arjun 1990: Disjuncture and Difference in the Global Cultural Economy. In Mike Featherstone (ed.), *Global Culture: Nationalism, Globalization and Modernity*. London and Newbury Park, Ca: Sage, pp. 295–310.

Beck, Ulrich 1992: *Risk Society: Towards a New Modernity*, trans. Mark Ritter. London and Newbury Park, Ca: Sage.

Beck, Ulrich, Giddens, Anthony and Lash, Scott 1994: *Reflexive Modernization: Politics, Tradition and Aesthetics in the Modern Social Order*. Cambridge: Polity Press.

Boyer, Pascal 1990: *Tradition as Truth and Communication*. Cambridge: Cambridge University Press.

Boyle, Andrew 1972: *Only the Wind will Listen: Reith of the BBC*. London: Hutchison.

Canclini, Nestor García 1989: *Culturas Híbridas: Estrategias para Entrar y Salir de la Modernidad*. Mexico, D.F.: Grijalbo.

Cannadine, David 1983: The Context, Performance and Meaning of Ritual: The British Monarchy and the 'Invention of Tradition', c.1820–1977. In E. Hobsbawm and T. Ranger (eds), *The Invention of Tradition*, Cambridge: Cambridge University Press, pp. 101–64.

Chaney, David 1983: A Symbolic Mirror of Ourselves: Civil Ritual in Mass Society. In *Media, Culture and Society*, 5, pp. 119–35.

Dayan, Daniel and Katz, Elihu 1992: *Media Events: The Live Broadcasting of History*. Cambridge, Mass.: Harvard University Press.

Gadamer, Hans-Georg 1975: *Truth and Method*. London: Sheed and Ward.

Giddens, Anthony 1991: *Modernity and Self-Identity: Self and Society in the Late Modern Age*. Cambridge: Polity Press.

Gillespie, Marie 1989: Technology and Tradition: Audio-Visual Culture among South Asian Families in West London. In *Cultural Studies*, 3, pp. 226–39.

Gross, David 1992: *The Past in Ruins: Tradition and the Critique of Modernity* (Amhurst, Mass.: University of Massachusetts Press.

Heidegger, Martin 1962: *Being and Time*, trans. John Macquarrie and Edward Robinson. Oxford: Basil Blackwell.

Hobsbawm, Eric and Ranger, Terence (eds) 1983: *The Invention of Tradition*. Cambridge: Cambridge University Press.

Kepel, Gilles 1994: *The Revenge of God: The Resurgence of Islam, Christianity and Judaism in the Modern World*, trans. Alan Braley. Cambridge: Polity Press.

Lerner, Daniel 1958: *The Passing of Traditional Society: Modernizing the Middle East*. Glencoe, Ill.: Free Press.

Lull, James 1994: *Media, Communication, Culture: A Global Perspective*. Cambridge: Polity Press.

Porter, Roy (ed.) 1992: *The Myths of the English*. Cambridge: Polity Press.

Reith, J. C. W. 1949: *Into the Wind*. London: Hodder and Stoughton.

Schramm, Wilbur 1964: *Mass Media and National Development*. Stanford, Ca.: Stanford University Press.

Shils, Edward 1981: *Tradition*. London: Faber and Faber.

Thompson, John B. 1990: *Ideology and Modern Culture: Critical Social Theory in the Era of Mass Communication*. Cambridge: Polity Press.

Thompson, John B. 1994: Social Theory and the Media. In David Crowley and David Mitchell (eds), *Communication Theory Today*, Cambridge: Polity Press, pp. 27–49.

Thompson, John B. 1995: *The Media and Modernity: A Social Theory of the Media*. Cambridge: Polity Press.

Weber, Max 1978: *Economy and Society: An Outline of Interpretive Sociology*, vol. 1, Guenther Roth and Claus Wittich (eds). Berkeley: University of California Press.

7

Identity, Meaning and Globalization: Detraditionalization in Postmodern Space–time Compression

Timothy W. Luke

Since the Enlightenment, as the Lancaster international conference of social theorists indicates, very few ideas have proven themselves to be as enduring in Western social theory as the continuous struggles between 'the powers of tradition' and 'the forces of modernity'. Like the theme of organic nature confronting artificial culture, the binary opposition of tradition and modernity in the work of many social theorists remains fixed as a primary identity-creating and meaning-generating story. So let us begin our story by consciously writing and reading how thoroughly this story is, and can only be, not much more than yet another re-presentation of how thematic oppositions inter-play in the narratives of social theory. With this maneuver of mutual recognition, we might reset the scene here, enabling us to interweave fragments of analysis and bits of understanding into a new story about the dynamics of 'detraditionalization' in the midst of 'postmodernization'. These notations of discursivity are essential, because it is the storied-ness of various situations/conflicts/settings/characters/symbols in all of these long-running social-theory discourses about 'tradition' and 'modernity' that have been all too often forgotten in accounts attempting to establish what these ideas mean.

Most tellings of the tradition/modernity tales almost always keep this contradictory couplet of concepts fused. Indeed, holding this combination together is a strongly fixed tradition in social theory. Like the opposition of nature to culture, 'tradition' is opposed to 'modernity' in an apparent inter-play of contradictions: *Gemeinschaft* versus *Gesellschaft*. From their mutual antagonism and respective incompatibilities, the new identities and innovative meanings of becoming modern are pushed against old identities and established meanings, which are, at the same time, pulling toward being traditional: *Gemeinschaft* becomes *Gesellschaft*. Outside of this story, however, there are actual intra-plays of many other identities and differences in which one finds tradition-in-modernity or modernity-as-tradition that clearly can tell another story. This discussion, then, will doubt the social-theory tradition expressed in fusing tradition and modernity so strongly together in *Gemeinschaft* and *Gesellschaft* relations. Instead, this account builds its stories around the problematic of space–time compression to draw an alternative account of 'detraditionalization' and 'postmodernization' in the workings of social theory today.

TRADITION/MODERNITY: CONTRADICTIONS AND CONFLICTS

In most instances, the tradition/modernity binary plays out as little more than a classic epic of social and political struggle, centered most commonly upon the prescriptive coding of modernity as 'positive new-ness' posed over-and-against tradition as 'negative old-ness', although there also are conservative constructions that would reverse the locations of these positive and negative polarities (Blackburn, 1990). From Adam Smith and Jean-Jacques Rousseau to Jürgen Habermas and Francis Fukuyama, this story has captured the imagination of social theory within a confining cage of complex cultural contradictions. Even today, many social theorists are still caught behind its bars, spinning their conceptual yarns from within its confines. Yet, the strongly centered world system of liberal bourgeois capitalism, which once pretended to be all-that-is-new in order to impose its beliefs and practices upon what then was presumed to be all-that-was-old, has 'ended' this history. By enveloping almost everything that remained resistant as *other-ness* (the South/the Orient/the East) within *it* (the North/the Occident/the West), the spaces of the 'old' and the 'new' are becoming fused into 'the now' of globalization, leaving the identity and meaning of both zones in crisis (Robertson, 1992; Luke, 1989). Agencies of change no longer can pretend credibly either to be what is 'positive new-ness' or to become meaningful in eradicating what was 'negative old-ness'. All that exists is mired in the same global now-ness, which is a much more uneasy, de-centered, unfocused, de-based amalgam of detraditionalizing/postmodernizing social exchange after 'the end of history' (Fukuyama, 1992).

The 'tradition versus modernity' story runs on a volatile rhetorical fuel in which various definitions, identities and meanings are mixed in unstable combinations. For example, the primary conceptual con-ference of theoretical reasons to our gathering in the 'conference rationale' prescriptively reads the character of 'tradition' and 'modernity' as having very particular attributes (Center, 1992, pp. 1–3). Tradition, as the conferents are told, is: (i) 'a set of conventions, a set of rules which regulate cultural and social life'; or (ii) 'organically emerging rules of the village *Gemeinschaft*'; or (iii) 'the God-given rules of religious authority'; or (iv) 'the unchallengeable rules of the more secular authority of an ancient empire or absolutist state'; or (v) 'the norms inscribed, as it were, in some sort of natural order' (Center, 1992, p. 1). Modernity, on the other hand, is: (i) 'The discursive creation and legitimation of reflexive subjects'; and (ii) 'old hat' (Center, 1992, p. 2). Or, in other words, it is *Gesellschaft*. This foundational archive can be read in many different expansive fashions, but these definitions all tend to reveal some problematic assumptions. On the one hand, they assert that tradition is essentially conventional, organic, God-given, authoritative, or natural; yet, on the other hand, they also suggest that modernity is normally reflexive or discursively generated by critical conscious subjects.

These divisions and distinctions, however, are basically unsustainable. The discursive creation and legitimation of reflexive subjects through *Gesellschaft* cannot happen in a vacuum, even if it is 'old hat'. It inevitably requires a fixed set of conventions, a stable set of rules which regulate cultural and social life, or perhaps something pulled from an old hat, namely, 'traditions.' Likewise, in this account, other questions are left open: who sets conventions, who sets rules, who regulates cultural and social life? What organically emerges in the rules of village *Gemeinschaft*? Who gives, receives, hears, enscribes God's rules? What rules these tradition-bound old empires or absolutist states? Who reads the norms of Nature in the natural order? In the final analysis, it would appear to be reflexive subjects: or people, who make, break, follow, depart from conventional rules in living their socially-interconnected existences. So, why do we allow this sort of semantic volatility to continue to be stabilized in these kinds of conceptual prescriptions? Perhaps it is because these strategies for effacing ambiguities cloak even more elaborate contradictions and deeply held convictions that are nested at the heart of modern social theorizing.

At this juncture, then, the tradition/modernity binary is a register of old battles won, current conflicts still undecided, and future struggles yet to be openly declared. The impulse to continually oppose tradition to modernity should be re-read as a contradictory archive of political struggle, cultural nostalgia, social surveillance, and moral remorse. On one level, it carries traces of the old bourgeois opposition to the putatively 'unchallengeable rules' of organic order and natural authority used by ancient empires or absolutist monarchs. Suspicions about these rules strongly linger in social theorists' analyses of such systems of moral legitimation. On a second level, it repeats nostalgic urban/suburban images of village *Gemeinschaft* that are attractive to modern city-dwellers, clutching for authoritative guidance in ethical conventions derived from these old ways. On a third level, it marks that presumption of power by administrative experts in core regions around the world as leading-edges of 'progress' to police and protect the trailing edges of 'reaction' in global semi-peripheries and peripheries. And, on a last level, it shows signs of many intellectuals' frustrations with the often baffling dictates of modern technologies, which decisively structure everyone's increasingly artificial environments, as they force ordinary people into wistfully searching for solid moral norms inscribed in some sort of natural order.

THE PAST IN RUINS?

All of these contradictions in the tradition/modernity binary are well-represented in *The Past in Ruins: Tradition and the Critique of Modernity* (1992) by David Gross. Consequently, a closer analysis of this text might help us elaborate more of our story about contemporary social theory. He expertly retells the standard stories about the demise of tradition and the rise of modernity, while, at the same time, anticipating the problematic of 'detraditionalization' in his rendering of 'postmodernity.' Drawing on the best insights of classic sociological theory, modern European history, and Frankfurt School critiques, Gross recounts the stories of how traditional feudal agrarian society with its organic stability, at once insured and guided by authoritative traditions, was swept aside by modern industrial capitalist society with its new normalized standards enforced and managed by the nation-state, consumer capitalism, and mass-media culture. Affirming nearly two centuries of sociological narrative, Gross asserts, 'One might say that in 1650 the overall cultural framework of the West was traditional . . . By contrast, in 1850 the overall cultural framework had become modern. Though substantial pockets of tradition survived they tended to be viewed through the lenses of modernity' (Gross, 1992, p. 42).

Such tales of modernity are widely regarded now as definitive, but, unlike other writers working over the same topic, Gross does not exaggerate the destruction of tradition by modernity, even though traditions largely were reduced in his view to a fragmentary mosaic composed of disconnected pockets of persistence a hundred and fifty years ago. Indeed, he argues that tradition still survives, only it does so beside, behind, between, or beneath the practices and structures of modernity. From our perspective, this argument is quite interesting in as much as Gross turns to a spatial register to define where and why tradition does or does not persist. It might be difficult to discover such spatial zones, but naturally surviving traditions are allegedly alive, and maybe even well, at four different sites: at the center of society, in religious, educational, political, and cultural institutions; at the periphery of society, in ethnic enclaves, rural areas, or urban bohemias; at the cracks and interstices of society, in family practices, kinship institutions, or personal emotional ties; and in the underground of society, where religious sects, linguistics minorities, tribal groups, secret societies, and revolutionary political movements operate. Elsewhere, however, Gross argues that space is occupied by the expectations and actions of modernity. The modernizing rules embedded in capitalist exchange, statist managerialism, and electronic imagery have prevailed in these regions, where they reign triumphantly over the crushed debris of the traditional past. —*territory vs-reterritory*

This account, however, raises some doubts. If tradition 'only' persists at the center, in the joints, on the margins, and deep underground, then, one must ask, where does it *not* survive? One might see this openly pessimistic summary of the current situation as positive. Tradition, as Gross understands it, really thrives almost everywhere except in those undetermined sites he places above ground, inside the margins, along the cracks, and not quite in the center. Even though there is much to admire in his epic portrayal of tradition defeated by modernity, it is clear that this account can be fundamentally challenged simply by reading it positively rather than negatively.

On the one hand, Gross introduces the appropriate evidence, calls many convincing witnesses, and provides a compelling case against modernity in favor of tradition. Still, his initial bill of particulars, identifying the failures of tradition and flaws in modernity, which was sworn out by the conceptual courts of sociological theory, seems, on the other hand, very suspect. We must raise questions, then, stirring doubts and challenging assumptions in responding to what is in many ways a very admirable account of tradition's alleged demise. The strands that Gross, and many other contemporary social theorists, weave together in the tales of contradictions rooted in the tradition/modernity couplet were first spun by Rousseau, Smith and Kant, then braided by Marx, Durkheim and Weber, and most recently retied by Foucault, Lyotard, and Habermas. Like those before him, Gross's telling of his story is often authoritative, wide-ranging, and exhaustive. Yet, it is precisely this powerful scope that calls it into question. Is *The Past in Ruins* an accurate account of modernity and tradition or is it essentially a sweeping rhetorical rehearsal of a conventional script? Is it truly persuasive or is it convincing because this script rests at the heart of many modern critiques of society,

economy, and the state? In other words, has only a thin theoretical model of
what might have happened been mistaken for a thick historical record of *what
did happen*?

Seeing the past (tradition) in ruins and the present (modernity) as its
ruination is now 'traditional' for us. It lives as a set of practices, a constellation of beliefs, and a mode of thinking that we inherit from Rousseau,
Marx, and Weber. Because we often wish to stand (explicitly or implicitly)
with these authors as critical critics of all that exists, we re-read their old
scripts in performing their/our traditions of social theory once again. The
basic story line of a *Gemeinschaft* to *Gesellschaft* narrative survives in our
conceptual clans and thrives among our theoretical tribes as a set of observances about history, a collection of teachings about change, a way of thinking
about us in our world, and a way of interpreting the reality of the past/
present/future.

Unfortunately, in choosing to follow this script, Gross falls victim, like
those before him, to an objectified modernist vision of tradition, which is
constructed as 'something' valuable that is passed on to posterity, from the
past to the present. This reified interpretation of tradition begins with the
first definitions given by Gross, but it continues to be a problem throughout
the book. To identify tradition, Gross goes back to the Latin verb *tradere*,
which implies transmitting or giving *something* up or over to another, since
Roman jurisprudence saw this practice as what legally constituted making a
bequest or inheritance. *Traditio* is the process of giving, and *traditum* is the
thing being transmitted. Hence, what tradition means is that '(A) something
precious or valuable is (B) given to someone in trust after which (C) the
person who receives the "gift" is expected to keep it intact and unharmed out
of a *sense of obligation* to the giver' (1992, p. 9). These webs of obligation in
giving and receiving 'something' of value through every successive generation, in turn, provide Gross with characters to appear as the cohesive agencies
of authority that once gave life meaning, purpose, and foundation. That is,
'it told people what they should do in order to be in harmony with the
world . . . it made clear that the authoritative was always that which was
handed down from the past through the medium of tradition' (1992, p. 10).
Here, perhaps, one sees 'the pregiven, natural order' designated by the reasoning of the conference rationale as the 'meaning' of tradition (Center,
1992, p. 2).

The thing-like quality assigned to tradition, however, essentializes and/or
subjectifies a set of beliefs and practices that are always no more than an
objectified set of contingent values and actions. Like classical sociological
theory, Gross sees tradition as 'something valuable,' and it must, like a thing,

be preserved in form and content to retain this value as it is passed on through at least three generations. Traditions, as thing-like containers, therefore become discrete vessels 'carrying' a certain cargo of spiritual value or moral meaning. And, this freight of moral, spiritual, cultural prestige creates a sense of continuity, 'as if one were a link in a chain stretching back in time' (1992, p. 10). Thus, Gross sees the value-laden vessels of tradition as conveyances, loading and unloading their prestigious wares of spirituality or goods of morality at the close and advent of each new human generation. In turn, the recipients are obliged to portage these containers and their contents through time to the commencement of the next new generation.

Of course, Gross does not fall victim completely to the expectation of changelessness in his original definitions. In dragging these vessels over the rocks and snags in the river of time, scrapes and dents are put into the thingified vessels of tradition, while minor alterations, and even major modifications, get made every time a new generation unpacks, uses, and repacks 'the somethings' being transmitted to the ages. Gross notes that 'nothing historically engendered ever remains fixed or static . . . . Hence, no tradition is ever taken over precisely as it was given, or passed on precisely as it was received' (1992, pp. 13–14). As traditions are conveyed, their transmission or giving over can be contested, accepted, challenged, or assimilated with complete acquiescence or all-around conflict. To picture this process, then, Gross enlarges his original reified version of tradition by casting it also as a subjectified process, or as a 'conversation' between the generations. Yet, this disembodied supplement to the original embodied vision of tradition does not go far enough. Conversations are about something. The manner in which Gross describes traditions as essentially unchanging vessels discharging their wares and ways into the everyday lifeworld of every new generation leaves one looking at such conversations as those that happen when one rummages through the trunks in grandma's attic, roots through the tool boxes in grandpa's garage, or unwraps their bequests at the reading of another relation's last will and testament. Old containers, ancient chests, and sacred closets are opened to reveal contents of continuity, cohesion, and community that are named and passed along in discussions via some immanent traditional grammar.

The thing-like quality that social theory grants to tradition also gives it a vital essence in Gross's discussion that frequently distorts his narrative. Looking back into the depths of time, for example, he argues that 'tradition defined values, established continuities, and codified patterns of behavior' (1992, p. 20). That is, traditions act, and human beings react. He claims that people came together to survive, but then people nearly disappear as actors, as tradition takes over the role of binding them together culturally and emotionally. Along with most *Gemeinschaft* to *Gesellschaft* theories, Gross forgets that tradition cannot act or think, only people actually engage in action and thought. *The Past in Ruins* repeatedly suggests that the disembodied agency of tradition did what nothing (or nobody) else was able to do. That is, it supplied categories, provided order, stabilized society, preserved heritages, fortified community, fostered dispositions, gave cohesion, produced respect, and encouraged piety (1992, pp. 20–3). Yet, this narrative reconstruction of tradition's powers misplaces cultural concreteness and mistakes social agency. In fact, people, and only people, can do these activities. The question is why and how did they do them in complex contexts of discursive interplay and reflexive cooperation defined by traditional categories?

Traditions are no more than traces of practices, signs of belief, and images of continuity revealed in human thought and action, which are continuously sent and chaotically received throughout all the generations. All the members of any generation are not identical in either their reception or their transmission of tradition. What any ritual, every value, all interpretations, or each practice ultimately means is impossible to determine with any real continuity or total certainty. Tradition does not, as Gross claims, 'rule' through the millennia as an authoritative subject (1992, p. 20). Rather, human subjects in authority over others use tradition as rules through the millennia to organize collective understandings of thought and action. Traditions are always at work in the residues, additions, modifications, and emendations of human beings' activities. There is no essential core that can be either regarded as a constant core of cohesion or reduced to some immutable gold standard of meaning.

Tradition, therefore, should not be regarded – to give it another prescriptive reading – as being necessarily static, backward, and conservative. Traditions also must be seen as very dynamic, contemporary, and forward-looking, because they are actively part of everyone's daily life in the modern world. Actually, there is 'a modernity' to tradition and 'a tradition' of modernity that social theorists or cultural historians, like Gross, almost entirely miss by choosing to retell their tales of the old *Gemeinschaft* becomes *Gesellschaft* narrative, which discursively digs a deep gulf between the substantive unity of what apparently was and the instrumental fragmentation of what seems to be now. Hence, the possibility of having 'modernistic' beliefs and practices in the traditional past is dismissed as unlikely, and the probability of seeing new 'traditionalistic' beliefs and practices in the modern present is regarded as impossible outside of vestigial pockets of old otherness within the nooks and crannies, at the margins, or in the underground of existing society. One need not necessarily coin neologisms, such as 'modition' or 'tradernity,' to present these alternative possibilities, but the conceptual customs of social theory that respect the prevailing disciplinary theoretical traditions of dividing the world into static tradition and dynamic modernity should be ignored.

Social theory, as long as it sticks with these concepts, often overlooks how 'traditional' modernity itself has become after six generations of nearly complete dominance as the organizing force in social institutions and practices. Perhaps more complex theoretical accounts, such as those given by Gross, would dodge this claim by asserting such routines are merely 'customs' rather than 'traditions.' Nevertheless, there might be more than state power, corporate greed, and slick images holding together what Gross calls modernity. Modernity is not some irresistible juggernaut that continuously paves over the ruins of the past, leaving tradition to survive only *in cognito* or *sub rosa* at the margins, in the cracks, or all the way underground. The empiricism and rationalism of modernity never fully embrace 'a clear, unbiased perception of the world as it really is' (1992, p. 24) nor totally endorse 'reason as the single most reliable authority and guide not only to life, but to truth as well' (1992, p. 25).

Much of modernity is, was, and will be, traditional in its make-up. Rationalistic reconstructions of tradition as rationality in the modern era do a great disservice to tradition and to modernity. Believing in the possibility of capturing a clear, unbiased perception of 'what really is,' in fact, is nothing more than a biased presumption of a world cleared for this sort of discovery. And the tests of reason continually turn out to become 'a rational scheme' dependent upon having rationalistic schemers to selectively decide what facts or fancies will have their feet held by the fire of unchecked ratiocination. In view of these limits, maybe tradition and modernity constantly coexist in the modernity of traditions and the traditions of modernity? In other words, modernity itself perhaps develops traditional properties as new generations adapt its premises and implications to their everyday life.

THE PRESENT IN RUINS?

Gross, of course, does not stop with modernity and its powers. He also makes a great deal out of the tremendous pace of change that apparently characterizes today's 'postmodernity.' Bobbing along in streams of signs across a world of images, postmodern society now 'exalts the immediate over the temporally distant, the new over the old, the present over the past' (1992, p. 59). Plainly, the developments that Gross identifies as inhospitable to tradition –

the globalization of production and consumption, the robotization/ cyberneticization of work, the advertising imagery as ideal culture, and the informationalization of society – are pervasive forces. Yet, there also is a tremendous changelessness behind many of these changes. The basic forms and functions of everyday life in the 1990s, ranging from systems of transportation, communication, production, administration and consumption to styles of clothing, shelter, food, drink and leisure, are in many ways more similar to those of the 1890s than they are to these vaguely dangerous pomo menaces of the immediate, the new, and the present.

Depending upon how one numbers the grouping of a human generation, we now are three, four, five, or six generations into the reproduction of urban-industrial capitalism, which has had exurban/global/informational tendencies working within it since the rise of streetcar suburbs, predatory imperialism, and finance capitalist cartels during the 1880s. The 'reign of images' (1992, p. 59) perhaps now is becoming one of autocratic absolutism, but petty pretenders to this throne were known to our forebears in the 1850s, 1870s and 1890s. With postmodernism, Gross argues, 'the battle against tradition is over, that modernism was victorious, that the new not only won, but became institutionalized everywhere' (1992, p. 59). On the one hand, this might mean tradition, as he sees it, is vanquished. Yet, on the other hand, it might mean *the new* also becomes its own substantive tradition, 'institutionalized everywhere' as a way of regarding others, a way of thinking about the world, a set of observances, and a type of behavior. Are distinctions between 'elite and popular culture,' or self 'as a desiring machine' (1992, p. 60), really recent innovations of postmodernism? Or are they features of a traditionalized modernity with roots in impressionism, big city department stores, silent films, and the Sears and Roebuck catalogue?

Indeed, one might peruse the recent wave of Burkean laments about the corporate clerics in Chicago issuing a writ of execution to the Sears' mail order catalogue business to fix this point. The Sears' catalogue 'dream book' provided a pre-given natural order, with its own elaborate set of practices, constellation of beliefs, and mode of thinking, for nearly five generations, to millions of desiring machines eager to become something other than they already were. The 'big book' clearly institutionalized the new, and directly specified how the scattered, disconnected, interchangeable, and ephemeral selves of America could fit into the changing forms of its commodity culture since 1895. As a printed guide, encoding visual statutes, sacred imagery, and exacting authorities of consumption, the Sears' dream book perhaps is done a major disservice by Gross, who claims that 'whenever a tradition is acquired textually, it tends to be grasped as abstract knowledge rather than something immediately, palpably present. Although this might help sharpen an understanding of tradition, at the same time it is likely to weaken allegiance to it' (1992, p. 16).

If we had a nickel for every recent op-ed obit or tearful letter to the editor confessing how the female or male writer-as-desiring-machine dreamed away the hours about having some flashy Sears outfits or inspecting the unshrouded mysteries of Sears bra and panty products, we could retire tomorrow in considerable comfort. Moreover, it is also clear that these desiring machines used the dream book in this fashion because ma and pa, grandma and grandpa, if not great-grandma and great-grandpa, did so as well, as part of their pre-given, natural order. In fact, these real heart-felt testimonies tell of ordinary life all across the land virtually stopping for a festival-like day or week of dreaming by all of the family's members when the catalogues came out every year. Sneaking off into the back bedroom to fantasize in the always immediately, palpably present, about Craftsman tools, Cheryl Tiegs leisure wear, Kenmore freezers, DieHard batteries, Roebucks intimate apparel, or Ted William's fishing gear has been a connecting tissue holding together 'those who are living, those who are dead, and those who are to be born' in America for nearly a century.

In a sense, these rituals of consumption happen 'in the nooks and crannies of modern life' (Gross, 1992, p. 4). Yet, in another sense, these ritualized practices emerge within and for consumer capitalism. Gross tells us modernity destroys tradition; yet, the demise of the Sears catalogue leaves us with written traces from pomo-selves, or 'chaotic masses of energies and intensities' (p. 60), recording how a substantive tradition emerged as part of modernity, continued through generations of desiring machines, and organized life in each generation around values and practices passed on from earlier generations.

One need not stop with the Sears catalogue. The forms and functions of the urban built environment, the protocols of motorized transportation, the codes of ordinary dress, the concoction of any family's diet, or the reception of many mass-media performances have traditional qualities. Perhaps Gross would dismiss these tendencies as custom, but there are traits of tradition in hi-rise skyscraper design, traffic systems, family-meal recipes, suburban fashion, Grateful Dead concerts, and watching *Casablanca* – to mention only a handful – that now tie three or more generations into cohesive communities of continuity. These practices did not exist in pre-capitalist feudal societies; instead, they have emerged only with the allegedly minimal selves of modernity operating as desiring machines. However, it is a rhetorical reach to reduce these linkages between generations to empty simulacra of traditionality manufactured by the state, corporations, and the mass media.

An immanent critique of the present will, or should, find people everywhere enacting and valuing practices and beliefs that are traditional, modern, and postmodern. Some are obvious, a few are obscure, and most are already operating. Yet, it is always difficult to decide definitely what is mainly past, what is purely present, and what is largely future, because all of these judgments are made in the present by people whose understanding of the synchronous/non-synchronous, the old/new, and the traditional/modern oppositions is actively constructed now. They are not passive transmitters of the essentially unchanged past or unchallenged creators of the overdetermined future. Instead, people construct tradition and modernity in thought, speech, feeling, and action, whose authenticity can be judged only in these actually lived terms rather than those drawn out of the dead disciplinary discourses in Rousseau's *First Discourse*, Marx's *Capital*, or Weber's *Protestant Ethic*, which are, in turn, only thinly disguised in *The Past in Ruins*.

Traditions, old and new, ancient and modern, in code and in practice, are an actually, not a potentially, integrative force. Gross is wrong: not all substantive traditions are traditional, not all substantive traditions are destroyed, not all substantive traditions are instrumentalized. Hence, the alleged decline of tradition and ascendance of modernity as mutually exclusive tendencies is wholly contestable. Traditions are manifest, not latent. They are not buried treasures, awaiting excavation like old pirate chests to be forced open and spent as valuable essences of 'old ways' to fix our 'new ways.' Nor are traditions fragmented bits and pieces of a dead past to be cobbled together on the lab-tables of social theory, lifted lifelessly into the thunderstorms of popular protests, struck by lightning bolts of reanimating communal energy, and then awakened to redeem the otherwise lost souls of modernity. Authentic traditions do exist in particular face-to-face relations at a micro-level in personal ties, family life, work practices, political groups, religious sects, educational institutions, intellectual discourses, and regional culture.

While the old *Gemeinschaft* becomes *Gesellschaft* story is fascinating, it hardly provides a definitive means of certifying what is and what is not an authentic tradition. Instead, as Gross himself concedes, the realization of authentic community, cohesion, and continuity can be attained or missed only in particular micro-level relations on a face-to-face level. And here is, again, the spatial problematization that may be the source of these disruptions. Space does not exist as such; it too must be fabricated continuously in the production and reproduction of society. The apprehension about a pre-given, natural order is, in large part, the sense of loss arising from the disappearance of pre-given, natural borders, as space and its containment of action is rapidly compressed in contemporary society.

The tradition-becomes-modernity narrative in social theory, as this retelling by Gross indicates once again, runs on simple scripts of 'then-and-now,' 'before-and-after,' or 'here-and-there' in order to suggest a simple moral. That is, once upon a time, this theoretical tale suggests, God, Nature or Ancestors established authoritative sets of rules to regulate cultural and social life then/there/before. And, now/here/after, for better and/or for worse, these pre-given divine/natural/ancestral orders are being contested, lost, ignored, or forgotten. Social theory, then, exploits the tradition/modernity binary by expounding alternative series of opposing statements employing these scripts. The relative contention of statis and change, presence and absence, fullness and emptiness, loss and recovery in 'traditional community' becoming 'modern society' affords the theorist judgmental opportunities to positively or negatively tag various aspects of the process and results of these transformations.

Undoubtedly, this rhetorical richness, which enables social theorists, on the one hand to slip into tradition-versus-modernity discourse, while covertly allowing them, on the other hand, to comment upon class and power, complexity and simplicity, technology and nature, accounts for the persistence of this thematic trope in social theory. In many ways, the tradition/modernity discursive formation is now a pre-given, natural order for social theory, regulating cultural and social discussions of macrological change with its own set of conventions inscribed in the discursive habits of sociology, politics, and anthropology. Such habits hide in rhetorical turns of theoretical phrasing, like those in the conference rationale as being 'largely understood,' having 'in common,' presuming 'a taken-for-grantedness,' which empower the social theorist-as-narrator to talk from the perspectives afforded by such alleged understandings at large, common possessions, or granted for the taking.

DETRADITIONALIZATION AND SPATIAL ORDER

How can social theory move away from the tradition/modernity narrative? Perhaps social theorists could move away from temporal terms, such as tradition and modernity, and look to spatial transformations as a means of accounting for large-scale social changes. In turn, shifts in the spatialized siting of power, community, and identity could be explored as a critical factor in this regulation of social order (Harvey, 1989; Luke, 1989). By re-examining cultural and social shifts as instances of 'time–space compression' (Harvey, 1989, p. 241), these linkages between time–space comprehension, cultural code construction, and actual behavioral practices around the opposition of tradition to modernity might be more fully understood. In other

words, the technological and commercial acceleration of most means of transportation, communication, production, and administration introduces 'processes that so revolutionize the objective qualities of space and time that we
are forced to alter, sometimes in quite radical ways, how we represent the
world to ourselves' (Harvey, 1989, p. 241). This expansion of 'the now', until
time horizons 'shorten to the point where the present is all there is (the world
of the schizophrenic)', brings along with it 'an overwhelming sense of *compression* of our spatial and temporal worlds' (Harvey, 1989, p. 241).

Traditional practices, as they are memorialized in modern social theory,
are spatially-specific and spatially-defined, even though the spatial dimension
is often explicitly ignored in theoretical discussions. Stable sites, permanent
places, or long-lasting locales often make what is recognized as tradition
possible; the site itself is a projector or container of traditional action. Without the original definition of natural/organic site-logics, site-languages, and
site-layouts, the substance of tradition perhaps cannot be intellectually coded
and decoded, or correctly enacted and reacted to, with any enduring predictability. Destabilizing sites, then, de-traditionalizes practices by collapsing
the settings and accelerating the meter of human action. To explore these
possibilities in a very provisional manner, a short story of some fundamental
shifts in space could be told, using some poetic license, in terms of how and
where spatial order is housed, by using different sorts of wares as a register
of order: the 'wetware' of organic bodies, the 'hardware' of engineered
architectures, the 'software' of informational telematics.

Organic Spatial Orderings: 'First Nature'

In as much as the social relations of a traditional society can be understood
from stories we weave today, it is clear that time and space ran then-and-
there by different social meters and measures (Ermarth, 1992). The taken-
for-grantedness of authority in a pre-given, natural order rests, in large part,
upon the taken-for-grantedness of not moving far beyond a natural organic
body's modes of making a day's travel from its immediate spatial locale. The
pre-given, natural order of organic limits is read into and/or read off the
terrain, weather, vegetation, and animal life of the immediate locale. Space
is relative/fixed/primordial/specific. The natural organic 'wetware' of human
bodies anchors the time-sense and space-consciousness of traditional lifeworlds
(Virilio, 1991, pp. 29–68). Time, then, also is marked in registers marked
in organic/astronomical/generational/particular terms.

Space is here an absolutely relative phenomenon as each settlement, band,
hamlet, village or croft defines its own place by its own crops, herds, or

ranges; the inhabitants' local knowledge of this tree, that hill, this brook, or that meadow, which often is what Nature *is* for them. A natural organic domain defines their space as they use it economically, symbolically, socially, and economically. Such knowledge, in turn, divides their space/settlement/ society from the surrounding communities next to them as well as defining who they are, how they will act, what they can do, and why others are different. The terrestriality of first nature is the spatial setting of/for the wetware of human agents. These particular constructions of time and space, in turn, anchor the expanse of human time and social space by settling upon an individual human being's rates of locomotion, levels of exertion, expectations of lifespan, faculties of sensation, and techniques of communication as the basis of time-marking and space-forming.

Consequently, the spatiality of traditional societies typically is organized around the mostly unmediated capacities of ordinary human bodies. This rendering of space embodies communal control, conventional understandings, and authoritative rules for each organic community with its own conventions and rulers. Nature is not as abstract providence, it is the qualities of this or that locale, known by and open to all by its specific/peculiar/local features. Directly engaging in manual production, oral communication, visual representation, tactile association, verbal justification, and grounded identification does determine the individual's and group's sensing of time and shaping of space. These constraints also set limits on the scale and energy of society. Authenticity here derives mostly from its em-body-ment of order. As Gross observes, there is a closeness and readiness to the highly embodied immediacy of tradition. Traditional visions of action often resort to organic metaphors for their allusions: conflict was chin-to-chin. Combat was hand-to-hand. Justice was an-eye-for-an-eye, a-tooth-for-a-tooth. Debate was heart-to-heart. Solidarity was shoulder-to-shoulder. Community was face-to-face. Friendship was arm-in-arm. And, change was step-by-step. The wetware of the human body measured space, marked distance, metered time, and defined order with infinite variation in the contemporary manifestations of each traditional society.

Identity, therefore, was perhaps more easily grounded. Organically emerging rules were set out by organically established and confirmed ruling forces: the weather, water, the soil, sun, the herd, fire, and the people. On this ground, the first nature of Nature defined much of the second nature of Society. Even so, the rules were not totally fixed and not completely fluid; reflexive, unstable, pluralistic, and unclosed possibilities in traditions continually confronted every human being as he or she became engaged in cycling through the contemporary times of his or her lifespan. Choice always existed, and choices required selecting the correct traditions and aptly adapting to these circumstances in practicing complex games of elaborate cultural reflexivity.

Engineered Spatial Orderings: 'Second Nature'

The practices of primordial communities in organic space prevailed before the invention and/or beyond the implementation of city-building, city-living, and city-expanding. With city-formations, space becomes much more processed/centered/organized/normalized. The 'hardware' of urbanism in-cites itself into once natural sites, rendering space more abstract/fluid/artificial/ universal. A trans-formed, artificial order is encoded into materialized hardwares, or the engineered sites and architectured edifices made possible by more organized trading links and/or ruling systems that take for granted moving people and products far beyond a day's travel from their origin. Such hardware, then, becomes the base for generating new senses of time and space in new materializations of spatial technics. Time is redominated in registers measured in civic/dynastic/administrative/universal terms.

Plainly, the spatial expression of traditional society can, and does, persist in small, early, or weak cities. Yet, once city-building and city-expanding give a new artificial relief to once natural settings and topography, a second nature of territoriality emerges wherein the (capital) city rules its immediate space/territory by 'urbanizing' territory (Mumford, 1970, p. 193). The hardware of city formations becomes the architectural armature for transforming existing domains of rural country into formally in-stated countries with urban(izing) centers. States, then, essentially try to citify/urbanize/townify space, turning normalized territorial space into their 'real' estate (Luke, 1991). The state's geographical boundaries are its walls, its various regions are its quarters, its capital cities are its citadels, its denizens are its citi-zens. The nation-state, the absolutist state, the imperial state, or the corporate state are all variations, therefore, of the city-state.

Mumford (1970; 1961; 1934) sees roots of these systems in ancient empires, but, as Foucault suggests, these shifts in thinking and acting developed in their most complete expression during the sixteenth and seventeenth centuries with the formation of Europe's absolutist monarchical states. As Foucault makes clear, for example,

> at the beginning of the seventeenth century ... the government of a large state like France should ultimately think of its territory on the model of the city. The city was no longer perceived as a place of privilege, as an exception

in a territory of fields, forests, and roads. The cities were no longer islands beyond the common law. Instead, the cities, with the problems that they raised, and the particular forms that they took, served as the models for the governmental rationality that was to apply to the whole of the territory. There is an entire series of utopias or projects for governing territory that developed on the premise that a state is like a large city; the capital is like its main square; the roads are like its streets. A state will be well-organized when a system of policing as tight and efficient as that of the cities extends over the entire territory. At the outset, the notion of police applied only to the set of regulations that were to assure the tranquility of a city, but at that moment the police become the very *type* of rationality for the government of the whole territory. The model of the city became the matrix for the regulations that apply to a whole state. (Foucault, in Lotringer, 1989, pp. 259–60)

With this shift in organizational agendas, then, the technics of space are transformed. A range of pre-given, natural (b)order(s) are submitted to the policing/engineering/administering of formal disciplinary discourses in elaborate built environments, creating a more artificial, cultural (b)ordering of space.

The wetware of human bodies in organic nature, when recontextualized in these rapidly evolving hardware complexes of urbanizing reason, can become changed into something different: nature and humanity are recast as 'natural resources' and 'human populations' occupying territory. Other hardware systems, beyond urban architectural technics, also then are deployed to extract and manage these newly recognized assets: railroads, electrical grids, steamships, hard-surface roads, canals, and telegraph/telephone systems. The space projected by such technics is radically different: engineered, not God-given; artificial, not natural; mediated by hardware, not immediate to wetware; rationalized, not communalized; national, not local. Disorder, flux, and contingency do develop in the spaces projected by these new technics of power; but an order, a permanence, and a necessity also emerge with the planned rationalization of space. So, systems of direction and meaning, once provided by tradition, also lose their spatial referents and action zones as space is reconfigured to suit the designs of state bureaucracies, accumulated capital, and technical experts. Pre-given, natural (b)order(s) in space degrade, and with them, many see the pre-given, natural order of tradition declining.

Sets of conventions or rules that regulate cultural and social life always exist as authoritative *doxa*. Yet, their implementation or enactment in specific places and particular spaces become problematic or contested as the technics of space change. A spatial technics that might entirely remain immediately local and organically grounded is keyed practically to the wetware of human bodies. The vernacular categories of dwelling, family, village, and locale resonate a more embodied ecological/natural/bioregional sense of space that remains largely pre-technical, pre-rational, pre-organizational. As long as space is framed in these terms, the drift of tradition as rules that regulate cultural and social life can usually proceed without tremendous interruption. However, the intrusion of a spatial technics which is scaled in terms of great distance, national expanses, mechanical artifice, and disciplinary abstractions, brings a register of urbanistic hardware to the management of space. Cultural and social life are regulated by the projecting/fabricating/policing/centering of such spaces bureaucratically, scientifically, professionally, technically. Architecture best represents these spatial technics, because 'it is an instrument of measure, a sum total of knowledge that, contending with the natural environment, becomes capable of organizing society's time and space' (Virilio, 1991, p. 22). The wetware of 'Nature' in these spatial technics becomes socially reworked in the hardware of 'Culture.'

Gross perhaps senses this difference in his division of space into sites of/for the survival of tradition and zones of/for the dominance of modernity. Where there are immediate, local, organic spaces remaining resistant to rationalized discipline – associational folkways, rural areas, family ties, or underground – Gross believes that tradition lives (1992, pp. 10–20). However, he sees this survival as a function of some innate persistence rather than peculiar spatial qualities that permit or foster the continuation of what Gross calls tradition. And where he sees the spatial technics of modernity on a loose rein is where the urbanistic hardware of the citified-state is most deeply rooted – above ground, at the center, outside of the family, in institutional procedures. Nevertheless, it is the shaping of space, and not the survival in time, which is important; for the everyday practice of the conventions that regulate cultural and social life is what is most critical for understanding detraditionalization.

Cybernetic Spatial Orderings: 'Third Nature'

Space, however, is now again being disrupted and transformed by an acceleration of the social means of production, consumption, administration, and destruction in a new global system of 'fast capitalism' (Agger, 1989; Attali, 1991). These shifts in space started during the 1950s and 1960s, when the global impact of mass telecommunications, electronic computerization, cybernetic automation, and rapid transportation first began to be experienced broadly around the world (Luke, 1983, pp. 59–73). Soon, systems of 'software,' as cybernetic codes, televisual images, and informational multimedia, sublate the central importance of hardware. They are neither soft organic bodies nor hard artificial edifices, but rather, rapidly changing materializations of complex mental designs. This shift toward informationalization also marks the coming of 'late' or 'disorganized capitalism.' As Jameson claims, this is a global change 'which is somehow decisive but incomparable with the older convulsions of modernization and industrialization, less perceptive and dramatic somehow, but more permanent precisely because it is more thorough-going and all-pervasive' (1991, p. xxi). Most significantly, these changes often are experienced as being part of 'the End of Nature.'

Informational systems change the structures of social action as well as institutional sites of cultural process in several different ways (Luke, 1989). A third nature of telematicality emerges where informationalization rapidly pluralizes the spatialized operational potentialities of existing cultures and societies. The logic of informational commodification demands constant expansion, turning everything into an object of communication. More and more national subcultures, local personalities, fundamentalist sects, and ethnic groups gain a voice and presence in the software of telematics and mass media. Thus, 'the West is living through an explosive situation, not only with regard to other cultural universes (such as the "Third World"), but internally as well, as an apparently irresistible pluralization renders an unilinear view of the world and history impossible' (Vattimo, 1992, p. 6).

Global infostructures begin to refocus the location and impact of social changes through their interactive connection of dynamically expanding informationalized zones and aggressive containment of static or collapsing non-informationalized zones (Baudrillard, 1983). Castells, for example, argues that 'what is facilitated by information technologies is the interconnection of activities, providing the basis for the increasing complexity of service industries, which exchange information relentlessly and ubiquitously . . . Whatever becomes organizationally and legally possible can be technologically implemented because of the versatility of the technological medium' (Castells, 1989, p. 142). These shifts split cultures, economies, and societies between the demands of nominal nationality and actual transnationality as both local and regional communities become integrated into truly transnational rather than essentially national modes of production. In these global economic changes, as Reich claims, 'Barriers to cross-border flows of knowledge, money, and tangible products are crumbling; groups of people in every nation are joining global webs' (1991, p. 172).

Informationalization links various global zones in the flows in codes of performativity: 'that is,' as Lyotard claims, 'the best possible input/output equation' (1984, p. 46). Shifts toward the performative provide new criteria for determining what is strong, what is just, and what is true in the operational workings of information flows. The normativity of laws, then, is gradually supplanted by the performativity of procedures (Lyotard, 1984, p. 46). Walls of code fabricated out of data bricks and digital mortar in cyberspaces, then, can now divide states and societies as effectively as walls of steel or stone once did in architectural space.

In the global flows of informational capitalism, 'the world of generalized communication explodes like a multiplicity of "local" rationalities – ethnic, sexual, religious, cultural, or aesthetic minorities – that finally speak up for themselves. They are no longer repressed and cowed into silence by the idea of a single true form of humanity that must be realized irrespective of particularity and individual finitude, transience, and contingency' (Vattimo, 1992, p. 9). Emancipation, in the informational order, 'consists in *disorientation*, which is at the same time also the liberation of differences, of local elements, of what generally could be called dialect' (Vattimo, 1992, p. 8). Through the multiplicity of dialects and their different cultural universes, living in this unstable, pluralistic world 'means to experience freedom as a continual oscillation between belonging and disorientation' (Vattimo, 1992, p. 10).

Gaining access to these disorienting but connecting transnational flows, with their flexible sites of operationalization as a 'mode of information' (Poster, 1990), grows in importance when establishing control over national space and its mode of production with rigid borders of organization. Again, as Castells asserts,

> there is a shift, in fact, away from the centrality of the organizational unit to the network of information and decision. In other words, *flows, rather than organizations*, become the units of work, decision, and output accounting. Is the same trend developing in relation to the spatial dimension of organizations? Are flows substituting for localities in the information economy? Under the impact of information systems, are organizations not timeless but also placeless? (1989, p. 142)

The depths and directions of these flows constitute a new system of spatiality of thought and action. Flows in most respects represent *capital in motion*, circulating money, labor, products, and technology (as well as information about them in audio, video, and data form) throughout the global economy. In these discourses, then, we witness a pluralizing reinterpretation of the world in as much as 'the images of the world we receive from the media and human sciences, albeit on different levels, are not simply different interpretations of a "reality" that is "given" regardless, but rather constitute the very objectivity of the world' (Vattimo, 1992, pp. 24–5).

As the jump from a wetware-base to a hardware-base altered the pre-given, natural (b)order(s) of space, so too does the jump from hardware-sets to software-sets in the ruling conventions of cultural and social life transform spatial order. Informationalization implodes the city, and with it, telematics arguably is now imploding the citified state. In the flows of information, energy, and imagery, 'places' are formed where viewers–listeners–users turn-on, tune-in, or log-on to the flow. Each different site of transmission and reception is highly variable and ultimately interchangeable. Virilio (1991), for example, argues:

> If the metropolis is still a place, a geographic site, it no longer has anything to do with the classical oppositions of city/country nor center/periphery. The city is no longer organized into a localized and axial estate. While the suburbs contributed to this dissolution, in fact, the intramural–extramural opposition collapsed with the transport revolutions and the development of communication and telecommunication technologies. (p. 12)

Once more, the pre-given, natural (b)order(s) of the existing nation-state regime are shifting in the transnational interfacings of the flow (Luke, 1993). Virilio's spin on these events parallels our readings of detraditionalization as he pins these shifts on the implosion of one spatial technics in the explosion of a new technics of space:

> With the screen interface of computers, television and teleconferences, the surface of inscription, hitherto devoid of depth, becomes a kind of 'distance,' a depth of field of a new kind of representation, a visibility without any face-to-face encounter in which the *vis-à-vis* of ancient streets disappears and is erased. In this situation, a difference of position blurs into fusion and confusion. Deprived of objective boundaries, the architectonic element begins to drift and float in an electronic ether, devoid of spatial dimensions, but inscribed in the singular temporality of an instantaneous diffusion. From here on, people can't be separated by physical obstacles or by temporal distances. With the interfacing of computer terminals and video-monitors, distinctions of *here* and *there* no longer mean anything. (1991, pp. 12–13)

The software of cyberspaces, telenets and infostructures, as a result, warp space and time once again.

Still, there is no reason to doubt that many of the conventional rules now regulating cultural and social life will be able to re-emerge from cybercustoms and teletraditions. At this juncture, however, the postmodernization of informational flows directly highlights the detraditionalizing of organic and architectonic practices (Toulmin, 1990). If living occurs in and around telematic spaces and places, then the traditions of material space/physical place will inevitably come up short. Identity and meaning in these globalizing flows perhaps cannot be precisely located or definitively stabilized. On the contrary, their bases are becoming cinematic/telematic/informatic, or essentially immaterial. Hence, conventions and rules for encoding them inevitably must employ other values: 'representations, images and messages afford neither locale nor stability, since they are the vectors of a momentary, instantaneous expression, with all the manipulated meanings and misinformation that presupposes' (Virilio, 1991, p. 22). And, in the last analysis, many more people will live and work within 'cities of quartz' as silicone chips, satellite relays, and fiber optics dematerialize urban sites, replacing many interactions in urban infrastructure with those made possible in the virtual spaces of global infostructures continuously (de)(re)materializing at telematic sites (Davis, 1990).

SOME PROVISIONAL SPECULATIONS

Such postmodernizing wrinkles in the texture of space, then, might account for many of the anxieties experienced by social theorizing as to the outcome of 'detraditionalizing' processes. Pre-given, natural (b)order(s), whether they are taken as organic inscriptions in the terrestriality of first nature or as ruling conventions projected materially onto the territoriality of second nature, become indistinct in the un-given, artificial zones ciphered into the telematicality of third nature.

As the technics of shaping space change, many of the modalities of social action and personal meaning or the regulations of cultural and social life also (de)(re)modulate their formations. Still, even in 'the now,' there are no necessary constraints against traditions guiding reflexively-interacting human beings in/through modernized spaces, even though it becomes more difficult in the constantly shifting spaces of the present. Detraditionalization, therefore, can be connected to the time–space compression of perpetual global change (Harvey, 1989). In large part, it operates within a continual process of respatialization, in which there are varying pressures toward a reinsitement and retemporalization of cultural and social life, where Gross's 'desiring machines' are multiplexed within the flows of virtual space inter-operating in televisual media, global commerce or informational software. The national/statal/industrial time–space of modernity is compressed by speed, leaving the constructs of ecological/natural/bioregional time–space as well as cybernetic/informational/telematic time–space as disruptive and/or corrective alternatives for reconstructing spatial technics. Cybernetically or televisually, *Gemeinschaft* and *Gesellschaft* melt and fuse again into amalgams of each other, giving tradition to modernity and modernity to tradition.

The plot of this story, then, has unfolded in successive sections. First, the binary opposition of tradition/modernity has been re-read closely to root out some elliptical dynamics in its rhetoric. While it stands as a modern theoretical construct, it also is used as a set of traditional conceptual practices. Secondly, the seductive power of this traditionalized rhetoric of modernity has been re-examined by re-tracing many of the tales told of it/by it in a recent representative example, namely Gross's *The Past in Ruins*. And thirdly, the current anxiety about tradition/modernity *qua* 'detraditionalization' has been traced to derivations from ill-defined apprehensions about 'postmodernization.'

Some might see a new binary opposition emerging here as the phenomenon of time–space compression addles once predictable certitudes anchored in more stable spatial orderings. Yet, the detraditionalization problem finally might be reframed provisionally in terms of what is behind the destabilizing of these sites of spatial definition, a reframing which serves to contrast the warehousing of social processes and structures in terms of cybernetic metaphors – like the constructs of wetware, hardware, and software – to explicate different spatial orderings involved in regulating cultural and social life. By turning from a modernist time-shift trope, such as the prevailing tales of *Gemeinschaft* versus *Gesellschaft* oppositions, to a site-location trope, or stabilizing and destabilizing the frames of spatial expression, one can perhaps outline more apt logics of social interpretation. Centered upon tales of spatializing structures emerging in 'the now' rather than relying on stories of time passing into 'the new,' this alternative register of change could prove much more suggestive for further discussions of how identity, meaning and space interact without returning to the traditional oppositions of 'tradition' and 'modernity.'

NOTE

1   Parts of this chapter have appeared in *Telos* (1992–3).

REFERENCES

Agger, Ben 1989: *Fast Capitalism*. Urbana: University of Illinois Press.

Attali, Jacques 1991: *Millennium: Winners and Losers in the Coming World Order*. New York: Random House.

Blackburn, Richard James 1990: *The Vampire of Reason: An Essay in the Philosophy of History*. London: Verso.

Baudrillard, Jean 1983: *Simulations*. New York: Semiotext(e).

Castells, Manuel 1989: *The Informational City: Information Technology, Economic Restructuring, and the Urban-Regional Process*. Oxford: Blackwell.

Center for the Study of Cultural Values 1992: Conference on Detraditionalization, 8–10 July 1993. Lancaster University: Mimeo.

Davis, Mike 1990: *City of Quartz: Excavating the Future in Los Angeles*. London: Verso.

Ermarth, Elizabeth Deeds 1992: *Sequel to History: Postmodernism and the Crisis of Representational Time*. Cambridge: Cambridge University Press.

Fukuyama, Francis 1992: *The End of History and the Last Man*. New York: Free Press.

Gross, David 1992: *The Past in Ruins: Tradition and the Critique of Modernity*. Amherst: University of Massachusetts Press.

Harvey, David 1989: *The Condition of Postmodernity*. Oxford: Blackwell.

Jameson, Fredric 1991: *Postmodernism, or the Cultural Logic of Late Capitalism*. Durham: Duke University Press.

Lotringer, Sylvere 1989: *Foucault Live (Interviews, 1966–84)*. New York: Semiotext(e).

Luke, Timothy W. 1983: Informationalism and Ecology. *Telos*, 53 (Summer 1983) pp. 59–72.

Luke, Timothy W. 1989: *Screens of Power: Ideology, Domination, and Resistance in Informational Society*. Urbana: University of Illinois Press.

Luke, Timothy W. 1991: The Discourse of Development: A Genealogy of 'Developing Nations' and the Discipline of Modernity. *Current Perspectives in Social Theory*, 11, pp. 271–93.

Luke, Timothy W. 1992–3: Neo-Populism: Fabricating the Future by Rehabbing the Past? *Telos*, Special Issue on Traditions, 94, pp. 11–18.

Luke, Timothy W. 1993: Discourses of Disintegration, Texts of Transformation: Re-Reading Realism. *Alternatives*, 18 (forthcoming).

Lyotard, J.-F. 1984: *The Postmodern Condition*. Minneapolis: University of Minnesota Press.

Mumford, Lewis 1934: *Technics and Civilization*. New York: Harcourt Brace Jovanovich.

Mumford, Lewis 1961: *The City in History: Its Origins, its Transformations, and its Prospects*. New York: Harcourt Brace Jovanovich.

Mumford, Lewis 1970: *The Myth of the Machine: The Pentagon of Power*. New York: Harcourt Brace Jovanovich.

Poster, Mark 1990: *The Mode of Information: Poststructuralism and Social Context*. Chicago: University of Chicago Press.

Reich, Robert B. 1991: *The Work of Nations: Preparing Ourselves for 21st-Century Capitalism*. New York: Knopf.

Robertson, Roland 1992: *Globalization: Social Theory and Global Culture*. Newbury Park: Sage.

Toulmin, Stephen 1990: *Cosmopolis: The Hidden Agenda of Modernity*. New York: Free Press.

Vattimo, Gianni 1992: *The Transparent Society*. Baltimore: Johns Hopkins University Press.

Virilio, Paul 1991: *The Lost Dimension*. New York: Semiotext(e).

8

Detraditionalization and the Certainty of Uncertain Futures

Barbara Adam

INTRODUCTION

Most contemporary social theorists agree that the world within which we are situated is different from the one in which social science originated. A significant number of them would further agree that those changes limit the scope of a theoretical tradition that originated with the democratic and industrial revolutions in the West, with capitalism and socialism, with Newtonian science and Cartesian philosophy, and with realism in art and literature. They would concede, in other words, that the social sciences today encounter conceptual and methodological difficulty when they face a world of rising uncertainty; when they are confronted on the one hand by constructed futures that outlast their creators by millennia and on the other by information technology operating at the speed of light, which facilitate simultaneous, networked responses across the globe. They tend to acknowledge the limitations of traditional theories when they encounter situations where local actions have global effects, when many of the hazards we face today are no longer linked to the time and space of their genesis/inception, and when simultaneity, instantaneity, in/visibility, im/materiality, multiplicity, the loss of 'other' and the construction of the future are confronted with the characteristic assumptions of traditional social science. Consequently, there is a widespread consensus amongst social scientists that we need theories that can encompass the contemporary condition and facilitate active engagement with its processes.

'A rethinking of the nature of modernity', writes Anthony Giddens (1991, p. 1), 'must go hand in hand with the reworking of basic premises of sociological analysis.' Similarly, Ulrich Beck (1992, p. 12) argues that we need 'ideas and theories that will allow us to conceive the new which is rolling over us in a new way, and allow us to live and act within it. At the same time we must retain good relations with the treasures of tradition.'

In this chapter I therefore want to consider the detraditionalization thesis in the light of the requirements identified by Beck and Giddens. That is to say, I want to explore to what extent the thesis allows us to conceptualize the new while retaining 'good relations with the treasures of tradition' and, moreover, consider whether it can be classified as a 'reworking of the basic premises of sociological analysis'. A leaflet advertising the Lancaster conference on the theme of detraditionalization stated that 'the process of detraditionalization provides a useful way of reflecting on the nature of, and relationship between, the pre-modern, modern and post-modern'. I want to question this belief and ask whether the conceptualization of these changes in terms of detraditionalization and the implicit schema of 'once there was and now there is' can really provide us with the wherewithal to grasp the complexity of social life in the age of cultural uncertainty. Furthermore, I want to query whether such an explicit focus on the past can help us to understand and engage with the future. Finally, I want to take issue with the idea that the detraditionalization thesis is an empowering conceptual tool.

My critique of the detraditionalization thesis is not a denial that something resembling detraditionalization is taking place but an argument that such processes need to be conceptualized in terms other than the oppositional thought tradition of the Enlightenment. As such, my analysis takes me in a direction different from the detraditionalization thesis and suggests an alternative agenda for social theory. Not before-and-after analyses of fixed states, established retrospectively, but interpenetration as a process, as well as the capacity to construct the future, seems to me to be the conceptual task for contemporary social science. Not the replacement of tradition, order and control by reflexivity, disorder, flux and uncertainty, but their simultaneous existence and their mutual implication, therefore, need to become its focus.

This means I am concerned neither to discuss the different approaches to the thesis of detraditionalization nor to arbitrate between the various critical responses to it. Nor am I interested in establishing or refuting the 'correctness' of the thesis. Instead, I want to focus on the tool itself in order to explore detraditionalization in terms of principles and strategies for knowing. Attention on the detraditionalization thesis as a conceptual tool and its implicit assumptions becomes important as soon as we acknowledge the constitutive nature of social science knowledge. That is to say, the tool and its underlying premises require attention once we accept as fact that social scientists change and construct the worlds they study through the very process of description and explanation, that the knowledge they produce is constitutive of the social world they study. Social science, as Giddens (1990, p. 16) puts it, 'spirals in and out of the universe of social life, reconstructing both itself and that universe as an integral part of that process'. Finally, focus on the conceptual tool is important because social scientists are fundamentally implicated in the process of detraditionalization. As definers of social reality and as authoritative guides to action our theories have become substitutes for tradition: we are contemporary voices of authoritative knowledge, tied up in the construction of the world we investigate. As such, our theories, concepts and base assumptions need to be *appropriate* to their role as constructors of immediate and long-term futures. Looked at in this way, the detraditionalization thesis needs to be scrutinized for its capacity to facilitate an active involvement with uncertain futures.

This chapter forms part of a wider project where I seek to articulate taken-for-granted assumptions that guide our seeing and understanding. Throughout this project, I use the focus on time to demonstrate the in/appropriateness of our theories and basic premises for grasping the complexity and contingency of today's life and for their potential to engage, in a practical/political way, with the ephemerality, networked multiplicity and far-reaching uncertainty of contemporary social processes. The future, however, is not a popular social science subject, since, as I show below, it cannot be encompassed by theories that have their gaze firmly fixed on the past.[1] This means that my analysis, in so far as it emphasizes the future in terms of contingency, un/certainty, project/ion, and social science responsibility for posterity does not have much other work to draw on for conceptual support.

ONCE THERE WAS AND NOW THERE IS — CONCERN OVER THE BINARY CODE

The first thing to be noticed when we examine the concept of detraditionalization is its reliance on dualistic analyses and either-or frameworks of meaning: authority based on tradition *or* reflexivity, located without *or* within, in pre-given *or* (self-)constructed orders. Detraditionalization is constituted with reference to tradition, which is the source of its being, a source with which it is no longer identified and which is conceived as its 'other'. This means that the conceptual tool with which we are to grasp and explain reflexively organized authority in an age of uncertainty, disorder, flux and contingency is *fixed* with reference to a postulated past condition and narrowly defined in terms of what it is *not*.

At this point it may be worthwhile to pause and consider the concept of tradition – the 'other' against which detraditionalization is being established. In *Keywords*, Raymond Williams (1981, pp. 268–9) explains how tradition is derived from the Latin root *tradere*, to hand over or deliver, and how the word has survived in the English language as 'a description of a general process of handing down' with a 'strong and often predominant sense of this entailing respect and duty'. In temporal terms, therefore, it conveys tradition as an active process, something that is created afresh at each moment of renewal. The creative aspect of tradition, however, is seldom at the forefront of social science's engagement with the subject matter. Max Weber (1964, p. 116), for example, emphasized the habitual and automatic aspect of tradition, suggesting that it therefore lies on 'the borderline of what can justifiably be called meaningfully oriented action'.

In *The Metronomic Society*, Michael Young (1988) writes extensively on the subject of habit, custom and tradition and seems to agree with Peter Medawar, who defines tradition as 'the transfer of information through non-genetic channels from one generation to the next' (cited in Young, 1988, p. 163). Young sees tradition as repeating cyclical processes that immobilize time (p. 99), as unquestioned and familiar actions that take us 'out of time and into timelessness' (p. 81). Like Weber, he stresses the fact that traditions, habits and customs do not seem to require conscious thought, which, in turn, facilitates a relatively effortless reproduction and maintenance of the past in the present. Finally, there is in the wider social science literature an emphasis on the externally located, authoritative dimension of tradition, its binding normative character – how we should live and how things should or should not be done – and its role in upholding social structures and perpetuating existing power relations. Pre-given unalterable authority, power located external to the individual, information transfer across time and space, as well as unquestioned and unthinking action are thus the backcloth against which the contours of detraditionalization are drawn and defined.

From the vantage point of the detraditionalization thesis, however, tradition becomes generalized. From this perspective, tradition implies something stable and self-evident, whilst temporality – the fact that tradition constitutes *renewal* at every moment of active reconstruction of past beliefs and commitments – is ignored. In order to appreciate the problem associated with the detraditionalization thesis's a-temporal and dualistic tenets we briefly need to focus on the context within which the concept of detraditionalization has been developed.

Detraditionalization is utilized as an explanatory tool for a world of increased contingency, massively expanding as well as decreasing choices, and 'experts' for every sphere of social life. It is employed for a social existence where spectatorhood – the ability to look on as 'objective observers' – has become habitual (Ermarth, 1992, p. 39) while, simultaneously, we are forced to recognize that each of our actions makes a difference and connects us to the global network of social relations: television, electronic communication, global business and finance link each of us inescapably to the mis/fortunes of peoples across the globe. In an even more striking way, environmental hazards connect us to brother worm, sister meson and daughter of a thousand years hence. The detraditionalization thesis is used in a social context where a previously 'natural' reality has to be recognized as constructed – our language, knowledge, truth, the body, reproduction. It is to aid our understanding of a world in which certainties are steadily shattered, a world in which the unthinkable becomes plausible and everything seems open to change and revision. It is put to use in societies permeated by the knowledge of science where technologies designed according to rational, linear and calculable principles contribute to the fracturing and indeterminacy of outcomes, where unintended consequences become the driving force for socio-political action. This is a context in which the moral foundations are shaken and countervailing, fundamentalist tendencies develop in the hope that they may protect against the excessive contingencies, the uncertainties, and the potential destruction of the future. This means, the vast array of choices, future potentials and *Angst*, the explosion of the future into our present which constitutes the context of the changes under discussion, is to be forced into a backward-looking distinction between tradition and modernity, control from without and restraint from within. Complexity is to be explained through the simplicity of a binary code; contingency and transience through comparison with an a-temporal past.

I am sceptical about the utility of this dualistic explanatory tool on several levels: it is problematic at the level of conceptual principles and implicit assumptions, and it does not work at the substantive level. While this chapter is not focused on the substantive debate around detraditionalization, it seems nevertheless worthwhile to allude to a few examples before paying more sustained attention to the shortcomings of the thesis at the level of conceptual principles.

First, all societies and their members, no matter how progressive and keen on change, have traditions that they hold dear and sacred: scientists still chase after certainty and proof irrespective of Heisenberg's uncertainty principle and in spite of facing countless phenomena that are not suited to this traditional mode of analysis. Moreover, scientific innovation, as Thomas Kuhn (1970) so persuasively argued, is premised and dependent on a commitment to traditions, rules and standards. Without them scientists could not even recognize an anomaly. As Young (1988, p. 153) puts it, 'innovators succeed with the aid of tradition even when they set themselves against it'. Examples of such complexity and the interpenetration of tradition in contemporary de- and post-traditional conditions abound: The Catholic Church today persists with its traditional stance against birth control irrespective of the world's over-population. The more extensively the world becomes globalised the greater seem the instances of newly erected boundaries to redefine and reassert traditional identities based on language, region, religion, and other cultural and racial heritages.

Secondly, the more the future impinges on and predefines our present the more intense seems to become our concern with the past – immediate, mediate and long-term – in print, television and electronic records, in museums and heritage parks, through the collecting of art and artefacts, through the dating of species, the earth, the universe. Young (1988, p. 237) talks of an explosion of collective memory marked by a proportional incapacity of individuals to absorb even the tiniest fraction of it.

Thirdly, just as tradition is central to contemporary society, so reflexivity is ontological to all of humanity, to what it means to be human: irrespective of the strictness of the rules that regulate social life, there is always room to redefine situations and act in the light of experience and new knowledge. Moreover, I find it difficult to think of a situation where it has not been possible to take on some personal responsibility for social processes.

Fourthly, all social orders are constructed, including those that are pre-determined by tradition, while, equally, there is overwhelming evidence, even today, for people having to comply with pre-given orders, conventions and sets of rules determined by tradition, religion, state and social exigencies. These pre-set, externally enforced orders remain compelling irrespective of whether or not people are aware of the fact that their actions make a difference, be they compliant or otherwise.

Fifthly, it is possible, furthermore, to identify a shift from traditional to new and different *external* authorities. I am thinking here of experts who hold authoritative knowledge (including social theorists), the media in its multiple guises, and even money. The proffered shift from external to internal authority, in contrast – from waiting for instructions to taking on board the concept of personal responsibility, which constitutes one aspect of detraditionalization – seems to remain more an agreed need than an all-pervasive fact of modernity.

And lastly, instead of detraditionalization we could equally talk of re-traditionalization since the age of uncertainty, contingency and flux seems to bring with it a yearning for the stability of tradition. When essential and unvarying components of human experience are no longer natural facts but social constructions; when unintended, hazardous consequences are proportional to their rational, calculated actions; when our social environment is technologized, disenchanted and devoid of intrinsic moral qualities; then it is not surprising that social scientists identify countervailing tendencies to the detraditionalization processes of reflexive modernity: Young (1988, p. 144) calls them anti-habits and sees them as embedded in the compulsion for individuals to 'question existing tools, ideas, and institutions', and to 'think things out for themselves'. Beck (1993) identifies them as counter-modernity, Giddens (1991) as countervailing tendencies. For Wolfgang van den Daele (1992) and others these processes culminate in foundationalism and fundamentalism, whilst others critical of the detraditionalization thesis prefer to label them re-traditionalization. In an environment where social structures become increasingly fluid and optional, tradition acts as a metaphor for something that requires no justification: reliability, stability, order, predictability, familiarity, trustworthiness and controllability.

Thus, we can see that the dualism of the detraditionalization thesis is untenable. It remains a problem, moreover, even when authors intersect comments about it being only a heuristic and an analytical tool. The difficulty is overcome neither by admitting that in 'reality' such dualisms always overlap, nor by Giddens's (1990, p. 4) acknowledgement that 'obviously there are continuities between the traditional and the modern, and neither is cut of a whole cloth . . .'. Furthermore, since the social world is infinite in its complexity – even in its most localized personal interactions and transactions – explanations in terms of dualisms provide an ideal basis for debate in the social sciences and politics. Such debate has the capacity to go on *ad infinitum* since each 'supportive evidence' has against it a potential array of data to refute it, either through its opposite or through showing that we are not dealing with a case of 'either–or' but possibly 'both and/or neither'. Explanations in the binary code, therefore, tend to be unsuitable to grasp conditions where there is an interpenetration and coexistence of tradition and self-conscious construction as well as all possible variations in between.

Beck, in *Die Erfindung des Politischen* (The Invention of Politics) (1993), discusses these very problems and distinguishes between theories of simple and reflexive modernity. While I am not sure that his terminology is helpful, particularly since it is bound to lead to a lot of confusion with opposing theories that have already claimed the conceptualization of reflexive modernity for themselves, his analysis is centrally important to my critique of detraditionalization as a conceptual tool. Beck identifies theories of simple modernity with the oppositional politics of left and right, public and private, individual and society, right and wrong, with the key assumptions of nation-state, class, objectivity and truth, and with the problematic practice of understanding complex social phenomena in terms of either-or choices. Theories of simple modernity refer to the dissolution and replacement of tradition by industrial society, which, he suggests, tends to be conflated and treated as interchangeable with the concept of modernity (1993, pp. 71–5). In conjunction with the postulated loss of tradition, they assume the need for self-construction without acknowledgement of counter developments, simultaneous existences and ambivalences. Beck (1993, pp. 189) calls such theories *autistic* because they abstract and separate what is fundamentally connected, networked, interpenetrating and related.

Theories of reflexive modernity, in contrast, stress a multitude of modernities which include regressive and counter developments. For these theories, conceptualizations of de- and post-traditionalization would be meaningless. In reflexive modernity, suggests Beck, the motor for change is no longer Weber's *Zweckrationalität* but the unintended outcomes of those networked rational actions which centrally include risks, hazards, dangers as well as benefits at the local/global level.

I want to propose that dualistic analyses are fundamentally unsuitable for grasping a globalized reality where everything is linked to everything else. Theories in the binary code, in other words, are highly inappropriate conceptual tools for conceptualizing a world enmeshed in networks of information, transport, finance capital, and industrial technologies, with their environmentally damaging effects. Dualistic analyses have no purchase, moreover, on situations where actions in one place can have effects at different historical times and distant places, or on situations of global environmental change which are characterized by a loss of 'other' – irrespective of whether this 'other' is nature, another species or, for example, a regional 'other' based on socio-geographical divisions of North and South. The detraditionalization thesis, therefore, tends to be unsuitable for encompassing conditions where there is an interpenetration and coexistence of tradition and self-conscious construction, of rational control and endless damage-limitation exercises to cope with unintended consequences, of expanding knowledge and increasing uncertainty, as well as all possible variations in between. With dualisms, in other words, we cannot handle complexity, implication, simultaneity, and temporality. Dualisms are static and linear; they fix and generalize into an atemporal, decontextualized form processes and relationships that are specific, embodied and embedded. Moreover, the detraditionalization thesis and its backcloth of tradition is totalizing in its sweep and by implication total in its exclusions. Such totalizing tendencies in social science have been extensively and persuasively discredited in feminist and postmodernist writings. There is no need therefore to rehearse these arguments here; it is sufficient to align myself with those critiques.

Beck (1993) draws on a 1927 paper by Wassily Kandinsky in which he suggested that the age of 'either–or' is being replaced by the age of 'and' in a fundamental shift in which the hegemony of objectivity, specialization, abstraction, simplicity, calculability and control is fractured, subverted, negated even, by the prevalence of simultaneity, multiplicity, uncertainty, ambiguity, networked relations, mutual implication, synthesis and a fusion of incompatibles (see also Adam, 1995). Focus on the 'and', Kandinsky proposes, perforates boundaries; it opens up and out towards those aspects of cultural life which are excluded in the 'either–or' mode of being, thus allowing for ambivalence, contingence and transience to come to the fore and take their rightful prominent positions within theories of socio-cultural life. The difficulty we face today is that we live in a world of 'and' but still think and theorize with the conceptual tools of a previous age: we still think in the categories of 'either–or', East–West, left–right, individual–society, suggests Beck (1993, p. 61), but we live in a world of multiple ambiguity and un/ certainty, a world no longer centrally constructed around those Enlightenment principles. To understand the contemporary through the conceptual tool of detraditionalization is clearly one such incidence where the tool is out of step with the reality it seeks to explicate. Instead of binary thinking we need code combinations and code syntheses, 'neither–nor' approaches and others; we need to embrace uncertainty, ambiguity and multiple meanings. Finally, we need to recognize that our frames of meaning influence and delimit what we can see. This means we need to turn the reflective attitude onto ourselves and allow our theories, concepts and assumptions to become subjects of our scrutiny.

THEN AND THERE, HERE AND NOW — TAKING ACCOUNT OF TIME

When we thus home in further on the principles and assumptions that underpin the concept of detraditionalization we find a number of temporal issues worthy of our attention: its analysis on a 'before-and-after' basis, its focus on the past, its disregard of scale, and its construction of historical 'others'. Together, those aspects not only predispose analyses based on the concept of detraditionalization towards conventional modes of thinking but also make it near enough impossible to deal with open, uncertain futures.

First, the prefix *de-* fixes the temporal scope of any analysis; that is to say, detraditionalization is defined with reference and in opposition to social organization governed by tradition. The *before* is traditional society: the *after* is that which is 'other', that which is *not* tradition. This applies equally to the prefix *post-*, as in post-traditional society, postmodernity, post-structuralism, post-Enlightenment, all of which are defined with reference to their earlier 'other': traditional society, modernity, structuralism, and the Enlightenment. The prefixes of de- and post- therefore not only delimit the substantive scope of the subject matter but also transform ongoing and embedded processes into disembedded, static states. Moreover, there is a tendency in such analyses to generalize the 'other' into an a-historical, a-contextual, hierarchically positioned caricature that bears no resemblance to the complexity of contextual, embedded societies.

The 'before' connotes a simpler, less developed phase than its successor state of detraditionalization. Yet, as I suggested above, such an understanding is substantively unviable and politically problematic. 'It is enough to remember', argues Katherine Hayles (1990, p. 213), 'how a few European cultures have been equated with mankind; how mankind has been equated with humankind; how humankind has been equated with intelligent consciousness.' The task, therefore, is not to achieve comparisons on a hierarchical 'before-and-after' basis but to find ways to conceptualize the complexity, the *and*. Social theory needs to encompass theoretically the mutual interpenetration of continuously changing multiple new and old developments. As Daele (1992, p. 547) points out, 'new stages carry on the heritage of older structures and with it the types of knowledge and technology that fit these structures. Specialization takes place within and in addition to the diffuse contexts of everyday life that continue to exist.' We may even talk of a fusion of incompatibles – not adding on and replacing, not moving from tradition to de- and post-tradition, but rather, conceiving of resonances and multiple readjustments where the old figures in the new and the new modifies the old. Today, for example, even 'tradition' is infused with science and technology. It is verified and stored through scientific research, electronics, film, print, and even freezing techniques.

Mutual implications and resonances cannot be absorbed into binary opposites. Thus, sensitivity to complexity, interpenetration, and difference is only possible if we move away from 'before-and-after' analyses and general, decontextualized statements about static states, and focus in addition on the praxis of contextual, embodied and embedded persons. Hayles gives us an indication of what might be involved in a complex and temporally sensitive conceptualization of the contemporary when she argues:

Older epistemes do not disappear; rather, they continue as substrata valid for organizing restricted spheres of experience. When I drive to the store or play volleyball, for example, I am a Newtonian, never doubting that the laws of motion apply unequivocally. I know this not only intellectually but kinaetheticly and intuitively. When I wonder why the price of gasoline has risen ten cents this week, I contemplate the complex mutual interactions most economically expressed through the field concept that also serves as a metaphor for global society. When I watch fractal forms being constructed on a computer screen, I am aware of yet another kind of thinking, distinct from the other two, with a wide domain of applicability to natural forms and complex systems. In what episteme do I live? Not in a single epistemology, but in a complex space characterized by multiple strata and marked by innumerable fissures. (1990, pp. 220–1)

The second aspect of concern relates to the detraditionalization thesis's focus on the past and its implicit bounded a-temporality. Let me explain. Detraditionalization is past-based because it defines contemporary phenomena and processes with reference to a previous condition – tradition – in the same way as postmodernism defines them with reference to modernity. Both are conceptualizations that are tied to bounded, static states, which makes both these theoretical approaches to the contemporary inherently non-temporal. Compare the two terms – detraditionalization and postmodernism – with a focus on 'the contemporary', 'the now', or 'the present'.

While detraditionalization and postmodernism are tied to the absolute, external grid of historical time and chronology, terms such as 'the contemporary', 'the now' and 'the present' are mobile, relative and flexible: they wander and develop with us, so to speak, accompanied by their fluid boundaries and horizons. They are not pre-fixed by the conceptual tool into specific historical locations. Rather, their boundaries are job-specific: they move with the present and they are defined variably by the task at hand. As such they evade fruitless academic debate about definitions of temporal boundaries: no need here for arguments, for example, about the length of the present – whether it spans the time it takes you to read this paper, all of today, the post-Thatcher era, or the period since computerization. Unlike detraditionalization and postmodernism, concepts like 'the present' or 'the contemporary' are infinitely adaptable to the job at hand. Such temporally open conceptual tools, I want to suggest, not only avoid the danger of losing sight of the subject matter through getting caught up in arguments over definitions, but are also more appropriate than their more bounded counterparts for analyses that deal with the interpenetration of past, present and future. They are suitable to convey the multi-layered, complex, ever-shifting phenomena of globally networked social processes and their effects. Furthermore, one of the key features of contemporary, science-based existence is its *unknowability* from the location of the past: computerization, satellite TV, Chernobyl and the depletion of Ozone, for example, bear witness to this. They were not predictable on the basis of knowledge available at the beginning of the twentieth century. Such developments make the past a poor source of definition for the present. When science and technology are creating fundamentally unknowable outcomes then it seems highly unfitting to use a conceptual tool such as detraditionalization (which fixes pasts) for definitions of ephemeral presents. To do so is analogous to the choice of a specific, single-job tool for a task that is still awaiting specification.

With respect to the third issue, of scale, I merely want to point to the importance of explicitly recognizing that this makes a fundamental difference to what we see. That is to say, the time scale of observation will determine whether or not we can discern processes that resemble detraditionalization. Classical science-inspired theories are indifferent to scale; with Einstein's Theory of Relativity the time frame of observation made a difference at very high speeds; with chaos theory we recognize that scale is inextricably involved in the observation of complex systems. The social system is, of course, the complex system *par excellence*. If Britain's coastline expands without limit as the measuring ruler decreases (Hayles, 1990, p. 210; Adam, 1995, pp. 160–5) then difference of scale will clearly influence our social analyses. Detraditionalization, however, seems to be insensitive to those crucial differences; it still uses the language of absolutes for phenomena that are fundamentally dependent on the framework of observation, and thus relative.

Finally, the fourth temporal feature of the detraditionalization thesis relates to the understanding of 'then and there', 'here and now', which constitutes the past as 'other'. Here, the dualistic approach is continued in relation to the past: detraditionalization implies a then-and-there, here-and-now dichotomy that is not only premised on assumptions of them (then and there) and us (here and now), but which precludes, as I argued above, any acknowledgement of the past permeating the present or any more complex conceptualizations of past–present–future interpenetrations. Moreover, it inhibits an understanding of selves and societies as *being* their pasts and it prevents theories that acknowledge pasts and futures as creations of the present (Adam, 1990, 1995; Mead, 1932/59).

Furthermore, when socio economic relations, risks, and environmental effects are globally networked, 'others' dissolve into selves; the classical 'others' become meaningless. As the source of our dualisms, the 'other' – other species, other cultures, other genders, races, and classes, other geo-political locations, other levels of being – loses its meaning as a conceptual tool once we appreciate our connectedness in conjunction with difference. Again, there is no either–or choice: difference remains crucially important, as is clearly demonstrated in the former Yugoslavia, Northern Ireland, or Afghanistan, for example, where it is re/defined and re/established with such harrowing consequences.

ENGAGEMENT WITH FUTURES: TOWARDS SOCIAL SCIENCE AS A MORAL ENTERPRISE

The detraditionalization thesis, with its past-based and dualistic analyses, as I have shown, is to be located in the Enlightenment tradition. It is an integral part of the disembedded, disembodied, detemporalized and objective tradition of the Enlightenment, a discourse which is so effectively criticized by post-structuralist, postmodernist and feminist theorists. 'The power of this consciousness and temporality' as Elizabeth Ermarth (1992, p. 29) points out, 'is "Nobody's" power: at once human and unspecific, powerfully present but not individualised.' In this objectified discourse the observer, the voice, and the narrator are always outside their respective subject matters. They are free-floating in some mythical hallowed space in which participants are transformed into neutral observers who pronounce on differences between 'others'. Irrespective of the intents of the proponents of the detraditionalization thesis, therefore, the use of detraditionalization predisposes social scientists towards traditional modes of thinking. The detraditionalization thesis belongs to the objectivist thought tradition of the Enlightenment and is thus deeply incompatible with its subject matter, with reflexivity, awareness of construction and personal responsibility. Thus, taken together, the characteristics of the detraditionalization thesis – its inherent dualism, its analysis on a 'before-and-after' basis, its focus on the past, its construction of 'others' – present a strong case against its usefulness for 'conceiving the new that is rolling over us' whilst allowing us 'to live and act within it' (Beck, 1992, p. 12).

The loss of 'other' needs to be conceptualized in relation to, and inclusive of, distinctions and differences, not as a choice between 'other' and implicated self, or between spectator and participant. Not before-and-after analyses of fixed states, established retrospectively, but interpenetration as a process seems to me to be the conceptual task for contemporary social science. Not the replacement of rationality, order and control by disorder, flux and contingency, but their simultaneous existence and their mutual implication, therefore, need to become its focus. This, as I have already said above, is in no way to deny that something resembling detraditionalization is taking — or more accurately has taken — place. But it is to argue that detraditionalization need to be conceptualized in terms other than the traditional dualisms of materialist Enlightenment thought.

Ironically, however, the detraditionalization thesis comes to its conceptual limits precisely where analyses of contemporary societies become interesting: when they face globalized relations, the certainty of an uncertain future, the in/visibility and im/materiality of contemporary hazards, the loss of the 'other', and questions of value; these are the issues that require the 'reworking of the basic premises of social science analyses'. They pose the challenge for contemporary social science to produce theories that allow us to be effective, responsible, embedded and embodied participants in that contemporary world of cultural uncertainty. This, of course, necessitates that the constitutive power of social science knowledge is not only something that is theorized but something to be centrally taken account of in social science praxis. As constructors of social reality, in other words, we are obliged to take a moral and political stand. It requires that we, as contemporary social scientists, come to terms with values and the need for engagement with the future; taking account of the future and responsibility for posterity becomes an inescapable moral imperative.

NOTE

1   Ulrich Beck (1992, and 1993) being one of the notable exceptions.

REFERENCES

Adam, Barbara 1990: *Time and Social Theory*. Cambridge: Polity; Philadelphia: Temple.
Adam, Barbara 1995: *Timewatch. The Analysis of Time*. Cambridge: Polity.
Beck, Ulrich 1992: *Risk Society. Towards a New Modernity*. London: Sage.
Beck, Ulrich 1993: *Die Erfindung des Politischen*. Frankfurt a. Main: Suhrkamp; translated as *The Invention of Politics*, Cambridge: Polity (forthcoming).
Daele, Wolfgang van den 1992: Concepts of Nature in Modern Societies and Nature as a Theme in Sociology. In M. Dierkes and B. Bievert (eds), *European Social Science in Transition. Assessment and Outlook*, Frankfurt a. Main: Campus, pp. 526–60.
Ermarth, Elizabeth 1992: *Sequel to History. Postmodernism and the Crisis of Represential Time*. Princeton: Princeton University Press.
Giddens, Anthony 1990: *The Consequences of Modernity*. Cambridge: Polity.

148   *Barbara Adam*

Giddens, Anthony 1991: *Modernity and Self-Identity. Self and Society in the Late Modern Age*. Cambridge: Polity.

Hayles, Katherine 1990: *Chaos Bound. Orderly Disorder in Contemporary Literature and Science*. Ithaca: Cornell University Press.

Kuhn, Thomas 1970: *The Structure of Scientific Revolutions*. Chicago: Chicago University Press.

Mead, George Herbert 1959/1932: *The Philosophy of the Present*, A. E. Murphy (ed.). La Salle: Illinois.

Weber, Max 1964: *The Theory of Social and Economic Organisation*, Talcott Parsons (ed.). London: Macmillan.

Williams, Raymond 1981: *Keywords. A Vocabulary of Culture and Society*. London: Fontana.

Young, Michael 1988: *The Metronomic Society. Rhythms and Human Timetables*. Cambridge, Mass.: Harvard University Press.

9

Detraditionalization, Character and the Limits to Agency

Colin Campbell

INTRODUCTION

The argument presented in this chapter is that the positive claims surrounding the detraditionalization thesis should be regarded as suspect on the grounds that it is a mistake to imagine that a decline in the power and influence of tradition automatically leads to a world in which individuals engage in more reflexive forms of conduct. Consequently it is suggested that the image of the contemporary social actor as someone who, armed with extensive discursive knowledge, is free to choose all his or her actions (which is common to both the modernist and postmodernist versions of social life) is simply implausible.

One reason for scepticism in this regard is that the decline of tradition can just as easily lead to an increase in the extent to which individuals abandon themselves to whim or impulse, or indeed succumb to the appeal of addictions, as it can to an extension of deliberation and hence rational, informed choice. The other is that there are inherent, natural limits to an individual's power of agency, limits which no amount of knowledge or self-awareness can overcome; with the result that the disappearance of traditional sources of authority cannot simply be equated with the absence of taken-for-granted patterns of conduct. Before this argument can be developed, however, it is first necessary to consider what is meant by 'action', and especially how it is constituted in individuals in the form of 'character'.

CHARACTER

Warren Susman has described the nineteenth century as manifesting a 'culture of character' (1984, p. 273), but the term might equally be applied to the modern age as a whole. For throughout the eighteenth and nineteenth centuries the dominant theme in the huge and burgeoning field of self-improving manuals concerned how individuals could transform their lives by first 'building their character'. Indeed this was widely regarded not only as the primary means through which individuals could realize their own dreams but also as the means through which society itself could be improved.[1] In effect, the programme of reconstructing society through the reconstruction of the person (and in which, as Susman shows, the term 'character' was always closely allied to those of 'work', 'duty', and 'manners' (1984, pp. 273–4)) was a moral crusade to turn 'behavers' into 'actors'; something which lies at the very centre of the modernist dream of using reason and science to create a utopia. For what 'building character' essentially consisted of was the development of a strong-willed self-control by means of which all impulsive behavioural responses were to be replaced by deliberately chosen actions.

Of course, in one sense, all societies could be said to rely on a process in which behavers are turned into actors. For this could be regarded as the primary purpose of the processes of socialization. Yet this view is misleading, because in traditional societies socialization largely involves turning respondent behaviours into unreflective conditioned ones (whilst also leaving many inherited tendencies unmodified). That is to say, the uncontrolled impulses of the human infant are channelled into traditional ways of behaving rather than suppressed in order that the adult will develop the capacity to perform willed and self-determined actions. Hence traditional behaviour, as Max Weber makes clear, 'lies very close to the borderline of what can be called meaningfully oriented action, and indeed often on the other side' (1964, p. 116). Thus replacing respondent behaviours with conditioned ones is a quite different process from replacing behavers with actors and is not by any means simply equatable with any form of 'socialization'.

The replacement of behavers by actors is not just a feature of the modern world; it is its central defining characteristic. Indeed, for Weber, it was this revolution which enabled the modern world to be built. For although there has been a tendency to regard such institutions as the nation-state, rational–legal bureaucracy or market capitalism as the key features of modern society, for Weber these were all merely consequences of the more fundamental change in the nature of human beings, one which turned impulsive and traditional behavers into rational agents. What is more, Weber regarded the primary locus for this change as the person, and not the social role or the institution. The displacement of behaviour (both impulsive and traditional) by action was thus not something which occurred first in the sphere of economic conduct and subsequently spread to other spheres of life. On the contrary, the initial revolution, as initiated by the Puritans, was one which aimed to turn the whole person into a rational agent.

This point is made very clearly by Weber. He stresses that the important feature of Protestant asceticism lay in its systematic method of rational conduct 'with the purpose of overcoming the *status naturae*', that is to say,

> to free man from the power of irrational impulses and his dependence on the world and on nature. It attempted to subject man to the supremacy of a purposeful will, to bring his actions under constant self-control with a careful consideration of their ethical consequences. (1930, pp. 118–19)

After describing this ideal as embodying an 'active' or 'quiet' self-control, he continues:

> The Puritan, like every rational type of asceticism, tried to enable a man to maintain and act upon his constant motives, especially those which it taught him itself, against the emotions. In this formal psychological sense of the term it tried to make him into a personality. (p. 119)

As he stresses, a commitment to this programme meant in practice the elimination of spontaneous and impulsive conduct, namely behaviour, and its replacement with a degree of self-control which enabled the individual to 'act' at all times. In other words, the Puritan personal ideal was equivalent to that of man the actor, as opposed to man the behaver. Indeed Weber is very specific about this, observing that the reason why Lutheranism was, in comparison with Calvinism, relatively ineffective as an influence on the development of a modern rational ethic of conduct, was because it 'left the spontaneous vitality of impulsive action and naive emotion more nearly unchanged'; the consequence being that 'the motive to constant self-control and thus to a deliberate regulation of one's own life . . . was lacking' (1930, p. 126). Again and again, Weber refers to the 'destruction of spontaneity' (p. 127) and 'the methodical rationalization of life' which Calvinist asceticism brought about; in other words, to the displacement of behaviour by action. Now although Weber uses the term 'personality' in the above quotation, referring to the Puritan's determination to develop complete self-control as involving the 'making' of a personality; the more apt term for that aspect of the person which has been constructed in this way, at least in English, would be 'character'.

Character is not a term one normally finds in the conceptual tool kit of the average sociologist. Indeed the term is notable in sociological discourse only by its absence. Thus it is not listed as a heading in *Sociological Abstracts*, nor included in the majority of sociology dictionaries or encyclopedias. (For example, it is not listed in Nicholas Abercrombie et al., *Dictionary of Sociology* (1985).) On those odd occasions when it is encountered, it is usually accompanied by the view that it is better dealt with under some other heading. Thus the entry for 'Character' in *The International Encyclopedia of the Social Sciences* (1968) reads 'See "Character Disorders"; "Ethics", "Moral Development"; "National Character"; "Personality"; "Psychopathic Personality"; "Traits".'[2] The clear message here would appear to be that either the concept is so marginal to the concerns of sociologists that there is really no need to discuss it, or there is no particular need for the term, as there are others (the notable candidate being 'personality') which are considered better adapted to serve the same purpose.

The issue here is not the absence of a sociological tradition in which the term 'character' (or, more often in practice, 'social character') is actually employed.[3] In reality, however, these studies are ones in which 'character' is actually little more than a synonym for 'personality'. Now although these are commonly treated as if they were closely synonymous terms, there is a critical difference between them, one which corresponds to an important conceptual distinction in social theory, that between action and behaviour. Occasionally one encounters sociologists who display some awareness of this fact. Thus George Theodorson and Achilles Theodorson's *A Modern Dictionary of Sociology* (1969) provides a definition of the term 'character' which successfully distinguishes it from personality, whilst also noting, quite correctly, if somewhat plaintively, that the term 'is not often used in [this] technical sense by sociologists' (p. 44). The simple yet important point they make is that it refers merely to the 'moral and ethical aspect' of an individual's personality. In fact, the critical difference between the two terms is first that 'character' has a more restricted application (such that personality may include character but not vice versa), whilst secondly, it has a specifically moral referent.

That this definition roughly corresponds to common usage is revealed in the fact that employers (together with other persons in positions of power or influence) are commonly asked to supply character references rather than personality references for those in their employ. Now whilst it is true that such references may indeed include remarks about an individual's personality, it is undoubtedly the character of the applicant which is usually of greater concern to any prospective employer. Thus while there is some interest in the fact that Mr X is described as an 'extrovert', or that Ms Y is deemed to be both 'intelligent' and 'impulsive', much more attention is given to comments about conscientiousness, diligence, punctuality, honesty and the like. The principal reason for the greater interest in these traits is that they are viewed as indices of the moral or ethical standing of the applicant. They are, as it were, features of conduct which are considered to permit an ethical 'reading' of the person.[4]

Now in saying that character relates to the moral and ethical aspects of personality it is clear that, as in the above example, one is referring to those features of an individual's conduct for which they are likely to be held responsible (and indeed, for which they hold themselves responsible). Individuals are regarded as responsible for those qualities which are judged to comprise their character in a way that is not true for the nature of their personality. It is for this reason that qualities such as diligence and punctuality may actually be of more interest to a prospective employer than such innate abilities as intelligence. Thus 'character' in this sense refers to those aspects of an individual's conduct which (a) are regarded as falling under the individual's willed control, and (b) are judged, by the standards of the day, to be morally significant. Hence the nature of an individual's character will consist of the summation of all those qualities judged to be capable of being controlled by will. The point about a character reading of an individual's conduct is that a given situational act is used as the basis for an inductive generalization about the possession of certain qualities by the person performing it. 'Personality', by contrast, is a concept which, since it refers to all the behavioural and mental characteristics of a person, obscures the important distinction between that which is willed and that which cannot be willed. Consequently personality is a term which refers to all forms of behaviour, including action; whilst character is the term which refers specifically to a system of action.

CHARACTER AND ACTION

In suggesting that personality and character refer to systems of behaviour and action respectively, both of which centre upon the person rather than the social role, the reference is (initially at least) specifically to Weber's original formulation of this contrast. That is to say, action is conceived as 'all human behaviour when and in so far as the acting individual attaches a subjective meaning to it' (1964, p. 88), as opposed to 'merely reactive behaviour to which no subjective meaning is attached' (p. 90). Now although some theorists have subsequently advanced alternative views concerning the way that action should be envisaged (for a valuable summary of these, see Turner, 1985), whilst Schutz (1967) in particular sought to make important modifications to Weber's conceptualizations, Weber's still remains the classic statement on how action should be distinguished from behaviour; and as such has served to influence the approach adopted by others. (See, for example, Merton, 1936, pp. 895–6) and Ludwig von Mises (1949, p. 11).) Thus although some have queried the value of the contrast, it still remains widely accepted. Indeed the case for a theory of action necessarily rests on the claim that action differs from behaviour in certain fundamental respects. Generally it is argued that action is meaningful in the sense of being purposive, voluntaristic, reflective or decisional in the sense that the weighing of means and ends is involved. Thus, as Jeffrey Alexander observes, 'all action . . . inherently involves weighing of means and ends, norms and conditions' (1982, p. 67). It will be argued below, however, that rationality is not the only, or even the most important, criterion of action.

What is so surprising (and not a little mystifying), is that the majority of sociologists who have followed Weber in focusing on the study of action have largely ignored what one would have supposed would have been their central object of study, that is, the system of action centred around the person; in other words 'character'. Instead, most sociologists have preferred to focus either on that system of actions which corresponds to an individual's position in a system of social interaction (that is, upon the concept of 'role' or 'status'), or upon discrete actions or action-sequences and the decisions underlying them (as in rational-actor and rational-choice theories). Consequently, either the actions of an individual are related to those of others or to their institutional context (as in the interactional or social situational paradigms), or the actions of an individual are related to the actor's state of knowledge, powers of reasoning, or beliefs, desires and wants. Finally, in those instances where the person is taken as the focus of study, the concentration on action is commonly abandoned for the more embracing phenomenon of behaviour: with the consequence that analysis proceeds by reference to personality theory.[5] What is conspicuously not studied, therefore, is the relationship between the different willed actions of the same individual performed under different social situations or circumstances.

Although there are several possible explanations for this strange lacuna in the sociological theory of action,[6] it would seem that the principal reason lies in the rather one-sided interpretation which has been given to the concept of action by successive generations of action theorists. For there has been far too much emphasis placed upon the cognitive and ratiocinative features of action, especially upon the single criterion of rationality. And the consequence of this is that the dimension of most relevance to the concept of character has been largely overlooked or down-played.

Although Weber identifies four ideal types of conduct (somewhat misleadingly all labelled 'action'), two of these — traditional and affectual — are, as we have seen , treated as 'limiting cases' (1964, p. 116) in the sense that they are 'on the borderline of what can be considered meaningfully oriented'. Hence they are actually not so much types of action as mixtures of action and behaviour, because they come close to resembling either an 'uncontrolled reaction to some . . . stimulus', or an 'automatic reaction to habitual stimuli' (1964, p. 116): which is merely another way of saying that they approximate either to respondent or to conditioned behaviour. Hence it would seem that in Weber's scheme, action proper necessarily means 'rational action', in the sense of being either *zweckrational* or *wertrational*. If we accept that these are ideal-type formulations, then *zweckrational* seems the furthest from being pure behaviour and thus represents the most ideal type of action. Ideal, that is, in the sense of being conduct in which all aspects have been 'planned'. Hence, the more that conduct is calculated in this sense (that is, chosen from among alternatives) the more it resembles action rather than behaviour.

However, this formulation merely embodies one dimension of the phenomenon of action, that of its reflective or decisional character, and as such deals only with the cognitive features of action. But action is not simply equatable with the cognitive processes of thinking, anticipating and calculating, even though generations of action theorists seem to have assumed as much. If action were purely equatable with cognitive processes no acts would ever be performed. Individuals might calculate or plan (although whether they would have any reason to do so is another matter) but they would not *act*, and indeed, so-called 'rational-actor' and 'rational-choice' theories are not actually theories of action at all, but merely theories of decision-making.

However, since Weber has already identified behaviour as 'reactive' or 'uncontrolled' it follows that action is also distinguished by the fact that it is controlled or willed. To the extent therefore that conduct approximates to the ideal type of action, it must do so to the extent that it is *willed* and not merely to the extent that it is planned or chosen. After all, to plan to do something is one thing; doing it is quite another. Now Weber did not take the ability of human beings to act for granted. That is to say, he did not presume that they possess the capacity as agents to implement their will whenever they wish. On the contrary, two of his types of 'action' actually came close to corresponding to forms of unwilled behaviour. At the same time, unlike several subsequent action theorists, he clearly recognized that individuals achieve their actions despite the inertia, resistance or distraction which stems from their status as biological organisms. Hence his conception of action recognizes that conduct is action to the extent that it involves the actor in successfully carrying out decisions despite behavioural resistance. This second ideal type of action is best described as an ideal type of agency: and the concept of character clearly relates primarily to this dimension of action.

Now it is precisely because sociologists have tended to neglect this meaning of 'action' that the concept of character has been so consistently overlooked. For character refers directly to an individual's overall power of agency. Thus to say of individuals that they have a 'strong character' is to indicate that you are of the opinion that a high proportion of their overall conduct is subject to willed control (i.e. is action); whilst by suggesting that someone has a weak character we would be implying that they frequently experience a breakdown in willed control. Character is, in this respect, a measure of a person's willpower, which is in itself nothing more than a popular term for an individual's general power of agency. Thus action is conduct which has occurred because it was willed as well as freely chosen, and the former is at least as crucial to the accomplishment of an act as the latter.

It is helpful in this respect to realize that in the first instance the reason why individuals perform any true action is not because they have good reason to do so, nor because they are motivated to do so, nor even because they feel constrained to do so, but because they will it; and it is this faculty of 'willing' which is commonly regarded as distributed unequally between individuals. Some people are regarded as able to exercise great 'will-power', or even to be possessed of an 'iron-will', whilst others are said to be 'weak-willed'. Since it is this very same faculty of volition which makes human beings capable of acting in the first place such comments can be seen as reflecting an awareness that individuals vary in their capacity as actors. However, one has to look hard to find any similar awareness among action theorists. All too often, their principal presumption, (and it is, of course, one which is commonly inherent in their assumptions) is that all mature, normal, human beings are competent actors; and that if there are variations in the degree of this competence it can have no particular bearing on the theory itself. Clearly this is not very plausible. It is hard to see how there can be a satisfactory theory of action which is not at the same time a theory of the actor as agent, and therefore also a theory of character. In addition, recognition of the fact that action competence varies from actor to actor directs attention to the social, historical and cultural preconditions for action.

This observation serves to bring us back to the thesis which Weber outlined in *The Protestant Ethic and the Spirit of Capitalism* (1930). For, as we have seen, this is primarily an account of the socio-cultural (and psychological) conditions necessary before character can come to dominate over personality, which is to say, before human beings can come to resemble 'actors' rather than 'behavers'. But of course, this process did not cease with the revolution which was Protestantism. On the contrary, it continued under the secular revolution called the Enlightenment, where it became, as was stated at the beginning of this chapter, the very centre of the modernist programme.

THE LIMITS TO AGENCY

But, of course, the modernist dream of a world in which 'personality' is replaced by 'character', with human beings completely transformed into totally rational actors, reflexively monitoring and consequently willing every feature of their conduct, is an impossibility. For there are very clear limits to the extent to which human beings can be changed from behavers into actors and hence to the extent to which the modernist programme of character-building can ever be implemented. (Whether it would be desirable to strive to realize such an ambition is, of course, another matter.) It is important to understand the nature of these limits because in addition to undermining the modernist dream they also serve to render the detraditionalization thesis unconvincing.

Although there are several reasons why human beings cannot be actors in the full sense, the most obvious limits are set by the fact that they are not gods, but biological organisms. Consequently all individuals are programmed with certain primitive respondent behaviours which are intrinsically resistant to willed control. Naturally this sets limits to the extent to which an individual can gain control of his or her own body, thereby determining what behaviours it manifests. Such reflex responses as blinking (as opposed to winking) or salivating, for example, will clearly never become willed acts. In addition, those impulses and emotional reactions which adults find that they can control most of the time, will inevitably, under some circumstances, be experienced as uncontrollable. This is to say no more than that everyone, even the most strong-willed of people, has their 'breaking point', and on encountering it, will necessarily discover the limits to their own power of agency.

These boundaries – both that which separates what can be controlled from what cannot, and the one beyond which control over normally willed responses can no longer be maintained – may be hard to draw with any precision. Some individuals possess a degree of control, both over specific bodily organs or processes and over their emotional reactions and impulses, which others do not; some people can wiggle their ears or do the splits, whilst others cannot. In addition some spiritual virtuosi seem to be able to control such physiological processes as heart-beat and respiration as well as to maintain immense self-control over their emotions. But despite these qualifications and the fact that human beings have comparatively little 'programmed' conduct compared with most animals, it is none the less clear that there are biological limits to the extent to which behaviour can be turned into action. Paradoxically, however, the real limits to action and thus the main obstacle preventing individuals from becoming complete reflexive, rational actors are not those stemming from this irreducible component of behaviour, but rather those which stem from the phenomenon of action itself. For, strange as it may seem, it is the very fact that human beings possess the power of agency which actually ensures that the whole of their conduct could never be made up entirely of action.

This can be seen, in the first place, by noting that under certain conditions some adult human beings actually have *less* control over specific behaviours than do animals. This follows from the fact that reflexivity often has clear dysfunctions, ones which can actually inhibit an individual's ability to perform natural respondent behaviours at will. If we think about the phenomenon of impotence in men, for example, as well as the difficulty which some people have in urinating in the presence of others, we can observe that in both cases what are supposedly natural respondent behaviours do not function normally. Thus what is for a behaver (such as an animal or an unsocialized human) an unproblematic 'natural' response, has here become a problem for an actor. What of course has made it a problem is that very power of self-awareness which is critical to the power of agency, whilst any attempt by the actor to employ self-conscious willed action to prompt such natural responses will only serve to aggravate the problem. Consequently these represent situations where the presence of the power of agency actually serves to restrict the goals which an individual can voluntarily realize.

However, these examples are in fact merely special cases of a more general category of goals or states which simply cannot be willed, and in relation to which, willing merely serves to render them more elusive. The classic examples would be sleep, contentment, happiness and spontaneity. Elster calls these states that cannot be willed 'by-product states', since they are 'out of reach of intentional action' (1983, p. 56). Whilst Faber provides an extensive list, in each case contrasting the by-product state with one which is within reach of instrumental rationality:

> I can will knowledge but not wisdom; going to bed, but not sleeping; eating, but not hunger; meekness, but not humility; scrupulosity, but not virtue; self-

assertion or bravado but not courage; lust, but not love; commiseration, but not sympathy; congratulations, but not admiration; religion, but not faith; reading but not understanding. (cited in Elster, 1983, p. 50)

Since those listed here contain some of the more important human goals, it should be clear that their invulnerability to any direct instrumental assault strongly suggests that human beings would be foolish even to try to translate all their behaviour into rational action. For from this perspective, reflexivity – in the sense of a continuous monitoring of one's own behaviour – is necessarily a self-defeating practice, something which merely serves to impair an individual's power of agency. Yet the main obstacle preventing the modernist dream of transforming all humans from behavers into actors concerns the intriguing (and much neglected) phenomenon of habit, and it is this which is most pertinent to a critique of the plausibility of both the modernist and the postmodernist world-views.

HABIT

Habit is a concept which, whilst central to the conceptual schemes and theoretical arguments of the founding fathers of the discipline, is strangely neglected by present-day sociologists.[7] Generally speaking, habit can be viewed as a learned act which has, through repetition, become automatic and hence easily and effortlessly carried out. Theodorson and Theodorson (1969) define it as 'a learned response that is automatically repeated by an individual in appropriate situations with a minimum of deliberate effort or reflection (p. 86), and it is of course this last point which is critical in this connection. Hence whether the conduct concerned was deliberately acquired and intentionally performed is less pertinent than the fact that it occurs with little or no prior reflection on the part of the individual. Obviously the development by the individual of certain habits (and especially skills) is functional, aiding the individual to accomplish complex tasks by enabling them to be performed automatically and thus releasing processing capacity for other tasks. In this sense, acquiring skills and developing habits is part of any programme aimed at producing a rational, reflexive actor. However, such skills and habits, once developed, constitute crystallized patterns of behaviour which are extremely resistant to change. Such established behavioural routines are indeed exceptionally hard to alter, for the individual has, in effect, relinquished the power of will with respect to such acts. Thus, should the needs or circumstances of the actor change, such habits can become dysfunctional and hence represent a marked limitation on the individual's freedom to act.

What this means is that at any one time there are likely to be many actions which it is extremely difficult for the actor to will, even though *theoretically* it is within his/her power to do so.[8]

Of course, intentionally and unintentionally acquired habits and skills, whilst representing an inevitable constraint on an actor's ability to will any action, also enable other, more complex, actions to be performed at ease. However, there are other habits which actors develop without intending to do so, and these may not have any very positive benefit to offset their constraining influence. In this respect it is important to remember that individuals rarely ever simply do one thing at a time (even though sociologists, and especially philosophers of action, regularly seem to assume that they do). If this were true then it might just be possible for individuals to perform nothing but conscious, willed and rationally chosen actions. But the reality is different; individuals commonly engage in several coterminous 'behaviours', some of which are the intentionally-acquired habits mentioned above. Thus individuals talk to their passengers while driving a car; eat while watching television; walk while gazing into shop windows, or run while listening to music on their Walkmans. Also people typically perform one action in the course of doing another. I may scratch my head or utter 'umm' and 'aah' in the course of delivering a paper, for example: behaviours which I do not intend and yet which others tell me I regularly perform. The implication of this simple observation is very important. For it means that some aspects of an individual's conduct will necessarily always be relatively unattended and therefore tend to lie outside of willed control. Consequently not all those aspects of conduct which an individual actually possesses the capacity to control will be controlled all the time.

Now whilst sociologists have been quick to study the limits to action set by the actions of others (or by social structure more generally), they have tended to ignore those limits set by the unattended behaviour which accompanies the actor's own actions. However, not only is this a feature of all action, but the more intensely an individual acts – that is to say, the more that concentration tends to narrow the range of attention – the *larger* will be the range of conduct which goes unattended. In other words, the more intensely we concentrate on doing one thing, the more we fail to notice all the other things we are also engaged in 'doing'. What is more, only if these accompanying 'behaviours' have very obvious consequences will individuals become aware of them and thus act to prevent them from being repeated. Consequently, those aspects of our behaviour which go unattended and yet which apparently have no significant consequences for us at the time (at least, ones of which *we* are aware) will naturally be those which will tend to re-occur. This means that not only do we do things once or twice which we had never decided to do, but that we often come to make a habit of doing them. And this, of course, is the reason why we unintentionally develop particular mannerisms, such as my 'umming' and 'aahing' during the course of delivering a lecture.

HABIT AND TRADITION

Weber is one of those founding fathers, mentioned earlier, who did discuss the phenomenon of habit, although he tended to identify it with 'tradition'. This, however, would seem to be a mistake and the subsequent failure of contemporary sociologists to appreciate the significance of habit has served to prevent the confusion from being corrected. For habit and tradition are very different phenomena; and it is their erroneous close identification which has probably led some sociologists to presume that a decline in the extent and significance of traditional conduct necessarily implies an extension in rational, reflexive action.

In referring to 'traditional behaviour' as 'action to which people have become habitually accustomed' (1964, p. 116), Weber may well be partly correct, and yet habits and traditions cannot be directly equated. For habits are predominantly personal practices, ones which may or may not be shared with others, whilst typically possessing a life-span of no more than the lifetime of the individual. In fact, the time period may be as little as weeks (such as the habits people may develop when on holiday), although it would normally cover months or years. What is more, such practices and routines (for example, brushing one's teeth; reading before going to sleep) usually lack any moral or ethical significance for the actor. Thus although such personal patterns may well be common to the members of a given social group or collectivity, and hence serve to distinguish them from other groups, they differ from traditions proper. Social classes, ethnic groups, or nations may be characterized in terms of differences in their prevailing personal habits. (Americans have a habit of eating food with a fork in their right hand, as opposed to the British, who typically hold it in their left while using a knife in their right.) Although such shared habits are commonly referred to as 'customs' – and may, because they are seen to be shared, come to be accorded some degree of moral significance – the important point about habit is that it necessarily relates to the actor's frame of reference and is therefore defined in terms of that actor's prior conduct and manner of performance. What is more a habit cannot be identified in terms of what is done, but only in terms of how it is done.

By contrast, 'a tradition' necessarily refers to shared and acknowledged social practices; usually ones which have endured over several generations. Furthermore, traditions usually possess an obvious normative significance. Traditions are therefore identified in terms of how long they have been followed, together with the fact that they represent institutional and not merely structured ways of behaving. Here one is using a societal and not a personal frame of reference. Hence there is no particular implication concerning how actors may carry out traditional practices. One can refer to the 'tradition' of burial or of marriage in church without implying that in either case participants in these ceremonies either choose to take part or indeed play their parts in an 'habitual' manner (except possibly the officiants).

In fact engaging in traditional ceremonies may well constitute highly self-conscious and deliberate actions on the part of the participating individuals, and be in no sense 'habitual': even though they may indeed not feel free to modify their form. This is because, from the point of view of individuals, 'traditions' are often singular rather than routine acts and hence simply cannot be performed habitually. (The practice of sutteeism is, from the widow's point of view, an excellent example.) What is more, many of these traditional activities may be very demanding, removing any possibility that they could be performed in an effortless, automatic or unreflective manner.[9] The only way in which such 'singular' customs (from the individual's point of view) and personal habitual actions might be said to overlap is with regard to the taken-for-granted nature of the individual's participation in them. It might be, therefore, that a tradition could be described as a 'social habit' in so far as it is associated with an unreflective disposition to engage in it at the individual level. That is to say, there is a distinction between performing a deliberately chosen act in an habitual manner and habitually deciding to do something but performing it in a self-conscious and deliberate fashion. A 'habitual act' could refer to either of these.[10]

The critical point is that whilst the decline of tradition might imply a decline in decisions which previously would have been taken in an unthinking fashion, this has no special implication for the extent or incidence of conduct which itself constitutes habitual performances. Thus the fact that the decline of tradition opens up fresh options for actors in terms of the range of actions which they can now perform, does not mean that they are any more likely to escape from the force of habit than was the case in more traditional societies. It may well be true, as Ulrich Beck (1992) suggests, that the decline of class and the nuclear family has led to greater individualization and hence reflexivity in the sense that individuals now have to take decisions in areas where formerly tradition and custom ruled. Hence, in matters of personal relationships, for example, individuals now have to decide whether to marry or merely to co-habit, whether or not to have children, and whether, if the relationship fails, to divorce or merely separate; all questions which would not have arisen in earlier times. Such structurally necessitated decision-taking can indeed be seen as involving detraditionalization, in the sense that life-trajectories which were formerly mapped out in advance for all individuals now have to be selected. Consequently, in this respect, one can refer to individuals being 'constrained' to reflect on the lives they lead.

Yet it would be a mistake to equate the freedom to make these critical life choices with an escape from routine and taken-for-grantedness. Individuals may no longer take-it-for-granted, for example, that they will get married in church, or that they will have their children baptized, as, in all probability, their parents or grandparents did. Similarly, couples may decide that they will not follow the established traditional pattern whereby the woman stays at home and looks after the children whilst the man goes out to work, but that, on the contrary, the man will do the housework and mind the children whilst the woman goes out to work. In this respect one could say that a 'tradition' has been overthrown. But neither the man nor the woman will escape the 'routines' of work (whether of the house or salaried variety) and hence of the habits which invariably accompany them. To focus on bio-graphically significant life choices is to forget that they are few and far between, whilst everyday life is made up of myriad minor decisions which rapidly crystallize into routine. In this respect one could say that modern society offers individuals a greater variety of choice in terms of those routines which serve to constrain their freedom of action, but it is not clear whether there is more freedom from routine in general than would be the case in a traditional society.

In this respect it is important to remember that every single deliberate, reflexive, freely-chosen, rationally calculated and willed action contains the potential to become the first step in the construction of an unconsidered and automatic, habitual routine of conduct. Indeed, if similar conditions repeat themselves, this is very likely to be the natural outcome. For all actions will necessarily decay over time into conditioned behaviours unless prevented through other equally self-conscious and deliberate acts designed specifically to halt the process. However, since habit is crucial to proficient and economical performance, a permanent revolution of this kind is no more likely to characterize the lives of individuals than it is to determine the fate of societies. Hence individuals quickly settle down to a situation in which only a small area of life becomes the focus for rational, reflexive, considered action, leaving much of their conduct to proceed on an habitual basis.

It follows that the conduct of individuals involves taking a great deal for granted: in a supposedly 'postmodern' society no less than in any other. First of all, it is impossible for individuals to engage in lengthy programmes of action without some aspects of their conduct being either unconsidered prior to commencement, or unattended during the performance, or unassessed once it has been completed. In that respect individuals simply cannot monitor every facet of their conduct. And secondly, it is equally impossible for individuals to act without developing patterns or routines of action which themselves quickly become taken-for-granted. In this very basic sense not only is the modernist dream of a completely reflexive actor an impossibility, but so too is the idea of a personal and social world without traditions. It is therefore largely only in theory that the decline of traditional sources of authority can be said to lead to a world in which the individual is entirely 'reflexive' and free to choose almost any action and hence any identity. Quite simply, the absence of traditional external sources of authority does not mean the absence of taken-for-granted patterns of conduct. The individual, even in a supposedly 'postmodern' world, is never located in a context in which some aspect of conduct is not taken for granted.

But then 'taken-for-granted' has at least two different senses. It may, on the one hand, mean that it has never occurred to the individual to query the correctness of a given course of action. In this sense what is taken for granted is the assumption that one should behave in a particular fashion, and it is this quality of 'unchallengeability' which has so notably disappeared from the contemporary social world. If this is all that detraditionalization is taken to mean, the thesis is plausible enough. On the other hand, the fact that some aspects of conduct are 'taken for granted' may mean that, from the perspective of the individual actor, they remain unconsidered, unattended and hence unexamined. Thus they constitute the background – or more often, perhaps, the accompaniment – to an individual's actions. They are 'taken for granted' simply by being unnoticed rather than by dint of possessing some special authority. Hence, should they come (or be brought) to the actor's attention, they may well be changed. But then this will simply cause some other aspect of the individual's conduct to fall into the category of being 'taken for granted'. Therefore, what traditions and habits can be said to have in common is that the conduct referred to is performed because it *did not occur to the actor or actors to do otherwise*. Thus if we are 'in the habit' of going to bed at a given time, then on many occasions we will do so without it occurring to us that we could act otherwise. Theoretically we could go to bed whenever we liked; in practice we are constrained by our own previously repeated actions.[11] In this case, although we are acting in a 'taken-for-granted' fashion, it is not because of the moral authority of tradition, but simply because of the inertial power of habit.

The tendency to overlook the central place occupied by habit in everyday conduct appears to stem from the enormous significance accorded to voluntarism and choice in both the modernist and the postmodernist visions of contemporary life. Interestingly, in this respect postmodernist theories can be seen to embody the same assumptions as those which characterize economics and rational-choice theory. That is, they presume that the behaviour of individuals is governed by conscious decision-making; that it is on this basis that individuals proceed to interpret their conduct. The only difference between the two theoretical frames is that whilst the latter assumes that conduct is oriented to the utility which goods and services provide, the former tends to assume that it is oriented to symbolic meanings. However, in both cases such an ubiquity of choice is postulated rather than established. The presumption is that this ubiquity follows both from the decline of tradition and from the increased availability of discursive knowledge.

Yet neither of these processes *logically* implies that individuals make a greater range of deliberate, informed choices than would have been the case in earlier times. Certainly options exist today which were closed to the majority of people in former eras, just as late capitalism provides a wider range of goods for consumers to choose from than was the case in earlier decades. Yet the apparent extension of life choice, like that of consumer choice, is mainly a function of market segmentation, such that diversity indicates the development of a plural society rather than a widening of the parameters of choice facing each individual. At the same time, limited resources, peer and family pressure, together with limited educational opportunities, as well as the natural limits to agency, all act as constraints on the degree of choice experienced by the majority of people.

CONCLUSION

The fact that more and more areas of human life have come under the critical and sceptical scrutiny of the modernist gaze, with the consequence that they have lost any 'natural' legitimation which they might once have possessed, should not be confused with the claim that actors are more reflexive than ever before, or that they possess the freedom to act in ways which involve taking less and less for granted. For there are very real limits on the degree to which actors can *in practice* be reflexive, as there are, too, on the extent to which they can *in practice* avoid acting in a taken-for-granted fashion. It is therefore vital to distinguish between the intellectual realm of speculative discussion – in which 'everything is up for grabs' – and the real world of human action – in which very little is actually 'up for grabs'. For in reality individuals are continually engaged in the practice of creating their own constraining 'traditional' world and do so, what is more, without giving much thought to issues of legitimation or authority.

One might say that the 'traditional' emerges as a by-product of action itself, as a consequence of the Weberian processes of routinization, and that, once in existence, it accretes unto itself the authority which simple repetition can bring. For what individuals do, and more significantly, what they have repeatedly done, will in their own eyes necessarily carry a degree of legitimation, since authority is grounded in action more than it is in the self. For action is not thought: it necessarily involves commitment, and commitment carries its own form of authority. The postmodern world of flux and reflexivity is really a creation of intellectuals; it is not and can never be the world of real life. Hence neither the modernist dream nor the postmodernist nightmare bears much relationship to the waking lives of ordinary people.

NOTES

1　Samuel Smiles's *Self-Help*, which had long been out of print, was reissued in the 1980s with a foreword by Norman Tebbitt (1986).
2　Interestingly there was an entry under 'Character' in the 1930s edition of the *International Encyclopedia of the Social Sciences*.
3　Perhaps the best known text in this respect is the Hans Gerth and C. Wright Mills volume, *Character and Social Structure*, first published in 1954. Mention might also be made of the work of David Riesman and his collaborators, who, in *The Lonely Crowd* (1966), proposed the famous tripartite typology of 'social character' types (the tradition-directed, the inner-directed and the other-directed). In addition, there has been an attempt by Daniel Bell to rehabilitate the largely discredited tradition of analysing 'national character'. (See Daniel Bell's 1968 essay 'National Character Revisited', in *Sociological Journeys: Essays 1960–1980*.) Then there is that body of work which has traditionally been encompassed by the heading 'Culture and Personality' and which would embrace the work of Edward Sapir, Margaret Mead, Ruth Benedict, Ralph Linton and Cora DuBois. This could also be regarded as dealing with 'character'.
4　There is another usage of 'character'; one which refers simply to the intensity of individuality which marks a given person; as, for example, in the phrase 'she's a real character'. For an earlier attempt by this author to draw attention to the concept of character, see Campbell (1993).
5　Action theorists seem to become behaviourists as soon as they turn to studying

the person. Probably the most famous example of this would be Talcott Parsons. Although originally taking his cue from Weber, he subsequently drew on the personality theory of Edward C. Tolman (see *Toward a General Theory of Action*, 1951), and later upon the work of Freud (see *Family, Socialization and Interaction Process*, 1955), in the course of what was supposedly an attempt to develop a general theory of action. (For an attempt by this author to 'rescue' Weber's original formulation of the concept of action, see Campbell, 1992.)

6   One reason might be that some sociologists hold the view that the 'person' is not a sociological concept; but that the sociological perspective merely involves the study of role-occupants and inter-actors. It should be obvious that this author does not accept such an argument. Another possible reason may be the absence of a 'theory of character' in psychology; with the result that sociologists are necessarily forced to draw upon theories of personality when it is theories of character which are actually required.

7   See Camic's observation that 'contemporary sociology has virtually dispensed with the concept' (1986, p. 1040). His explanation for this state of affairs is that 'the concept of habit was a casualty of sociology's revolt against behaviorism — a casualty whose effects are still to be seen' (ibid.). Among the leading figures who regarded habit as an important concept, one would have to include John Dewey, William James, George Herbert Mead, W. I. Thomas and Thorstein Veblen, as well as Durkheim and Weber.

8   William James mentions the example of the old soldier who cannot stop himself saluting if anyone shouts 'Attention!'. Since such patterns of behaviour have become deeply ingrained they can be exceptionally hard to alter, as anyone who tries to 'break a habit' discovers (1950/1890 (vol. 1), p. 114).

9   In Britain it is the custom at a wedding for the best man to make a speech, and for those faced with this prospect it would be a godsend if they could accomplish it 'automatically' and 'effortlessly'.

10 A 'social habit' may, of course, also be a personal one. For example, the fact that the British have the 'habit' of greeting each other by just shaking hands whilst the French choose to kiss each other as well. These customs are also *probably* 'habits' for those who perform them, being learned responses performed automatically and unreflectively. But we cannot be sure of this without access to the actual subjective experiences of actors. It may also be the case, as both Durkheim and Weber observe, that customs and conventions could originate in patterns of habitual conduct. What started as mere shared habit may thus become an expected pattern of conduct, hence acquiring a binding normative quality.

11 One could say that ethno-methodology has specialized in studying the 'taken-for-granted' features of social life. However, because this perspective focuses on interaction it tends to lead to a stress on the extent to which the conduct of actors is based upon taken-for-granted assumptions concerning the expectations and responses of others.

REFERENCES

Abercrombie, Nicholas, Hill, Stephen and Turner, Bryan 1985: *The Penguin Dictionary of Sociology*. London: Penguin Books.

Alexander, Jeffrey 1982: *Theoretical Logic in Sociology,* Vol. 1: *Positivism, Presuppositions and Current Controversies*. Berkeley: University of California Press.

Alexander, Jeffrey 1988: *Action and its Environments: Toward a New Synthesis*. New York: Columbia University Press.

Beck, Ulrich 1992: *Risk Society: Toward a New Modernity*, trans. M. Ritter. London: Sage.

Bell, Daniel 1980: *Sociological Journeys: Essays 1960–1980*. New York: Free Press.

Benedict, Ruth 1934: *Patterns of Culture*. Boston and New York: Houghton Mifflin.

Camic, Charles 1986: The Matter of Habit. *American Journal of Sociology*, 91, pp. 1039–87.

Campbell, Colin 1992: In Defence of the Traditional Concept of Action in Sociology. *Journal for the Theory of Social Behaviour*, 22, pp. 1–23.

Campbell, Colin 1993: Understanding Traditional and Modern Patterns of Consumption in Eighteenth-Century England: A Character–Action Approach. In John Brewer and Roy Porter (eds), *Consumption and the World of Goods*, London: Routledge, pp. 40–57.

Drever, James (ed.) 1952: *The Penguin Dictionary of Psychology*. Harmondsworth, Middlesex: Penguin Books.

Elster, Jon 1983: *Sour Grapes: Studies in the Subversion of Rationality*. Cambridge: Cambridge University Press.

Gerth, Hans and Wright Mills, C. 1954: *Character and Social Structure*. London: Routledge & Kegan Paul.

Goffman, Erving 1971: *The Presentation of Self in Everyday Life*. Harmondsworth: Penguin Books.

Hanks, Patrick (ed.) 1979: *Collins English Dictionary*. Glasgow: Harper Collins.

James, William 1950: *Principles of Psychology*. New York: Dover.

Linton, Ralph 1945: *The Cultural Background of Personality*. New York: Appleton-Century-Crofts.

Mead, Margaret 1939: *From the South Seas: Studies in Adolescence and Sex in Primitive Societies*. New York: Morrow.

Merton, Robert K. 1936: The Unanticipated Consequences of Purposive Social Action. *American Sociological Review*, 1, pp. 894–904.

Mises, Ludwig von 1966: *Human Action*. Chicago: Regnery.

Parsons, Talcott and Shils, Edward (eds) 1951: *Toward a General Theory of Action*. New York: Harper Torchbooks.

Parsons, Talcott, Bales, Robert F. Olds, James, Zelditch, Morris and Slater, Philip E. 1955: *Family, Socialization and Interaction Process*. Glencoe, Illinois: Free Press.

Riesman, D. et al. 1966: *The Lonely Crowd: A Study in the Changing American Character*. New York.

Sapir, Edward 1949: *Selected Writings in Language, Culture and Personality*, edited by David G. Madelbaum. Berkeley: University of California Press.

Schutz, Alfred 1967: *The Phenomenology of the Social World*, trans. George Walsh and Frederick Lehnert, with an Introduction by George Walsh. Northwestern University Press.

Sills, David (ed.) 1979: *International Encyclopedia of the Social Sciences*. New York: Macmillan.

Smiles, Samuel 1986: *Self-Help*. Harmondsworth: Penguin.

Susman, Warren 1984: *Culture as History: The Transformation of American Society in the Twentieth Century*. New York: Pantheon Books.

Theodorson, George A. and Theodorson, Achilles G. 1969: *A Modern Dictionary of Sociology*. New York: Thomas Y. Crowell.

Turner, Jonathan H. (1985): The Concept of 'Action' in Sociological Analysis. In Gottfried Seebass and Raimo Tuomela (eds), *Social Action*, Dordrecht: D. Reidel, pp. 61–88.

Weber, Max 1930: *The Protestant Ethic and the Spirit of Capitalism*, trans. Talcott Parsons. London: Unwin University Books.

Weber, Max 1964: *The Theory of Social and Economic Organization*, trans. A. M. Henderson and Talcott Parsons, edited and with an Introduction by Talcott Parsons. New York: Free Press.

Part III

Detraditionalization, Human Values and Solidarity

10

The Foreigner

Richard Sennett

For Isaiah Berlin

MANET'S MIRROR

Edouard Manet was a painter of the city but no realist, as we commonly understand that term. He did not seek to achieve in painting the effect of surprising life in the raw, as did photographers of his time. Nor did Manet's record of Paris share much in spirit with Zola's declarative, indignant literary portraits of the city's whores, abandoned children, or families dining on roasted rats. Manet's art is capable of stunning direct political statement, as witness the painting he made in 1868, *The Execution of the Emperor Maximilian*, but the artist's vision of the city relies upon other means for its effects.

In recording the life he saw in Paris Manet made use of visual gestures which trouble the eye, which wrench it from object to object within the frame of the painting, and which often suggest that the real story of the painting is happening elsewhere, off the canvas. In painting the city, Manet is an artist of displacements. It is in his understanding of displacement that the artist speaks to us socially, today as in his own time; his art challenges certain assumptions we may make in describing people who are displaced economically or politically: the immigrant, the exile, the expatriate.

These words name the differing reasons a person may live abroad, but the result of such displacements seems, today, a fate in common. To be a foreigner is to live ill-at-ease abroad — the immigrant who is culture-shocked and clings to his or her own, the exile who hibernates indifferently in a city barely touched, the expatriot who soon dreams of returning . . . Such images sentimentalize the need for roots and the virtues of the hearth. More, they deny to those who become foreigners the will and capacity to make something humane from the very experience of displacement, even if forced initially to migrate. A painter completely at his ease in his city, interested in the smells and shadows of its everyday life, Manet yet imagines what is positive about the experience of displacement. The duality of 'home' and 'foreign' comes apart under his brush, since the imagery of familiar places becomes itself increasingly strange and foreign.

Manet's eye for displacement is given full rein in his last major painting, *The Bar at the Folies Bergère*, done over the winter of 1881–82. The painting has an interesting history. In 1879 Manet proposed himself to the Municipal Council of Paris as the painter of murals for the new Hôtel de Ville; these would show the effect on the life of the city of new constructions – the steel bridges, the poured-cement sewers, the wrought-iron buildings – murals of modern Paris. Manet's proposal was rebuffed, and it is significant that this, the great work he turned to after his denial, does not present one of the scenes envisioned for his murals of Paris, but rather, turns to something seemingly more sentimental, more kitsch even, a picture of the Folies Bergère. What Manet would seek to do is infuse this banal scene with the force of all the changes he felt at work in Paris, changes which had spurred the development of a modern sensibility.

It is important for us to understand, in retrospect, what the Folies Bergère of Manet's time was, and was not. It was a place of sensual license: both female and male prostitutes drifted among its crowds, and there were performances of the Can-Can, which in its nineteenth-century version was nothing like its more modern, sanitized descendant. (The Can-Can, introduced into Paris in the 1830s, was usually danced by women with no underclothing beneath their loose, short skirts, so that every time they kicked their legs their mounts of Venus were disclosed to view.) The Folies Bergère was not itself, however, a whorehouse, though conveniently located to several, a fact which meant that it was possible for women to frequent it for amusement – which surprisingly respectable women in surprisingly respectable numbers did. This, then, is a risqué place but a public one, filled with noisy crowds drinking and flirting, the air perfumed by cigars, coffee, and cheap Beaujolais. Parisians went to the Folies when they wanted to relax. It was comfortable and homey, a home away from – very far away from – the rigors of the family home.

Such is the scene Manet will take apart. We are shown a woman standing behind a bar, pensive, sad, unsmiling, an isolated figure in the midst of noise (the painted figure is based on Suzon, a barmaid at the Folies Bergère whom Manet knew). The viewer is drawn into this scene through the use Manet makes of mirrors, mirrors which create a special experience of displacement.

The barmaid is painted so that she stares directly out at the viewer. The mirror in front of which she stands is also directly opposite the viewer; Manet reinforces this full-frontal alignment by how he places the barmaid's arms and hands on the bar; her arms are extended and her hands are turned out, as a ballet dancer would turn out the legs in the full-frontal 'address' of the body. Directly to the right of this figure we see her back reflected in the mirror, the flat mass of her black dress exactly the size of the body, so that the reflected figure lacks perspectival diminishment; the reflection seems in the same dimensional plane as the body. I say we see her reflection in a mirror, although optically this is impossible; we could not be facing her directly and seeing her reflection to the right of her at the same time. Today the viewer accepts this impossibility; it seems visually logical if optically impossible. However, Charles de Feir, in his *Guide du Salon de Paris 1882*, spoke for many of Manet's contemporaries in finding this strange mirror a sign of the painter's faulty technique.[1]

In many of Manet's late paintings, the modern viewer's sense of optical displacement is reinforced by some seemingly minor, arbitrary gesture which further detaches the scene from representational fact. In *The Bar at the Folies Bergère*, this occurs in the way Manet paints two gaslights reflected in the mirror; they are disks of pure white, white disks which lie flat on the picture plane; these lanterns cast no shadow, they show no penumbral refractions as mirrored lights usually do, nor indeed are they even painted in the round. Again, Manet's contemporaries found in these strange lights a sign of the painter's weakness. In *L'Illustration*, Jules Compte (1986) remarked of them that, 'Monsieur Manet has probably chosen a moment when the lamps were not working properly, for never have we seen light less dazzling . . .'. (p. 240).

Today we can see these white disks to serve the same purpose as the displaced reflection of the barmaid's black dress. They set up the painting so that we focus on the only significant experience of depth and recession in it. In the upper right corner of the painting, reflected in the mirror, we see the man the barmaid is looking at, staring intently into her eyes. However, just as the barmaid's back cannot possibly be reflected to her immediate right, this intent gentleman in his top-hat asking her a question with his eyes, who inspires in her a look of such sadness, cannot exist optically, for he would entirely block out our direct, unobstructed view of Suzon, who is in turn looking straight in front of her. The painting is set up so that the viewer, you or me, is standing in front of her. But of course you or I don't resemble the particular person reflected in the mirror. Because of the full-frontal positioning of the subject in relation to the viewer, there is no way to look at *her* without this reflexive disturbance occurring. The drama Manet creates in this painting is: I *look* in the mirror and see someone who is not myself.

This aspect of the painting did speak to Manet's contemporaries. Some sought to pass off the disturbance with a joke (the *Journal Amusant* of 27 May 1882 made a woodcut of the painting with the gentleman reflected in the mirror drawn in, standing before the barmaid and blocking our view) but most critics reacted with anger to the disturbing questions about the viewer created by Manet's painting: 'Is this picture true? No. Is it beautiful? No. Is it attractive? No. But what is it, then?'[2] Their distress could have most to do with the story being told by the painting; a man propositions a young barmaid, who responds to him with a look of infinite sadness.

Of course such a story is as apt a Victorian homily as one could imagine. The lonely young woman in a vice-tainted public realm was a homily Edgar Degas painted more directly, for instance in *L'Absinthe* of 1876. In Manet's painting the optic disturbance relieves the woman of serving such a neatly moralizing purpose. A question is raised about the story of the painting by making the viewing of it, by men and women in other costumes, times, and places, inseparable from the story being told. In the same painterly way, the objects placed on the bar are given a heightened life. The bottles on the bar are painted fully in the round; they contrast with the abstract disks in that mirror which shows us another self than the one we might prefer to call our own. Although the mirror runs full-length across the painting, Manet allows only two of this crowded collection of objects to show in the reflection, even though optically *all* should show. These optical ghosts of bottles, flowers, and fruit seem the most solid objects in the painting.

This is how displacement works in the *Bar at the Folies Bergère*. Displacement creates value: reflexive value, that is a value given both to the viewer as part of the thing seen, and again to the very physical world itself, whose character and form we are forced to see by looking at its transmutation in a distorting mirror. By contrast, there is but an illusory solidity to those objects which have not been subjected to this displacement. Were Manet a philosopher – which he would emphatically protest he was not – he might point to this as the real purpose of his painting: the solidity of undisplaced things, as of selves which have not experienced displacement, may indeed be the greatest of illusions. This painting certainly makes a modern promise: disturbance will infuse value into experience. But how could this promise of displacement be kept off the canvas, in the street?

A CHANGE IN EXILE

Were we able to walk the streets of Paris in Manet's youth – the streets contained between the Rue de Rivoli and the Boulevard St Germain north to south, and what are now the bridges of St Michel and Carrousel east to west – we might see the method of Manet's painting setting one scene of life.

In this section of Paris were contained a crowd of foreigners mixed among the students of the Beaux-Arts, the medical and the law faculties of the University of Paris. The largest and oldest contingent were central Europeans, Poles and Bohemians who had been steadily displaced from their homelands in the 1830s. Throughout the 1840s Italian political *émigrés* poured into this part of the city, joined in 1846 by a contingent of Greeks. Most were in Paris because of their politics at home; most were intellectuals, though the Greeks included a large number of sailors who had been caught up in the War of Independence a generation before.

We might think of this as a pre-modern world of foreigners. The Parisians idealized the resistance of local burghers elsewhere to aristocratic and royal exploitation. Though a people not notably accessible to outsiders, the French thus received the Poles and later the Greeks warmly; the upheavals in both these countries were perceived as middle-class revolts rather than upheavals of the poor. During the 1830s the universities of France were opened to foreigners, and the right of political asylum was first codified in its modern form (in which an individual can apply for this status through an established state bureaucracy, rather than plead for it as a favor from a ruler). Under these conditions the *émigrés* of the 1830s and 1840s sought to mobilize the Parisians on behalf of their various causes, hoping to gain both money and the pressure of public opinion which would in turn move the French government to act. Today, we know the fashionable side of these efforts, such as the music Chopin wrote as *pièces d'occasion* for charity concerts, but there was a more popular enlistment of the public, as in the proselytizing of the Greek sailors among the stevedores and carters of the quais of the Seine for aid; they were so successful that Greek work costumes were worn on the docks as a sign of sympathy. Moreover, the Paris police on the whole approved, thinking foreign interests would deflect French workers from local discontents, a deflection of the Parisian proletariat which had worked effectively throughout the Napoleonic Wars.

It was, as I say, a curious situation, this xenophobic nation who found persecuted foreigners attractive, but it was also a historically pregnant scene. For it was in Paris that there first became apparent those changes which would produce the more modern image of the foreigner as a figure necessarily in pain. These changes, paradoxically, are due to the development of modern nationalism; a nationalism which has made those who leave their nations seem like surgical patients who have suffered an amputation.

It is of course true that from the Greeks onward belonging to a nation has been thought necessary to forming a whole human being; the foreigners in the Greek city-states – the *metics* – were considered by citizens to be slightly juvenile since they could not exercise the adult privilege of voting. But the meanings of 'a nation' have changed greatly in the course of Western history; nationality has been at times inseparable from a particular religious practice, at times defined by aristocratic dynasties, at times it has included the net of trading partners of a mother city.

The nationalism which began to find its voice in the Revolution of 1848 marks a distinct version of collective identity in our civilization: nationality becomes an anthropological phenomenon to which political activity is, at best, a servant: the nation becomes an *ethos*, the rule of *nomos*, in Greek terms, that is, the sheer rule of custom, and it is almost a crime to interfere with the sacredness of custom through political decision-making or diplomatic negotiation. It was due to this great change in the meaning of nationality that the exiles who lived in Paris in 1848 would find themselves having to rethink what it meant to be long displaced from 'home'. Their everyday lives abroad gradually lost contact with the rituals and customs of the homeland, the *nomos* becoming a memory rather than an activity. They would have to find a meaning for their lives in the very fact of their displacement, in being foreigners: they would need to look at their memories of the nation in something like Manet's mirror.

The Revolution of 1848 lasted four months, from February to June of that year. It began in Paris, but by March its repercussions were felt throughout Central Europe, where movements sprang up proclaiming the superiority of national republics over the geographic parcelling of territory made by dynasties and diplomats at the Congress of Vienna in 1815. Events had something of the same combustive character as did the disengagement from Russian hegemony which spread across these same nations in the last four months of 1989. The doctrinaires of 'the nation' who began to make a public impression in 1848 used a different kind of language than did those who had earlier argued for constitutional regimes, democracy, or other political ideals in their homelands, echoing the ideals of the American and French Revolutions. The language of the Slavophiles or the Sons of Attica was a triumph of anthropology over politics. In 1848, the idea of a nation as a political codex was rejected by the revolutionary nationalists because they believed that a nation was enacted instead by custom, by the manners and mores of a *volk*. The food people eat, how they move when they dance, the dialects they speak, the precise forms of their prayers: these are the constituent elements of national life. Law is incapable of legislating these pleasures in certain foods; constitutions cannot ordain *fervent* belief in certain saints; that is: power cannot make culture.

The doctrine of nationalism which crystallized in 1848 gives a geographic imperative to the concept of culture itself: tradition, habit, faith, pleasure, ritual – all depend upon enactment in a particular territory. More, the place which nourishes rituals is a place composed of people like oneself, people with whom one can share without explaining. Territory thus becomes synonymous with identity.

It is important to understand that the annals of mid-nineteenth-century Europe were filled with revolutionary nationalists preaching to a sometimes receptive, sometimes indifferent public, but always a public which was hearing something new: it heard ordinary rituals and beliefs praised, and everyday life celebrated, as collective virtue. An older code of national honor, for instance, would have found this celebration of everyday life degrading. In that older code, you placed a foot soldier in a blue-and-red flannel uniform fitted with gold braid, epaulets, and stamped ceremonial buttons. No matter that it was a useless costume or worse than useless during military engagement, no matter that he might be starving in barracks; this ceremonial robe gave him a place in something greater and grander than himself, it glorified his condition as a Frenchman. Similarly, in peacetime, monarchs such as Louis XIV sought to legitimate their politics through elaborate ceremonies; these 'progresses', 'turnings' and 'audiences' threw into dramatic relief the glory of the state, its magnificent constructions elevated far above, and so 'unnatural' in relation to the sphere of everyday life. National honor was to be found in artifice.

By contrast, the ideology of the nation preached by Kossuth, Manzoni, Garibaldi, Mieckewitz, or Louis Blanc – that the people should glory in themselves as they ordinarily were marketing, feasting, praying, harvesting – meant that honor was to be found in authenticity rather than in artifice.

The spirit of this new nationalism makes its appearance visually almost as soon as the revolutionary texts are printed in February and March of 1848. In the posters calling for national unity composed in the spring of 1848 by Chodluz and others, the People are shown responding to the call for uprising dressed in work clothes, or in peasant costume. This imagery is more complicated than simply identifying the People with the poor, for in the revolutionary posters of 1790 and 1791, the poor were often depicted in military uniforms, or wearing the colors of their political clubs. Two generations later, in responding to a great historical event, the People do not dress for the occasion. Nor in the posters of 1848 are the masses given especially dramatic expressions of rage or patriotic zeal: everything is done to signify that the people are not self-conscious, just being themselves. Gone, indeed, are even the allegorical, classical figures who emblazoned the posters of the revolutions of 1830, such as Delacroix's 'Liberty Leading the People'. For the revolutionary nationalists of 1848, the *volk*'s unawareness of itself, its lack of a mirror, was a source of virtue – as against the vices of self-consciousness and self-estrangement of the cosmopolitan bourgeois, whose mental outlook is upon a diorama of mirrors which reflect back endless hesitations and second thoughts.

This anthropological image of a *volk* is an epochal event in modern social imagery and rhetoric. Nineteenth-century nationalism established what we might call the modern ground-rule for having an identity. You have the strongest identity when you aren't aware you 'have' it; you just are it. That is, you are most yourself when you are least aware of yourself.

It is important to understand that this formula is indeed a rule for exercising power, even though it speaks in the name of a cultural unity, a folk-soul, beyond the reach of any political regime. The great imperialists of the nineteenth century, men like Livingstone, Stanley, and Rhodes, subscribed to this anthropological view; they too held the widespread view of the sacred character of everyday culture, they believed in the primacy of *nomos*, only they derived from it the principle that 'natives' should not be contaminated by too much contact with the foreign masters; the integrity of native culture would be diminished. Rhodes was in earnest. It is simply that the ground-rule of modern *nomos*: that you are most yourself when you are least aware of yourself, can be made both to serve revolutionary upheaval, as in 1848, or to orchestrate the forms by which one nation dominates others yet seeks to prevent cultural 'contamination'. In the same way a modern state can also capitalize upon anthropological virtue. Its institutions can be legitimated as reflections of popular impulse rather than as *constructions* which might be problematic and in need of constant discussion. Institutions such as the civil police or the neighborhood revolutionary committee can be declared permanent organs of spontaneity, the consequences of what 'everybody' wants welling up from the folk-life.

Rousseau's celebration of the 'noble savage', a century before 1848, was a bitter play on words. Rousseau seems to have been much struck by the stuffed figure of an American Indian in full ceremonial dress who was put on display in Paris by a taxidermist in 1741; this 'savage' Rousseau imagined to be a man whose reflectiveness was more acute and profound than the bewigged, gossipy, thoughtless Parisian who came to the taxidermist's shop. The Noble Savage — the eighteenth century's idealization of the authentic person — *thinks*. Again, the divide between the eighteenth-century revolutionaries and the nineteenth-century nationalists was marked by a difference in geographic consciousness. The political doctrines of 1789 transcended place; one did not have to live in Paris, or be French, to believe in the liberty, equality, and fraternity proclaimed in the French Revolution. Or again, in Kant's *Reflections of a Universal Citizen of the World* of 1784, he argued that a human being develops the more the person feels at home and derives stimulation among a diversity of other people. This 'universal citizen' seeks the stimulation of foreign scenes, and learns what is common, universal, in them all.

Of course no change in ideology occurs in a simple switch from one form of belief to another. In Manzoni's writings on the Italian peasantry, his rural countrymen sometimes appear as the real Italians because, removed from the cities which were the seats of Austro-Hungarian power, they have guarded the practices of an earlier, free Italy. In this they are like Rousseau's noble savage — self-conscious guardians of what is in fact a superior culture. And then, sometimes Manzoni writes as Tolstoy will later write: the peasantry is morally superior because peasants have no awareness of themselves in time and history, are free of the gnawing poison of too much thought, of thinking beyond the confines of life as it is given. The peasant does not look in the mirror of history: he simply is. The People are silent.

In the rhetoric of nationalism which took form in the nineteenth century, the spontaneity and lack of cosmopolitan self-consciousness of the people was linked in turn to a conception of national time. The nation, also, simply is. The rhetoric of nationalism took a people's rituals, beliefs and mores to represent forms of being rather than doing, to make Heidegger's distinction; the rituals, beliefs and mores which create the national ideal are celebrated as time-tested and permanently cohering — they belong to the very land, to the unity of human beings with 'their' soil. This notion of national being also entails a certain kind of silence. In Louis Kossuth's appeals for a Magyar revolt, the centuries-long interaction of Magyars with the Turks, Slavs, and Germans whom history had brought among them is excluded from the account of what it is to be Magyar; these historic encounters in fact colored the practice of religion, created a complex cuisine, and altered the structure of the Hungarian language itself. In place of this history, Kossuth preached a version of Magyar culture as if from generation to generation it had been both unchanging and self-sustaining. The corollary of national time, a time of being, was the concept of national purity.

As Isaiah Berlin was shown in his study *Vico and Herder* (1976), those two eighteenth-century forerunners of nineteenth-century nationalism, the framing of the nation in anthropological terms began for the most liberal of all reasons: it was an affirmation of the dignify of human differences. For Herder, in Berlin's words, 'it is [people's] differences that matter most for it is the differences that make them what they are, make them themselves' (p. xxiii). It is easy to forget how bold and how recent is the very assertion that human beings are creatures of particular cultures. Machiavelli whispered advice into his prince's ear drawing upon examples of ancient emperors and kings; these rulers, dead for thousands of years, could yet serve the prince as models because human nature does not change, or so Machiavelli and his contemporaries thought.

The assertion that human beings are culture-specific was, in the eighteenth century, more again than a plea for taking anthropological variation seriously. It was an attack on what we call today 'Eurocentrism'. Voltaire believed that 'It is terrible arrogance to affirm that, to be happy, everyone should become European' (cited by Berlin, 1976, pp. 197–8). In different places, different people find different ways to attempt happiness, that most difficult of feats. Yet the break between the affirmation of difference in the eighteenth century and its affirmation in the nineteenth lay just here: to Voltaire, the knowledge that others do not die of foods we are afraid to eat, that others in fact find happiness in tasting them, ought to give us pause about our own convictions, indeed ought to arouse our desire to taste the forbidden. The perception of differing values ought to make the perceiver more cosmopolitan. Whereas Herder understood something ahead of his time: the perception of difference might make people more ethnocentric, since there is no common humanity to which they can jointly appeal.

Place and displace; the virtue of being yourself in place, and the vice of looking at yourself somewhere else. Just here the problems of being a foreigner began. In the early spring of 1848, it seemed to Parisians such as 'Daniel Stern' (the *nom de plume* of Marie d'Agoult, Franz Liszt's one-time companion, whose chronicles of 1848 are a vivid record of the upheaval) that the 'foreign colony will empty in a few days, as our friends return to the places which call them' (1848, vol. 6, p. 353). Given the nationalism being trumped in the press, her expectation seems logical. The political question of this nationalism, posed to all those who had become foreigners – *émigrés*, ex-patriots, or exiles – is, why aren't you home among your own kind? How indeed could you be Russian, somewhere else? Yet by late April of 1848 Daniel Stern had noted that, oddly, few of the *émigrés* had left for home. 'They are still to be found arguing in the Palais Royal, receiving emissaries from abroad, hectoring; they are full of hope, but no one has packed his bags' (ibid.).

Perhaps the greatest of nineteenth-century exiles was a man who would make but a brief appearance on this scene, yet, from observing it, would capture in indelible prose the cursed relation between nationalism and the condition of being a foreigner. Alexander Herzen was the illegitimate son of an ageing Russian nobleman and a young German woman (hence his name, which is roughly equivalent to 'of my heart' [*herzlich*]). Inspired by the uprising of 1825, he was, as a young man, active in radical Russian politics as these politics were then understood, that is, he was a proponent of constitutional monarchy and liberal reforms. For this he suffered internal exile and eventually expulsion from the Russian Empire. Like others of his generation, he thought of himself at first as in temporary exile, expecting to return to his native land when political circumstances made it possible. But when at last this possibility arose, he held back. It was not out of social assimilation, or love for European culture, or personal ties like those of his friend Turgenev to Pauline Viardot, which kept him from returning. He remained passionately interested in the affairs of his country but felt no longer able to live in it. He perambulated the capitals of western Europe, passing his later years in London, where he published a famous newsletter about Russian realities called *The Bell*.

There is a certain kind of social thinking, falsely humane, which posits an inverse relation between consciousness and circumstance. In this kind of thinking, the sufferings of the poor make them intellectual victims of their necessities; poor thought is the sheer calculation of survival. The niceties of consciousness, the complexities of interpretation, are seen as luxuries of the affluent. In this way of thinking, the bastard son of an aristocrat can be no guide to the dilemmas faced by the wave upon wave of emigrants who would quit Europe in the nineteenth century, much less a guide for the conundrums faced by Mexican day workers, Korean grocers, Soviet Jews, or other foreigners today. Herzen, the friend of John Stuart Mill, diffident with the diffidence bred of attending many formal occasions; Herzen, so curious about the places in which he yet knew he did not belong . . . Herzen enters the story we have to tell in April of 1848. It was at this moment of delay that Herzen joined the exile colony in Paris; he did so to move away from Rome, which was in its own first moments of nationalist awakening.

It must not be thought that Herzen or the other Parisian *émigrés* who did not immediately respond to the call of their own nation were cowards; the lives of many *émigrés* read as a long series of prior imprisonments and tortures, particularly at the hands of the Austrian police. In part the answer to their immobility was to be found in a familiar cruelty, that of events passing them by. Their web of mutual contacts abroad was outdated, just as their political plans for constitutions and government agencies had no place in the new rhetoric of The People. But more than this, as Daniel Stern noted, something had happened to the foreigners themselves in exile. 'It is as though they have looked in the mirror and seen another face than the one they thought they would see', she wrote (1848, p. 466). It puzzled the *émigrés*, as well as her: something in them resisted returning, something held them back.

Her image strikingly recalls Manet's mirror, in which what is reflected back to us is so unlike what we expect to see. It was exactly this connection which Herzen would in the course of his life take up, seeking to understand how nationalism had forced people to look in something like Manet's mirror to find a liveable, humane image of themselves. Ritual, belief, habit, and the signs of language would appear far different in this displacing mirror than at home. The foreigner may indeed have a more intelligent, more humane relation to his or her culture than the person who has never moved, who knows nothing but that which is, who has not been obliged to ponder the differences of one culture from another. But that is not the pressing business of becoming a foreigner. It is rather that one has to deal creatively with one's own displaced condition, deal creatively with the materials of identity the way an artist has to deal with the dumb facts which are things to be painted. One has to make oneself.

This was, at least, the possibility that Herzen sensed, reading newspaper accounts of a wave of violence in Slovakia directed against the gypsies who had poured into the country; the gypsies believing in 1848, as in 1990, that a nation which rises against its masters might promise them freedom as well; Herzen sipping wine in the Café Lamblin, which even a century and a half later serves that beverage in the adulterated form which disgusted him; Herzen's companions plotting, telegraphing, arguing, and remaining; Herzen leading a foreign contingent in a march on the National Assembly, in support of the 'rights of man'. They would have to find a new way to be Russian.

THE SECOND SCAR

The fact on which the entire story in the legend of Oedipus the King turns seems of little artistic interest in itself; rather, just a cog in the machinery of the plot. There was a physical mark on the king's ankles resulting from a wound he received as a child. The name 'Oedipus' itself means, in Greek, 'one with pierced ankles'. The king has wandered, lost touch with his origins; when the characters in the legend come to the point where they must know the king's true identity, they are able to recover this truth by looking at his body. The process of identification begins when a messenger declares . . . 'your ankles should be witnesses' (Sophocles, 1954, p. 55).

Were the evidence King Oedipus is seeking not about incest, we might pay more attention to his scar. Despite the great migrations in his life, his body contains permanent evidence about who he 'really' is. The king's travels have left no comparable signatures upon his body. His migratory experience counts for little; that is, in relation to his origin.

This scar of Oedipus seems a source in Western culture for the indelible marks which the nineteenth century would read on the collective body of the nation. Origin becomes destiny. Indeed, it might seem, looking back to the beginnings of our civilization, that exile, dispossession, migration, have been of far less account than the marks of origins and of belonging. One would think of Socrates' refusal of exile as evidence of the belief that even death as a citizen was more honorable than exile. Or Thucydides' remark that foreigners have no speech, by which is meant not that they literally don't know how to talk well, but that their speech counts for little in the *polis*; it is the chattering of those who can't vote.

And yet the marks on Oedipus's ankles will not be the only marks on his body. He will answer the wounds others made on him at the beginning by gouging his own eyes out. If we again cast the sexual weight of this legend aside and examine it simply as a story, the second wound balances the first; the first is a wound marking his origins, the second marking his subsequent history. Twice-wounded, he has become a man whose life can literally be read in his face, and in this condition he sets out again into the world as a wanderer. Oedipus thinks in leaving Thebes that perhaps he could return to his origins, to the mountain, '. . . *my* mountain, which my mother and my father while they were living would have made my tomb' (ibid., p. 73), yet this return is not to be. As *Oedipus Coloneus* opens, he has come instead to the deme (village) of Colonus, a mile northwest of Athens, where the Delphic oracle has told him he will die instead; the prophecy will in turn be fulfilled differently than he had imagined at the opening of the play. The two wounds on Oedipus's body are thus a scar of origins which cannot be concealed and the wanderer's scars which do not seem to heal.

This second, unhealing scar signifies in Western civilization as much as does the scar of origin, which marks the value placed on membership in a particular place. The Greeks themselves would have understood Oedipus's unending journey as resonant with the Homeric legends, particularly the legend of Odysseus. In Greek practice, later to be codified in Roman law, there were certain circumstances in which foreign exile was in fact honorable, more honorable then Socrates' way; *exsilium* entitled the person convicted of a capital charge to choose exile instead of death, a choice which spared friends and family the shame and grief of witnessing one's execution. But Sophocles introduces to *Oedipus Coloneus* a moral dimension to the very act of migration, in depicting Oedipus as a figure who has been ennobled by his uprooting. The play makes of Oedipus the *metic*, the foreigner, a figure of tragic grandeur rather than an outsider lesser in stature than a citizen.

Becoming a foreigner means displacement from one's roots. Such uprooting has a positive moral value, indeed is central to the Judeo-Christian tradition.[3] The people of the Old Testament thought of themselves as uprooted wanderers. The Yahweh of the Old Testament was himself a wandering god, his Ark of the Covenant portable, and, in the theologian Harvey Cox's (1966) words, 'When the Ark was finally captured by the Philistines, the Hebrews began to realize that Yahweh was not localized even in it . . . He traveled with his people and elsewhere.' (p. 49). Yahweh was a god of time rather than of place, a god who promised to his followers a divine meaning for their unhappy travels.

Wandering and exposure were as strongly felt to be the consequences of faith among early Christians as among Old Testament Jews. The author of the 'Epistle to Diognatus', at the height of Roman Empire's glory, declared that,

> Christians are not distinguished from the rest of humanity either in locality or in speech or in customs. For they do not dwell off in cities of their own . . . nor do they practice an extraordinary style of life . . . they dwell in their own countries, but only as sojourners . . . Every foreign country is a fatherland to them, and every fatherland is a foreign country.[4]

This image of the wanderer came to be one of the ways in which Saint Augustine defined the two cities in *The City of God*:

> Now it is recorded of Cain that he built a city, while Abel, as though he were merely a pilgrim on earth, built none. For the true City of the saints is in heaven, though here on earth it produces citizens in which it wanders as though on a pilgrimage through time looking for the Kingdom of eternity. (1958, p. 325)

This 'pilgrimage through time', rather than settling in place, draws its authority from Jesus' refusal to allow His disciples to build monuments to Him, and His promise to destroy the Temple of Jerusalem. Judeo-Christian culture is thus, at its very sources, about experiences of displacement. It is a religious culture of the second scar.

The reason for this value put upon uprooting derives from a deeply felt distrust of the anthropology of everyday life; *nomos* is not truth. Ordinary things, in themselves, are illusory – as illusory to the Orphics and to Plato as they were to Saint Augustine. Such a devaluation of everyday behaviour appears at the haunting moment in *Oedipus Coloneus* in the speech Oedipus makes to young Theseus:

> Dear son of Aegeus, to the gods alone it happens never to die or to grow old; all else is confounded by almighty Time. The strength of the land wastes away, and the strength of the body; faith dies and faithlessness comes to be, and the same wind blows not with constancy either in the friendships of men or between city and city. To some now, and to others later, the sweet becomes bitter and then again pleasant. And if in Thebes it is now fair weather for you, Time in his course will break to pieces the present pledges of harmony for a small word's sake.[5]

This second scar which is the mark of the foreigner is a moral stigma, then, precisely because it does not heal. In both Classical and Judeo-Christian thought, those who cut free from circumstance, who led uprooted lives, could become consequent human beings. Wandering the world, they transformed themselves. They set themselves free from blind participation, and thus could enquire searchingly, could make choices for themselves, or, like the blind Greek king and the Christian martyr, could feel at last in the presence of a Higher Power. The two scars on the body of King Oedipus represent a fundamental conflict in our civilization between the truth-claims of place and beginnings versus the truths to be discovered in becoming a foreigner.

This is the context in which should be set the passions of modern nationalism, with its emphasis on sharing among similar people, on the dignity of everyday life, the value of identity. These passions argue for community at the expense of self-transformation. From the Homeric legends through the tragic playwrights, from the prophets of the Old Testament through the early Christian prelates, there has been a contrary passion for self-transforming experiences at the expense of community, a passion for displacement.

HERZEN'S MIRROR

On 27 June 1848 the Revolution came to an end in Paris. Troops swept through the city, indiscriminately shooting into crowds, deploying cannon in random barrages into working-class neighbourhoods; the forces of order had arrived. Herzen, like the other foreigners who had remained in Paris of their own free will, was now forced to leave. He went to Geneva, then back to Italy, then back to France, arriving finally in London in August 1852, an ailing middle-aged man whose wife was erotically engaged elsewhere, who had set himself publicly against the Slavophiles dominating radical discourse in his homeland, who spoke English haltingly in the manner of novels he had read by Sir Walter Scott. '[L]ittle by little I began to perceive that I had absolutely nowhere to go and no reason to go anywhere' (Herzen, 1968, vol. III, p. 1024). It is not inflating his suffering to say that at this moment Herzen became something like a tragic figure, a man who felt the second scar of homelessness which will not heal.

What is instructive about Herzen's writings is the sense he comes to make about how to conduct daily life in such a condition, how to make sense of being a foreigner. 'By degrees, a revolution took place within me.' In part he began to make a virtue of his very isolation in exile: 'I was conscious of power in myself . . . I grew more independent of everyone' (ibid.). And so he began to reconstruct how he saw the world around him: '[N]ow the masquerade was over, the dominoes had been removed, the garlands had fallen from the heads, the masks from the faces.' To explain the consequences of this new vision of others in this personal crisis of exile Herzen resorted to the same imagery of displaced vision that Daniel Stern had evoked. 'I saw features different from those that I had surmised' (p. 1025).

Rather than making of his exile a reason for spiritual transcendence of the world itself, as a Christian might, Herzen stayed on the ground; he tried to understand how a foreigner should cope with his or her own nationality. The nation, for a person who had become a foreigner, posed two dangers: one a danger of forgetting, the other of remembering; the one a condition in which the foreigner was demeaned by the desire to assimilate, the other in which he or she was destroyed by nostalgia.

In his own experience Herzen came, in the 1850s, to see these dangers exemplified by the two men who came from his past in the 1830s and the early 1840s. Ivan Golovin was, like Herzen, a political refugee of those years, but he had at first seemed to Herzen simply a despicable individual, a small-time crook barred after a few years from the Paris stock exchange, an exploiter of his fellow exiles, flitting from scene to scene. Herzen now came to see Golovin's personal vices magnified by the conduct of his exile: 'What had he left Russia for? What was he doing in Europe? . . . Uprooted from his native soil, he could not find a center of gravity.' (ibid., p. 1399). The importance of Golovin's character was magnified in Herzen's reflections on

London. Golovin's character, Herzen wrote, 'bears the stamp of a whole class of people', those whose very desire to assimilate had led to a loss of self:

> ... who live nomadic lives, with cards or without cards at spaces and in great cities, invariably dining well, known by everybody, and about whom everything is known, except two things: what they live on and what they live for. Golovin was a Russian officer, a French *braider* and *hobbler*, an English swindler, a German *Junker*, as well as our native Nozdrev Khlestakov [characters from Gogol]. (ibid.)

Abroad, such people see that their new compatriots cannot understand what it was like in the place they came from, or it does not interest them: understandably so, as it is all so far away, so long ago – in a word – so foreign. And so men like Golovin, afraid to risk alienating or boring the others, act as though it never was.

Herzen was much too civilized to regard those foreigners seeking to assimilate as necessarily morally tainted. He looked at them rather as people who were engaged in a kind of voluntary amnesia, and he feared that from this will to forget could come other acts of denial. In the painting the foreigner is making of his or her life, large patches are over-painted in white.

One might perhaps reformulate the insight Herzen had in looking at Golovin as follows: the desire for assimilation can be experienced as a force which creates a sense of shame about oneself, and so weakens one's ego strength. Of course the capacity to assimilate requires income, and educational and occupational advantages an aspiring 'new American', say, is likely to lack. But a person consumed by the desire to assimilate may also behave like a self-censor, screening out the full range of experiences and observations which he or she has lived; self-screening supposes there is something shameful, unacceptable in one's past to be kept from others. For the foreigner this cycle of censorship and shame can begin with no more than a feeling that the gesture of touching others when one talks to them, or the smell of foreign foods on one's breath, are behaviors which must be corrected. Shame about the fact that one's breath smells different when one eats foods from the old country is reinforced by the very fear of breathing into the faces of people who do not eat these foods. Feeling ashamed of oneself is indeed likely to lead to the loss of judgement, if not moral probity, which Herzen observed in Golovin. It is why, for us, the famous 'melting pot' of American myth may function more like a melt-down of the ego's ethical powers.[6]

Golovin is a significant figure in Herzen's own attempt to work out what it means to be Russian, somewhere else – the attempt to understand how to make a humane displacement of one's nationality. In a famous letter Golovin wrote to the editor of the *Moscow News* from Paris on February 1, 1866, he declared, 'I was a man before I was a Russian.'[7] Herzen prints this letter at the very end of his portrait of Golovin – and, indeed, of the first edition of *My Past and Thoughts*. The irony is meant to resonate. Such a declaration in the Age of Enlightenment could have come from Kant; now it comes from a stock-speculator and extortion artist, anxious only to fit in wherever he is. The revelations of exile surely cannot end this way. For the foreigner, the knowledge that he comes from elsewhere, rather than being a source of shame, should be a cautionary knowledge.

For Herzen, economic individualism was the great danger of the era of capitalist expansion he saw coming into being. Nationalism and capitalism could march hand in hand, as Herzen, a confirmed socialist, argued again and again in *The Bell*. By contrast, Herzen's hopes for a socialist movement were pinned on immigrants. Their very displacement gave them the experience, or at least the possibility, of looking beyond themselves, dealing in a co-operative fashion with others similarly displaced.

As a reader of Herzen, it is here that I find him at his most compelling. Herzen would have thought it perfectly comprehensible for ethnic groups in modern America to be at the center of liberalism of the American kind, feeble version of the democratic socialism in Europe that it is. He would have explained this relation between immigration and liberality, I think, by saying that the scars of displacement had liberally disposed those aware of themselves as foreigners, unlike the Golovins, who seek only to forget. Herzen's belief that socialism is most practicable by foreigners is an idealization of displacement, to be sure, but an ideal founded on a view both profound and profoundly skeptical that the evils of possessive individualism could ever be cured by communal relations of the nationalist, homogeneous, self-referential sort. Only the knowledge of difference and the experience of displacement can erect a barrier of experience to the appetites of possessive individualism.

In reading Herzen as a writer about our own times, one needs to think about the distinction between liberalism and pluralism. The modern ground-rule of identity threatens constantly to restrict personal freedom to cultural practice: your needs are legitimate in so far as they can be identified with what the Mexican community, or elderly Russians, or young black women, *do*. The liberal ideal can be degraded into mere pluralism through a particular application of this rule; pluralism becomes simply a matter of defining the borders between communities sharing abutting territories; within each, people live as though they have never left home, as though nothing has happened. Paradoxically, it is the vivid consciousness of oneself as a foreigner which is necessary to defeat this pluralist self-enclosure in ethnicity. Herzen recalls someone in England speaking to him: ' "In your words", a very worthy man said to me, "one hears an outside spectator speaking". But I did not come to Europe as an outsider, you know. An outsider is what I have become' (Herzen, 1968, vol. III, p. 1065). And for this same reason, in their recent book *Immigrant America* (1990) Alejandro Portes and Ruben Rumbaut flatly declare, 'Assimilation as the rapid transformation of immigrants into Americans "as everyone else" has never happened' (p. 141). Their assertion is more than a sociological observation; it is the affirmation of a necessary, enlightened consciousness.

Nostalgia, the opposite danger of amnesia, seems a simple condition. Indeed it seemed so to Herzen in Geneva in 1850 just after he had quitted Paris with the other Central European refugees. For the first time it dawned on many of them that they were in permanent exile, which triggered in them the dangers of nostalgia:

> All *émigrés*, cut off from the living environment to which they have belonged, shut their eyes to avoid seeing bitter truths, and grow more and more acclimatized to a closed, fantastic circle consisting of inert memories and hopes that can never be realized . . .

and again,

> Leaving their native land with concealed anger, with the continual thought of going back to it once more on the morrow, men do not move forwards but are continually thrown back upon the past . . .

From which he concluded that the exile could be enslaved as well by his or her own powers of memory, those 'questions, thoughts and memories which make up an oppressive, binding, tradition' (1968, vol. II, p. 686).

Fifteen years later, in London, Herzen again takes up in his memoirs the subject of *émigré* nostalgia, and now it, too, is transformed by his own transformation in exile. Herzen writes of his encounters with Father Vladimir Pecherin in a short portrait worthy of Chekhov. Pecherin is someone Herzen, like all people of his generation, knew about. In the mid-1830s the young Pecherin had taken up the Chair of Greek at Moscow University, and felt himself in the next few years suffocating in his homeland; in Herzen's words, '[R]ound about was silence and solitude: everything was dumb submission with no hope, no human dignity, and at the same time extraordinarily dull, stupid and petty' (vol. III, p. 1386). Pecherin, the young classics professor, decided to emigrate, which surprised none of his contemporaries, who were also suffocating in Mother Russia. Pecherin boarded a boat for England, landed . . . and suddenly entered a Jesuit monastery. In this he did surprise other young people around him, who could not understand how he could revolt against one system of authority only to submit to another.

When Herzen landed in England he sought out Pecherin, to make his acquaintance and to ask if some of Pecherin's youthful poems might be reprinted in Herzen's publication *The Bell*. They meet in the Jesuit monastery of Saint Mary's, Clapham; the two Russians begin by speaking French to one another, then, though Pecherin fears he can hardly remember his mother tongue, in Russian. He is avid for news, he disowns the value of his Russian poems yet is avid for the younger man's opinion. After their meeting, they begin to correspond, the Jesuit convert writing in French about materialism, science and faith, writing with an intensity to this stranger, assuming no boundaries stand between their full exposure to one another – as no Frenchman, whether devout or not, would presume to do.

Herzen tells us this as preparation for recounting an event he read about in the newspapers two years later, in 1855. A Jesuit monk, described in the press as a 'Reverend Father Wladimir Petcherine, a native of Russian', was on trial for burning a Protestant bible in a market place in an Irish town. Here is Herzen's digest of what happened at the trial: 'The proud British judge, taking into consideration the senselessness of the action and the fact that the accused was a Russian, and England and Russia were at war (the Crimean War), confined himself to a paternal exhortation to decent behavior in the streets in future' (vol. III, p. 1397).

Even more fascinating than the story Herzen recounts is the fact that he had got it all wrong by 1865, when he came to write this part of his memoirs. In point of fact, Pecherin showed that he had caused some pornographic literature to be burnt, not a bible, and he was acquitted. The sensation at the time was about a Jesuit taking 'direct action' when discovering smut; the future Prime Minister Gladstone, much interested in the conditions of prostitution in modern England, was intrigued by this 'direct action' against pornography. There is a reason for Herzen, in recalling it, to alter ['I do not suppose with conscious intent to deceive'] the story of Pecherin's trial. For to Herzen this is a story of how those displaced from their homelands can remain a prisoner of their past. It makes perfect sense to Herzen: a Russian messenger arrives who will print evidences of Pecherin's past life, the life of a young man passed in Moscow when Tsar Nicholas, abetted by the clergy, had organized police searches in the universities for heretical writings. For Herzen, the point of the story is that Pecherin suffered something like an atavistic seizure. The youthful victim of orthodoxy has become a policeman of heresy.

Pecherin is an exemplary figure of a disaster which Herzen has come to observe with even greater fear during his years of exile: it is what Freud was later to call the 'return of the repressed' (1973). The return of the repressed is of far greater danger to the foreigner than explicit longing for the past. This return of the repressed befalls those who do not work to transform that part of themselves which lives in memory. The foreigner must confront memories of home; memory must be displaced, refracted, so that he or she is not suddenly seized by the past, acting out the injuries received long ago, now playing instead another role in that old drama. But how is a transformation to occur so that the drama itself is rewritten?

The advice which thus gradually takes form in the pages of Herzen's memoir about how to behave in the countries where the foreigner lives, is something like: 'participate, but do not identify'. The admonition, 'participate, but do not identify' is a way for a foreigner to defeat the segregating game of pluralism. The impulse to participate is an assertion that one has rights as a political animal, a *zoon politikon*, wherever one lives. In place of the ancient device: nothing that is human is foreign to me, the device of modern identity could be: nothing that is foreign to me is real. The Japanese President Nakasane once asserted: 'Only those who understand one another can make decisions together.'[8] A foreigner's assertion of the right to participate, beyond what pertains to his or her national identity, is one way to force the dominant society to acknowledge that there is, on the contrary, a public sphere beyond the borders of anthropology. It is also the only way to survive being personally imprisoned in a Balkanized, unequal city of differences.

Herzen finds a way to create a picture of 'home' so as to make bearable his very yearning for it. In London, he says, suddenly he has become Italian:

> And now I sit in London where chance has flung me – and I stay here because I do not know what to make of myself. An alien race swarms confusedly about me, wrapped in the heavy breath of ocean, a world dissolving into chaos . . . and that other land – washed by the dark-blue sea under the canopy of a dark-blue sky . . . it is the one shining region left until the far side of the grave . . . O Rome, how I love to return to your deceptions, how eagerly I run over day by day the time when I was intoxicated with you! (1968, vol. II, p. 655)

'Home' is not a physical place but a mobile need; wherever one is, home is always to be found somewhere else. As Herzen's life unfolds in England, a sunless land of overly practical if kindly people, the home he needs will change countries, from a place of snow to sun, from the intimate village outside Moscow to the languid cafés of Rome. Herzen will always have a home, so long as he can change how it looks. This ironic, slightly bitter, knowledge about his need for 'home' came to Herzen as an older man; he acknowledged that he would never feel complete. Finally he came to terms with insufficiency: it is permanent, the scar does not heal. And this same power of displacing 'home' was what he hoped for others who did not pack their bags when the borders opened in March of 1848, who did not return to the loved world of their childhood, their language, their soil.

I have perhaps unfairly modulated Herzen's voice, which is that of a man who is more curious than censorious; as a writer he understood that moral 'points' are best left implicit in the stories of individual lives. Yet if I have done him this injustice, it is only because in his pages – detailing the disastrous schemes of *émigré* bankers, the rage of Serbian poets reading nearly accurate English translations of their work, the fight of many political *émigrés* to prevent the dissolution of socialist ideals in the acid of Slavic pseudo-religiosity – these portraits of foreigners struggling to create a life abroad which yet does not cut them off from the past seem emblematic lives, just as the assertions of nationalism which took form in the last century are emblematic of the dangers of other assertions, of racial, sexual, or religious assertions of identity.

In modern society, anthropology has become a threat to liberty. Anthropological man or anthropological woman withdraws from the impurities and difficulties of experiencing *difference*. His or her *nomos* is racial solidarity, ethnicity, sexual practice, age – an entire society of self-referential identities. But the foreigner conscious of the very fact of foreignness cannot so easily withdraw. He or she has to salvage, if possible, something from the voyage out. The very words of Daniel Stern, in observing the foreigners around her reluctant to leave Paris, might be conceived as this imperative: 'look in the mirror and see someone else'.

Like Manet, Herzen sought to understand displacement not as something gone wrong, but as a process which had its own form and possibility. In particular Herzen saw that his displacement from Russia had created a new kind of freedom in his life, a freedom of self apart from place, a freedom he felt strongly, but felt to be so new, so modern, that he could not claim to define it. Indeed, that very inability to say neatly and precisely who he was added to his sense of freedom. In this, he became the first, the emblematic, and in the very qualities of his introspection and questioning of his condition, perhaps the greatest of foreigners.

In a way it is always a temptation for individuals who are displaced to idealize their roots as solid and secure, to make still photographs of the past while the present unfolds more like a film composed of abruptly shifting scenes. It was no accident that the passion of nationalism that swept through Europe in 1848 took such an anthropological form. This year marked a turning point in which large numbers of people were beginning to feel the unsettling effects of industrialism and rapid urban migration. The overt targets of the national upheavals were the dynasties of the *ancien régime* – the Habsburgs (especially its cadet branch in the House of Savoy), the Hohenlohes, the Hohenzollern and Hohenstaufen penetration of the Russian aristocracy. But those who took aim at the past in 1848 were people disturbed by a present whose terrors they could feel but not clearly name. The Italians who rose against the Habsburgs were northerners, living in cities like Milan, in which significant beginnings of manufacturing had occurred; the Poles, Bohemians, and Bavarians who rose against their monarchs lived in places where small farms were, throughout the 1830s and 1840s, being closed or incorporated into large estates, countries in which massive numbers of young people were leaving the land. From the onset of mercantile development after 1815, the cities to which immigrants came were less and less places of a settled 'native' population, settled in its position, habits , or domiciles; the imagery of 'native' versus 'foreign' was used by people who were themselves constantly migrating within the nation, 'restless unto death' as Tocqueville described them.

It was under these conditions that the ideal of a national *being* appealed to those who were displaced. Urban migration and its attendant economics was one of the forces which created nationalism, an image of somewhere fixed, necessary for those who were experiencing displacement. 'A world dissolving into chaos': against it the land stands as a measure of the enduring; its being is set against the trials of one's own becoming.

The 'chaos' of economic redeployment and the migration of labor which began in the mid-nineteenth century seem unlikely to abate in a globalizing world. The motive for cultural idealization will be as strong for us, perhaps stronger, than it was for the people who lived through the first great age of industrial capitalism in the nineteenth century. The era of the 'universal citizen' celebrated by Kant was an era which could not conceive of mass migration, and which imagined capital as comfortingly stationary when invested in land and estates. The era of the 'universal citizen' in the eighteenth century, which produced constitutional ideas seemingly applicable anywhere – in provincial, self-serious America equally as in the France of a thousand courtesies married to smiling ironies – this era celebrated balance, its social imagination was of equilibrium. In an unbalanced material world, the need arose instead for a being-in-place.

The foreigner is the figure who has to cope with the dangers that lurk in this need. Since the foreigner cannot become a universal citizen, cannot throw off the mantle of nationalism, then the only way he or she can cope with the heavy baggage of culture is to subject it to certain kinds of displacement, which lighten its burdensome weight. And in this effort to displace the imagery of culture and folkways the foreigner is engaged in a work akin to that of the modern artist, whose energies have, in the last century, been marshalled not so much to represent objects as to displace them.

THE CRACKING OF THE LARGE GLASS

I began this chapter with a work of art and I should like to end it with one. In 1926 *The Large Glass* of Marcel Duchamp was broken after being shown for the first time in public, at the Brooklyn Museum in New York. Accounts of what happened vary: some say a workman dropped this construction in glass by accident, others claim a janitor thought it was a piece of junk and pitched it into a garbage bin. Whatever the means, the result was surprising: the cracked panes of glass seemed appropriate additions to the wire, dust, aluminium foil and paint attached to the structure. Indeed , the cracking of the glass panes seemed to give new importance to these elements painted, pasted, or dusted on them.

Duchamp's great passion was chess: he was a member of the French Olympic Chess team in 1928, and the devisor of several innovative end-game gambits. This same strategic passion is manifest in his visual efforts. In the layer upon layer of clues, references, and false starts impregnated upon this construction over the course of ten years, from 1913 to 1923, *The Large Glass* has claim to be the more cerebrally complicated image of our time. If these meanings are obscure – a difficulty compounded by Duchamp's decision in 1923 to leave the piece incomplete – he was, as in a game of chess, constantly engaged in the intentional activity of moving with a reason. The obscure and the incomplete are not the same as the unthinking move which spells death to the professional chess player. The cracking of the medium in which Duchamp made his moves is thus all the more remarkable in its effect of binding the clues together.

The full title of this work is *The Bride Stripped Bare by her Bachelors*, a title which may suggest that the complicated moves Duchamp is engaged in are erotic as well as optical. By the time Duchamp stopped working on it, *The Large Glass: the Bride Stripped Bare by her Bachelors* contained an assemblage of malic molds, chocolate grinders, suspension rings, bayonets, neckties, toboggans, scissors, mortise joints and other signs which related the world of the bride in an upper glass panel to the world of the bachelors in the lower (as Duchamp labeled them).

That connection between these two panes of glass, in one way, would be as familiar to any French child today as in Duchamp's youth. In country fairs in France there is often a booth in which a bride doll is placed surrounded by male suitors, the suitors carved from bowling pins; the person who can knock all these pins down with a light ball made of twine is given the bride doll. In 1916 Duchamp had created a work called *With Hidden Noise*, in which just such a ball of twine is enclosed between two brass plates joined by four bolts. Hidden within this ball is a small object of some sort which rattles when the ball is shaken, again like the twine ball at the country fairs one uses to knock down the bachelors. At country fairs, as I say, this has always been a popular game, and Duchamp seems to have chosen the title of his own puzzle well, a game of sexual conquest played with the concentration and seriousness people invest in playing other games, and also the same detachment.

The moralizing connection to Manet's *Bar au Folies Bergère* which comes to mind is not perhaps as important as the relation between the use of a mirror in Manet's painting and the use of glass in Duchamp's construction. We know well enough from Duchamp himself what he intended by the use of glass. Duchamp sought to challenge 'the usual sensory evidence enabling one to have an ordinary perception of an object'.[9] By using glass, he could instead establish the character of objects in ways that subverted this retinal understanding; objects no longer existed as physical experiences, since the eye could look behind them, through clear glass; the glass took away from their substantiality. Within the reality established by glass, one would instead understand, 'from the point of view of mass, a plane (generating the object's form by means of elementary parallelism) composed of elements of light'.[10] Put another way, the use of glass was Duchamp's way to help the mind 'see' – in the sense we have when we speak of a mental act in terms of 'I see what you mean' – without dependence upon what the eye sees.

Glass was thus the medium through which Duchamp sought to gain power over the physical world, to break the dependence of the mind upon the information provided by the retina. And the breaking of the glass in 1926 was suddenly to reveal that he could not take power over the physical world in this way. The revelation was not exactly the dispelling of an illusion, but rather the physical thing reclaimed from Duchamp, the cracks and splints of glass reclaiming the reality of sensate experience beyond the stratagems of the maker. In the same way, Manet's mirror recovers the reality of those bottles and fruits on the bar which, seen in themselves, without the work of displacement, are ghost objects of no retinal reality.

To re-envision others and oneself as concrete, particular human beings rather than as cultural types, may also depend upon such unexpected turns: not the destruction of frames of reference but rather something like their cracking. That unexpected turn, that displacement, is what makes it possible for a foreigner to become a Russian somewhere else, and for a work of modern art to become modern.

NOTES

1   Charles de Feir (1882, p. 23); for a full list of contemporary criticisms of this painting see T. J. Clark (1986, pp. 310–11, footnote 65). Though my analysis of this painting is radically at odds with Clark's, I wish to acknowledge the ever-provoking analysis of my ever Marx-izing colleague.
2   Henri Houssaye (1883, p. 242). I have used Clark's translation, though the diction of the French original is much more emphatic. See Clark (1986, p. 243).
3   In the following four sentences I have taken the liberty of quoting myself; they open my book *The Conscience of the Eye*, 1991, pp. 5–6.
4   Translated and quoted in Jaroslav Pelikan (1985, pp. 49–50).
5   Sophocles, *Oedipus Coloneus*, pp. 607–720.
6   It is an insight which may bear on a large study of Mexican immigrants and Mexican-Americans which found 'the *higher* the level of acculturation (or "Americanization") the greater the prevalence of . . . alcohol and drug abuse or dependence, phobia, and antisocial personality'. Portes and Rumbaut (1990, p. 169.)
7   Printed in Herzen (1968, vol. III, p. 1418).
8   An 'off the record' remark at the Council on Foreign Relations – but why should it be?
9   Quoted in Gloria Moure (1988, p. 21).
10 Ibid.

REFERENCES

Augustine 1958: *The City of God*, trans. Gerald G. Walsh, et al. New York: Image.
Berlin, Isaiah 1976: *Vico and Herder: Two Studies in the History of Ideas*. London: Hogarth Press.
Clark, T. J. 1986: *The Painting of Modern Life: Paris in the Art of Manet and his Followers*. Princeton: Princeton University Press.
Compte, Jules 1986: in Clark, T. J., *The Painting of Modern Life*.
Cox, Harvey 1966: *The Secular City*. Rev. edn, New York: Macmillan.
Feir, Charles de 1882: *Guide du Salon de Paris 1882*. Paris.

Freud, Sigmund 1973: *New Introductory Lectures on Psychoanalysis*. Harmondsworth: Penguin.

Herzen, Aleksandr Ivanovich 1968: *My Past and Thoughts*, trans. Constance Garrett and Humphrey Higgens, in four volumes. New York: Alfred Knopf.

Houssaye, Henri 1883: Le Salon de 1882, *L'Art français depuis dix ans*. Paris.

Moure, Gloria 1988: *Marcel Duchamp*, trans. Joanna Martinez. New York: Rizzoli.

Pelikan, Jaroslav 1985: *Jesus through the Centuries*. New Haven: Yale University Press.

Portes, Alejandro and Rumbaut, Ruben 1990: *Immigrant America: A Portrait*. Berkeley, Cal.: University of California Press.

Sennett, Richard 1991: *The Conscience of the Eye*. New York: Knopf.

Sophocles 1954: *Oedipus the King*, trans. David Greene. Chicago: University of Chicago Press. Original, *Oedipus Tyraneus*, Loeb: pp. 1030–5; p. 1453.

Sophocles: *Oedipus Coloneus*. Cambridge, Mass.: Loeb Classical Library.

Stern, Daniel 1848: *Oeuvres*. Paris.

11

On Things not being Worse, and the Ethic of Humanity

Paul Heelas

'The God of humanity has arrived at the gates of the ruined temple of the tribe'

Tagore, 1961, p. 101

'[I] have been brought up without religion, but not without respect for the so-called "ethical" demands of human civilization'

Freud, 1960, p. 367

'This human person, the definition of which is like the touchstone which distinguishes good from evil'

Durkheim, 1973, p. 46

'As the archeology of our thought easily shows, man is an invention of recent date. And one which is perhaps nearing its end'

Foucault, 1992, p. 387

In this chapter a number of claims are first introduced, to do with the loss of the tradition-informed and adding up to a pretty bleak view of the moral and existential reliability of our time. Attention is then paid to a major reason why things are by no means as bad as they could be. This reason has to do with the development of an 'ethic of humanity'. Taking place together with detraditionalization, the ethic has played a crucial role in ensuring that the outcome has not involved the collapse of 'the good' in life. Furthermore, the ethic provides a crucial bulwark against those processes which encourage forceful, differentiating traditions and all the distress which they can cause.

THE DOOM-AND-GLOOM SCENARIO

According to many, cultural metanarratives are well on the way to collapse. Thus Peter Berger writes that modernity brings with it 'a weakening of every conceivable belief and value dependent upon social support . . . modern societies are characterized by unstable, incohesive, unreliable plausibility structures . . . certainty is hard to come by' (1979, p. 19). Anthony Giddens writes of 'the radical turn from tradition intrinsic to modernity's reflexivity' (1990, pp. 175–6), claiming that 'In conditions of high modernity, in many areas of social life – including the domain of the self – there are no determinate authorities' (1991, p. 194). And Fredric Jameson refers to 'the extinction' of that once significant realm of the metanarrative, 'the sacred and the "spiritual"' (1991, p. 67).

An interrelated way of portraying the collapse thesis is to focus on the kinds of judgements which people make when they are disinclined – or are simply unable – to rely on tradition-informed value identification, prioritization and differentiation. Thus Alasdair MacIntyre argues that 'we live in a specifically emotivist culture', his contention being 'that in moral argument the apparent assertion of principle functions as a mask for expressions of personal preference' (1985, pp. 22, 19). Or we might think of Allan Bloom, ostensibly discussing the relativization of 'the true' but also making a more radical point concerning scepticism. Having claimed that 'There is only one thing a professor can be absolutely certain of: almost every student entering the university believes, or says he believes, that truth is relative,' Bloom continues, 'The true believer is the real danger. The study of history and of culture teaches that all the world was mad in the past; men always thought they were right, and that led to wars, persecutions, slavery, xenophobia, racism, and chauvinism. The point is not to correct the mistakes and really be right; rather it is not to think you are right at all' (1987, pp. 25–6).

Another interrelated way of presenting the doom-and-gloom thesis is to focus on arguments to do with the fate of the self. The basic claim is that selves have become disembedded, the disintegration of culturally determinate or confirmed modes of identity provision ensuring that individuals are no longer able to rest secure with any over-arching, authenticated order of things. As formulated by Arnold Gehlen (1949/1980), for example, 'Any individual transplanted into our own times from the vigorously concrete cultures of antiquity, of the Middle Ages, or even the baroque era, would find most astonishing . . . the lack of structure and form in which the people of our time are forced to vegetate; and would wonder at the elusiveness and abstractness of our institutions, which are mostly "immaterial states of affairs"' (1980, p. 74). Or again, and in a fashion similar to more recent theorizing to do with the 'de-centring' of the subject, Gehlen wrote of 'The lack of stable institutions' and those processes which, 'by demolishing the bulwarks of habit, exposes . . . ["man"] defenseless to the casual flow of stimuli' (ibid., p. 77). Then there is Giddens's argument, namely that 'The loss of anchoring reference points deriving from the development of internally referential systems creates moral disquiet that individuals can never fully overcome' (1990, p. 185).

Not all the authors under consideration are systematically inclined to pessimism. Giddens, for instance, writes about 'emancipatory politics' (1991, pp. 209–31). However, the overall thrust is that we have lost those cultural formations which once served to provide fundamental values; which once provided life-plans, identities and visions; which once determined a sense of worthwhile duty. And, as it naturally follows from this scenario, we are left with an increasingly de-differentiated (difference becoming simply 'the different'), disorganized or relativized culture: a 'culture' increasingly unable to adjudicate between that which is true, good, or valuable and that which is not; unable to provide 'reliable' plausibility structures; unable to regulate the 'anything goes' tendencies ascribed to its detraditionalized or consumerized occupants. No longer determinately informed by 'the Cultural', our lives are instead informed by the exercise of personal preference. The 'value' ascriptions and selections of 'emotivist "culture"' are what have come to count. So have those of the 'culture of contentment' (Galbraith, 1992), 'the postmodern consumer culture' (Jameson, 1991) and the 'narcissistic' culture of 'the minimal self' (Lasch, 1985).

THE ETHIC OF HUMANITY

Is it possible to discern enough tradition-maintenance, traditionalization or re-traditionalization to undermine, if not invalidate, claims concerning radical cultural collapse? Of all the evidence – and there is a great deal – which counts against the unidirectional view that we have entered a quasi-cultural state of self-centredness, emotivism or relativism, attention is now focused on that provided by the establishment of a culturally pervasive ethical formation. The ethic of humanity, it is argued, has come to serve as perhaps *the* dominant tradition of our time.

Durkheim's Portrayal

To begin with, what are the characteristics of this ethic? Durkheim's account of what he called 'the religion of humanity' (or 'the cult of man', etc.) provides a useful introduction. A key extract from *Suicide* (1952) helps provide a way of coming to terms with his rather unsystematically presented thoughts on the topic. The passage runs:

> This cult of man is something . . . very different from . . . egoistic individualism . . . Far from detaching individuals from society and from every aim beyond themselves, *it unites them in one thought, makes them servants of one work.* For man, as thus suggested to collective affection and respect, is not the sensual, experiential individual that each one of us represented, but *man in general*, ideal humanity as conceived by each people at each moment of its history. None of us wholly incarnates this ideal, though none is wholly a stranger to it. So we have, not to concentrate each separate person upon himself and his own interests, but to *subordinate* him to the *general interests of humanity*. Such an aim draws him beyond himself; impersonal and disinterested, it is above all individual personalities; like every ideal, it can be *conceived of only as superior to and dominating reality*. (pp. 336–7; my emphases)

A number of points can now be elaborated, relevant passages from elsewhere in Durkheim's corpus being drawn upon to give a more complete picture of his thoughts on the topic.

First, as reference to 'man in general' – or to what is sometimes spoken of as the 'intrinsic quality of human nature' (1992, p. 112) and the like – serves to indicate, the ethic involves a universal basis (however idealized) concerning what it is to be truly human. The second, closely related point, is that this notion of what it is to be human serves to ground or inform a universally applicable morality. We should all 'subordinate' ourselves to 'the general interests of humanity'; in another formulation, 'the only moral ways of acting are those which can be applied to all men indiscriminately; that is, which are implied in the general notion of "man"' (1973, p. 45). As Durkheim also makes quite explicit, cultural relativism or contextual ethicality is thereby rejected: 'I am sure of acting properly only if the motives which determine my behavior depend not on the particular circumstances in which I find myself, but on my humanity in abstract. Inversely, my actions are bad when they can be logically justified only by my favoured position or by my social condition, by my class or caste interests, by my strong passions, and so on' (ibid.). The third, also closely related point, concerns the rejection of that relativistic utilitarian ethicality associated with 'egoistic individualism'. As it is put, 'duty consists in disregarding all that concerns us personally, all that derives from our empirical individuality, in order to seek out that which our humanity requires and which we share with all our fellowmen' (ibid.).

Another feature to be highlighted concerns the fact that the ethic is seen to be grounded in that which 'can be conceived of only as superior to and dominating reality'. Durkheim frequently used religious language to characterize this reality, for example writing of the 'human personality' as 'sacred, even most sacred' (1952, p. 333). One way of interpreting such usage is that he is intent on emphasizing the authoritative nature of the ethic. In the religious sphere in general, 'the sacred' is held to be that which cannot be violated by utilitarian considerations. Accordingly, the term can be used to emphasize the claim that the religion of humanity speaks with a force which cannot – or should not – be questioned. Finally, and following on from this, Durkheim sometimes writes as though the ethic exercises 'sacred' authority over everybody, in all cultures (recall 'it unites them in one thought, makes them servants of one work'). However, as his reference to 'egoistic individualism' serves to indicate, he also acknowledges that 'sacred' authority is indeed ignored by those intent on pursuing their utilitarian expediences, or aims which do not exist 'beyond themselves'.

Turning now to the moral content of the religion, much hangs on the claim that 'human personality' is of 'incomparable value' (1952, p. 336). The 'sacrosanct quality' (ibid., p. 334) attributed to the person is manifested in the values of 'dignity' and 'respect'. 'The dignity of the person', we are told, 'is the supreme end of conduct' (ibid., p. 363); 'there is in all healthy consciences a very lively respect for human dignity, to which we are supposed to conform as much in our relations with ourselves as in our relations with others', the passage continuing, 'we ought to respect human personality wherever we find it, which is to say, in ourselves as in those like us' (1964, p. 400). Furthermore, the intrinsic value ascribed to the 'human personality' entails that 'morality demands that to a certain extent we should be treated as though we were equal' (1979, p. 72).

The emphasis on intrinsic value, dignity, respect and (at least relative) equality goes together with a number of more specific 'duties', including that 'forbidding any attempt on the life of a human being and prohibiting homicide, except in cases allowed by law' (1992, p. 112). (As Durkheim continues, 'The reason why homicide is prohibited nowadays under threat of the most severe penalties provided by our code of law, is that the human person is the object of a sacred respect' (ibid., p. 113).) Another such duty concerns avoiding 'unlawful attack' on 'the property of the human person' (ibid., p. 121).

In sum, and here implying an unambiguous view of equality, 'I have to respect the life, the property, the honour of my fellow-creatures, even when they are not of my own family or my own country' (1992, p. 110). Finally, and now using the language of 'rights', Durkheim makes the more general claim that 'Nowhere [than in the religion] are the rights of the individual affirmed with greater energy, since the individual is placed in the ranks of sacrosanct objects; nowhere is the individual more jealously protected from encroachments from the outside, whatever their source' (1973, p. 46).

On the one hand, then, there is a moral imperative not to offend the dignity or rights of fellow humans. On the other, however, there is the moral imperative to act for the good of the whole. Deriving from the fact that we *belong* to sacralized humanity, this humanity 'is an object of love and aspiration that we are drawn towards' (1953, p. 48). 'The greatest good is in communion with others' (1953, p. 37). There is 'sympathy of all that is human, a broader pity for all sufferings, for all human miseries, a more ardent need to combat them and mitigate them, a greater thirst for justice' (ibid., p. 49). And 'the acts inspired in us' by the 'human personality' are seen as leading to 'sacrifices and privations' (1952, p. 335).

In sum, the religion comprises a mode of evaluation to do with those duties, obligations, freedoms, rights and sentiments which are taken to be bound up with the fact that we are all humans.

The Ethic as Tradition-informed Liberalism

As Durkheim himself observes, the religion of humanity is a form of 'liberalism' (1973, p. 46). In order to argue that it serves as a moral tradition, thereby counting against the radical detraditionalization thesis, however, it is important to distinguish it from another version of liberalism: one which, it is claimed, has played a central role in undermining substantive morality.

Albeit to varying degrees, the version which serves to undermine is of a deontologized nature. The basic idea is that liberty is best ensured by formulating justice in terms of 'rights' rather than 'goods'. Kant provides a maximally deontologized rendering, claiming that the right is 'derived entirely from the concept of freedom in the mutual external relationships of human beings, and has nothing to do with the end which all men have by nature (that is the aim of achieving happiness) or with the recognized means of attaining this end' (cited by Sandel, 1982, p. 5). The good, whether construed by reference to human nature or in some other fashion, is seen as too coercive to be accorded a role in the management of human affairs.

Although such a 'pure' liberalism has largely remained in the hands of philosophers, it has been claimed that a somewhat less minimalistic liberalism has become rife at the cultural and political level. 'Equality', a substantive 'good', enters the picture. And the interplay between liberty and equality (with its associated values of 'toleration' and 'respect') serves to generate relativism. The assumption that people are free to hold different values, together with the assumption of equality, ensures that one cannot judge those whose values deviate from one's own. Instead, one must maintain equality (respect or toleration) by supposing that, in context, such values are actually justified. From the 'moral' point of view, the different is simply 'the different'. This, then, is the liberalism which Bloom – it will be recalled – finds among students. It is also the version which MacIntyre has in mind when he writes of 'the dominant liberal culture about education' (1991, p. 16). As he puts it, 'an education which purports to teach a morality neutral between rival controversial standpoints concerning the virtues will end up teaching a largely indeterminate morality – that morality of the rhetoric of commonplace usage which lacks determinate answers to those questions in terms of which any substantive and determinate account of the virtues has to state its positions'.

Durkheim's portrayal, however, is of a morality which is some distance removed from the 'respect or tolerate the other' relativized version. Grounded in what adherents believe to be a universal absolute – the ideal of humanity – the religion is informed by a basic ontological good. The ideal, as we have already noted, is held to be 'like the touchstone which distinguishes good from evil'. (See also, for example, 'If he be the moral reality, then it is he who must serve as the pole-star for public as well as private conduct' (1992, p. 56).) Human rights, we have also seen, are held to be derived from the 'sacrosanct' nature of the person. So is the importance attached to 'respect', 'dignity', 'love', 'sympathy' and so on. Indeed, far from facilitating relativistic manoeuvrings to sustain respect, or toleration of that which the religion holds to be wrong, the ethic actually has a decidedly illiberal edge to it. Albeit derived from an inclusivistic, egalitarian premise – the 'intrinsic quality of human nature' is held to be a universal – the ethic nevertheless serves to distinguish between those who are good and those who are bad; those who have dignity and those who do not; those whose freedom should be respected and those who should be criticized. The ethic, that is to say, is also exclusivistic, this in the sense of refusing to accord 'respect' (to concentrate on a key value) to all ways of life: a feature implied by Durkheim when he writes that the ethic holds that 'we ought to respect human personality wherever we find it, which is to say, in ourselves *as in those like us*' (my emphasis).[1]

The value ascribed to what is taken to be the truth is clearly much more important than the value of allowing people the freedom to adopt wrong truths. The religion of humanity might have liberal characteristics, but central ones – including 'freedom' and 'respect' – only operate among those who have adopted the frame provided by 'man in general'. That those who deviate from the religion – who deviate from what it is be be truly human – must be judged accordingly shows how far it has moved along the path running from respecting all others, to tolerating what is nevertheless taken to be morally wrong, to rejecting ill-informed ways of life.

A Dominant Tradition of Our Times

A great advocate of the ethic himself – not least in that he did not believe that all societies are of 'equal moral value' (1961, p. 79) – Durkheim clearly took delight in noting that great numbers in the West thought in terms of what he clearly considered to be a *tradition* of substantively humanistic and universally applicable tenets. In one formulation, for example, he claims that the ethic 'has become a fact, it has penetrated our institutions and our mores, it has blended with our whole life, and if, truly, we had to give it up, we would have to recast our whole moral organization at the same stroke' (1973, pp. 46–7). Indeed, and in stark contrast to cultural-collapse theorizing, Durkheim argues that the ethic is ever-gaining in potency: 'Shall we find some people saying that the cult of the individual is a superstition of which we ought to rid ourselves? That would be to go against all the lessons of history; for as we read on, we find the human person tending to gain in dignity. There is no rule more soundly established' (1992, p. 56).[2]

One way of supporting claims of this kind is to draw attention to the history of human rights. There has certainly been a proliferation of rights – civil, political, economic, social and cultural – since the eighteenth century; rights which have become inscribed in constitutions and international law, and which inform the activities of bodies such as the Red Cross (founded 1863), the International Labour Organization (1919) and the United Nations (1945). As Scott Davidson, for example, concludes, 'Few areas of national or international life now remain untouched by the influence of human rights' (1993, p. 163).[3] But what is the significance of this history for the ethic of humanity? The question is raised by the fact that many rights (as Davidson points out) have to do with 'liberty'; more specifically, those 'first-generation rights' associated with the English, American and French Revolutions which emphasize 'the right of individuals to be free from arbitrary interference by the state' (ibid., p. 6). It is thus possible to see rights as a component of deontologized, morally vacuous liberalism: an interpretation, it might be noted, which would appear to inform Bauman's observation (chapter 3, this volume) that human rights have to do with 'the right to be left alone'.

However, there are very good reasons for supposing that the cultural history of human rights is in fact closely bound up with the ethic of humanity, its history thereby serving to indicate the growing significance of this ethic. First-generation rights – let alone the 'second-generation' (emphasizing 'equality' and 'the right to the creation of conditions by the state which will allow every individual to develop their maximum potential') or the 'third' (emphasizing 'fraternity' and those international rights which 'will guarantee the right to development, to disaster relief, to peace and to a good environment') (Davidson, 1993, p. 6) – would not have developed had they not been fuelled by cultural assumptions and values concerning the nature of the self and, more recently, belief in a universal community of humankind. The importance attached to protecting individuals from state interference, for example, could not have come into play were it not for the cultural value which had come to be attached to the individual *qua* individual; to the individual as significant in its own terms rather than in terms of how the state might construct and regulate its identity. In like manner, the development of rights emphasizing equality surely presupposes a particular view of the person. And the development of all those rights which emphasize 'the right to . . .' surely presupposes an even more determinate view of that to which we are all entitled by virtue of being human. (See, for example, Durkheim, 1992, p. 56.)

The fact that rights involve 'goods' determined by what human nature is taken to be is clearly seen in the great documents of the human rights movement. The Preamble of the Universal Declaration of Human Rights (1948), for example, commences, 'Whereas recognition of the inherent dignity and of the equal and inalienable rights of all members of the human family is the foundation of freedom, justice and peace in the world . . .'; and Article 1 states, 'All human beings are born free and equal in dignity and rights. They are endowed with reason and conscience and should act towards one another in a spirit of brotherhood.'[4] It can also be observed that the ethic expressed in rights documentation has the same substantive, and thus illiberal, aspect as the religion of humanity. The Declarations and International Conventions of the United Nations, for instance, are replete with statements which do not serve to respect all others; which are intolerant with regard to deviant ways of life. The countless numbers of people – say in castist and communalist spheres of India – who fail to 'act towards one another in a spirit of brotherhood' must be judged accordingly.

If the world were populated by the kind of people described by Bloom, it is inconceivable that the United Nations, together with other international bodies, would be able to mount their – for the arch-liberal, 'intolerant' – campaigns against what is judged to be wrong. Bloom's relativists, having no strong views on such matters, would cry 'respect the other' and have done. However precisely because the world is populated with large numbers holding substantive beliefs to do with what it is to be human, and what it is to belong to a universal community of humankind, the United Nations – and a great many other organizations, including states – are legitimated and encouraged in their political and interventionistic attempts to bring about what they consider to be the just order of things.

A simple question further reveals the potency of the ethic of humanity: 'what is wrong with racism?' 'Racism', as we know it, has been considered perfectly acceptable in innumerable cultural settings. It is more the norm than the exception for groups of people to 'fail' (as we would see it) to recognize that others are essentially the same as themselves.[5] But as William Pickering, with Durkheim in mind, puts it, 'The most "sacrilegious" attitude a person may take today is to be anti-humanistic, to be racialist . . .' (1984, p. 498). That this is so only makes sense if it is assumed that the great majority of us are now profoundly committed to 'humanity'.

The vitality of the tradition of humankindness is also revealed by turning to the 1960s. This might appear to be a strange place to look. Many see the 1960s as a key point in the collapse of the cultural, the rejection of traditions generating antinomian, relativistic, and self-centred outlooks. However, although there is much truth to the contention that established orders were rejected – at least by sectors of the population – the fact remains that significant numbers were committed to beliefs, values and practices which, in various ways, are bound up with the ethic of humanity. An obvious example is the civil rights movement. Whites supported black demand for 'the equality that belongs to them as human beings by natural and political right' (Bloom, 1987, p. 33). (The Civil Rights Act was signed in 1964.) A similar example is provided by all those who opposed the American presence in Vietnam, the North Vietnamese and the Vietcong being supported in the name of brotherhood and their right to self-determination. More generally, many in the 1960s adopted a clear set of values, liberal in nature whilst being shaped by their commitment to a Romantic or expressivist rendering of the ethic of humanity.[6] Far from respecting all others in relativistic fashion, this commitment ensured that core values – equality and freedom of expression – only applied to those seen to be living the true kind of life, namely one to do with authenticity, love, peace and community. Those living wrong ways of life – belonging to 'straight' society, for example – were harshly criticized.

Developments since the 1960s provide further evidence of vitality. One might consider new social movements, including the environmentalist and the spiritual.[7] In New Age circles, for example, the true self, seen as a holistic universal lying at the heart of all people, is explicitly sacralized. Furthermore, this true self is experienced as providing a 'touchstone which distinguishes good from evil' (to recall Durkheim's formulation), it serving to provide 'inner wisdom'. And in New Age-cum-environmentalist quarters, humanity is extended to the natural order as a whole and vice versa; all is held to share the same spirituality. Or one might consider the development of multi-culturalism. Multiculturalists emphasize difference. Radical forms aside, however, this is fuelled by faith in equality. (Most) ways of life are equally worthy of respect. And finally, one might consider the closely related development of political correctness. A primary aim of many of its advocates is the eradication of wrong kinds of differentiation. Those who are victimized should be enabled to exercise their rights; those who are politically incorrect should mend their ways. On the one hand, it will be noted, political correctness involves profound faith in human equality. On the other, however, it has an arguably illiberal, dogmatic edge to it. Couched in terms of substantive (often socialist) versions of what it is to be human, wrong ways of life are readily identified; freedom of speech is restricted; and measures – such as 'positive discrimination' – taken to enforce equality can serve to generate a sense of injustice. The politically-correct movement thus serves to highlight the egalitarian and exclusivizing aspects of the ethic of humanity.[8]

Overall, it cannot be doubted that humanistic liberalism serves as a powerful tradition. The importance attached to equal opportunities or to positive discrimination (as in the great Indian Mandel reforms), the role played by bodies such as the European Human Rights Commission, the establishment of the category 'crimes against humanity', the development of prizes – for example the Nobel – for contributions to 'humanity', and the activities of human rights groups, all serve to indicate the extent to which the ethic has become institutionalized. Its inclusivism, at the level of 'intrinsic human nature', informs the sentiments of all those who value, respect or strive to assist others, in particular those who suffer. Its discriminatory role in judging whether or not people are living the human life paves the way for action. And rather than 'perhaps nearing its end' – as Foucault and others suggest[9] – everything indicates that the ethic is growing in strength. It is difficult, today, to think of a nation where a substantial number of the population do not speak with this voice. One nation in particular serves to emphasize the point: India. Until quite recently dominated by exclusivistic caste ('untouchable' v. Brahmin), religious (Hindu v. Muslim), ethnic (tribal v. the rest) and imperialist (the West v. Indian) traditions, the ethic of humanity is now institutionalized in any number of ways; including the fact that it is a central component of the politically-dominant Congress Party.

DETRADITIONALIZATION AND THE DEVELOPMENT OF THE ETHIC

Detraditionalization involves loss of faith in established orders. For this to happen, a person has to become disengaged, that is, has to cease to be dominated by authoritative 'others'. More exactly, detraditionalizaton involves a shift to the authority of the 'individual' because the person has to acquire new 'individualistic' values – different from those provided by established orders – in order to lose faith in what has been on offer. As we have seen, most accounts of detraditionalization suppose that these values are of a self-centred, utilitarian, relativistic variety. However, and here Durkheim is re-introduced, it can also be argued that detraditionalization provides something approaching the necessary – although not necessary and sufficient – condition for the construction of the ethic of humanity.

In an especially significant passage, which will therefore be cited in its entirety, Durkheim states:

> Originally society is everything, the individual nothing. Consequently, the strongest social feelings are those connecting the individual with the collectivity; society is its own aim. Man is considered only an instrument in its hands; he seems to draw all his rights from it and has no counter-prerogative, because nothing higher than it exists. But gradually things change. As societies become greater in volume and density, they increase in complexity, work is divided, individual differences multiply, and the moment approaches when the only remaining bond among members of a single human group will be that they are all men. Under such conditions the body of collective sentiments inevitably attaches itself with all its strength to its single remaining object, communicating to this object an incomparable value by so doing. Since human personality is the only thing that appeals unanimously to all hearts, since its enhancement is the only aim that can be collectively pursued, it inevitably acquires exceptional value in the eyes of all. It thus rises far above all human aims, assuming a religious nature. (1952, p. 336; see also 1973, pp. 51–2)

An initial observation derives from the claim that 'the individual' is 'nothing' in societies where the 'collectivity' is all-important. However exaggerated this might be, a considerable amount of evidence suggests that embeddedness is associated with exclusivistic outlooks. Many socio-cultural orders, that is to say, serve to value their occupants so as to generate contextualized inequalities. To the extent that people are defined – or constituted – in terms of a particular socio-cultural formation, that formation serves to characterize their true way of being. Other socio-cultural formations, with their different ways of life, are accordingly seen to be associated with alien – and therefore invalid – modes of being. Such perceptions, it naturally follows, count against those experiences which might serve as the basis for holding a notion of the human which transcends socio-cultural differentiations.[10]

To the extent that 'strong' traditions serve to exclusivize what counts as human nature, the inclusivistic outlook can only develop under circumstances of detraditionalization. By definition, it goes without saying, the ethic is incompatible with strong tribal or national identities. Hence the importance Durkheim attaches to the claim that 'the moment approaches when *the only remaining bond* among the members of a single human group will be that they are all men' (my emphasis). But does detraditionalization provide something akin to the necessary *and sufficient* conditions for the construction of the ethic of humanity? Why should it not simply result in egoistical individualism? Durkheim argues, it will be recalled, that 'Since human personality is the only thing that appeals unanimously to all hearts, since its enhancement is the only aim that can be collectively pursued, it inevitably acquires exceptional value in the eyes of all.' Unfortunately, the argument is patently circular or tautological. What is supposedly being explained, namely the exceptional value ascribed to the human personality, is actually explained by the same thing, namely the unanimous appeal of human personality.

Durkheim's explanation hangs on an ontological commitment; a commitment even more clearly seen in such passages as 'The obligations laid upon us by both the one and the other arise *solely* from our intrinsic human nature or those with whom we find ourselves in relation' (1992, p. 3).[11] Detraditionalization thus serves to reveal an authentic human nature, an inner 'voice' which can direct detraditionalized selves in the right direction; whose virtues explain the construction, form and authority of the religion of humanity. And, it can be noted, such a Romantic or expressivist approach has played an important role among other theorists of the development of human values. One might think of the work of Peter Berger et al. (1974) on the expressivist-orientated 'homeless mind', David Harvey (1993) on 'ecosocialism' and Marx's 'species being', Charles Taylor (1991) on the 'ethic of authenticity' or Victor Turner (1974) on 'communitas'. Or one might think of Zygmunt Bauman, arguing that 'the end of morality as we know it' has enabled 'the moral capacity of the self' to come into its own (chapter 3; see also Bauman, 1993, pp. 248–9).

Detraditionalization has clearly played a role in paving the way for the construction of the tradition of humanity. The degree of value attributed to the self *qua* self is surely incompatible with socially-dominated views of personhood. The idea that there is a self 'above society' (as Durkheim (1952, p. 333) puts it) is surely incompatible with those selves generated by socio-cultural differentiations. And it is certainly safe to conclude that detraditionalization has played a crucial role in facilitating the operation of the ethic: human rights, for example, have only been able to come to serve as a virtually universal ethical standard – possessing validity across states and therefore entitling intervention – because the self-determining authority of nations has become weaker.[12] But appeal to 'intrinsic human nature' or a 'moral self' – to provide that inner authority which explains why detraditionalization has not simply led to egotistical, anarchical individualism – will only convince the converted.

What precisely has fuelled the ideology, in the West let alone elsewhere, that the 'non-social' self – belonging to humanity rather than to the differentiated cultural realm – is of primary value, constitutes a formidable task for intellectual inquiry. Indeed, rather than there being anything demonstrably 'natural' or self-evident about the notion of intrinsic human nature, the historical record of ideologies of inequality shows that much has counted against the idea.[13] There are no easy answers as to what has served to fuel a somewhat exceptional feature of cultural life. Christianity, for example, might appear to provide a ready solution, it being argued that the ethic has been inspired by relevant Biblical passages and subsequent teaching. However, the Bible can be read in many different ways (including those of an exclusivistic variety). Indeed, as John Passmore (1970) has argued, Christianity has very often taken an 'Augustinian' form, emphasizing the difference between those who are saved and those who are not. Considerations of this kind, together with the fact that the ethic of humanity did not become significant until relatively recently, suggest that widespread adoption of the 'humankind' interpretation of the Bible has almost certainly been determined by other factors.[14]

To complicate matters further, theorization of those processes which have fuelled the ethic of humanity cannot ignore all those other processes affecting moral beliefs. The ethic cannot be understood in isolation from all that it has to contend with. Exclusivizing tendencies are widespread in the West, let alone elsewhere. What counts as 'being properly human' is defined contextually, in terms of strong tradition-informed religious or ethnic criteria. The

'I am a man' slogans of the civil rights movement of the 1960s have in measure been replaced with the slogans – to do with 'Black consciousness' and 'Black nature' – of the radical, differentiating multiculturalist.[15] Then there are those tendencies involving another kind of contextualism, the self-referentiality of egoistic individualists taking precedence over humanistic values. In addition, and recalling the kind of claim made by Bloom, there are also tendencies encouraging that form of relativistic liberalism which emphasizes 'respect for the other'.

Furthermore, 'the problem of solidarity' has to be handled. As Durkheim (1915) argued forcefully, morality thrives when people *belong* to collectivities. Assemblies, rituals, a diverse range of group activities and communal practices, serve to generate and enhance commitment to moral values. Communitarians today argue along much the same lines. As Richard Bellamy (1992) puts it, 'They point out that we only acquire the capacity for judgement through living in real societies embodying those conceptions of the good which give our lives their particular purpose, meaning and character' (p. 236).[16] Bearing in mind that the ethic of humanity is associated with detraditionalized circumstances, the problem is thus one of identifying what has served to fuel its ethic of solidarity. The only answer, it would seem, is that its *own* practices – for example those taking place in schools – suffice to account for its potency.

ON THINGS NOT BEING WORSE AND THE VIRTUES OF HUMANITY

It is easy to criticize the ethic of humanity. Deconstructionists and proponents of more radical versions of multiculturalism and communitarianism have been having something of a field-day. It is argued that the ethic is a contingent construction rather than being informed by 'intrinsic human nature'. It is noted that the ethic is historically situated. It is pointed out that it is impossible to demonstrate that there is such a human nature. Or it is argued that human nature is itself constructed – by the socio-cultural – differences in this realm thereby ensuring that there is no such thing as the intrinsic or invariant. It is also argued that the ethic contains values which pull in different directions. As controversy over abortion serves to indicate, the right to choose can clash with the right to life; the value attached to toleration is contradicted by those values – including freedom – which ensure that certain forms of life cannot be countenanced. Furthermore, those seeking to propagate the ethic are accused of engaging in cultural imperialism. They are seen as seeking to impose their own view of what counts as 'being human' on those who hold different assumptions.[17]

However, such criticisms are not too worrying. The fact that it is not possible to 'ground' or demonstrate the ethic is a difficulty which faces all forms of ethicality. The ethic of humanity, in this regard, is no better or worse than any other. The fact that it is internally tension-laden or contradictory, it can be suggested, is not such a bad thing. Debate – for example over the exact limits of toleration – serves to ensure that the ethicality is vitalized. And as for the criticism concerning assimilatory cultural imperialism, an obvious point to make is that virtually every nation now has powerful political parties or organizations advocating human values. To suppose that those in the West who have sought to encourage human rights in, say, South Africa, are behaving as cultural imperialists is to ignore the fact that such countries have their own liberation movements. By definition, those holding *human* values do not believe that politics should end at Dover or Heathrow; and only feel gratified when international intervention succeeds.[18]

As for arguing in favour of the ethic, the case is that it stands as the best bulwark – at least the best that we have – against two harmful tendencies. One concerns the development of strong, exclusivizing traditions. The historical record, especially of this century, shows quite clearly that such traditions – whether religious, quasi-religious or secular – do more harm than good. Serving to distinguish between those who belong and those who do not, the latter are demeaned. Most radically, they are not held to be human. A great many of the estimated 200 million killed by conflict during this century would not have died were it not for the fact that they were embroiled in attempts to construct utopian traditions. And today – a time when, as Edward Said (1994) puts it, 'a new and in my opinion appalling tribalism is fracturing societies, separating peoples, promoting greed [and] bloody conflict' – *belief* in the ethic of humanity is as important as ever. Thinking of India, for example, there is little doubting the fact that communal violence would be much greater than it is were it not for the powerfully institutionalized politics of humankindness carried out by the – necessarily 'secular' – state. In short, the *cultural* differentiations of pluralistic or multicultural societies are one thing; strongly traditionalized differentiations, where cultural distinctions come to erode faith in shared human nature, are another.[19]

The other harmful tendency has to do with the opposite process, namely loss of tradition. Attention is here directed to the development of self-interest. Instead of those dangers which ensue from too strong an attachment with a collectivity, the danger now is associated with the individual coming to take precedence over what it is to belong to humanity. Rather than being prepared to exercise commitments for the public good, those involved are only concerned with their own, immediate gratifications.

Overall then, the ethic of humanity might only be a great myth. But this tradition plays a crucial role in curtailing tendencies which lead beyond 'being human': either to the 'I' which is fundamentally differentiated from others because it *belongs* to a tradition, or to the 'I' which simply dwells on *itself*.

CONCLUSION

Thinking of the main themes addressed in this volume, material has been presented which shows that radical detraditionalization theory is wrong: minimally to the extent that it ignores a central tradition of our times, and one which has helped arrest undoubted tendencies leading to cultural collapse. The development of the ethic of humanity, together with a range of other factors which cannot be explored here, serves to ensure that our cultural history is much too complicated to be captured in terms of designators marking periods in the fate of tradition. Contra Giddens (1994), we are not 'living in a post-traditional society'. Traditions come and go and come; relativizing processes co-exist with those fuelling cultural identity politics; different moral trajectories – as described by Durkheim (1973), Charles Taylor (1989) or Robert Bellah et al. (1985) – compete for attention. Theorization of detraditionalization must interplay with theorization of tradition-maintenance, construction and re-construction.

Considering the value of the ethic of humanity, the argument has been that we are living in a world where this ethic is *effective*. The liberal state has always been faced with a dilemma. On the one hand there is the emphasis on freedom, the ideal being to allow individuals to live according to the dictates of their own rational consciences. Accordingly, the state should have as little authority as possible; indeed, should be as value-open as possible. On the other hand, there is the liberal emphasis on certain substantive values, including equality and the prevention of unnecessary suffering. Accordingly, state intervention is encouraged. During the last two centuries, the emphasis on freedom has certainly meant that the liberal state has dismantled certain strong traditions which previously reigned supreme. The public sphere has been detraditionalized, this in the sense that religious and monarchical underpinnings have been marginalized. At the same time the state has had to exercise control. The ethic of humanity has become the dominant tradition of the democratic state, providing, as it does, a compromise solution to the problem of freedom and authority. Freedom, that is to say, is important, but only if it takes the right kind of form. If properly sustained, in particular through educational practices, the humanist tradition of cultivating freedom should serve well for the future. Given where the autonomy of difference can lead, the identification of selfhood with universal values of humankindness is surely a pressing cultural imperative. The voice of human authority must counter the processes whereby cultural factors serve to discriminate at the level of human 'nature'.

NOTES

1 Another illustration (of which there are many) of how universalistic liberal values are qualified is provided by the passage, 'So long as his conduct has not caused him to forfeit the title of man, he seems to us to share in some degree in that quality *sui generis* ascribed by every religion to its gods' (Durkheim, 1952, p. 333).

2 Others who have drawn attention to the growing importance of substantive liberalism include Louis Dumont (who writes of 'the independent, autonomous, and thus essentially nonsocial moral being, who carries our paramount values and is found primarily in our modern ideology of man and society' (1986, p. 25)), and J. Salwyn Schapiro (who begins with Hobhouse's view that liberalism has become 'an all-penetrating element of the life-structure of the modern world' (1958, p. 3)). For a more critical portrayal, see Richard Bellamy (1992); for a more optimistic one, see Francis Fukuyama (1992).

3 Or as Max Weber puts it, liberalism and 'the old individualistic principle of "inalienable human rights" which to us in Western Europe seem as "trivial" as black bread is to the man who has enough to eat' (1978, p. 281).

4 Antonio Cassese (1990) in particular sees human rights as being bound up with notions of what it is to be human rather than simply being associated with the idea of obtaining 'freedom from' the state. He notes, for example, that the American Declarations of 1776–89 and the French Declaration of 1789 'emphatically proclaim a particular *conception of man and society*' (1990, p. 24). More generally, the role played by the cultural value of human 'potential' is also noted (e.g., p. 62).

5 According to Dumont, for example, 'the human individual as a value appears only in the ideology of modern societies' (1986, p. 215). See also Michel Foucault, on what he considers to be the quite recent appearance of 'the figure of man' (1992, p. 386). Edmund Leach notes that as late as 1870 'polygeny was the dominant orthodoxy in scientific circles throughout Europe and America' (1982, p. 71); and, more generally, that the notion that 'man' is 'born free and equal' is 'not shared by humanity at large' (p. 58). Not until this century were people in the West seen as equal enough for them all to obtain the right to vote. There

were an estimated 15,000 slaves and runaways in Britain just two hundred years ago.

6   The Romantic movement is profoundly imbued with the ethic: Schiller's 'Ode to Joy', put to music by Beethoven (the fourth movement of the Ninth Symphony) and, it might be added, now rendered as the European Union anthem, serves as an indication. The value Schiller attached to the phrase, 'All men become brothers' or, elsewhere, 'the inner unity of human nature', was widely shared by Romantics. See, for example, M. H. Abrams (1971) and Richard Unger (1975).

7   Stephen Crook et al. draw on research which indicates that some 20 per cent of the adult population of Western Europe declare support for such movements (1992, p. 141). For a general account, see Meredith Veldman (1994).

8   The Prince of Wales has recently drawn attention to what he considers to be political correctness's excessive exclusivism, writing of the 'fashion for . . . testing everything . . . against a predetermined, pre-ordained view, and rejecting it if it does not measure up, so that people feel intimidated and brow-beaten . . .' (*Daily Telegraph*, 5 May 1994, p. 1).

9   Gilles Lipovetsky (1992), Jean-François Lyotard (1986) and Zygmunt Bauman (1993) are among those who go further than Foucault in proposing that the grand metanarrative to do with emancipating humanity has been de-legitimated; has fallen into ruin.

10 The classic anthropological analysis of this is provided by K. E. Read: the Gahuka-Gama (Eastern Highlands of New Guinea) do not 'separate the individual from the social context and, ethically speaking, [do not] grant him an intrinsic moral value apart from that which attaches to him as an occupant of a particular status' (1967, p. 196). Concerning the general point being made, see Dumont's claim concerning 'the exclusivism or absolute ethnocentricism that accompanies every holistic ideology' (1986, p. 207). The ethnographic record, it can be added, contains countless examples of 'traditional' societies which, like the Gahuku-Gama, operate with contextually embedded moralities which serve to devalue others.

11 See also his contention that, 'It is this quality ["their intrinsic quality of human nature"] that quite naturally becomes the supreme object of collective sensibility' (Durkheim, 1992, p. 112).

12 As Davidson observes, the situation today 'stands in stark contrast to the pre-1939 era when the systematic and large-scale violation of human rights by governments went unacknowledged and unaddressed by other members of the international system' (1993, p. 163).

13 As Durkheim himself notes, 'in fact we are unequal. We have neither the same physical force, nor the same intellectual power, nor the same energy or will' (cited in Pickering, 1979, p. 72). Furthermore, as we have seen, members of many societies assume that cultural differences are bound up with differences between 'us' and 'them'. Even for the 'enlightened', it is not clear how 'Man'

can be discerned among the culturally different. In a famous passage, 'I have seen in my time Frenchmen, Italians and Russians. I even know, thanks to Montesquieu, that one may be a Persian, but as for Man, I declare that I have never met him in my life; if he exists it is without my knowledge' (Joseph de Maistre, cited by Leach, 1982, p. 56).

14 Durkheim himself thought that Christianity had played an important role in the development of the ethic. (A useful summary of his views is provided by Pickering, 1984, pp. 422ff). Dumont also emphasizes the role played by Christian teachings (1982); see also the responses by Bellah (1982) and S. N. Eisenstadt (1983). Another kind of explanation, concentrating on the development of egalitarianism, is provided by Ernest Gellner (1983). The argument is that 'the overwhelming thirst for economic growth' requires population mobility; and this in turn results in egalitarian values (p. 25; cf. Durkheim, 1964, p. 400). A problem in this regard, however, is that mobility increases pluralism; and there is evidence to suggest that traditions – with their differentiating tendencies – thrive in pluralistic settings. (See, for example, Finke, 1992.) Barrington Moore (1967) is succinct: 'No bourgeois, no democracy' (p. 418). Francis Fukuyama (1992), influenced by Hegel, argues that 'the quest for recognition' has played a crucial role in the development of the liberal ethic. Charles Taylor (1989) provides an account of how a number of philosophers have attempted to ground human values (e.g., pp. 410–12).

15 As Allan Bloom says of the Black Power movement, 'Its demand was for black identity, not universal rights. Not rights, but power counted. It insisted on respect for blacks as blacks, not as human being simply' (1987, p. 33). See also John Fiske on the '"weak" racism' advocated by some of those engaged in cultural identity politics (1993, p. 267).

16 See, for example, Richard Rorty (1989); cf. Norman Geras (1994).

17 The cultural-imperialism criticism is perhaps the most frequently encountered today. It is especially forcefully made by those multiculturalists who emphasize the value of difference. Gianni Vattimo (1992), for example, claims that 'ethnic, sexual, religious, cultural, or aesthetic minorities' have been 'repressed and cowed into silence by the idea of a single true form of humanity that must be realized irrespective of particularity and individual finitude, transience, and contingency' (p. 9). See also the criticisms made by John Fiske (1993). (James Hunter (1994), especially chapter 7, provides a useful summary.) Zygmunt Bauman (1993) engages in a more wide-ranging critique of the ethic, arguing that 'while universal values offer a reasonable medicine against the oppressive obtrusiveness of parochial backwaters . . . [the] drug when taken regularly turns into poison (p. 239). John Carroll (1993) provides a quite spectacular attack on humanism. Jean Baudrillard (1993) claims that 'discourse on the rights of man . . . is pious, weak, useless and hypocritical' (p. 85). Edmund Leach (1982) provides a considered assessment of human-based values, agreeing with Gramsci – '"human nature is the totality of historically determined social relations"' – and therefore

concluding, 'we have tried, by political coercion and propaganda, to impose on man, as cultural moral being, a . . . sense of unity which contradicts the very essence of our *human* nature' (pp. 78, 85).

18   Are we not entitled to be proud that Nelson Mandela's victory speech, on winning the 1994 election, specifically thanked those outside the country who had helped end apartheid: 'To the people of South Africa and the world who are watching: this is a joyous night for the human spirit. This is your victory, too. You helped end apartheid, you stood with us through the transition.' Another way of objecting to the cultural-imperialism critique is that the world's great religious traditions have their *own* ethics of humankindness (see Leroy Rouner (ed.), 1988).

19   Seyla Benhabib (1992), some of the contributors to Judith Squires (ed.) (1993), and Paul Yonnet (1993) are among recent authors to have argued for universalized values.

REFERENCES

Abrams, M. H. 1971: *Natural Supernaturalism*. London: W. W. Norton.

Baudrillard, Jean 1993: *The Transparency of Evil*. London: Verso.

Bauman, Zygmunt 1993: *Postmodern Ethics*. Oxford: Blackwell.

Bellamy, Richard 1992: *Liberalism and Modern Society*. Cambridge: Polity.

Bellah, Robert 1982: Responses to Louis Dumont's 'A Modified View of our Origins: The Christian Beginnings of Modern Individualism'. *Religion*, 12, pp. 83–91.

Bellah, Robert, et al. 1985: *Habits of the Heart*. London: University of California Press.

Benhabib, Seyla 1992: *Situating the Self*. Cambridge: Polity.

Berger, Peter, et al. 1974: *The Homeless Mind*. Harmondsworth: Penguin.

Berger, Peter 1979: *The Heretical Imperative*. New York: Anchor Press/Doubleday.

Bloom, Allan 1987: *The Closing of the American Mind*. New York: Simon and Schuster.

Carroll, John 1993: *Humanism: The Rebirth and Wreck of Western Culture*. London: Fontana.

Cassese, Antonio 1990: *Human Rights in a Changing World*. Cambridge; Polity.

Crook, Stephen, et al. 1992: *Postmodernization. Change in Advanced Society*. London: Sage.

Davidson, Scott 1993: *Human Rights*. Buckingham: Open University Press.

Dumont, Louis 1982: A Modified View of our Origins: The Christian Beginnings of Modern Individualism. *Religion*, 12, pp. 1–27.

Dumont, Louis 1986: *Essays on Individualism*. London: University of Chicago Press.

Durkheim, Emile 1915: *The Elementary Forms of the Religious Life*. London: George Allen & Unwin.

Durkheim, Emile .1952: *Suicide*. London: Routledge & Kegan Paul.

Durkheim, Emile 1961: *Moral Education*. Glencoe: Free Press.

Durkheim, Emile 1964: *The Division of Labor in Society*. London: Collier Macmillan.

Durkheim, Emile 1973: Individualism and the Intellectuals. In Robert Bellah (ed.), *Emile Durkheim. On Morality and Society*, London: University of Chicago Press, pp. 43–57.

Durkheim, Emile 1975: *Durkheim on Religion*, edited by W. S. F. Pickering. London: Routledge & Kegan Paul.

Durkheim, Emile 1992: *Professional Ethics and Civic Morals*. London: Routledge.

Eisenstadt, S. N. 1983: Transcendental Visions – Other Worldliness – and its Transformations. *Religion*, 13, pp. 1–17.

Finke, Roger 1992: An Unsecular America. In Steve Bruce (ed.), *Religion and Modernization*, Oxford: Clarendon, pp. 145–69.

Fiske, John 1993: *Power Plays Power Works*. London: Verso.

Foucault, Michel 1992: *The Order of Things*. London: Routledge.

Freud, Sigmund 1960, in Ernest L. Freud (ed.), *Letters of Sigmund Freud*. London: Hogarth Press.

Fukuyama, Francis 1992: *The End of History and the Last Man*. Harmondsworth: Penguin.

Galbraith, John Kenneth 1992: *The Culture of Contentment*. London: Houghton Mifflin.

Gehlen, Arnold 1980: *Man in the Age of Technology*. New York: Columbia University Press.

Gellner, Ernest 1983: *Nations and Nationalism*. Oxford: Basil Blackwell.

Geras, Norman 1994: Richard Rorty and the Righteous among the Nations. In Ralph Miliband and Leo Panitch (eds), *Socialist Register 1994 (Between Globalism and Nationalism)*, London: Merlin Press, pp. 32–59.

Giddens, Anthony 1990: *The Consequences of Modernity*. Cambridge: Polity.

Giddens, Anthony 1991: *Modernity and Self-Identity*. Cambridge: Polity.

Giddens, Anthony 1994: Living in a Post-traditional Society. In Ulrich Beck, Anthony Giddens and Scott Lash, *Reflexive Modernization*, Cambridge: Polity, pp. 56–109.

Harvey, David 1993: The Nature of Environment: Dialectics of Social and Environmental Change. In Ralph Miliband and Leo Panitch (eds), *Socialist Register 1993*, London: Merlin Press, pp. 1–52.

Hunter, James Davison 1994: *Before the Shooting Begins*. Oxford: Maxwell Macmillan International.

Jameson, Fredric 1991: *Postmodernism*. London: Verso.

Lasch, Christopher 1985: *The Minimal Self*. London: Picador.

Leach, Edmund 1982: *Social Anthropology*. London: Fontana.

Lipovetsky, Gilles 1992: *Le Crépuscule du Devoir*. Paris: Gallimard.

Lyotard, Jean-François 1986: *The Postmodern Condition: A Report on Knowledge*. Manchester: Manchester University Press.

MacIntyre, Alasdair 1985: *After Virtue*. London: Duckworth.

MacIntyre, Alasdair 1991: How to Seem Virtuous without Actually Being So. Lancaster University: Centre for the Study of Cultural Values, Occasional Papers Series.

Moore, Barrington 1967: *Social Origins of Dictatorship and Democracy*. London: Allen Lane.

Passmore, John 1970: *The Perfectibility of Man*. London: Duckworth.

Pickering, William (ed.) 1979: *Durkheim: Essays on Morals and Education*. London: Routledge & Kegan Paul.

Pickering, William 1984: *Durkheim's Sociology of Religion*. London: Routledge & Kegan Paul.

Read, K. E. 1967: Morality and the Concept of the Person among the Gahuku-Gama. In John Middleton (ed.), *Myth and Cosmos*, New York: Natural History Press, pp. 185–230.

Rorty, Richard 1989: *Contingency, Irony, and Solidarity*. Cambridge: Cambridge University Press.

Rouner, Leroy (ed.) 1988: *Human Rights and the World's Religions*. Indiana: University of Notre Dame Press.

Said, Edward 1994: Cited by Stephen Amidon, The Closing of the Liberal Mind, *The Sunday Times*, 'The Culture Essay', 6 November 1994, pp. 10–12.

Sandel, Michael 1982: *Liberalism and the Limits of Justice*. Cambridge: Cambridge University Press.

Schapiro, J. Salwyn 1958: *Liberalism. Its Meaning and History*. London: D. Van Nostrand.

Squires, Judith (ed.) 1993: *Principled Positions*. London: Lawrence & Wishart.

Tagore, Rabindranath 1961: *The Religion of Man*. London: Unwin Books.

Taylor, Charles 1989: *Sources of the Self*. Cambridge: Cambridge University Press.

Taylor, Charles 1991: *The Ethics of Authenticity*. London: Harvard University Press.

Turner, Victor 1974: *The Ritual Process*. Harmondsworth: Penguin.

Unger, Richard 1975: *Holderlin's Major Poetry*. London: Indiana University Press.

Vattimo, Gianni 1992: *The Transparent Society*. Baltimore: Johns Hopkins University Press.

Veldman, Meredith 1994: *Fantasy, the Bomb, and the Greening of Britain*. Cambridge: Cambridge University Press.

Weber, Max 1978: in W. G. Runciman (ed.), *Selections in Translation*. Cambridge: Cambridge University Press.

Yonnet, Paul 1993: *Voyage au Centre du Malaise Français*. Paris: Gallimard.

12

Community Beyond Tradition

Paul Morris

'WHAT CONSTITUTES THIS WE?' (LYOTARD, 1992, p. 25)

Everyone, but everyone, is for community. Our politicians, of the old and the new, Left and Right; our political philosophers; our religious leaders; our modern and postmodern theorists appear to share little but their pious promotion of 'community'. The demands on us to (re)create community are incessant and ubiquitous. We are besieged by calls to support community: our local community; our regional community; our national community; the European Community, and the international community. We are to support community policing; community medicine; community planning; community care; community architecture; community churches, and community schools. As Raymond Williams notes, community, 'unlike all the other terms of social organization (state, nation, society, etc.) . . . never seems to be used unfavourably, and never to be given any positive opposing or distinguishing term' (Williams, 1976, p. 66).

'Community' has myriad meanings ranging from the most benign, if all too often misguided, general social concern ('the hermeneutics of the warm tummy') to the New Right's cynical dismantling of statutory welfare provision and services in the name of the 'autonomy of local communities'. We hear two often repeated refrains that highlight the popular ambiguity about community. The first (the story of liberal freedom) reports a communal authority and tradition that challenges the right of an individual to be her own authority and undermines the individual's freedom of choice, as in the case of arranged marriages, or the children of Jehovah Witnesses who are refused blood transfusions. The only antidote to this tale of the coercive nature of all 'traditional' communities is the autonomous, free-to-choose, liberal individual. The second (the organicist) stresses the intensification of individualism, fostered by the institutions of an absolute and impersonal modern capitalism. This 'selfishness' serves to render the traditionless self utterly alone, bereft of personal connections, de-politicized, without clear guidance or certainty, and raises the very question of the possibility of any community at all in today's world. The only antidote to this woeful narrative is to try to overcome this loss of community by striving for a renewed sense of collective purpose, shared values and the common good.

DETRADITIONALIZATION, RE-TRADITIONALIZATION AND COMMUNITY

The parallel processes of detraditionalization and re-traditionalization allow us to grasp something of our contemporary ambivalence concerning community. The first refers to the complex process of the undermining of established communal authority, resulting in the dis-embedding of particular traditions and specific customary practices within the life of a given community. Re-traditionalization is the parallel process in which the 'tradition' to be overcome (detraditionalized) is constructed in opposition to, and normally as an earlier stage of, the detraditionalized present. This redefining and reworking of the past actually creates that past. Community, whatever our understanding, in order to be community, must have duration and thus must necessarily entail some notion of tradition.

One can trace, for example, the transformation of modern Jewish communities since the granting of citizenship rights in the aftermath of the French Revolution. This process of detraditionalization involved: the redefinition of 'Jew', formally at least, on individual rather than communal grounds; the loss of earlier communal authorities; the 'modernization' of synagogue services; the development of rational forms of Judaism; the relativization of the importance of the existing education and its hierarchies; the breakdown of the cultural barriers between Jews and gentiles; and the creation of a Judaism compatible with citizenship, modern education, and professional life. In order to legitimate the new forms and views there was a simultaneous reworking, or re-creation, of the traditions of the past (re-traditionalizing). The past was re-envisaged in either prejudicial or romantic ways. Prejudicially by many, the past was reconstructed as the time of isolation before the modern freedoms. Romantically by others, the past was re-figured as a perfect model of a community life offering security, certainty and a place in the grand scheme of things. The past ('tradition') was thus invented (re-membered) to suit current purposes.

These two intimately connected, and mutually constitutive, processes redefined a new mode of detraditionalized 'identity' *and* constructed a re-traditionalized model of the tradition that was to be 'overcome'. Parallel to the modern discourse of the freedom of the individual, and a necessary part of it, we also find the organicist model of the traditional life that it claimed to supersede (prejudicial for some, romantic for others). As a community undergoes detraditionalization, its 'past' becomes frozen, as it were, in its re-traditionalized ('pre-modern') form. The ancient traditions, that the conservatives among us seek to revive and recover, are the co-products of the very detraditionalizing held to account for their demise. So, for example, the calls for a return to the timeless ways of traditional Judaism usually require a return to the early or mid-nineteenth century, as in the case of 'traditional' seminary syllabuses, or forms of communal organization. Are these the only options – coercive community or an un-collection of isolated individuals?

Modernity in this fashion can be viewed as a particular, historical intensification (and increased frequency) of the processes of detraditionalization. Recently, we have begun to recognize and theorize the beginnings of the widespread detraditionalization of modernity – something akin to what Seyla Benhabib calls the 'disenchantment of modernity itself' (Benhabib, 1992, p. 68). The established and embedded practices and discourses of modernity are now being challenged and modernity re-traditionalized in a variety of ways. But whether we refer to our times as high modernity, late modernity or postmodernity, it is clear, as Joseph Heller entitled his novel, that, *Something Happened* (Heller, 1972). The calling into question of all forms of authority and tradition, including those of modernity (for example, the liberal consensus, the state, and the autonomous individual), leads us to the consciousness that something indeed seems to have happened to our communities. In addition, there are a host of new communal forms evident within our midst. These concerns are reflected in the renewed interest in the issue of community in recent years across a range of academic disciplines and practices.[1] Zygmunt Bauman is surely right when he writes that postmodernity, which he glosses as the 'age of contingency' is also 'the age of community': 'of the lust for community, the search for community, the invention of community, imagining community' (Bauman, 1991, p. 246; and this volume).

In this chapter I intend to argue for two positions. First, not all communities are of the same type, and we therefore need differential understanding of 'community'. This issue is addressed in the last section of the chapter, where two radically different models of community are developed. Secondly, in the present liberal era with our growing suspicions concerning the various modernist programmes for the creation of *community beyond tradition*, paradoxically, we find that the attempt to go beyond tradition actually (re)constructs those very traditions and leads us back to 'traditional' communities. The community beyond tradition is tradition itself.

The new focus on community is both a critique and a re-formulation of a number of the classical themes of modernity. The various modernizing projects were all concerned with the construction of new and improved, detraditionalized, communal forms (such as the Marxist aim of restoring the alienated individual to community), that is, *community beyond tradition*. Presently there is a growing awareness that the conceptual schemes of modernity serve only to obscure and conceal the nature of community. The liberal 'doctrine' of individual freedom (from tradition), and the subsequent attempts to generate the world from the 'subject', became incorporated in dominant versions of the grand progressive narratives of modernity. One form of this is to be found in the discernible shift from community to association, from tradition to modernity, from the care and understanding of family, friends and neighbours to connections based on a recognition of the separateness and independence of a set of actors involved in a diverse set of relationships. Although the crudity of this story of the detraditionalization and transformation of community into association has long been recognized and its modifications are legion, it is the attempt itself – of theorizing the collective starting from the individual – that is problematic.[2]

Beginning from the assumption of the existence and reality of the individual, who then, and only then, forges links between herself and other separate and discrete individuals, it becomes all but impossible to conceive of any sort of community at all. One plus one plus one plus one plus one just never seem to add up to more than a number! This separating out of individuals, so well portrayed by Michel Foucault, just does not let us put Humpty Dumpty together again (Foucault, 1980). These attempts flounder from the first and require the development of all sorts of strange notions, linking individuals to each other, in order to account for the reality of community: Emile Durkheim's 'collective consciousness'; Geog Simmel's 'shared social *a priori*'; Ferdinand Tonnies' 'organic will', and Talcott Parsons's 'values orientation'. (See Birnbaum and Leca, 1990, pp. 62–92.)

It is important to note that *each and every theory of the individual necessarily entails some account of how individuals become, or should become, aggregated*. Our difficulty is with these models of aggregation. Individual subjects can only form collectivities by association, by covenant, by contract, by agreement, and by consent. The 'tradition' of liberalism insists that this consent be freely given. Even the language of collectivities betrays an incipient individualism by begging the question: a collection of what? Individuals/subjects. There is in all this a recognition that something has happened, something has been lost. But to commence with the individual subject can only lead to conceptual impoverishment and, at best, most inadequate accounts of community.

Christianity can be seen as a two-thousand-year quest for the creation of a wholly non-violent, non-coercive, perfect and equal community (Milbank, 1990). Here, we intend only to briefly examine one modern alternative to 'traditional' forms of community, an alternative that developed, in part, out of these Christian reflections. We will return to Christian notions of community more fully below. The Pauline model of a new community, consisting of relatively isolated individuals (detraditionalized Jews and Greeks) reconstituted in Christ as the New Israel, was re-presented by later Christian thinkers (Galatians, 3: 28–30). In Augustine, the separate individuals are to be reconstructed, through the *mysterium* (mystery) of the sacrament of the Mass, into the unity of the body of Christ, so that each single one participates by overcoming his isolation in the single communion-body. It is this repeated re-enactment that creates and re-creates the Christian community. In this sense, Christian(s) and Christ are mutually constitutive (Augustine, 1977).

The seventeenth- and eighteenth-century theorists of the 'state' revived this Augustinian model, replacing the individual Christian who overcomes his isolation by participating in *corpus Christi*, the life (body) of Christ, with the individual citizen who overcomes his separateness by participation in the 'body politic', in the life of the state. This participation was to create the national community. Paul's demand that the participants (in Christ) be detraditionalized in terms of *ethnos* and gender, is paralleled in the modern state by insistence that the differences of occupation, locality, dialect, race, gender and religion are irrelevant to the individual's absolute status as a participating citizen. This is the basis of the claim that the modern liberal programme created a 'neutral' space – *beyond tradition and community* – in order to allow for the 'new community'. An alternative formulation of this thesis is that 'democracy' requires 'the absence of community' as its foundation (Lasch, 1991, p. 464). The state and the citizen are mirror images of each other – each is an absolute subject in a philosophical sense. The model of the nation-state as national community has been a most significant alternative to 'traditional' community.

NATION AS COMMUNITY

The nation-state is presently being detraditionalized. The impending, or at least threatened, collapse of the self-determining state is intimately linked to a parallel 'deconstruction' of the self-determining citizen (individual). The

modern state is challenged from above by the promise of 'communities' of
states, and from below by the growth of sub-national 'communities', often
calling for their own national status (Hobsbawm, 1990, pp. 182–3). While
the fragility of one form, at least, of the modernist state is clearly evidenced
in the case of the former Yugoslavia, the sub-national challenge is manifest
globally as the communal identification of 'citizens' assumes more concrete
and local forms (Friedman, 1989, pp. 61–2).

The nation-state has failed to produce the promised new community. The
state is being re-thought and re-configured, in part, because of the perceived
failure of the universality, effect, and impact of its modes of participation.
The language (including the symbols and rituals of participation) of the
nation-state is being interrogated in terms of other more inclusive and less
coercive understandings of community. So, for example, Benedict Anderson
contrasts a notion of 'real', that is, local community – where each knows his
neighbour – with the imagined national community where all citizens can
only have an imaginary 'image of their communion' with each other (Anderson,
1983, p. 6). This challenge also holds true, of course, for the so-called ethnic,
sub-national communities – Anderson argues that every community beyond
the face-to-face village community is 'imagined', and he even questions whether
this too might be imagined. The fiftieth anniversary of the end of the Second
World War serves to remind us forcefully of the other face of the nation-state
– National Socialism. In the totalitarian state, the Leader becomes the single
authority and all other voices are suppressed. Here, individual identities
(those defined as acceptable) are submerged in the absolute subject of the
Leader and participation is reduced to obedience. This represents a common
life of shared values, but is this what we mean by community? The spectre
of Nazism (and, to a lesser degree, Stalinism) continues to haunt the discourse on community and has led to a series of reflections on the organicist,
single body (or subject) model of community and, perhaps, to the premature
conclusion that all such communities are by definition not only coercive but
potentially totalitarian. This is the national community/nation-state as inverted Augustinian nightmare.

'. . . A PERSON NECESSARILY BELONGS' (A. HELLER, 1984, p. 34)

The hope that out of the modern, liberal, so-called democratic nation-states
something of the past sense of community can be retrieved and, at least, a
core of values held in common can be recovered, is associated with a group
of thinkers collectively known as communitarians. Their heart-felt lament at

the loss of community – a shared culture of institutions, moral values and practices – leads them to envisage new modes of participation in order to recover the public sphere for the citizen and thus regenerate her political agency. *The Responsive Community*, a communitarian journal edited by Amitai Etzioni, seeks to bridge the gap between communitarian thinking and political practice and has been influential in shaping the agendas of the political parties of the centre both in the United States and in Britain. (See Atkinson, 1994, for a recent British example.) Etzioni's new study highlights a number of the major communitarian themes: the strengthening of family life (making divorce more difficult, promoting more active parenting supported by appropriate legislation), encouraging political participation at all levels (particularly the local but also the regional and national), and shifting the liberal emphasis on rights to responsibilities (Etzioni, 1994).

Although communitarians have constructed elaborate histories of communitarian thought, their recent career begins with a series of critical reactions to Rawl's work on justice (Rawls, 1971; MacIntyre, 1985; Walzer, 1983, 1990; Taylor, 1989, 1991, 1992; and Sandel, 1982). The communitarians object, albeit in different ways, to Rawl's argument that justice requires that the state ensures the *rights* of the individual, who should then be free to rationally pursue his chosen goals. They argue that this view rests on a view of the individual that not only entails an illegitimate evacuation of history and memory but denies the possibility of community by pitting the individual's rights against society. They contend that individuals are not separate and atomistic at all, but formed, and constituted, in, and by, their families and local communities. The self, they argue, is a much richer and more contextualized notion than the liberals will allow, and prioritizing the justice of the rights of the individual is an unwarranted reduction of the reality and complexity of the self and its attachments. For example, MacIntyre contends that the liberal rejection of tradition and its insistence that values are an individual concern entails that morality too becomes a matter of individual choice. He argues that a liberal society cannot generate virtue, the foundation of any community.

Communitarians tend to be somewhat politically conservative and the programme to shore up communal and family values can easily degenerate into a backward looking ('back to basics') campaign, with the rejection of many of the hard won liberal freedoms. Some communitarians are quite explicit about their willingness to sacrifice individual 'rights' to the greater communal good. Others insist that this modern conflict between the individual and social collective will dissolve when their relationship is correctly understood. Yet others struggle to advocate strong communities while maintaining select individual freedoms. Nowhere is this tension more evident than in the work of Charles Taylor. His 'romanticism' entails a more positive evaluation of the 'expressive self' than is usual among communitarians and leads him to defend central features of these individual freedoms while seeking to redefine them in communitarian terms.

Taylor focuses on what he calls the 'culture of authenticity', a peculiarly modern and now dominant development (Taylor, 1991, p. 25). So dominant, in fact, that he finds it inconceivable to contemplate a return to a pre-authentic era. Authenticity is an awareness (or experience) of our own authentic nature, which Taylor likens to a 'revelation' ('a revelation through expression') that no-one else can live my life for me – it is my life based on my choices (cf. the popular record 'It's My Life') (ibid., p. 61). We no longer seek the God or Good ('the model of how to live') outside of ourselves, but 'within' (ibid., pp. 26, 29). Authenticity (as a form of 'individual self-fulfilment'), when set within the framework of atomistic notions of the self and an 'instrumental reason' colonizing all aspects of our lives, leads inevitably to our present malaise – widespread de-politicization and the reduction of all relationships to the instrumental utilization of other people. This renders any 'strong' sense of community an impossibility and represents the complete breakdown and fragmentation of our culture, reducing it to a 'system' of pluralized, unbridled self-determining freedoms, where the only value is choice itself.

Taylor seeks to rescue authenticity from liberalism. He argues that for our values (indicated by choice) to be meaningful at all, some values (choices) must be more significant than others. We cannot just 'invent' these values and choose to act accordingly, for this would indeed be 'crazy', and anyway empirically this is just not the case (1991, p. 36). Our choices only make sense against the background of our language and culture, our embeddedness in our communities and their prior hierarchical ordering of the relative importance of the particular values to be found, and/or desired, in that community. We work out our values and choices in a 'dialogical setting that binds us to others' (ibid., p. 62). He advocates re-establishing the links between authenticity and its communal contexts so that we recognize the bonds of solidarity and the communal demands entailed by our choices.

For Taylor, community already necessarily exists. But we need to recognize it and the part that it plays in generating the very possibilities of authenticity. We are already connected, but live under the sway of a rhetoric that explicitly denies this. This recognition of our existing communal relationships will regenerate our sense of community as the moral demands beyond pure choice (that is, beyond our selves), and the facticity of our unconditional relationships become the conscious basis of our thought and action. Taylor asks us to recognize that 'we are embodied agents, living in dialogical conditions, inhabiting time in a specifically human way, that is, making sense of our lives as a story that connects that past from which we have come to our future projects' (1991, pp. 105–6).

How does Taylor propose to bring this recognition of the moral dimension of our choices to effect the regeneration of community? How do we return from the *novum* of authenticity to 'strong' community? As communal values cannot just be imposed by some authority or other without fatally undermining authenticity,[3] he calls for a (public) debate over the meaning and significance of authenticity. Those who do recognize their communal obligations should seek to think and act accordingly and take upon themselves the task of 'persuading' others of the reality of their embeddedness and the demands incumbent upon them. It is hard to imagine, given the asymmetry of power, such persuasion having much effect without actually becoming coercive. Etzioni's 'persuasion', by means of policy changes in family law (including enforced time off work for both mothers and fathers to encourage responsible parenting) and changes in the structure of local government, appears to be as coercive as any other programme of socio-cultural engineering, certainly on a par with his detested, liberal welfare policies.

Taylor's is a community whose existence requires its 'members' to be persuaded that it exists at all! At least part of this confusion arises from the slippage in 'community', from the community of birth and formation, to the wider political community. Taylor's examples of acting in the light of moral demands tend to be the latter, as do the public scale of 'choice values', while the intimacy of relationships and realities of the 'dialogical setting' suggest family, neighbours and friends. Might it not be the case that the level of 'community' required for authenticity is not strong community in his sense at all? He admits that authenticity is central to our culture and yet it appears to have become so with little direct reference to community. Do the mass media serve as a partial substitute for a dialogical community? Returning from authenticity to community will not be easy.

While we can recognize the value in Taylor's (Kantian) strategy that community *must* be assumed in order to give a plausible account of authenticity, it is much harder to see this understanding of community as the basis for the generation of a much more integrated type of community. Even if we assume that Taylor is successful in persuading reasonably large numbers of authentic selves of their communal obligations, the nature of this community is entirely dependent on the authentic choice of its 'members' to continue to be so! At any given time the reality of community rests only on the immediate authentic choices of authentic selves who could just as authentically choose to reject community. It could be argued that this is just the choice that large numbers of moderns have in fact made. While Taylor succeeds in arguing his case for the necessary recognition of the communal foundations of our selves and the continued importance of this connection as a basis for our freedoms, he fails to convince that this weaker sense of community can be translated into the strong community that he is so concerned to promote.

'BEING-IN-COMMON', OR COMMUNITY

Postmodern and post-structuralist theory has, in a sense, been the attempt to re-think community, although often this has been rather obliquely. The rejection of the metaphysics of subjectivity (the deconstruction of the subject of modern capitalism/liberalism) and the collapse of 'traditional' collectivities have led to a call for a more inclusive democracy that has a place for those groups that were marginalized by the modernist model of the state and its limited and abstract modes of participation. (See, for example, Young, 1986; Mouffe, 1993.) There is a new stress on 'locality' ('locality of culture . . . a form of living more complex than "community"; more symbolic than "society"; more connotative than "country" . . . more collective than the "subject"'), and the newer and looser communal forms (Bhaba, 1990, p. 292). There has been little attempt, however, to reflect philosophically on the nature of community.

One of the most provocative attempts to do just this has been the work of Jean-Luc Nancy (1991). Nancy begins from the Heideggerian notion of *mitsein* and the closure of the metaphysics of subjectivity and tries to portray community in a non-essentialist fashion, within the framework of a philosophy of finitude. He wants to go further than Heidegger, whose 'spirit of the people' he suspects of not yet being free of the seductive power of community still thought of in terms of some form of subject. Nancy also desires to go beyond our current awareness of de-colonized, multicultural and information communities, which he rightly accuses of still being excessively 'humanistic' in their failure to recognize that 'the sovereignty of the subject thwarts a thinking of community' (ibid., p. 23). Can we think of community without locating its origin in some notion of the subject (individual or collective)? Defining his task, he asks: 'How can the community without essence . . . be presented as such?' (ibid., pp. xxxix–xl). Like the communitarians, he argues that our singularity arises only out of community and that the loss of community to 'political and technical economies' heralds the loss of our 'selves'. He rejects any idea of an immanent self, speaks of the 'singular being', and addresses the question: 'How can we be receptive to the meaning of our multiple, dispersed, mortally fragmented existences, which nonetheless only make sense by existing in common?' (ibid., p. lx).

Nancy denies that the answer to this question lies in any fusion of singular beings into a common substance (people, spirit, nation, fatherland, destiny, or generic humanity). Such substantial definitions of community entail a completed or 'infinite' identity. This unicity is the failure of community, the failure to recognize the singular being. He labels this 'realisation of the essence of a community' (as 'common being'), 'communion'. Communion has an ultimate and fixed identity and as such cannot accommodate the 'exposure' of the temporal, singular being. He contrasts 'communion' with 'being-in-common' and insists that 'existence in common . . . gives rise to the existence of the singular being'. Being-in-common is not some feature added on to the life of the singular being but is integral and constitutive. We are only separate (singular) because of our being-in-common – 'without community we are deprived of our finite existence'. Communion can only generate common being but never the being-in-common of singular beings.

Whilst recognizing the horrors of living without community ('The gravest and most painful testimony of the modern world . . . is the testimony of the dissolution, the dislocation, or conflagration of community'), Nancy parts company from most of the communitarians over their narrative of the loss of past community (transformed into 'an association of forces and needs', that is, 'society') and the need to regain or reconstitute it. He is too much of a modern to fail to recognize the re-traditionalized picture of the paradise that we have lost as just that: a world in which goods and services were fairly distributed, authority was justly exercised, and where 'each member identifie(d) with the living body of the community', should be viewed with suspicion (1991, pp. 10–11). These models of the past, where members of a community engage in intimate communication, share an authoritative culture (rituals, symbols and institutions), and enjoy reliable and close personal bonds (family, village, Athens, Rome, the Christian communion, communes, guilds, corporations and various fraternal associations), represent for Nancy only the effacing of the singular being in 'communion'.[4]

These reconstructed images of the past have led to a series of modern attempts to re-create communion. The most notable example of this is Communism, with its striving for community beyond 'social divisions and domination'. Moderns have imagined the utterly discrete and absolutely separate individual, and her emancipation as the only antidote to the perceived coercion of the past, but then found themselves unable to give a plausible answer to the question of why such individuals necessarily form groups. The only allowed aggregations of individuals have, according to Nancy, been forms of communion. But what is this individual? Nancy insightfully defines the individual as 'the residue of the experience of the dissolution of community'. The demise of community leaves the isolated individual (1991, p. 3).

Although in one sense the story of the West is a history of the loss of some ideal community, this has become so acute that modernity can almost be defined by its images of lost community. Nancy locates the origins of this obsession: 'the true consciousness of the loss of community is Christian' (1991, p. 10). The Christian promise that human beings could penetrate into 'true immanence' marks the invention of the dominant narratives of a single, human family inevitably set on a historical course towards its own final immanence (salvation). In this vein, he characterizes the fascist attempt at re-creating communion as a 'convulsion of Christianity' (ibid., p. 16). He even suggests that 'the thought of community may be only the modern with-drawal of God' and that community has now come to occupy the place formerly inhabited by the sacred (ibid., p. 35).

Rousseau, Schlegel, Hegel, Marx and Wagner et al., fulfilling the 'destiny of modern thought', re-presented this project of human immanence in their attempts to recover our now lost communion in the mystical body of Christ. These undertakings give us the 'immense failure' that is the history of com-munities as they attempt to combine beings in an absolute beyond relation and community – 'the domination, oppression, extermination and exploita-tion of all collectivities where the "excess of transcendence" is presented and instituted as immanence' (ibid., p. 19).

Our mistake, Nancy contends, is to confuse the loss of the communion of all (Christian) believers with our consciousness of our loss of intimacy and immanence. The craved-for resurrection of communion ('communal fusion') can only serve to destroy community and communication, and dissolve the 'irreducibly singular'. He dismisses the various theories of intersubjectivity, communication and consensus as inadvertent forms of communion, which even against the intentions of their proponents fatally compromise the sin-gular being. Nancy associates this immanence with death (the suicide of lovers; death for king/Kaiser and country; or death here, for the sake of immanence in the hereafter). Community, he reiterates time and again, is not a product of fusion; in fact, it is not a project at all.

'Finitude, or the infinite lack of infinite identity . . . is what makes commun-ity', writes Nancy. Community comes about as a retreat from the completed, infinite identity of community (communion). This retreat, he defines as resistance – 'resistance itself: namely to immanence' (ibid., p. 35). Nancy understands community to be a rupture of the totality of Being, a violation of the subject (individual or state). This rupture breaks the totality and 'undoes the absoluteness of the absolute', leaving community, relational and non-absolute. He likens this breaking to Heidegger's distinction between the ontic and the ontological (ibid., p. 7). Community is finite, composed of finite singular beings ('the singularity of being keeps open a space . . . within immanence'), and thus, without community we would be 'deprived of our finite existence'.

While it is the singular being that dies, the meaning of death is not individual but reciprocally revealed in community. It is the death of the singular being that allows a community to reject the seduction of under-standing itself as a corporate being, or subject – that is, to resist immanence. Community is what takes place 'through others and for others'. Nancy, draw-ing on Georges Bataille, writes of community as space (space opened up in totality/immanence) – 'the spacing of the experience of the outside, outside-of-self'. This is not the space of egos, immortal subjects and substances, but 'the Is, who are always others' (ibid., p. 15). In this way, community presents to us our births, deaths, and existence outside of ourselves. Thus, Nancy can write, 'outside of the community there is no experience'. He therefore con-siders the loss of community to be an ontological disaster, nothing less than the 'privation of being' (ibid., pp. 21, 57). Community consists in the expo-sure of finite singularities, a finitude that cannot be overcome by the com-munion of these singularities in a totality immanent to their common being. Singularity in community is not an external connection of discrete, separate subjects or substances, nor a 'common or fusional interiority', but being 'together' ('being-in-common'). Nancy refers to the plurality of singularities ('there is no singular being without another singular being') as 'an originary or ontological sociality' (ibid., p. 28). It is for this reason that community is not something to be produced but a single ontological order where finite identity is shared, an experience that is constitutive of singular beings.

Myth is necessary for community but also its greatest danger. Nancy defines myth as totalitarian and immanentist. The myth ('the unique speech of the many') of a community is always a communion narrative, and serves as the means by which the many come to recognize each other and 'com-mune' together in myth. As the origin, will and destiny of the absolute community is narrated, the community is revealed to itself. The repeated recitation of myth founds and re-founds the community. Communion is the submerging of all singular beings in one completed, common identity of all in one body. The community on the very brink of communion (totality) can be ruptured ('interrupted'); when at the edges of the communion, the singularity of those present reveals itself. This takes place when singular beings reach out to one another, touch one another and separate themselves from each other, 'thus communicating and propagating their community', that is, their being-in-common (ibid., pp. 63–71). The interruption of community has 'a singular voice'. The interrupted (inoperative) community is the community as it resists the immanence of communion.

While myth is the voice of the common body, Nancy considers literature to give 'voice to being-in-common'. Literature is the re-telling of myth, its subversion and inversion by singular beings. Literature is the interruption of myth. While myth is the voice of the communion, literature is always the voice of a singular being. The 'meaning of the community' is not communicated by literature, but rather by 'an infinite reserve of common and singular meanings' (ibid., p. 79). 'Nonetheless', writes Nancy, 'we only understand that there is no common understanding of community, that sharing does not constitute an understanding, . . . that it does not constitute a knowledge, and that it gives no one, including community itself, a mastery over being-in-common' (ibid., p. 69).

Nancy, like the communitarians, assumes a prior existing community in order to account for the singular being. And, like the communitarians, he slides between the community as the place of our birth and death, and a much wider almost universalistic designation – 'our community . . . our modern and postmodern humanity' (ibid., p. 52). His designation of literature as the interrupter of myth also suggests that this broader understanding is of the greater significance. Whilst he is certainly correct in locating the origin of the modern state in Christianity, he has rather overstated his notion of communion. Christian history is replete with examples of just the sort of communion that Nancy describes, although the other side of this story comes awfully close to his own position regarding the interrupted community. The mass only has to be endlessly re-enacted in order to re-create the communion, time and again, *because it was, and is, interrupted* countless times by countless singular (Christian) beings.[5] And the requirement that the communion be provisional, until its future completion and perfection beyond the world, suggests that it has yet to overcome its interruption. It is provisional in another sense too, in that the absolutely universal communion will always be resisted by the last heathen still to be converted. Christianity is the history of singular attempts to resist the totalizing of a church that all too often sought to engulf all communities. This resistance is in the repeated formation of a host of smaller communities (for example, the religious orders, the

Anabaptist believers' or gathered church). Viewing the Reformation in this fashion too, might be valuable.

Nancy offers us the most original and insightful re-thinking of community as the relational, differential being-in-common of innumerable singular beings. The inoperative community does allow for singular difference. While Nancy is right in that communitarians (in spite of Taylor's great efforts) cannot allow such difference and that their shared codes (recognition of the moral demands of their choices) must necessarily entail the suppression of singularities, it is by no means clear that this inevitably leads to a fascist communion. Nancy's community is a secularized and inverted postmodern version of Christian communion. It is also constructed as an antidote to that communion, in that, as there is no longer a God (for Nancy), we are finally liberated from the 'unattainable communion' of Christianity (and its modern, secular successors), leaving us free to 'share in community' – *community beyond tradition* (ibid., pp. 110–50).[6] Although Nancy does not intend to present a new politics of community, and it would miss the point to criticize him for this omission, the broad thrust of his political concern is clear. If Nancy is right and community is not some*thing* that can be produced, this is a most pertinent critique of communitarianism.

Nancy's attempt to theorize community while paying due regard to singularity raises important issues as to this very possibility. Aristotle claimed that there can be no science of that which is unique. Giorgi Agamben takes up this issue in a most suggestive way in his recent book on community (1993). He offers a sustained interrogation of the philosophical stranglehold of the antinomy of the individual particular and the human universal. He seeks to deconstruct this binary option in order to create a space ('unrepresentable space') *between* its terms. Agamben develops a series of notions constructed to create just such a space. For example, in an outline of 'the coming community', he writes of a community entered by singularities who manifest the 'perfect exteriority that communicates only itself'. (1993, pp. 62–4). He also develops the idea of an 'inessential commonality' expressing the universal (essence) but one in which differences are not lost and can, and do, reappear (ibid., pp. 16–19).

In a meditation on identity, the state and Tiananmen Square, Agamben contends that while the state can recognize any identity and allow any singularity that can be included in some identity, it cannot allow singularities to form a community without affirming any identity at all. He imagines a community where singularity is 'not mediated by any condition of belonging . . . but by belonging itself'. These singularities cannot, by definition, form a society and as they have no discernible identity of belonging they do not, and cannot, seek recognition by the state. Even a peaceful demonstration by such a community leads to the suppression of this dire threat from the 'principal enemy of the state' (ibid., pp. 84–6). He envisages the impending collapse of the state undermined by the 'coming community', the *community beyond tradition*. Agamben's work highlights the difficulties that arise from an exploration of singularity in community and the subversive nature of such considerations for thought (and institutions?) still bound by a metaphysics of identity.

COMMUNITIES OF ASSENT AND DESCENT

In this last section, I want to propose two different heuristic models of community, drawn from the Jewish and Christian traditions. Jews, like other groups, have been historically much exercised by the need for a mechanics of continuity. Jewish discussions of cultural continuity, until most recently, have always assumed an already existing community, a community conceived of as familial. Among Jews (again, until most recently) communal affiliation was usually by birth to a Jewish mother (matrilineal descent) or by a conversion that granted fictive descent. I refer to this Jewish model (there are also Hindu and other parallels) as a community of descent. Culture and religion significantly overlap in a community of descent and are often closely identified. Communities of descent are essentially non-missionary but always recognize conversion as a possibility, and tend towards 'legal' forms of culture. They look back to the past where descent has its 'origin'. Most significantly, descent communities are inherently pluralistic as identity does not depend on ideology but is vouchsafed by descent.

Communities of assent, on the other hand, are based on the Christian model (there are mainstream Buddhist and Islamic parallels). The model here is the Pauline one discussed above. The development of a non-familial community is shown in the novel, and perhaps unprecedented, teaching of Christianity. The Greek word used for this new community was *ecclesia* (church), literally 'called out', that is, called out from the 'old Israel', the community of assent. Assent communities are always built out of, and posterior to, communities of descent. To use anachronistic terms, the assent community is a voluntary association, or something akin to the Kantian notion of an 'aesthetic community'. Assent communities are always 'new', orientated towards the future completion of their communion, and are thus continually engaged in the process of their own formation.

Communities of assent are based on strategies of successful rhetorical persuasion, designed to lead to assent to a body of shared truths, or values. The communities of assent are normally missionary, reflecting their potential universality. Religion and culture become distinguishable, the former being the 'assent package'. Such communities are by their very nature cross-cultural and assent is neatly packaged (Christian doctrines, dogmas and creeds; the Five Pillars of Islam; the Buddhist Four Noble Truths and Eightfold Path) to facilitate expansion into different cultural contexts. The communities of assent replace familial relations with metaphorical brothers, mothers, sisters and fathers. The stress in these communities is on the assent package – for example, purity of doctrine becomes the substitute for the descent community's physical purity laws of contact and descent. Most importantly, identity *is* dependent on assent to the foundational truths and/or doctrines. This focus on assent renders this model of community fanatically anti-pluralistic and intolerant of heretics. The community of assent necessarily requires a progressive narrative of its own temporal supersession and replacement of the community of descent.

It is important to recognize that these two models of community represent two fundamentally different types. All of the authors that we have examined offer but a single, definitive model of community. The recognition that there are two (and, of course, other) different types of community entails that discussions of community be differential. The danger is to create a single, progressive model of community (whether pre-modern, modern, or postmodern): 'having assumed a universal history, the humanist inscribes the particular community into it as a moment in the universal becoming of human communities' (Lyotard, 1992, p. 34). The call for the recognition of singularity, or authenticity, at the personal level should require that deliberations are also about the singularity, or 'authenticity' of communities. Almost all models of community are of the assent type, that is, specific content is given to the shared values or truths, whether this be in the language of justice and rights, or of the common good. The exception to this is, of course, Nancy, but even he smuggles 'justice' and 'equality' into his characteristics of being-in-common. It is the assent that raises the issue of what to do with dissenters. Nancy is right that all assent communities suffer from the inherent danger of understanding themselves as totality: one completed, fixed, unicity, or subject – in his terms, this represents the perils of the 'immanence of communion'. Assent communities suppress singularity by giving at least minimal content to their forms of assent and, therefore, have a 'totalitarian' dimension. The community of believers necessitates that every single singularity assents to the creed of that community. Failure to do so leads to marginality, exclusion, or death.

The significance of the descent model is the way in which 'identity' is assured by birth, and, as such, is (very nearly) unnegotiable. Descent communities collectively assent to all kinds of shared truths, but identity/membership does not depend on this assent. In communities of descent, assent formulations are secondary and there is typically a looseness about such formulations, about which universal agreement is always resisted. In the history of Jewry, there have been numerous attempts to construct the essence of Judaism: as the three basic principles; the six hundred and thirteen commandments; the thirteen principles of faith; the Law (*halakhah*); belief in God, or the *sui generis* identity of the Jewish nation. Each one of these in turn has been contested and denied universal assent. As the question of the identity of the community (or its members) does not depend on this universal assent, dissent is not a challenge, or threat, to identity.

The Talmud tells of a Rabbi *Aher* (Rabbi 'Other') who is in opposition to most assent formulations, and Jewish authoritative sources include 'unorthodox' and dissenting, as well as 'orthodox' views. The traditions of biblical exegesis generate plural meanings for every verse and there is a great latitude in matters of belief. The ascription of identity by birth raises paradoxical issues, such as the case of a secular Jew (today, this is both a possibility and a widespread actuality) who converted to Catholicism, later becoming a priest. As a 'Jew', he applied to immigrate to the land of Israel. The Rabbinic position was that his identity was most anomalous but intact! Descent requires plurality and allows for a wide degree of assent singularity. Jewish communities have maintained conformity in other ways, usually behavioural. Transnational diaspora Jewry survived two millennia in essentially non-coercive communities, without benefit of police-force or army. The community did, however, have the final sanction of *herem* (a ban of excommunication, which led to exclusion from the community, as in the famous case of Spinoza).

Descent communities tend to be non-hierarchical (there are courts and legal authorities but identity is beyond their brief, except for the cases of conversion or disputed identity). In contrast the hierarchies of assent have to decide on the orthodox form of assent, that is, who is in and who is out. One of the great paradoxes of assent communities – a structural or design fault? – is that their assent hierarchies define assent packages in terms of external challenges, which serve to create and name outside groups (heretics or heathens), so that the very attempt to formulate the conditions of universal communion is thwarted by the parallel construction of those still beyond assent! The formulations of assent are always idealized and thus create the political task and agenda for these communities. Their principal political task is to include those who, by definition, they have excluded, by force if necessary. This is in stark contrast to the communities of descent, whose community already exists and whose politics are concerned with the much more limited task of attempting to ensure its continuity.

Assent, as the formation of the single subject, leads to unicity, coercion and imperialism. It can also lead to education and 'progressive' programmes as it seeks to coerce and remake those outside into perfect assenters. The descent model, with its pre-social, pre-linguistic, self-understanding of its own connectedness, can lead to indifference to those with different lines of descent. In the former, community is always an unfinished task. While in the latter, community has the character of concrete, physical facticity.

The communities of assent and descent are, of course, just models and both operate in almost every historical context. Historically, even if the foundations were still on the basis of descent, assent has played a major role in Jewish communities, especially as new forms of community have developed (such as the growth of the Hasidic movement in the late eighteenth and early nineteenth centuries). And it is hard to construct the history of Christian communities without the most extensive reference to the ties and bonds of descent. The tensions that we examined above, for example, in the communitarian literature, can be seen as being caught between the communities of birth and formation, and the new not-as-yet community of assent.

Nancy (and Taylor) seem to come, at times, very close to a notion of descent in their deliberations about the underlying and necessary assumption of the existence and formative power of the community of birth, experience, and death. Does 'descent' ultimately derive from (descend into) the detested categories of 'biology' and 'race?' Is descent not just another construction, intelligible only in terms of some originary narrative? Was not the liberal programme designed to overcome just these contingencies of birth? All communities necessarily have a discourse of descent, and it is significant to note that these differ greatly in different communities. It is important to distinguish between 'biology' and 'race' as part of the nineteenth century's triumphant, grand narratives of European supremacy, and descent *per se*.

That descent is a constructed category is not in question. But in every community we find a hierarchy of such constructions. The discourse of descent has a specific history in each particular community. It is always a contested category and a great degree of flexibility over descent has been evidenced in most communities as they attempt to respond to historical contingencies. So, for example, from Ezra returning to the Land of Israel from the Babylonian exile, to the discussions over the immigration of new groups to the modern State of Israel (Ethiopian Jews, Bombay Jews, and currently the issue of those from the former Soviet Union), the 'traditional' limitations on descent have been debated and usually relaxed. If one wants to use biological terminology, descent communities conceive of descent in terms of what we might call 'open geneotypes'. Not all constructions are of equal weight in a community. Descent is at (or towards) the top of these communal hierarchies of constructions in the communities of descent, and other constructions are often interpreted in the light of this.

For some theorists of postmodernity the most effective resistance to the tyranny of the coercion of the liberal state is the concentration upon locality, the local community. The local 'community' satisfies Anderson's condition of face-to-face encounter. Many communitarians, likewise, advocate a return to the personal contact of local communities as the most effective resistance to the tyranny of capitalist forces on atomized individuals. The problems of immanence, however, occur at the local level in much the same way as they do at the state level. Issues of boundaries, qualifying periods of residency, and the construction of the consensus and compromise necessary for political action, all tend to be just as effective at creating outsiders as they are at constructing the unitary subject (body) of the 'community'. These are, of course, communities of assent, and thus still require not only formulations of assent but authorities that decide on the correctness or otherwise of the assent of others. Territorialized communities prioritize territory ('dying for it') over and above other values. The image of a plethora of overlapping communities still entails at each and every instance a common form of assent.

Descent communities are inherently local. Jewish law, for example, operates only at the level of the specific local community. As communities of descent understand their community by descent and not by *locale* (or common interest), they are rarely defined, or confined, territorially. Diaspora Jewry represents a model of a de-territorialized community which existed for nearly two millennia without benefit of state or fixed hierarchy. The community was, however, never just the local Jewish community.[7] It was connected to each and every other Jewish community by descent; each community was a local instantiation of the whole community of descent. In the language of Judaism, each community existed under the 'tabernacle' of the 'Community'.

There are, thus, two levels of community, both of which are vital if we are to understand the communities of descent. First, at the local level, 'community' can be strived for as an object of production, in terms of institutions, practices, and even common beliefs formed by common formation. Secondly, we find the already defined and existing Jewish 'community' (of descent) on the firm basis of which these efforts are made. It might even be argued that local Christian descent communities operated in a similar fashion in relation to the greater assent communion of Christendom. For the local level to operate effectively at all, it requires that the community itself be part of some greater already-existing community and that this already-existing greater community be the basis of identity.

There are two issues that need to be highlighted, by way of conclusion about descent. First, the historically dominant discourse of (Christian) assent has tended to obscure the realities of descent in the literature of the West. Communities continued to function in terms of descent but this was rarely discussed in these terms. It is only very recently that historical studies of the family have surfaced. The difference between assent and descent is reminiscent of its modern parallel – the distinction between community and association. And, in a similar way, the dominant discourse of association has tended to conceal the continued existence of communities. Many of the issues that used to be discussed under the rubric of class, might helpfully be reexamined in terms of descent. When we challenge the controlling notion of association (assent), we discover considerable evidence of descent communities. Just as communities of descent are misunderstood and distorted by attempts to understand them in assent terms (i.e. what do the Jews believe, assent to?), so modern 'communities' are all too often misconceived and our grasp warped by viewing them solely in terms of assent.

Secondly, while I have constructed descent in opposition to assent (this being quite plausible with regard to Judaism and Christianity), descent could be couched in terms less explicitly opposed to assent. In the attempt to broaden the discussion to other communities, we might try to think of descent outside of its specificities of a particular historical discourse. What is significant about descent is that it is not very negotiable, representing not identity in the modern sense (conceived of as 'assent') but a given, something beyond personal construction (what we referred to above, as descent as a high-level communal construction). Descent in this way might be taken to be any prior 'identity', prior to self-construction, namely, the community into which one was physically born and the link between that and the community in which one's formation took place. This descent community is a physical community (made up of particular beings, and, as in the case of Jewry, conceived in a specific way) and not a metaphorical community (as in the case of all communities of assent where the community consists of all believers). In assent communities there is a metaphorical appropriation of 'naturalness' (or, descent), which serves to efface the physical dimensions of the connections of birth (one form of the detraditionalization of descent – 'to be born again', or the prioritizing of class, or other assent category over 'descent'). We can see this metaphorical appropriation most clearly in the case of the construction of ethnicity, when it takes the form of a detraditionalization of the community of birth and formation, reconstructed as the unicity of the *ethnos* (a communion, or absolute subject).

Descent, in this sense, is the limit-concept of the liberal notion of self-making.[8] It is that which cannot be wholly constructed, that which is undeniably the case that serves to link a singular being to her community of birth, experience and death. Communities of descent in this way obscure and conceal their own origins. No individual or group of individuals can found such a community – for only communities of assent have such originary events. Communities of descent do have myths but only myths of their eternal descent, not of their point of inception. For every single person their community is already in existence before them and continues with, or without them. Taylor writes of the 'politics of recognition' (Taylor, 1992), that is, of the call for recognition made by 'communities' in a multicultural and pluralistic society. His argument assumes that there are authorities who assent to this recognition. The reality of communities of descent suggests another model of recognition.

It is not that members of descent communities (in actuality, all of us) eschew self-making, it is just that we cannot choose our own community of descent. They have already chosen us. Our only freedom with regard to this choice is the simple binary opposition, between acceptance or rejection, of the community's recognition of us. If we choose to recognize this external recognition then we accept the obligation that this entails. Each community of descent defines status in its own way, and extends recognition to those that fall under this definition of membership by descent. And within each community of descent the issue of status is constantly being debated and reworked as new anomalies and challenges arise. To be a Jew, for example, is to be included in a descent community's recognition of itself. It offers an opportunity to respond affirmatively and join a local instantiation of the community, or, alternatively, to reject this recognition (a relatively new option). Other communities offer parallel recognition, although each community has different modes of 'membership'. The problems of recognition in Taylor's sense are issues of assent.

The debate between modernists and postmodernists is not really about the affirmation of reality by the former versus its denial by the latter. It is rather that postmodernists deny that there is a single formulation of reality. This is not a claim that there is nothing out there, but that what is out there is much richer and more diverse than modernists (can) acknowledge. We are witnesses to a reversal of the last one hundred and fifty years of denial of the importance of descent communities. Increasingly large numbers of people have heard the 'call of their geneotype', that is, they have responded affirmatively to their recognition by their community of descent. Rather than finding refuge in their descent identities (as in a sociological version of Fromm's 'fear of freedom' thesis (Fromm, 1960)), many today are celebrating that fixed element beyond their own constructive possibilities.

The level of personal communal commitment is rather implausible when explained in terms of assent. It is difficult to account for the priority of belonging over the details of assent, without reference to some notion of the 'given', along the lines of descent. To interpret descent in terms of assent – the most usual approach – leads to the attempt to explicate belonging in terms of cost–benefit analysis, or Taylor's 'instrumental reason'. Such accounts do little justice to a belonging that appears to be prior to any reasoning at all. The axiomatic character of descent makes little sense when analysed in terms of rational calculation. There is, however, a recognition of the possibility of non-assent communities in the work of a number of theorists. Bataille's formulation of such a 'community' beyond assent is that of two lovers. The contemporary revival of interest in friendship and intimacy also reflects this concern. Nancy attempts to extend the non-assent community beyond the pair to a more general account of community. It is important to note that descent communities understand the connections between members in a similar fashion – that is, they are unasked for, unquestionable, beyond construction.

Plural identity is a feature of our world. Which is the descent community of those that appear to have more than one descent possibility? In some cases it will depend on the particular status accounts of the communities concerned (patrilineal, matrilineal, or other). It is important to recognize that new communities of descent are always in the process of being formed, and re-formed, so that plural communities of the recent past can become 'new' descent communities. Historically, the discourse of each descent community contained a recognition of the existence of other descent communities (the seventy 'families' of the Hebrew Bible). It is possible to conceive of the various descent communities, internally and externally, engaged in various programmes of assent.

CONCLUSION

Once we remove the strait-jacket of the modernist thinking about evolutionary development from descent to assent communities (*community beyond tradition*), and the conflation of assent and descent, we can begin to recognize that these are not alternatives but different communal forms. There are, of course, many other communal forms but these certainly need to be studied and theorized. The current critiques of modernity allows us to re-think *community beyond tradition* (the traditions of the modern) and to recognize the importance of communities of descent: not as an anachronism but as another form of community. The issues of assent are still posed but they are the attempts to create communities that require as their basis communities of descent. A recognition of the foundations of descent, as well as the attempt to construct communities of assent on this basis, generates the very possibility of new communal forms. Programmes, efforts, self-making (singular and collective) can proceed from the ground of descent without the identity of the community being challenged or compromised by assent. Only such a model can allow for the unique singularity of each member. Membership, in this sense, will no longer be tied to assent, and thus those who are unquestionably connected are free to be their singular selves.

Assent also needs to take place between communities and this must only be facilitated by the rejection of unitary notions of (the) community. We are not faced with the binary choice between the fascist mass or unrelated individuals. 'Individuals' are already connected to existing communities, and the recognition of assent *and* descent allows us to maintain difference while consciously constructing communities of assent. In Ricoeur's terms, descent gives us the 'short connections', and assent gives us the 'long connections' (Levinas, 1994, pp. 71–2). Levinas contends that modern professional life is not a mistake or lacking in care, and that we should take its attempt to construct solidarity through regulations and law seriously. But he also notes that such communities of assent are more about leading us to 'walk together', than about turning our 'faces towards one another' (ibid.). We are bound to work collectively for an assent *community beyond tradition* that will actually allow us to walk together, but this should not be at the expense of our already-existing communities of descent.

NOTES

1   The new concern with community is not the 1960s sociology of community (see, for example, Sanders, 1966; Koenig, 1968; French, 1969) where traditional societies or local communities were targeted for sociological study, nor the anthropological study of community (for example, Misra and Preston, 1978; Cohen, 1985), but an attempt to theorize community outside of the existing, modernist grand narratives. It is interesting to note that a recent study in this mould (Crow and Allan, 1994), whilst advocating a revival of research on local communities, reports little supporting the 'romantic' imaginings of the 'spirit of community'. The connection between local community and 'society' is often formulated along

the lines that the 'linkages between communities make up the network called society' (Arensberg and Kimball, 1965, pp. 3–4). On the relationship of community to ideology, see Plant (1974). The importance of the different notions of community for sociology are discussed in Nisbet (1953).

2   For example, Max Weber wrote, 'Sociology itself can only proceed from the actions of one or more separate individuals and must therefore adopt strictly "individualistic" methods' (quoted in Birnbaum and Leca, 1990, p. 33).

3   MacIntyre's recognition that even 'traditional' communities must be open to debates about values (virtues) leads him to distinguish between 'tradition' and a 'tradition in good order', one where such debates can and do take place (MacIntyre, 1985, p. 206). For an anti-liberal, anti-moral pluralist, defence of rights theory, see Moon (1993).

4   See von Gierke (1990) for an analysis of the associations of 'comradeship' in European, especially German, history. Otto von Gierke offers a model of pluralism based on the place of these associations (distinguished from 'institutions') within the framework of the state. For an attempt to incorporate a number of von Gierke's insights into a contemporary political framework, see Black (1988).

5   For general views on Christian community, see de Vries (1966). For an interesting, if misguided, attempt to justify liberal rights theory on the basis of natural theology, see Dyck (1994); and for an evangelical view of community, see Grenz (1993). Consult Rouner (1991) for a collection of essays on community in a number of different religious traditions.

6   There are a variety of post-subject accounts of community (see, for example, Lingis, 1994). On Nancy, see the collection of essays in Miami Theory Collective (1991). Nancy draws quite heavily on Blanchot's work on community (Blanchot, 1988).

7   Consult the following volumes for a spectrum of contemporary views on Jewish community: Frank (1992); Goldberg and Krausz (1993).

8   E. Yeo and S. Yeo take the opposite position (On the Uses of 'Community': From Owenism to the Present, in S. Yeo (ed.) by making a distinction between common identities and national or state identities. The latter are held to 'already exist'. While they are right about the constructed nature of common identities, they appear to have misunderstood the links between descent 'identity' and national (or state) identity. The latter is a modern secularized version of the former, and while both of these appear similar in the sense that they 'already exist' (i.e. are not constructed), descent identities are physical and familial while nation/state identities are only metaphorical.

REFERENCES

Agamben, G. 1993: *The Coming Community*. Minneapolis: Minnesota University Press.

Anderson, B. 1983: *Imagined Communities*. London: Verso.

Arensberg, C. and Kimball, S. 1965: *Culture and Community*. New York: McGraw-Hill.

Atkinson, D. 1994: *The Common Sense of Community*. London: Demos.

Augustine, Bishop of Hippo, 1977: *City of God*. New York: E. P. Dutton.

Bauman, Z. 1991: *Modernity and Ambivalence*. Oxford: Polity.

Benhabib, S. 1992: *Situating the Self*. Oxford: Polity.

Bhaba, H. K. (ed.) 1990: *Nation and Narration*. London: Routledge.

Birnbaum, P. and Leca, J. (eds) 1990: *Individualism*. Oxford: Oxford University Press.

Black, A. 1988: *State, Community and Human Desire*. Hemel Hempstead: Harvester Wheatsheaf.

Blanchot, M. 1988: *The Unavowable Community*. Barrytown, New York: Station Hill Press.

Cohen, A. 1985: *The Symbolic Construction of Community*. London: Tavistock.

Crow, G. and Allan, G. 1994: *Community Life*. Hemel Hempstead: Harvester Wheatsheaf.

de Vries, E. (ed.) 1966: *Man in Community*. London: SCM.

Dyck, A. J. 1994: *Rethinking Rights and Responsibilities: The Moral Bonds of Community*. Cleveland, Ohio: the Pilgrim Press.

Etzioni, A. 1994: *The Spirit of Community*. New York: Crown.

Foucault, M. 1980: *Power/Knowledge*. New York: Pantheon.

Frank, D. (ed.) 1992: *Autonomy and Judaism*. Albany, New York: State University of New York Press.

French, R. M. (ed.) 1969: *The Community*. Itasca, Illinois: Peacock.

Friedman, J. 1989: Culture, Identity and World Process. *Review*, 12, 1.

Fromm, E. 1960: *Fear of Freedom*. London: Routledge and Kegan Paul.

Goldberg, D. and Krausz, M. (eds) 1993: *Jewish Identity*. Philadelphia: Temple University Press.

Grenz, S. J. 1993: *Theology for the Community of God*. Nashville, Tennessee: Broadman and Holman.

Heller, A. 1984: *Everyday Life*. London: Routledge and Kegan Paul.

Heller, J. 1972: *Something Happened*. London: Black Swan.

Hobsbawm, E. J. 1990: *Nations and Nationalisms since 1870*. Cambridge: Cambridge University Press.

Koenig, R. 1968: *The Community*. London: Routledge and Kegan Paul.

Lasch, C. 1991: *The True and Only Heaven*. New York: Norton.

Levinas, E. 1994: *Beyond the Verse*. London: Athlone.

Lingis, A. 1994: *The Community of Those who have Nothing in Common*. Bloomington, Indiana: Indiana University Press.

Lyotard, J-F. 1992: *The Postmodern Explained*. Minneapolis: Minnesota University Press.

MacIntyre, A. 1985: *After Virtue: A Study in Moral Theory*. London: Duckworth.

MacIntyre, A. 1981: *After Virtue*. London: Duckworth.

Miami Theory Collective (eds) 1991: *Community at Loose Ends*. Minneapolis: Minnesota University Press.

Milbank, J. 1990: *Theology and Social Theory: Beyond Secular Reason*. Oxford: Basil Blackwell.

Minor, D. and Greer, S. (eds) 1970: *The Concept of Community*. London: Butterworth.

Misra, B. and Preston, J. (eds) 1978: *Community, Self and Identity*. The Hague: Mouton.

Mommsen, W. 1965: Max Weber's Political Sociology and his Philosophy of World History. *International Journal of Sociology*, 17.

Moon, J. D. 1993: *Constructing Community: Moral Pluralism and Tragic Conflicts*. Princeton: Princeton University Press.

Mouffe, C. 1993: *The Return of the Political*. London: Verso.

Nancy, J-L. 1991: *The Inoperative Community*. Minneapolis: Minnesota University Press.

Nisbet, R. 1953: *The Quest for Community*. Oxford: Oxford University Press.

Plant, R. 1974: *Community and Ideology*. London: Routlege and Kegan Paul.

Rawls, J. 1971: *A Theory of Justice*. Cambridge, Mass.: Harvard University Press.

Rouner, L. S. (ed.) 1991: *On Community*. Notre Dame, Indiana: University of Notre Dame Press.

Sandel, M. 1982: *Liberalism and the Limits of Justice*. Cambridge: Cambridge University Press.

Sanders, I. 1966: *The Community*. New York: Ronald Press.

Taylor, C. 1989: Cross-Purposes: The Liberal–Communitarian Debate. In N. Rosenblum (ed.), *Liberalism and Moral Life*, Cambridge, Mass.: Harvard University Press, pp. 159–83.

Taylor, C. 1991: *The Ethics of Authenticity*. Cambridge, Mass.: Harvard University Press.

Taylor, C. 1992: *Multiculturalism and the 'Politics of Recognition'*. Princeton: Princeton University Press.

von Gierke, O. 1990: *Community in Historical Perspective*. Cambridge: Cambridge University Press.

Walzer, M. 1983: *Spheres of Justice*. New York: Basic Books.

Wlazer, M. 1990: The Communitarian Critique of Liberalism. *Political Theory*, 18, 1, pp. 6–23.

Williams, R. 1976: *Keywords*. London: Fontana.

Yeo, S. (ed.) 1988: *New Views of Cooperation*. London: Routledge.

Young, I. 1986: The Ideal of Community and the Politics of Difference. *Social Theory and Practice*, 12, pp. 1–26.

13

Tradition and the Limits of Difference

Scott Lash

INTRODUCTION

A number of different thinkers across a spectrum of disciplines and pursuits have maintained, either implicitly or explicitly, that we live in a more or less fully post-traditional order. Thus sociologists such as Ulrich Beck and Anthony Giddens suggest that we live in an age of 'reflexive modernity', in which the last traditional vestiges of an earlier simple modernity have reflexively been eliminated (Beck, Giddens and Lash, 1994). Thus philosophers such as John Rawls and Jürgen Habermas have proposed a rational ethical order in which all talk of values, all talk of traditions is either systematically set aside for a focus on procedures and constitutionalism, or relegated to the disused junkyard of 'background assumptions'. Thus Neo-classical, social-democratic and Marxist economics have conceived the individual as a rational-choosing, tradition-free agent possessing preference schedules and 'interests' in the market place. Thus a great number of architects and planners have forsaken history, place and meaning for the sake of doctrines in which the only meaning that counts lies in the form-and-function-making practices of the architects themselves. The assumption here is very much of a piece with Max Weber's famous pronouncements on the ethics of responsibility in a culture in which rationalization had systematically eliminated the traces of tradition in each of the contemporary life orders.

Another group of thinkers has aspired to 'deconstruct' these notions of rationality. Yet in doing so they have not in any sense taken seriously or even re-problematized the issue of tradition, but have pushed the destruction of tradition even further. Thus the rationalism of Marxist and capitalist neo-classical economics had already understood embedded economic practices of making and using things to be superseded by the fully detraditionalized exchange value of the commodity. This second group, these deconstructors, proffer an even more thorough dismantling of tradition; and de-territorialize even the commodity in favour of the anarchistic practices of the libidinal revolution. If the rationalist and Freudian unconscious is already detraditionalized in eroding the symbolic exchange of the *part maudite* in favour of the abstract forces and relations of drives and the Oedipus, then its subsequent deconstruction renders even the symbolic order of the unconscious placeless, without a home, with no possible ground (Baudrillard, 1994). Deconstruction in architecture for its part, at least initially, appears to be restoring a place for tradition in its allusions to classical, gothic, Romanesque and even Eastern sources. Yet these remain the allusions of a playful and formalist bricolage, without genuine history, meaning, value or content. In short, without *tradition*.

It is this second cultural paradigm that, under the sign of deconstruction, difference, the other or alterity, seems to be making all the running today. This is so, as their opponents such as Giddens and Habermas have not failed to note, in academic life across a variety of disciplines. It is noticeably so in a whole host of spheres of popular culture, in which fragmentation of the self and hypostatization of the other constitute core, if unspoken, assumptions in contemporary cinema, pop music and magazines. But contemporary culture is not simply marked by such a 'metaphysics of difference' in its leisure pursuits but also in the ethics, the politics of everyday life. Thus the identity politics of feminism, anti-racism, 'queer politics' and ecological movements are much more at home in the language of alterity, deconstruction of the subject, the critique of logocentrism than they are in the language of democratic interest aggregation and construction of a rational social order. If 1968 opened up the floodgates for such a politics of expression and fragmentation in the West, then 1989 did so in the East. But the demise of Marxism and the Berlin Wall ushered in not primarily a reassertion of the Enlightenment's as yet unrealized project. Instead, we have seen the proliferation of the vastest and wildest iterations of – intellectual, subcultural and national – alterity. And in the 1990s in the South (and the South in the West) as well, discourses of modernization and uneven accumulation are progressively being displaced by the deconstructive language of hybridity, diaspora and postcolonialism (Laclau, 1990, 1994).

What, however, is meant in this context by 'difference', the pivotal concept for such an ethics or politics of deconstruction? Difference has very little to do with the value pluralism of liberalism. This must first of all be emphasized. This is underscored by Homi K. Bhabha (1990) in his development of an analytic distinction between 'diversity' and difference. Diversity, on this view has to do with the subject–object-type thinking of the Enlightenment and liberal thought. Diversity presumes an Archimedean point (subject), outside of the 'world' (object), from which the variance of lifestyles and properties of persons and groups in the world can be categorized. Difference, in contradistinction, notes Bhabha, presumes a radical alterity, one in which the other cannot be judged, categorized and pigeonholed. To be in the position of an Archimedean point vis-à-vis the other is not to respect the other. Difference thus denies the existence of such an Archimedean point as well as 'our' capabilities of knowledge of the other. Difference is a politics leaving a third space, a space reducible neither to subject or object, universal or particular – a space open to the radical alterity of the other.

So far so good. But a contemporary radical political culture cannot have its core assumptions only in ideas and practices of difference. It must just as much have its basis in the thought and practice of *solidarity*. That is, solidarity is as crucial in any reconstructed radical contemporary political culture as difference. At issue here is, in the first instance, solidarity within the same. I do not think that abstract collective interests – as liberalism and Marxism presuppose – are a sufficient basis for collective action, for solidarity within the same. That is, not common interests, but shared practices, shared meanings and shared traditions constitute solidarity. Solidarity is based on value, and the core values of deconstruction, as of liberalism, do not concern so much the revaluation but rather the irrelevance of values. Thus shared understandings, a genuine intersubjectivity, and shared – albeit often invented – traditions are a basis of solidarity within the same. But tradition is also important for solidarity with the other, whether this other be female, ethnic, 'queer' or nature; difference is not enough. There must also be *recognition*. And recognition presupposes not just blind alterity but understanding, a certain kind of intersubjectivity, and some sort of shared tradition. The problem is that the most inspiring of today's intellectuals, the organic intellectuals of deconstruction politics, give us only a notion of difference, to the neglect of solidarity and tradition.

What I want to suggest in this chapter is that it is no accident that the politics of difference, no more than of Marxism or contemporary social-liberalism, is weak when it comes to solidarity and tradition. I will argue that this absence of tradition is at the heart of the most fundamental philosophical assumptions of the politics of difference. I want to argue that this is because the notion of difference, at its very core, excludes any coherent notion of *intersubjectivity*. Although deconstruction does speak the idiom of same and other, of the 'I' and the 'Thou', I shall claim that its fundamental assumptions are not of intersubjectivity, not of same and other but of same and text, not 'the I' and 'the Thou' but 'the I' and 'the It'. I want to argue that without a notion of tradition the politics of difference, like liberalism and Marxism, cannot talk meaningfully about temporality or values.

Because radical identity politics today takes its inspiration from these intellectuals whose core assumptions are deconstruction and difference, I want to challenge these core assumptions where they are thought through at their strongest – in the work of Derrida, Heidegger and Levinas. All three of these writers begin, not from reflexive modernity, but from a refusal of reflexivity, and specifically from a refusal of reflexivity as found in the work of Husserl. Husserl spoke of the counterposition of the reflexive and natural attitude. His phenomenology is based on the constitution of meaning from the reflexive attitude. All three of these thinkers – Heidegger, Levinas and Derrida – turn the tables on Husserl and deconstruct the reflexive attitude in favour of the natural attitude. The problem is that none of their versions of deconstruction gives space for intersubjectivity within this natural attitude. Thus their notions of difference lack tradition and exclude the possibility of solidarity.

DECONSTRUCTION: PHENOMENOLOGY VERSUS FINITUDE

What exactly is meant by 'difference'? What does Jacques Derrida mean by '*différance*'? There have, in the Anglo-Saxon world, in fact, been two waves of reception of Derrida. The first took place primarily in literary criticism and the study of modern languages. Here Derrida was understood as a post-structuralist, who deconstructed crucially the structuralism of Saussurean linguistics. Here for Saussure meaning was a matter, not of the relation of signifier to signified, but of the difference among signifiers in a *langue*. Derrida followed Saussure's structuralism this far. He was characteristically post-structuralist in deconstructing the distinction between *langue* and *parole*. Thus difference became no longer just a question of the spatial relations among signifiers, but took on a temporal dimension. *Ecriture* or writing, displacing the *langue/parole* distinction, took on not the synchronic and static character of *langue* but the diachronic and temporal character of *parole*. And in *écriture*, meaning, as the differential and spatial relation among signifiers, became also always temporally postponed. Because of the temporal non-contiguity of signified and signifier, meaning is constantly alluded to but never quite achieved.

To be sure, critical literary theory derived a lot of mileage from this idea of difference. Only they got it, I think, wrong. This was not fundamentally what Derrida meant by difference. Paradoxically the basic meaning of difference in

Derrida is a lot more applicable to literary theory than it is to the human sciences (ethics; non-positivist sociology, or politics and cultural studies; post-colonialism and the like). This is because it addresses the relation between statements and things or experience. It is thus applicable to texts but is very bad at addressing intersubjectivity. But more on this below. For the moment let us address what Derrida fundamentally meant by difference. The point of reference – as second wave Derrideans such as Critchley (1992), whose background typically is philosophy, have understood – is not Saussure, but Husserl. Derrida was not trained as a linguist or in literary studies but as a philosopher. For some fifteen years, in his twenties and his early thirties, he was primarily a Husserl scholar. His concept of language comes from Husserl and not Saussure. It has a lot more to do with the notions of language involved in logic, and especially in Frege, than in linguistics or literary theory.

Given this context, not of Saussurean semiotics but of phenomenology, what can the theory of deconstruction mean by 'difference'? Although heavily influenced by Heidegger, Derrida, unlike Levinas (1973), does not give us a primarily 'ontological' reading of Husserl. He focuses, unlike Levinas, not on a possible notion of being, nor on the undermining of positivism and naturalism in Husserl, but instead on Husserl's theory of the sign. Readings of Husserl can be divided into 'ontological' and 'logical'. Heidegger, for example, and the phenomenological sociologists Max Scheler, Alfred Schutz and arguably Harold Garfinkel, and ethnomethodology as well as Levinas, proffer an ontological reading of Husserl. (See Srubar, 1988.) Derrida, however, like other French theorists such as Ricoeur, as well as most Anglo-Saxon philosophers, gives us a reading as much in the context of logic as of ontology. I will argue below that some of these ontological Husserlians – in particular Schutz and Gadamer (1976) – who work towards a theory of intersubjectivity, also have strong notions of tradition and hence solidarity. But let us stay with our discussion of Derrida and Husserlian signs for the moment.

Now Derrida's (1978a) initial breakthrough, in his mid-thirties, into the non-specialist literature was via his critique of structuralism in a book edited by Jean Piaget.[1] Here he criticized the notion of 'finite totality' – shared by Saussure, Lévi-Strauss and Althusser – presumed in the idea of structure. For structuralists the relation between elements of such a finite totality, or system, determine the place of various instances of the system as well as the value of statements and meanings inside the system. For Derrida, Husserl's transcendental, and in this sense 'infinite', ego offered the possibility of breaking out of this structural and finite totality (Critchley, 1992, p. 64). Here we can see an implicit critique not only of structure as finitude but of the phenomenology of finitude of the generation of Derrida's teachers, of Merleau

Ponty and Ricoeur (1981). Both these philosophers want to reconceive Husserl in terms of not so much the theoretical attitude of the transcendental ego but rather the natural attitude of the body, desire and perception.

What can Derrida (1978a, pp. 156–7) mean by this claim that Husserl's transcendental ego offers a way out of structuralism's 'finite totality'? He clearly does not mean a move from structuralism's immanence to a transcendental instance, in the sense that the world religions – in contradistinction to the immanentism of animism and totemism in tribal societies – were transcendental (Weber, 1963; Parsons, 1968). Derrida would understand structuralism's assumptions of the finite to be very much of a piece with Kant's idea of finitude. Kant uses the word transcendental in many senses. He speaks for example of the 'transcendental aesthetic', the 'transcendental analytic', the 'transcendental dialectic' and 'transcendental argument'. But each of these terms is used not in the realm of infinitude but in that of finitude. All of these entities are conditions of the possibility, not of metaphysical or infinite knowledge but of empirical and finite knowledge, of synthetic *a priori* judgements for which experience is necessary. Kant counterposes this realm of the 'understanding', of empirical knowledge, comprised of objective truths – on the model of mathematics and physics – to the realm of 'reason'. He counterposes the 'empirical will' of such experiential knowledge (which can only know appearances and not things-in-themselves) to the pure practical will of the moral imperative. The will in the realm of finitude is for Kant heteronomous, while the will of infinitude is autonomous, the realm of freedom. And he places God in this critique of pure reason, this critique of metaphysics, firmly within the realm of reason as inaccessible to the understanding. The Kantian categories, such as cause, substance, existence – are mobilized in the knowledge of appearances of the understanding. The infinitude of reason contains God, freedom, ethics and noumena or things-in-themselves. They cannot be known, as the metaphysics of Leibniz and Descartes claimed. Their acceptance can only be on the basis of 'rational faith' (Walsh, 1975).

Derrida, in his initial Husserlian critique of structuralism, would seem to have a notion of transcendence and the critique of finitude that is quite similar to Levinas's (1973) early Husserlian phase. He would understand Husserl's transcendental ego as breaking out of the immanence and finitude in which Kant's synthetic unity of apperception is mired. This would entail a mode of thinking characteristic, not of the Kantian understanding, but of the realm of reason. But this would be a mode of thinking which is at the same time a departure from what Kant called metaphysics. The suggestion is that we can know noumena without metaphysics. Husserl implies that

Kantian objective knowledge (through the categories of the understanding) is not universal but only knowledge in the mode of natural science and mathematics. For Husserl Kant's objective knowledge of appearances through the logical categories is in fact the way that the natural sciences know things. Such knowledge (of appearances) is in fact knowledge of things-themselves to the extent that such things possess the categorial structure presumed by the natural sciences. Husserl encourages using the phenomenological method to know things, not according to the categorial structure of the natural sciences, or according to how these things are for the natural sciences, but according to their own categorial structure; their own mode of existence. Such knowledge is the intuition of their essences; the knowledge of noumena. It is also the transcendence of the finitude and immanence of consciousness (Levinas, 1973, pp. 42–3). For Derrida the scientistic assumptions of structuralism, as well as their substantialist conception of the relations of elements, would be very much in the tradition of Kantian finite totality.

The Sign: Difference and Natural Attitude

In *Speech and Phenomenon* Derrida first develops the notion of 'difference' through deconstructing Husserl's theory of the sign. This notion of the sign, whose basis is the distinction between expression (*Ausdruck*) and indication (*Anzeichen*) is dependent on, though surely not derivative of, the Fregean distinction between sense (*Sinn*) and reference (*Bedeutung*). Frege had already effected a major departure from the epistemological tradition, that is from the high modernist and substantialist tradition which located meaning in the mind of the knowing subject. Frege displaces this for a logical notion of meaning. For him meaning is more closely identified with truth and validity. It is attached to statements themselves rather than to images in the minds of epistemological subjects. Meaning is defined instead in terms of certain logical truth conditions of statements. Meaning here comprises both sense and reference, though Frege makes no secret of his privileging of sense. Frege was a major influence not just on Husserl but on logical positivism, on Bertrand Russell and Wittgenstein of the *Tractatus* (Searle, 1969, pp. 168–71; Thompson, 1981, pp. 50–7). In this context we should note Derrida's involvement with Husserl's logic, with Husserl's work at its most 'transcendental': with his *Logical Investigations* and *Ideas*, rather than the *Cartesian Meditations* and *Crisis of the European Sciences*, in which the transcendental attitude begins to give way to the 'natural attitude'. The point here is that Derrida, in contrast to other post-Husserlians, and especially Max Scheler, Schutz and Gadamer, not only privileges the 'I–it' relationship over the

'I–thou' (or intersubjective) relationship; he also, unlike them, tends often to privilege the theoretical attitude over the natural attitude. Both of these points are central to deconstruction's weaknesses on tradition and solidarity. We should further note that when Derrida speaks of logocentrism or 'phallogocentrism', though this might refer to the entire 'metaphysical' or 'onto-theological' tradition, it refers in particular to that break with classical epistemology effected by Frege, Husserl, and other 'later' modern philosophers in quite literally the name of logic, and in the sense of meaning as the truth conditions of statements.

Where, then, does *différance* come in? Frege and Husserl were agreed that in any empirical statement or sign there was some sort of mix of sense and reference, of expression and indication, but that analytically the two dimensions of meaning (the sign) were distinct from one another. Derrida deconstructs even this analytic distinction. He argues that expression and indication are inseparable even analytically; that they interpenetrate each other at their very core; that they are primordially joined (Derrida, 1973, p. 31; Critchley, 1992, pp. 169–71). In this first deconstruction of Husserl, Derrida is also introducing the concept of difference. What is being deconstructed is not so much the analytic distinction between expression and indication. What is being deconstructed in fact is expression and the transcendental reduction itself. The eidetic reduction is achieved by means of expression. Here the elements of indication in signs must be reduced in order to obtain pure expression. Indication is how signs function outside the reduction. If expression is primordially, at its origin, always contaminated by expression, then Husserl's phenomenological reduction is impossible. For Husserl the logical condition of the possibility of meaning is the reduction. That is, only when expression is purged of indication through the reduction is meaning possible. Only then can a sign have meaning. But because the contamination of indication can never be reduced, argues Derrida, there is always an irreducible difference between a sign and the meaning of a thing or experience.

For Husserl, expressions have a single meaning whilst indications have occasional meanings (Schutz, 1974, p. 169). Expressions meet logical truth conditions, while indications have a set of different meanings which may be trivial. For Husserl, only for the transcendental ego, only with the move out of the natural attitude into the theoretical or reflexive attitude, is meaning (and he means univocal and also logical meaning) possible. If the sign is always already also indication then the reduction is impossible and meaning must be delayed or deferred. The reduction is for Husserl how we can know things themselves. Knowing things themselves does not mean knowing the outer surfaces of trivial things such as a table. The sort of things whose categorial structure, whose mode of existence, is at issue are things like man, society, number, colour, consciousness, the world, and the like. The reduction means bracketing the succession of appearances, of *Abschattungen* of things, and thus grasping the categorial structure of things; thus grasping their essences. It is the 'intuition of essences'. Knowledge of the specific categorial structure of objects is knowing their meaning (Derrida, 1973, pp. 92–4; Levinas, 1973, pp. 9–10). For this the reduction and the sign as pure expression is necessary. And since the sign as pure expression is not even analytically possible, meaning in this more ontological sense of knowing the categorial structure of entities of major importance must always be deferred.

This is the crux of the original sense of 'difference'. As it stands it seems fine in order to critically analyse texts of literature as entities, as objects, perhaps even as experience. But it has got little to do with intersubjectivity, the human sciences, ethics, solidarity and politics. To understand solidarity, to understand recognition or respect for the other, it is necessary to think seriously about intersubjectivity, and to understand intersubjectivity, a notion of tradition is necessary. But any notion of intersubjectivity is excluded here. Let us look at this a bit closer. Derrida, in deconstructing the distinction of expression and indication, wants at the same time to privilege the second term over the first. He wants to privilege indication over expression, reference over sense, and rhetoric, in the classical sense, over logic (Garver, 1973, p. xxvii). He wants to privilege 'figural' over 'discursive' signification (Lash, 1990).

Now the notion of indication in Husserl may well be multivocal, may well be closer to forms of life, may well be uttered from the natural attitude, but it none the less has to do with the relations between people and things and not with intersubjectivity. It is a matter of I–it and not I–thou. Signification through indication bears extensive similarities with Peirce's notion of indexical signs. Peirce thus distinguishes between symbol, icon and index in terms, effectively, of a sign's closeness to the natural attitude, its situatedness, the extent of what anthropologists call the sign's 'motivation'. Indexes, like indicators, are not uttered from a transcendental position. Unlike indicators, indexes are not *per se* multivocal, but instead their meaning is determined by the concrete position from which they are uttered. Pronouns, for example, are thus indexes, in that they make no sense unless the concrete antecedent is already known, whereas a generic substantive like 'capitalism' may be meaningful without any reference to its concrete context. (See Eco, 1984, pp. 137–9; Habermas, 1971.)

The Peircean notions of index, more than Derrida's indicators, are a step towards the natural attitude in which any meaningful notion of solidarity and tradition must be explored. It is very much in the natural attitude that Heidegger addresses the sign in *Being and Time*. Heidegger addresses the sign specifically in the chapter on the 'Worldliness of the World'. Here, section 17 is entitled 'Reference and Signs'. Only reference is not, as in Frege, in semiotics and linguistic philosophy, rendered as *Bedeutung* but as *Verweisen* (Heidegger, 1986, p. 76). *Verweisen* in German is a much more concrete term than *Bedeutung*. It also means assigning. That is, *Bedeutung* can also be translated as 'meaning', while *Verweisen* would be 'with reference to', i.e. *Verweisung auf* or *Verweisung an* something. *Verweisung* has the sense of an 'arrow', literally an indicator, almost more like a signal than an index, in the sense that *Bedeutung* does not. Yet having introduced reference, Heidegger (1986, p. 77) says that the ontological structure of the sign is not to be understood in terms of reference, but that reference is at the heart of the ontological structure of relations. That is, that formal relations are derivative of this more basic structure of reference (*Verweisung*).

Heidegger then says that signs are in the first instance to be understood as equipment for indicating (ibid., p. 78). This is consistent with his understanding of the world as a ready-to-hand, spatially articulated structure of equipment (*Zeuge*). Because signs are equipment, their categorial structure or their being is determined as ready-to-handness (p. 78). Thus Heidegger's signs do have a prima facie resemblance to what Husserl and Derrida mean by indication. But Heidegger does not use the Husserlian term *Anzeichen* for indication, but instead uses *Zeigen*, which also means show or point (p. 78). Again, *Anzeichen* would be an abstract derivative of *Zeigen*. *An-zeichen* includes *zeichen* (sign) in its meaning, whereas *Zeigen* is like pointing with your finger. The example Heidegger uses is the turn-signal on a car (p. 78). Thus signs, to the extent that they are equipment, are *Zeigzeuge* (p. 78).

But Heidegger continues, and notes that signs are more than equipment. They are a particular kind of equipment that 'gives way' to something else (p. 79). Here, giving way is also raising to our circumspection the totality of equipment (p. 79). In this sense the sign is the way the ready-to-hand announces itself. This second aspect of the being of the sign is not the same as the being of equipment or the being of the world. It instead partakes of *Dasein*'s being and 'Dasein's Being in the world'. This second dimension of Heidegger's sign bears similarities, though placed fully in the natural attitude, to Husserl's notion of expression. In this sense a sign is still a *Zeigzeug*, that is, equipment for indicating. But it is not a thing, as it is in its capacity purely as equipment. Husserl's expressions allow us to intuit the essences of things, that is, to know their categorial structure. Similarly Heidegger's signs, to the extent that they do not function purely as equipment, allow us to orient ourselves in the equipmental totality of the world, bringing this totality to our circumspection.

This is indeed heady stuff. It is crucial for Heidegger's displacement of the Husserlian reduction, and is of the utmost centrality in any social or culture-theoretical discussion about the situatedness of knowledge. The problem is that all this goes on outside of any context of intersubjectivity. Heidegger's *Destruktion* of the sign, like Derrida's deconstruction and Husserl's original intention, is a matter not of intersubjectivity but of *Technik*. German philosophers today commonly stress the counterposition of *Philosophie der Moral* and *Philosophie der Technik*. Most schematically, *Philosophie der Moral* addresses relations between *Menschen und Menschen* while *Technik* addresses relations between *Menschen und Dingen*. And Heidegger, it is argued, is in this context very much a philosopher of the 'I–it' of *Technik*. Thus Heidegger's famous subsequent criticisms of the Third Reich are on the basis of its being caught up in the sending of Being as technology, while he steadfastly refused to criticize Nazis on the basis of morality.

This refusal of intersubjectivity is most apparent in the chapter on Being-In (*In-Sein*) in *Being and Time*. If the chapter on the worldliness of the world concerns the categorial structure, or being of beings (*Seienden*) and the being of the world, then the chapter on Being-In primarily addresses the categorial structure, the being, the 'existential analytic' of *Dasein*. Here we see how beings are disclosed to *Dasein*; that is, we see the 'ways of existence' through which beings are disclosed to *Dasein*. Heidegger addresses this through explication of the categorial structure of 'the there'. But in as much as *Dasein* is not a subject which is found inside some sort of abstract space, *Dasein* 'is', as Heidegger (1986, p. 134) notes, 'its there'. Here Heidegger is giving us a hermeneutic explication of notions of knowledge addressed in the Kantian categories and Husserl's intentionality. Here Husserl, as we noted, would understand the Kantian categories not so much as categories of the understanding, but as the categorial structure of things in so far as they are conceived in the natural sciences. For phenomenology, consciousness would have a very specific categorial structure, a very specific mode of existence. The categorial structure of consciousness, the essence of consciousness, lies in intentionality. That is, consciousness is the only kind of being that can intuit the essences of other beings, can assume the transcendental attitude and perform the eidetic reduction. Intentionality here, Levinas (1973, p. 41) stresses, does not at all mean the intentionality of a 'subject' in regard to an object. Consciousness is neither a substance nor subject. The notion of substance itself, in the categories of Aristotelian logic and the Kantian understanding, is naturalistic. And the idea of subject and object entails that of two substances. This is quite similar to Heidegger's Being-In. Instead of intentionality we have *Dasein* as 'the there', as 'that Being which carries in its inmost Being the character of not being closed off' (Heidegger, 1986, p. 132). It is also the being through whose illuminated opening the being of other beings is disclosed.

Heidegger, like Husserl, looks at knowing (or in this case disclosure) via a temporality of consciousness (*Dasein*). For Heidegger this contains moments of past, present and future. The past moment he calls *Befindlichkeit*, literally 'finding oneself', and specifically, for Heidegger, 'finding oneself thrown' (in a Kierkegaardian sense) into existence (p. 135). We should note here that *Dasein*'s access to truth via the past has nothing to do with tradition, with, as in Gadamer, a previous historical intersubjectivity of experience. It has to do with no intersubjectivity at all, but instead the immediacy of thrownness and mood. The future moment of the temporality of *Dasein*'s access to the truth of beings is called *Verstehen*, or understanding. It has to do with the projection of future horizons against which the being of beings disclose themselves (ibid., p. 145). But compare this with the notion of understanding (*Verstehen*) in other phenomenological accounts such as Schutz. For Schutz, as for Weber and Scheler, 'understanding' is specifically differentiated from 'meaning' in that it entails intersubjectivity. It has to do with *Verstehen* of the other, not of objects or experience (Schutz, 1974, pp. 137–8; Srubar, 1988).

The other thus plays a very small role in Heidegger's existential analytic. It is the I–it relation not the I–thou which dominates. Similarly, though Derrida (1978b, pp. 123–4) subsequently aligns himself with what he sees as intersubjectivity in Levinas, his initial deconstruction of Husserl was not of Husserl's lack of a notion of intersubjectivity. Difference had nothing to do with the same and the other. It had to do not with an exploration of 'the limit' or 'the frame' of Husserl's I–it relation in order to find 'the trace' of the I–thou. It was instead the displacement of Husserl's I–it relation with Derrida's own spatio-temporally deferred I–it. The other is nowhere in sight.

TEMPORALITY AND INTERSUBJECTIVITY

There are of course two senses to difference. The first, discussed at length above, is taken graphically, is spatial. The second is temporal. It is where Derrida speaks of the temporal deferral of meaning or *différance*, which is why difference is spelled with an a. Let us look at this temporal deferral, which again is a deconstruction of Husserl. As in other deconstructions, what Derrida does here is to find traces that, against a thinker's will, escape from the space of the metaphysics of presence and point to its outside, to its limit conditions. In this second temporal deconstruction of phenomenology the starting point is Husserl's *Phenomenology of Internal Time-Consciousness*. Here intentionality and the reduction is not the intuition of essences of objects, or knowledge of the categorial structure of objects. It is not even transcendental in Husserl's normal sense of the word. It is instead immanent. That is, intentionality is not exterior to consciousness in the intuition of the structure of objects, but is directed interior to consciousness at *experience*. So we are talking about an immanent, not a transcendental intentionality (Levinas, 1973, pp. 37–40).

This entails a notion of meaning based on the relationship between consciousness and immediate experience. Meaning here is dependent on fixing the flow of experience, through what Husserl calls the 'reflective glance'. Once fixed, units of experience become in principle discrete and repeatable. That is, experiences do not have meaning or only have trivial meaning until they are reduced through the ego 'ray' of the reflective glance in order to constitute the experiences as phenomena. Here at issue are two attitudes towards immediate experience. And Husserl (like Derrida) enjoins us to begin not with thought or the 'I think' but with the 'I experience'. The attitude of immediate experience is the 'natural attitude', and the attitude of the transcendental and eidetic reduction is the 'reflexive' or 'theoretical attitude' (Schutz, 1974, p. 68). In the natural attitude as Husserl describes it the ego undergoes a flux of experience, a sort of temporality that is very much, Derrida later noted, like Bergson's *durée*. The reflexive attitude – with its fixing and 'lifting out' of units of pre-phenomenal experience in order 'polysynthetically' to constitute phenomena and achieve meaning – involves a certain spatialization of time, though not that of the substantialism of naturalism and positivism (Game, 1991, pp. 92–8).

Now given the temporality of the natural attitude of immediate experience, of the ebb and flow of overlapping shadows, and confused images of *durée*, then where does 'difference' lie? It lies in the first place in that its meaning, for Husserl, can never be a matter of 'presence'. This is because even in the reflexive attitude, the ego itself cannot be lifted out of experience. That is, some units of the ego's experience are in the natural attitude whilst others are in the reflexive attitude. And because units of experience must temporally succeed one another, the ego cannot be in the natural attitude and the reflexive attitude at the same moment. Thus to create meaning in an act of eidetic reduction the ego must reflect on the immediate experience of a *past* moment. Thus meaning can never be a matter of presence, never a matter of identity, but must have the character of absence and difference. There must thus always be temporal difference or deferral between experience and the constitution of meaning. Meaning is even less a matter of presence and identity for those chains of acts that Husserl calls 'actions'. These involve a goal and a project. Here meaning is always delayed into the future of any given moment of experience. So again there is deferral or temporal difference. Only whereas with the reflexive 'act' temporal difference was a matter of memory or recollection, in the project-action it is a matter of anticipation (Derrida, 1973, pp. 63–5; Schutz, 1974, pp. 74–5).

There are two major problems with this idea of temporal difference. The first is that Derrida again does not very fully at all break with the reflexive attitude for the natural attitude. This was already characteristic of his deconstruction of Husserl's sign. Here, whereas Heidegger, as we saw above, fully left the reflexive for the natural attitude, Derrida stays in what he sees as an irredeemably corrupted reflexive attitude. Derrida does the same in regard to temporality. Bergson's temporality of *durée*, his *Lebensphilosophie*, pits the uncorrupted natural attitude of 'life' against the theoretical (reflexive) attitude of 'thought'. Derrida, however, still inside the reflexive attitude, goes no further than noting the unavoidable deferral of meaning.

The point is that to take solidarity and tradition seriously is not just strongly to thematize, not just the I–it but also the I–thou; it is also fundamentally to break with the reflexive for the natural attitude. Thus Habermas's intersubjectivity of the ideal speech situation is placed par excellence in the reflexive attitude. It counterposes itself to the tradition-based intersubjectivity of Gadamer. It will not speak the language of substantive values, only that of formalist procedural norms (Benhabib, 1992, pp. 72–3). Its notions of speech acts are lifted out from ongoing forms of life. Finally its idea of validity claims recalls the logical truth conditions of Fregean propositions. The problem is that the ostensible 'anti-Habermas', Jacques Derrida, though he is aware of its impurities, still partakes very significantly of the assumptions of the reflexive attitude.

There are a number of different ways of departing from the reflexive for the natural attitude. In *Lebensphilosphie* there is Bergson's move from thought to life, or Nietzsche's from (reflexive) slave moralities to the (natural) will to power. There is, for example, the late Wittgenstein's counterposition of (natural) forms of life with the early Wittgensteinian reflexive and descriptive logical positivism. There is Heidegger's counterposition of present-at-hand and ready-to-hand, and the corresponding opposition of the categorial and the existential. The notion of existence in existentialism, for example, partakes

of the natural attitude as opposed to the essences (substance) and thought of
the cogito. There is Jacques Lacan's counterposition of the unconscious to
(Anna) Freudian ego-psychology.

Likewise, there are different ways of conceiving temporality in the natural
attitude. Though Derrida's initial deconstruction of Husserl's notion of time
retains a stance largely in the reflective attitude, his later – and most of
deconstruction's – philosophy of temporality does pit natural against theoretical attitude. Here the viewpoint is largely Bergsonian, pitting time as
radical contingency versus time as abstract order. Here as *durée*, the natural
attitude's temporality is also the time of immediate experience (*Erlebnis*). It
is disconnected, follows no logic of its own; it is contingent and disruptive;
it starts and stops in fits; it erupts; its images or figures overlap. It is temporal without at all having any kind of narrative organization; it is fully de-
territorialized. But pivotal to all these characteristics of deconstruction's
temporality is *Erlebnis*, or immediate experience.

In contraposition to deconstruction, hermeneutics – still inside the natural
attitude – opens up a vastly different sort of temporality. The notion of
temporality in *Being and Time* is conceived as in the natural and not the
reflective attitude. Time, for Heidegger, is in the natural attitude in that it
is the horizon of *Existenz*, conceived in counterposition to the theoretical
abstraction of the metaphysical ('onto-theological') tradition. But in so far as
things are encountered against the background of an horizon, *Dasein* never
has immediate experience or *Erlebnis*, but experience is already mediated by
the horizon. Experience is then to be conceived not as *Erlebnis* but as *Erfahrung*;
as always mediated. Now Heidegger's temporality owes little to intersubjectivity, and *Dasein*'s horizon is that against which the being of beings
(*Seienden*, not other *Daseins*) is disclosed to *Dasein*. Further, the temporality
which forms this horizon is conceived not in terms of tradition, but instead
as defined by our finitude in regard to death, our thrownness, our falling and
our understanding as projection.

In *Being and Time* Heidegger gives very little space for intersubjectivity –
only in the small and weakly developed section on *Mitsein* does he address
this. *Mitsein* here is, *pace* Bauman (1993) and Levinas, not primarily a matter
of *Mit ein andersein* or a national and militaristic *mit ein andermarschieren*.
Mitsein, as Derrida notes, is not an ontic but an existential category. Yet the
point for us is not that Heidegger's notion of intersubjectivity partakes of
Black Forest tribalism, it is that he has little notion of intersubjectivity at
all. It is telling, however, that the short discussion of intersubjectivity in
Being and Time is followed directly by Heidegger's ominous introduction of
Das Man (Derrida, 1978b, p. 319; Heidegger, 1986, pp. 117–18).

The equivalent of what I here am calling *Erfahrung* – and my notion is principally drawn from Gadamer (1986, pp. 352ff; 1989, pp. 346–62) and Schutz (1974, pp. 111–12) – is conceived by Heidegger in *Being and Time* as exceedingly individualistic. Given the 'workshop model' of the world in *Being and Time*, one would have expected a notion of *Erfahrung* more like the everyday German idea of an *erfahrender Geselle*, an experienced journeyman. Such experience, such *Erfahrung*, in contrast to either the immediate experience of *Erlebnis*, or the heightened individualism of being-towards-death, is rooted in intersubjectivity and tradition, is already mediated by the *long intersubjectivity* of tradition and by the longer one of history (Ricoeur, 1981, pp. 127–8). Thus Bourdieu's 'habitus' and the notion of the body in Mauss are 'practical', and practice in this sense – which evades the reflexive and logocentric juxtaposition of theory and practice – is located in the natural and not the reflexive attitude. But in such notions of practice, the body – habitus – is not like a self or consciousness confronting immediate experience. Experience is always mediated through a body, an habitus, which itself is learnt and infused with the intersubjectivity of tradition.

TIME AGAINST BEING

Perhaps a better way into an ethics of difference, of deconstruction, is via the work of Emmanuel Levinas. Levinas explicitly draws on Buber's 'I–thou' to construct a notion of intersubjectivity which he calls 'sociality'. His work is explicitly an ethics and comprises a strong notion of temporality which is not ultimately that of the immediate *Erlebnis* of *durée*. Levinas, as we saw above, has a very strongly ontological reading of Husserl. Conversely his reading of Heidegger is phenomenological, in that focus is on the being of beings, that is the exisential structures of beings rather than on the 'sending' of being. Thus if Derrida should be read as primarily deconstructing the logical dimension of phenomenology, hence literally logocentrism, Levinas's deconstruction is indeed – as he specifies – literally a challenge to '*ontology*'. Levinas, though he recognizes a certain affinity between his work and Derrida's, does not view his work as exemplifying deconstruction, but instead phenomenology. That is, he wants to 'intuit the essence' of (Heideggerian) ontology. But in the course of this reduction Levinas finds no essence, no categorial or existential structure at all, but instead the 'I–thou' relation of the ethical.

Thus after his apprenticeship as a very young man to Husserl and Heidegger – resulting in that prescient book *The Theory of Intuition in Husserl's Phenomenology* – Levinas wrote *De l'existence à l'existant*. Existents and existence is, he says, a euphonious way of talking about being and beings (*Sein* and *Seiende*, *l'être* and *étants*). *De l'existence à l'existant* is Levinas's first major attack on the idea of being; his initial break with both Heidegger and Husserl. Here 'being' is developed in Levinas's famous notion of the '*il y a*'. Levinas (1990, pp. 10–11) specifically distinguishes his notion of being from Heidegger's '*es gibt*', in which being gives in a 'plenitude' of 'generosity'. It gives by filling and fulfilling the being of beings, as well as the being of *Dasein*, which it fills as the opening through which the being of beings is disclosed. Levinas notes that his notion of being as the '*il y a*' is not generous but empty and stingy. It is also impersonal in the sense that '*il pleut*' or '*il fait nuit*' is impersonal. The '*il y a*' is empty, like a desert, it is 'obsessive', 'horrible', 'insomniac', it is like a child who wakes up in a nightmare and sees not beings but monstrous shadows creeping about his bedroom (ibid., pp. 109–10). The *il y a* is also something that beings cannot escape. It follows beings, human beings, about like a shadow. That is, *Dasein* is oppressed by the Being of his being (p. 94). Levinas thought, in *De l'existence à l'existant*, to give some idea of the character of the *il y a* through a phenomenology of laziness and fatigue (pp. 41ff).

But Being is more than emptiness. It is a '*remue-ménage*', as Maurice Blanchot called it, a 'bustling', a household bustling, a bustling of equipment. The emptiness of being, of the *il y a*, its impersonal neutrality, is also that of the economy, of possession, of the 'war of all against all' of Hobbes, and of early liberalism's possessive individuals (Levinas, 1990, pp. 26–7). In this, subjectivity is the mastery of the ego over the anonymous *il y a* of being. Subjectivity entails a materiality and solitude of, not infinity, but immanence. 'Experience and solitude', Levinas (1983, p. 13) intones, 'in the light of knowledge absorbs all other.' Beings or existents for Levinas are not the condition of possibility of being, but the bustling of being is being without existents, being without beings. This is because existence denies existents by engulfing them. Being denies beings (or *Seienden*) of their alterity, of that part of them which is not captured by their essence, by their categorial structure, by their mode of existence. As *Dasein* or consciousness, Being for Levinas would force human beings to be 'transcendental reducing' or 'disclosing' animals. Those parts of us as human existents, which are exterior to our capacity as disclosing or reducing animals, is denied by Being.

There is, however, a way out, an exit, from Being, from the *il y a*, in an exteriority of 'the Good', which, as in Plato, is 'beyond Being'. Levinas (1974, p. 13) underscores that the movement by which an existent moves towards the good is not a move to a better existence but an exit from Being (existence) and all its categories. Levinas is pointing here to a movement out

of the 'inhuman neutrality' of ontology, whether as transcendental consciousness or as Being. He is invoking a movement outside the 'representation' of
beings as the same, towards a more tenuous 'desire' of beings as the other.
This is a 'de-neutralization' of being as the other becomes no longer mediated
but 'proximate' (1974, pp. 105ff). As proximate and unmediatable the other
becomes unrepresentable and unknowable. The other is thus 'infinite', in the
sense that the thing-in-itself, God and reason are unknowable and infinite in
Kant. Ethics and the Good outside of Being are a question of the ego's (*le
moi*) or *Dasein*'s relation to the other. This is a relation not of intentionality,
nor of mutual disclosure as in *Mitsein* (Heidegger, 1986, pp. 121–2). Levinas
is proposing effectively a shift towards the natural attitude, and to a sort of
intersubjectivity in the natural attitude. But unlike Schutz or Gadamer this
intersubjectivity is a matter of not knowing the other; it is not all based in
a notion of understanding. Without understanding, recognition, I submit, is
impossible and solidarity unattainable.

Levinas calls himself 'a metaphysician'. And indeed he is one in several
senses. First he is a metaphysician in that his ethics is a 'first philosophy'.
Secondly, he mobilizes the 'infinity' of metaphysics against the finitude
of ontology. Thirdly he is a humanist. But his humanism is ranged against
the universalisms of previous humanisms. It is defined against Early
Modern (Grotian) natural law, eighteenth-century liberalism and Marxian
(Feuerbachian) humanism. Levinas's humanism is not universalist but instead
proximal. He maintains that it is not our humanity but our inhumanity that
lies in our capacities as essence-intuiting (or being-disclosing) animals. Our
humanity is instead in that left-over part, our own *part maudite* that exits
from Being's neutralization.

Levinas has characterized his immediate post-war work as 'the Good and
Time'. Thus the lectures making up his *Le temps et l'autre* were written at the
same time as *De l'existence à l'existant*. Let us look at the temporality of the
Good which Levinas constructs in this. Time here is no longer a question of
existence's finitude of being-towards-death; rather the 'desire of the infinite'.
For Heidegger, Being is neither finite nor infinite, whereas *Dasein* and existence are pre-eminently finite. Care, propounds Heidegger in Division One of
Being and Time, is the being of *Dasein*. Division Two of the book is largely
devoted to rethinking care in regard to the horizon of temporality. Thus
Heideggerian temporality is, for Levinas, bound up with *Dasein*'s self-
consciousness, in that what Being gives to *Dasein* is a temporal structure of
disclosure and self-disclosure. These notions arouse Levinas's ire and condem-
nation. For him time is neither the ontological horizon of the being of *Dasein*
nor the synchronic time in which *Dasein* represents itself. Levinas castigates

Heideggerian time as a 'dispersion of being' in *Dasein*, consisting of 'moments, exclusive of each other, each which propels the preceding into the past, outside of its presence, but which still furnish the idea of this presence', suggesting 'meaning and non-meaning, death and life'. Levinas here would see Heideggerian time as effectively 'onto-theological'. He stands in opposition to such an 'intellectualist' conception of god, whose time as 'eternity is a unity', and whose dispersion as 'multiple' in Dasein is a result of 'the death of God' (Levinas, 1983, p. 9).

For Levinas, phenomenological and ontological time, the temporality of *Erlebnis* and *Erfahrung*, are instances of 'synchronic time' whose basis is the knowledge or 'representation' of the other. In Husserl this other is either the flux of immediate experiences or the objects intuited by the ego. In either case there would effectively be two temporalities: one of the reflective ego, and a second of either experiences or objects in which the first temporality 'synchronically' would 'represent' the second. In Heideggerian time it would be the horizon of the natural attitude which permits *Dasein*, synchronically, to know and represent beings. For Levinas (1983, p. 8), in contrast, time is a 'diachronic relation' of 'thought to the other', in which thought 'desires' the other as 'infinite'. On this view, 'dia-chronic' – in contrast to the synchronic time of ontology – precludes the knowledge or representation of the other. It also precludes the nullification of the other in a 'relation of "satisfaction" and "enjoyment"'. Levinas (1983, p. 8) here is speaking of a relation beyond satisfaction which 'signifies a surplus of sociality'. Who, then, is this other, and what sort of relationship are we talking about? The other is not a being (*Seiende*) or an experience or objects as in Heidegger and Husserl. The other is also not a consciousness, an ego or *Dasein*. The other, for Levinas, is either 'God' or 'the other man' (*l'autre homme*). Whether deity or human, this other is infinite in the sense of Kantian noumena in that he/she cannot be known. So if, because in this de-synchronization, thought cannot represent or cognize the other, then how does thought relate to this other? The answer is through 'desire'.

Thought's or the 'I's relation to either God or the human other is via desire. Desire here means a sensible relation, through the senses, rather than through reason, law, or even Kantian 'rational faith'. The locus classicus of this is in Kierkegaard's *Fear and Trembling*. It is the recounting of the story of Abraham from the Old Testament, in which God addresses Abraham: and not as if the latter were general ego, transcendental consciousness or even 'rational man'. God addresses Abraham in his flesh-and-blood singularity. Abraham cannot hide from his responsibility as Abraham before God. He must say 'Here I am.' Contrary to what might be understood as any sort of communion or covenant with God, contrary to any natural or codified law, contrary to reason, Abraham is asked to sacrifice his son. He is not even asked this via any legitimating pretext of reason or law, but through the senses, through the sensible voice, through the 'grain', in Roland Barthes's sense, of the voice of God (Bhabha, 1994, p. 184). He is asked via a word whose sensibility exceeds the realm of the sentence in a determinate and bodily signification. Kierkegaard understands this, not as the shame but as the glory of Abraham (Rose, 1992, p. 12). In this relation between God and Abraham, the Infinity that is God is not a 'supreme being' as in intellectualist versions of the Judaeo-Christian tradition. It is in no sense a substantive (and neither is it a verb or adverb). God, as the Jewish *Yahweh*, not only cannot be represented, it cannot be grasped (*com-pris*). It cannot even be pointed to as in Heidegger's *Verweisen*. Not only cannot knowledge grasp this Other, but thought itself is 'in-adequate' to such an Infinite (Levinas, 1983, p. 10).

My relationship with the other – a relationship in which both same and other are 'singular' (that is, neither universal nor particular) – is a relationship, writes Levinas, without terms; a relationship in which neither same nor other is a substance. What connects the temporality of the 'I' with that of the other is not intentionality, but 'a thread, a tenuous thread'. The 'I' here is so proximal to the other that signification cannot be very mediated at all. It must be immediate; it must be highly motivated. It must be more akin to index than to symbol, or icon. It must be more proximal than index, more immediate even than a signal. It is a relationship with, as Levinas says, the 'face' of the other, with the 'skin' of the other's face. This very, not discursive, but 'figural' regime of signification deals with meanings that, Levinas says, are '*non-figuré*', that is, that cannot separately be inscribed. This is a form of signification between bodies which are not substances, and are thus unassignable to speakers' positions in discourses.

In most instances Levinas's other retains its proximity and singularity, incredibly abstract in terms of its particular nature. Usually the other is God or *l'autre homme*, or a face which is at the same time singular and nameless. Yet he still insists that the other is a 'surplus of sociality' beyond the concept. This surplus further (1983, p. 8) takes the shape of a 'set of figures of sociality encountering the face of the other man: eroticism, paternity . . .'. He writes that the 'dia-chronic' describes the relationship of thought 'to otherness (*autrui*) – the feminine, the child, the ego's fecundity'. And that it is these latter which are the Good – 'and not the ecstasy in which the same absorbs itself into the other' – that 'is articulated by the transcendence of time' (1983, pp. 13–14). What 'opens up' time for Levinas is this transcendental alterity. Such temporal alterity does not understand difference, as does logocentrism, in terms of different attributes that similar substances have, but as different 'contents'; thus Levinas understands femininity, not as difference of quality in human beings, but as radical alterity of women from men. The ethical in 'the exceptional epiphany of the face', writes Levinas (1983, pp. 14–15) depends on this sensual *'socialité à deux'*. Here the 'radiance (*rayonnement*) of the ethical in eroticism' is instantiated in the alterity of the feminine, in the 'epiphany of the face' in which alterity is 'carried' by the 'thou shall not kill'.

CONCLUSIONS

But what kind of time is Levinas referring to? It is, in the first instance, a time that is constituted in opposition not only to historicity and historicism but to history itself. That is, history for Levinas must be relegated to the realm of the *il y a*. And illeity is exterior to any of that. It is exterior to the public realm of history. Hence perhaps the locus of incursions of illeity in the 'private sphere', in fecundity, generations, family and the feminine. The public realm is governed by the principle of the reduction, by economy, by all against all. And temporality, as opposed to history, is 'opened up' only where there is illeity. Further, even in the private, in the sensual of the feminine, it is the also, but otherwise, sensual and revelational 'thou shalt not kill' that is 'carried' in 'the epiphany of the face'. The sort of temporality that this invokes is not so much the disjunctive temporality of Bergson's (and Derrida's) *durée*, but instead that of eschatology. That is, the temporality of the Good finds its determinacy in revelation and ultimate redemption. It is here where illeity resides. This is, Levinas pronounces, 'older', more 'primordial' than ontology.

If we were to read this sociologically, with say Weber, we would understand what Levinas calls phenomenology in terms of the universalism of modernity, and ontology as the particularism of tradition. What Levinas is thus saying is that ontology or tradition is just as rationalist, just as cognitivist, just as epistemological as modernity. And that history – whether in tradition or modernity – must be rejected for this primordial moment of the time of the other – which is for him the only time that matters. He is saying by implication that this time is so old as to be not only pre-modern, but pre-traditional.

But how old indeed is Levinas's primordial sensual and singular moment of revelation, and the eschatological time it constitutes? This is not the place for sustained discussion, only for a few, perhaps sociological, suggestions. Is it more primordial than tradition, despite its insistence on sensible proximity versus the mediation of rational law? Or is it instead itself post-traditional and from the time of the birth of the world religions? Is it, despite its insistence on the proximity and materiality of God's word, 'onto-theological', or what sociologists following Weber call 'religio-metaphysical', in which the metanarrative of secular history is culturally prefigured by the big metanarrative of redemption and revelation? Surely this sort of reading of Levinas, can only be reinforced by his Kantian insistence on the infinitude, the unknowability of the ethical? Are we, at least in a very important sense, not back in the abstract ungrounded ethics and metanarratives that have made Marxism and liberalism so out of touch with the turn of the twenty-first century? Would not deconstruction in its Levinasian version be just as inadequate as Marxism and liberalism in conceiving solidarity?

I have argued for the limits of the philosophy of difference. The problem with an ethics and politics of deconstruction has been understood very help-fully by Gillian Rose (1992, pp. 263–4) as due to the very 'singularity' of its *problematique* in opposition to the universalism–particularism dichotomy of logocentrism. These three terms correspond, though cannot of course be reduced, to the Weberian trinity of tradition (the particular), modernity (the universal) and charisma (the singular). Here deconstruction is the negative dialectic, the heterodoxy of the prophetic singular. And this constitutes at the same time the richness and the limits of the theory of difference. This two-sidedness is instantiated in what is indeed one of the richest veins of deconstruction's re-thinking of contemporary political culture: post-colonial theory. Post-colonial theory, for example, in the work of perhaps its strongest proponent, Homi Bhabha (1994, pp. 142ff), proposes a politics of temporal-ity, of 'narrating the nation'. He proposes a temporality that takes place within the Derridian limit – in the 'in-between' – of the historicity of totalizing 'pedagogical' narratives of the nation and the disjunctive, dissemi-nating, 'performative' temporality of the excluded other of that narrative. As alterity, as difference, the other cannot of course be known by the same. This is original, provocative work, and Bhabha's notion of the 'limit' as the in-between of Western and post-colonial peoples is an advance on Derrida's and Levinas's notions of the 'limit' in terms of abstract exteriority. Yet once again we have the same pattern in which the pedagogical narrative is the atemporal yet historical *il y a*, and the performative, disjunctive incursions of the 'peo-ple without history' illeity. That is, the other of the nationalist narratives of universalism is not the particular but the *singular*.

Let this chapter stand as a plea for neither modernism's universal, nor the postmodern 'singular', but instead for this particular. Let post-colonial diaspora be understood not just in terms of 'routes', but also in regard to 'roots'. Let the realm of Being, including institutions, communities, economics, space of everyday life, be understood not as the barrenness of the '*il y a*', but as the plenitude of '*es gibt*'. If there is anything that militates against any possible notion of solidarity, any notion of 'the we' in a conceivable politics of deconstruction, it is – despite its name – its incessant constructionism. Hence not just gender but sex is constructed, science is constructed, identity is constructed, objects are constructed. But what about *es gibt*. What about 'the given'? To the extent that we are born or thrown or throw ourselves into a set of already existing forms of life, to the extent that we have a habitus, to the extent that we are our practices, human beings are not just 'anything goes' individualists, but alongside their constructions, find themselves substantially enracinated in this sort of 'given'. Without some sort of 'given', some sort of plenitude of forms of life which fill us up as subjects, no understanding, no recognition – either of same or other – is possible. Without some sort of given, values cannot be, but only the norms of procedure, or the anti-normative and anti-valuation of the 'anything goes'. But who then is the giver of this given? It need not be God, Christ, the state or the family. Perhaps we are all potentially givers of this given, of *die Gabe* or the gift. Perhaps the given has to do with the reciprocity of symbolic exchange – in which the gift is not only sweetness and light, but generations of revenge. But how can this be possible in an age, not of symbolic exchange, but of dead, digitized symbols; not of forms of life, but a virtualized habitus? This is what can be understood as the question of 'reflexive community', comprising a reflexivity radically divergent from the phenomenological reduction. I hope that we have taken some steps, in this chapter, at least in beginning to problematize this question.

NOTES

This chapter was inspired by debates and discussions at the Detraditionalization conference organized by the Centre for the Study of Cultural Values at Lancaster in July 1993. Its themes grew out of a Continental Philosophy reading group which met at Lancaster from 1992 to 1994. Let me thank the group's 'core', Mick Dillon, Alastair Black and Andrew Shanks for all I learned from them during the group's discussions. I have also learned a lot about Levinas during my joint supervision with Paul Morris of Nicky Chu. More recently, I am grateful for conversations with Celia Lury on non-semiotic forms of signification and with Linda Woodhead on 'the given'.

What has become this chapter was presented in sketch in papers at (a) the Foucault Conference organized at Goldsmith's College by Vikki Bell and Nikolas Rose in

April 1994 (under the title: 'The Cultural Prejudices of Radical Politics: Deconstruction versus Hermeneutics') and (b) at the International Sociological Association conference in Bielefeld, in a Sociological Theory group session chaired by Franco Crespi, held in July 1994 (under the title: 'Reflexive Community and Solidarity').

1 The initial draft of this paper, *'Genèse et structure et la phénoménologie'*, by Derrida, was written in 1959. It was re-drafted quite thoroughly and published in French in 1965. It was translated into English in *Writing and Difference* in 1978. (See Critchley, 1992, pp. 63ff.)

REFERENCES

Baudrillard, J. 1994: *Symbolic Exchange and Death.* London: Sage.

Bauman, Z. 1993: *Postmodern Ethics.* Oxford: Blackwell.

Beck, U., Giddens, A. and Lash, S. 1994: *Reflexive Modernization.* Cambridge: Polity.

Benhabib, S. 1992: *Situating the Self.* Cambridge: Polity.

Bhabha, H. 1990: The Third Space. In J. Rutherford (ed.), *Identity*, London: Lawrence & Wishart.

Bhabha, H. 1994: *The Location of Culture.* London: Routledge.

Critchley, S. 1992: *The Ethics of Deconstruction: Derrida and Levinas.* Oxford: Blackwell.

Derrida, J. 1973: *Speech and Phenomenon. And other Essays on Husserl's Theory of Signs.* Evanston: Northwestern University Press.

Derrida, J. 1978a: '"Genesis and Structure" and Phenomenology'. In J. Derrida, *Writing and Difference*, London: Routledge, pp. 154–68.

Derrida, J. 1978b: Violence and Metaphysics: An Essay on the Thought of Emmanuel Levinas. In J. Derrida, *Writing and Difference*, London: Routledge, pp. 79–153.

Eco, U. 1984: *Semiotics and the Philosophy of Language.* London: Macmillan.

Gadamer, H. 1976: *Philosophical Hermeneutics.* Berkeley: University of California Press.

Gadamer, H. 1986: *Wahrheit und Methode. Grundzüge einer philosophischen Hermeneutik.* Tübingen: JCB Mohr, fifth expanded edition.

Gadamer, H. 1989: *Truth and Method.* London: Sheed and Ward, second revised edition.

Game, A. 1991: *Undoing the Social: Towards a Deconstructive Sociology.* Milton Keynes: Open University Press.

Garver, N. 1973: Preface, to J. Derrida, *Speech and Phenomenon.* Evanston: Northwestern University Press, pp. ix–xxx.

Habermas, J. 1971: *Knowledge and the Human Interests.* London: Heinemann.

Heidegger, M. 1986: *Sein und Zeit.*, 16th edition. Tubingen: Max Niemeyer Verlag.

Laclau, E. 1990: *New Reflections on the Revolution of our Time.* London: Verso.

Laclau, E. (ed.) 1994: *The Making of Political Identities.* London: Verso.

Lash, S. 1990: *Sociology of Postmodernism.* London: Routledge.

Levinas, E. 1973: *The Theory of Intuition in Husserl's Phenomenology.* Evanston: Northwestern University Press.

Levinas, E. 1974: *Autrement qu'être ou au delà de l'essence*. Paris: Kluwer/Martinus Nijhoff.

Levinas, E. 1983: *Le temps et l'autre*. Paris: Quadrige/Presses Universitaires de France.

Levinas, E. 1990: *De l'existence à l'existant*. Paris: Librairie Philosophique J. Vrin, 2nd edition.

Parsons, T. 1968: *The Structure of Social Action*. New York: Free Press.

Ricoeur, P. 1981: *Hermeneutics and the Human Sciences*. Cambridge and Paris: Cambridge University Press and Editions de la Maison des Sciences de l'Homme.

Rose, G. 1992: *The Broken Middle. Out of our Ancient Society*. Oxford: Blackwell.

Schutz, A. 1974: *Der sinnhafte Aufbau der sozialen Welt. Eine Einleitung in die verstehende Soziologie*. Frankfurt: Suhrkamp.

Searle, J. R. 1969: *Speech Acts. An Essay in the Philosophy of Language*. Cambridge: Cambridge University Press.

Srubar, I. 1988: *Kosmion*.

Thompson, J. 1981: *Critical Hermeneutics*. Cambridge: Cambridge University Press.

Walsh, W. H. 1975: *Kant's Critique of Metaphysics*. Edinburgh.

Weber, M. 1963: *The Sociology of Religion*. Boston: Beacon.

Part IV

Dissolving Detraditionalization

14

Databases as Discourse, or Electronic Interpellations

Mark Poster

THE MODE OF INFORMATION AND DATABASES

In this chapter I shall underscore the way computerized databases function as discourses in Foucault's sense of the term, that is, the way they constitute subjects outside the immediacy of consciousness.[1] This effort contrasts with other critical positions on databases which miss their discursive effects, treating databases with categories that overlook the decentring operations of language on the subject. Such, for example, is the case with Marxist writings, such as those of Herbert Schiller (1981) and Tim Luke (1985), in which databases are seen as contributions to the power of major institutions, especially corporations. Here databases are a new instrument for capitalists to tighten their grip on the mode of production. Information in databases, Marxist critics advise, is not equally available to all, as the somewhat utopian proponents of this technology contend, but redound preponderantly to the benefit of the economic ruling class. Similarly, liberal writers on the subject, such as David Burnham (1983), James Rule (1974) and Gary Marx (1988), address in particular the appropriation of database technology by the state, warning of the considerable augmentation of centralized power it provides. Liberals are concerned in particular with the threats to privacy occasioned by databases in the hands of the government.

While these perspectives certainly offer much to consider, they fail to expose the cultural innovations brought about by the integration of database technology into existing political, economic and social institutions. In each case, Marxist and liberal perspectives incorporate the novel system of knowledge into their existing conceptual framework, revealing only that side of the phenomenon that fits within its grid of understanding. For Marxists databases are comprehensible only to the extent they are a factor in the struggle over the means of production; for liberals databases enter the field of politics as a component in the never-ending danger of autocratic central government. For both positions the novelty of databases is reduced to a minimum and the social individual or class as configured by the theory remains unchanged with the advent of the new. I posit that critical social theory must explore, in addition to these offerings, the relation of databases to the cultural issue of the constitution of the subject and that to do so Foucault's theory of discourse provides a most compelling guide.

With respect to the problem of culture, the chief limitation of Marxist and liberal theories is that they configure the social field primarily as one of action, minimizing the importance of language. With respect to databases, the action in question for Marxists is the relation of power between capitalists and workers, while for liberals it is the fate of political domination. Both positions forget that databases are composed of symbols; they are in the first instance representations of something. One does not eat them, handle them, or kick them, at least one hopes not. Databases are configurations of language; the theoretical stance that engages them must at least take this ontological fact into account. A form of language, databases will have social effects that are appropriate to language, though certainly they will also have varied relations with forms of action as well.

The poststructuralist understanding of language is of special relevance to an analysis of databases that proceeds from critical social theory because of the connection it draws between language and the constitution of the subject. Poststructuralists make a number of salient claims about the interaction of language and subjects: (1) that subjects are always mediated by language; (2) that this mediation takes the form of 'interpellation'; and (3) that in this process the subject position that is a point of enunciation and of address is never sutured or closed, but remains unstable, excessive, multiple.

The first proposition is to be understood neither as tautological nor as innocent. A human being is configured as a subject, is given cultural significance, in the first instance through language. The kind of bearing that society imposes on individuals, the nature of the constraint and the empowerment it operates, takes its effect in language. The significance of the proposition may become more clear if we remember that in our culture the bearing of language on individuals tends to be systematically obscured by the privilege we give (in language) to the subject as a point of origin of motivation, consciousness and intention. Since Descartes's articulation of the configuration of the subject, since the dissemination of this configuration in Enlightenment thought, since the inscription of this configuration in the major institutions of representative democracy, capitalist economics, bureaucratic social organization and secular education, it has become the cultural foundation of the West. Once understood as a subject, the individual is fixed in the binary opposites of autonomy/heteronomy, rationality/irrationality, freedom/determinism. The linguistic level of the configuration is actively forgotten or naturalized as the subject faces these binaries from the vantage point of interior consciousness.

At the micrological level of daily life the subject is continuously reconstituted as such through interpellation or 'hailing'.[2] In determinate linguistic acts the subject is addressed in a position and/or provoked to an enunciative stance in a manner that obscures the position or the stance. When a teacher calls upon an elementary school student to answer a question, the position of the student as an autonomous rational agent is presupposed, a position that the student must 'stand into' first in order to be able to answer, in order to be a student. The operation of linguistic interpellation requires that the addressee accept its configuration as a subject without direct reflection in order to carry on the conversation or practice at hand. Interpellation may be calibrated by gender, age, ethnicity or class or may exclude any of these groups or parts of them. The issue is not that interpellation is an invasion of society upon the individual that ought to be avoided; that objection already falls within the binary freedom/determinism and presupposes the constitution of the individual as subject. Rather what is important is that the process goes on at the level of language and that in Western culture it takes the particular form of the subject.

The third proposition is that the interpellation of the subject is always partial, incomplete, riddled with gaps and open to reconfiguration and resistance. The constitution of the subject in language is different from the Newtonian understanding of the world of material objects, in which matter is pushed and pulled into determinate positions by laws that are inexorable and unchanging. In the most trivial case, the subject is always multiple, interpellated into different positions: the student is also child, friend, pet's master. But in each instance of interpellation, the subject is configured as fixed, determinate, closed. In adult circumstances of some social weight, interpellation appears to be, or better is, structured as final, real, complete. The fixing of identities is not a matter of being pushed or pulled by gravity but of being invited to play a role in such a way that the invitation appears to have already been answered by the subject before it was proposed, but at the same time the invitation could be refused.

FOUCAULT'S CONCEPT OF DISCOURSE

An understanding of the poststructuralist sense of the relation of language to the subject is necessary to gauge the stakes at play in Foucault's concept of discourse, a concept that in turn is crucial to a critical approach to databases. Foucault employs the term discourse in most of his writings, especially in his work of the 1960s, *The Order of Things* (1966/1989) and *The Archaeology of Knowledge* (1969). In these works Foucault presents a critique of the human sciences and an alternative method of analysis. The term discourse is introduced above all as a counter-position to those who understand writing as the expression of a subject, those who, in their search for meaning in acts of reading or listening, move from words back to consciousness. Here is one of Foucault's more lucid statements of this position.

> In the proposed analysis, instead of referring back to *the* synthesis or *the* uni-fying function of *a* subject, the various enunciative modalities manifest his dispersion. To the various statuses, the various sites, the various positions that he can occupy or be given when making a discourse. To the discontinuity of the planes from which he speaks . . . I shall abandon any attempt, therefore, to see discourse as a phenomenon of expression – the verbal translation of a previously established synthesis; instead, I shall look for a field of regularity for various positions of subjectivity. Thus conceived, discourse is not the ma-jestically unfolding manifestation of a thinking, knowing, speaking subject, but, on the contrary, a totality, in which the dispersion of the subject and his discontinuity with himself may be determined. It is a space of exteriority in which a network of distinct sites is deployed. (1969, pp. 54–5)

The relation of writing to the subject is sharply reconfigured in this passage. The term discourse is used primarily as a way to register the difference of Foucault's theory of writing from that of humanism. It designates a move towards an exteriorization of the analysis which itself is strategic. Foucault's claim is not that he has discovered the one, true way to understand knowledge or even that his way is somehow epistemologically superior to other, human-ist ways. Only that if one seeks a critique of knowledge in our twentieth-century culture, if one seeks to distance oneself from our culture's way of regarding its own knowledge, the term discourse indicates the path of that move.

Many critics of Foucault, who are usually themselves within the humanist way of knowing, complain that Foucault does not adequately specify the term discourse as a field, does not carefully indicate the boundaries of discourse, or its object. Manfred Frank (1992), for example, even quotes Foucault as acknowledging this deficiency, except Frank takes it as an admission of failure rather than as an indication that the interest of the term discourse lies not in relation to a well-defined object but in relation to a level of analysis of any knowledge domain. Here is Frank's quote from Foucault:

> Finally, instead of making the rather hazy meaning of the word 'discourse' more distinct, I think that I have multiplied its meanings: sometimes using it to mean a general domain of all statements [*énoncés*], sometimes as an individualisable group of statements [*énoncés*], and sometimes as an ordered practice which takes account of a certain number of statements [*énoncés*]. (1992, p. 110)

Foucault appears to be suggesting that if the aim is a critique of knowledge in our society then the effort of theorization need not so much focus on delimiting the object but on specifying the level of meaning one is attempting, so that the relation of knowledge to the subject – in other words the cultural construction of the subject – can be raised as a question.

Beginning with the essay 'The Discourse on Language', first presented as his inaugural lecture at the Collège de France in 1970, Foucault introduced a connection between the terms 'discourse' and 'power'. From that point on, most effectively in *Discipline and Punish* (1977) and *The History of Sexuality* (1978), Foucault developed usages of the category 'discourse' that were distinct from those in his earlier works. In the 1970s and 1980s discourse was frequently used as a couplet, 'discourse/practice', an indication that Foucault refused the separation of discourse from the 'non-discursive'. He also introduced terms such as 'technology of power' and 'micro-physics of power' in which discourse was subsumed into arrays and articulations of various kinds of practices, institutional, disciplinary, resistive and so forth. The question of the relation of language to the subject was here considerably broadened: as language, discourse was configured as a form of power, and power was understood as operating in part through language.

THE PANOPTICON AS DISCOURSE

The question of discourse, with its imbrication to power, then, is about the cultural issue of the constitution of the subject. And in particular it is about the constitution of the subject as a rational, autonomous individual. Max Weber had also developed the thesis of the rational subject as a problem, as an index of domination rather than, as in liberalism and to a certain extent in Marx, as a sign of freedom. But Weber's understanding of rationality was burdened by its character as a universal principle. He was able to historicize the problem of reason and the subject only to a minimal extent. Foucault noted this difference in his position from that of Weber, attributing to him an understanding of rationality as 'an anthropological invariant', whereas Foucault's own effort was to analyse reason as historically constructed (Foucault, 1991, p. 79).

Foucault's problem then is to construct a theory of discourse that historicizes reason, reveals the way discourse functions as power and spotlights the con-stitution of the subject. Strictly speaking Foucault never provided such a theory because, he argued, theory reinscribes the rational subject at another epistemological level. Instead he demonstrated such a theory of discourse in his histories of punishment and sexuality. The closest he approached such a theory is found in brief statements, mostly in his occasional writings, such as the following given in a late interview:

> I do indeed believe that there is no sovereign, founding subject, a universal form of subject to be found everywhere. I am very skeptical of this view of the subject and very hostile to it. I believe, on the contrary, that the subject is constituted through practices of subjection, or, in a more autonomous way, through practices of liberation, of liberty, . . . on the basis, of course, of a number of rules, styles, inventions to be found in the cultural environment. (1988, pp. 50–1)

Discourse is understood as having a power effect on the subject even in movements of 'liberation'.

The power effect of discourse is to position the subject in relation to structures of domination in such a way that those structures may *then* act upon him or her. The chief characteristic of the power effect of discourse is to disguise its constitutive function in relation to the subject, appearing only after the subject has been formed as an addressee of power. A classic example of this operation of discourse is, for Foucault, psychoanalysis. The discourse/practices of Freud produce in the subject an Oedipalized child, an under-standing of one's childhood as, in the case of boys, a desire for one's mother. Once the child-subject is so constituted by psychoanalytic discourse, the child is then seen as being forbidden this desire, with the consequences of the Oedipal trauma and its deep effects on the personality. But the crucial point is that the effect of the discourse/practice is to name the child's desire, to configure the child as a libidinal subject with the particular aim of its mother (see Foucault, 1978, pp. 129–31). Discourse has the same function in *Discipline and Punish*.

The modern system of punishment, incarceration, is first of all itself not the result of a rational subject. Against liberals and Marxists, Foucault argues for a Nietzschean genealogy of prisons in which its origins are found neither in the ideas of the Enlightenment nor in the workings of early industrial capitalism. Foucault traces the origins of the prison to a multiplicity of non-related pieces of earlier history: Enlightenment critiques of Old Regime forms of punishment, military training practices and schedules, procedures of examination in schools, Bentham's architectural ideas for prisons – none of which is understandable as a cause of the prison. Foucault (1977) attributes the origin of the prison to a kind of non-agency, as follows: 'Small acts of cunning endowed with a great power of diffusion, subtle arrangements, apparently innocent, but profoundly suspicious, mechanisms that obeyed economies too shameful to be acknowledged, or pursued petty forms of coercion – it was nevertheless they that brought about the mutation of the punitive system, at the threshold of the contemporary period' (p. 139). Having dethroned the rational subject from the agency of the establishment of prisons, Foucault goes on to analyse its operations as discourse.

The story is by now well known. Prisoners reside in cells surrounding a central tower in which a guard is placed who can look into the cells but whom prisoners cannot see. An invisible authority is thereby instituted, one who is all-seeing (hence the term 'panopticon') but invisible. This instance is part of a complex articulation of discourse/practices which includes the juridical practices that sentenced the individual to prison, criminologists who study prisoners as individual cases, administrative schedules and routines for prisoner activities, evaluation procedures for possible parole, and so forth. Foucault characterizes the operation of the panopticon in these words: 'By means of surveillance, disciplinary power became an integrated system . . . it was also organized as a multiple, automatic and anonymous power; for although surveillance rests on the individual, its functioning is that of a network of relations from top to bottom . . . and laterally . . . this network holds the whole together and traverses it in its entirety with effects of power that derive from one another: supervisor perpetually supervised . . .' (1977, p. 177). Properly understood, the panopticon is not simply the guard in the tower but the entire discourse/practice that bears down on the prisoner, one that constitutes him/her as a criminal. The panopticon is the way the discourse/practice of the prison works to constitute the subject as a criminal and to normalize him/her to a process of transformation/rehabilitation. My argument is that with the advent of computerized databases a new discourse/

practice operates in the social field, a superpanopticon if you will, which reconfigures the constitution of the subject.[3]

DATABASES AS A SUPERPANOPTICON

Databases are discourse, in the first instance, because they effect a constitution of the subject. They are a form of writing, of inscribing symbolic traces, that extends the basic principle of writing as *différance*, as making different and as distancing, differing, putting off to what must be its ultimate realization. In its electronic and digital form, the database is perfectly transferable in space, indefinitely preservable in time; it may last forever everywhere. Unlike spoken language, the database is not only remote from any authorial presence but is 'authored' by so many hands that it makes a mockery of the principle of author as authority. As a meaningful text, the database is no-one's and everyone's yet it 'belongs' to someone, to the social institution that 'owns' it as property, to the corporation, the state, the military, the hospital, the library, the university. The database is a discourse of pure writing that directly amplifies the power of its owner/user.

And everyone knows this. Because they do know it, they resist it. A poll by *Time* magazine in late 1991 revealed that between 70 per cent and 80 per cent were 'very/somewhat concerned' about the amount of information being collected about them in databases, with the higher figure referring to the federal government, credit organizations and insurance companies, and the lower figure referring to employers, banks and marketing companies.[4] The population is now cognizant of being surveilled constantly by databases and it apparently feels ill at ease as a result. Database anxiety has not as yet developed into an issue of national political prominence but it is clearly a growing concern of many and bespeaks a new level of what Foucault calls the normalization of the population.

Examples of the politicization of databases multiply every day. The US federal government has developed FinCen (Financial Crimes Enforcement Network), with an awesome power that combines artificial intelligence programs with massive parallel processing to monitor bank transactions for the purpose of detecting criminal activity.[5] In the economic sphere, retailers that sell by modem regard the information they accumulate about customers as their property, as a valuable asset, gained as a by-product of the sale, which they may then sell to other retailers. But customers do not want such information about themselves travelling, beyond their ken, from one vendor to another. Although an effort by the Lotus corporation in the early 1990s to sell customer information was thwarted by consumer protests,[6] resistance to the use of these types of databases is likely to fail because it is based on the modern, political distinction between the public and the private. Consumers regard their purchases as private, as part of the capitalist system, which designates all economic transactions as 'private'. But databases are a postmodern discourse that traverses and cancels the public/private distinction.

Increasingly, economic transactions automatically enter databases, and do so with the customer's assistance. Credit card sales are of course good examples. According to the conventional wisdom of political economy, the consumer buys something in a 'private' act of rational choice. Yet when the credit card is extracted from the wallet or purse and submitted to the clerk for payment, that 'private' act has become part of a 'public' record. The unwanted surveillance of one's personal choice becomes a discursive reality through the willing participation of the surveilled individual. In this instance the play of power and discourse is uniquely configured. The one being surveilled provides the information necessary for the surveillance. No carefully designed edifice is needed, no science such as criminology is employed, no complex administrative apparatus is invoked, no bureaucratic organization need be formed. In the superpanopticon, surveillance is assured when the act of the individual is communicated by telephone line to the computerized database, with only a minimum of data being entered by the sales clerk. A gigantic and sleek operation is effected whose political force of surveillance is occluded in the willing participation of the victim.

Unlike the panopticon, then, the superpanopticon effects its workings almost without effort. What Foucault notices as the 'capillary' extension of power throughout the space of disciplinary society is much more perfected today. The phone cables and electric circuitry that minutely crisscross and envelope our world are the extremities of the superpanopticon, transforming our acts into an extensive discourse of surveillance, our private behaviours into public announcements, our individual deeds into collective language. Individuals are plugged into the circuits of their own panoptic control, making a mockery of theories of social action, such as Weber's, which privilege consciousness as the basis of self-interpretation, and of liberals generally, who locate meaning in the intimate, subjective recesses behind the shield of the skin. The individual subject is interpellated by the superpanopticon through technologies of power, through the discourse of databases that have very little if anything to do with 'modern' conceptions of rational autonomy. For the superpanopticon, this perfect writing machine, constitutes subjects as decentred from their ideologically determined unity.

If we look at databases as an example of Foucault's notion of discourse we see them as 'exteriorities', not as constituted by agents, and we look for their 'rules of formation' as the key to the way they constitute individuals. Databases in this sense are carefully arranged lists, digitalized to take advantage of the electronic speed of computers. The list is partitioned vertically into 'fields' for items such as name, address, age, sex, and horizontally into 'records' which designate each entry. A retailer's database has fields which record each purchase an individual makes so that in the course of time a rich portrait of buying habits is created, one that is instantaneously accessible and cross-referenced with other information such as the individual's location, and possibly cross-referenced as well with other databases keyed to items such as social security number or driver's licence. In effect these electronic lists become additional social identities as each individual is constituted for the computer, depending on the database in question, as a social agent.

Without referring the database back to its owner and his or her interests, or forward to the individual in question, as a model of its adequacy or accuracy, we comprehend the database as a discursive production which inscribes positionalities of subjects according to its rules of formation. In this way we see the database outside the dichotomy 'public/private' and outside the dynamics of the mode of production. Instead the discourse of the database is a cultural force which operates in a mechanism of subject constitution that refutes the hegemonic principle of the subject as centred, rational and autonomous. For now, through the database alone, the subject has been multiplied and decentred, capable of being acted upon by computers at many social locations without the least awareness by the individual concerned yet just as surely as if the individual were present somehow inside the computer.

Some readers may object that databases cannot be characterized as discourses in Foucault's sense since for Foucault discourses were large collections of texts. The examples he gives are psychology, economics, grammar and medicine, all of which include sentences and paragraphs strung together by arguments. The same can hardly be said of databases, which for the most part are not textual in this way but rather, agglomerations of isolated words or numbers whose location in the 'discourse' are paramount. The only places where sentences of any kind are found in databases is in the program or code language that constitutes them and in some types of fields that are textual. And yet the crucial features of discourse are indeed contained in databases even though they omit the standard features of prose. Databases are fully what Foucault calls 'grids of specification', one of the three 'rules of formation' of discourse. These grids are 'the systems according to which the different kinds of [the object in question] are divided, contrasted, related, regrouped, classified, derived from one another as objects of . . . discourse . . .'

(1969, p. 42). Nothing qualifies as a grid in this sense as well as databases; they are pure grids whose vertical fields and horizontal records divide and classify objects with a precision that more traditional forms of discourse such as psychology must surely envy.

But what is most important about discourses for Foucault is that they constitute their objects. His greatest concern is to avoid treating discourse as 'groups of signs', as texts or as writing perhaps in Derrida's sense, but to treat them 'as practices that systematically form the objects of which they speak' (1969, p. 49). His emphasis is on the performative aspect of language, on what language does rather than what it denotes or connotes. Computerized databases are nothing but performative machines, engines for producing retrievable identities. A feature of many databases that indicates their status as 'practice' is their 'relational' abilities. Two databases may function as one if one field in each is identical. Thus if a census database and an employee database both have fields for social security numbers (which is increasingly the identifier field of choice), the employer may use the census to discover whatever he might about the employee that is not in his own records but in the census. These kinds of linkages between databases have been used in the Parent Locator System, the effort to find divorced and separated men who do not support their children. Relational databases thus have built into their structure the ability to combine with other databases, forming vast stores of information that constitute as an object virtually every individual in society, and in principle may contain virtually everything recorded about that individual – credit rating data, military records, census information, educational experience, telephone calls, and so forth.[7]

The most sophisticated examples of the use of relational databases are in market research firms such as the Claritas Corporation. This company boasts the use of 'over 500 million individual consumer records from *several* leading databases'.[8] The company combines and analyses data from the following categories of databases: media and market research studies, newspaper research (including readership of newspapers, viewing of television and listening to radio), customer research studies, car and truck registration data, mailing lists and credit rating data. The company combines over 1,200 databases of both the private and public sectors. Claritas generates its own database, 'Compass', which it makes available to its customers for their own research. Its masterpiece though is a database called 'Prizm' that is an identity construction system. Prizm divides up the entire population into 'clusters', which can be as fine-grained as six households. Each cluster is then fitted into forty types such as 'rank and file', 'black enterprise', 'single city blues', 'furs and station wagons', and so forth. Each type is defined by income, per cent of the US population, age, class, size of household, and 'characteristics'. In the case of the identity known as 'bohemian mix', some 1.1 per cent of the population, characteristics are, for example, 'Buy, wine by the case, common stock; Drive, Alfa Romeos, Peugeots; Read, *GO*, *Harper's*; Eat, whole-wheat bread, frozen waffles; TV, *Nightline . . .*'. The company then provides a few sample zip codes where this species may be found.[9]

Databases such as Prizm constitute subjects in a manner that inscribes a new pattern of interpellation.[10] The 'hailing' of the individual is here quite distinct from that of the teacher and the student, the policeman and the perpetrator, the boss and the worker, the parent and the child. In these cases there is often a direct message sent and received in a face-to-face situation. With databases, most often, the individual is constituted in absentia, only indirect evidence such as junk mail testifying to the event. Interpellation by database in this respect is closer to the instance of writing, with the reader–subject being hailed by an absent author. But here again there are important differences: from the standpoint of the person being interpellated, the writer is known, even if only as a writer, and is an individual or finite group of individuals. The reader very often intentionally selects to be interpellated by the particular author, whereas in the case of computer databases that is rarely if ever the case. Interpellation by database is a complicated configuration of unconsciousness, indirection, automation, and absent-mindedness both on the part of the producer of the database and on the part of the individual subject being constituted by it.

More research needs to be done in order to specify the configuration of interpellation in various types of databases, to answer the question of just how centred or dispersed subjects are in these cases and the characteristics of this dispersion or multiplicity. However, the above discussion suffices to indicate the importance of databases in complicating the concept of interpellation. The computer database inaugurates a new era of interpellation far different from that of modernity with its discourses of print and its handwritten system of case files. The category of interpellation may serve as the leading thread in a critical interpretation of databases, one that specifies the attributes of subject constitution, reveals the domination inherent in the process, and indicates the path by which the positions of enunciation at which subjects are interpellated may be multiplied throughout social space, mollifying the noxious effects of the discourse.

Once the form of representation embodied in the database is understood, it may be compared to other regions of the mode of information – television viewing, computer writing, telephone conversation, video and audio recording, and so forth. Each of these cultural technologies also have discursive effects, the sum of which may be seen as slowly erecting the basis of a culture that is decidedly different from the modern. In each case the subject as a coherent, stable, rational centre is refuted by heterogeneity, dispersion, instability, multiplicity. The database is part of a larger, massive cultural transformation which positions the subject outside the framework of visibility available to liberal and Marxist theoretical orientations. No wonder Jean-François Lyotard struck a chord when he announced in *The Postmodern Condition* (1984) his 'incredulity toward metanarratives'. As daily life is pervaded more and more by the regions of the mode of information, the culture of modernity enjoys less and less verisimilitude. Though the effects of the mode of information are differential with respect to class, gender and ethnicity, they constitute a very general phenomenon that betokens a new play of power, a new dialectics of resistance and a new configuration of politics and its theorization.

Like television, music reproduction, computer writing and video art, databases generate discursive effects by simulating a reality, or better, to use Baudrillard's term, a hyperreality. The fields that compose the database construct representations of individuals. The fields, often consisting of a fixed amount of characters, are highly limited by the imperative of the technology, its rule of formation in Foucault's sense, which is retrieval speed. The database is effective only to the extent that its information is instantaneously accessible but at the same time it must be large and comprehensive in relation to its referent population. Near total coverage and instantaneous accessibility characterize a good database. Yet this accessibility refers to the constructions within the database, which function as simulacra of the population covered. To the database, Jim Jones is the sum of the information in the fields of the record that applies to that name. So the person Jim Jones now has a new form of presence, a new subject position that defines him for all those agencies and individuals who have access to the database. The representation in the discourse of the database constitutes the subject, Jim Jones, in highly caricatured yet immediately available form.

Another way of understanding the discursive nature of databases is to relate them to what Foucault calls governmentality. This is a form of power characteristic of welfare states. It is neither the micro-physics of power that characterizes local situations in everyday life, nor the grand state power of monarchs and presidents. Governmentality is a kind of bureaucratic power, one that relies upon knowledge of the populace to police society and maintain order. Foucault, in places, calls it 'biopower' and takes as its precursor the management of the family as in ancient Greece, the original meaning of economy (1991, pp. 87–104). He defines governmentality as follows: 'To govern a state will therefore mean to apply economy, to set up an economy at the level of the entire state, which means exercising towards its inhabitants, and the wealth and behaviour of each and all, a form of surveillance and control as attentive as that of the head of a family over his household and goods' (ibid., p. 92). Governmentality, or the form of power of the welfare states of the advanced industrial societies of the later twentieth century, is inconceivable without databases. The vast populations of these societies might well be ungovernable without databases. Databases provide contemporary governments with vast stores of accessible information about the population, which facilitates the fashioning of policies that maintain stability. An important political effect of databases, as they have been disseminated in our societies, is to promote the 'governmental' form of power, to make knowledge of the population available to coercive institutions at every level.

To counter this stabilizing effect of databases, Lyotard, in *The Postmodern Condition*, suggests that a new emancipatory politics would consist in giving everyone access to databases (p. 67). Certainly this policy, however utopian under present circumstances, would serve to democratize information. Each individual or group would have easy computer access to the same information as the government. Although such a prospect sounds utopian, given the increasing poverty, it is conceivable that at least in principle computer access to such databases could be widely extended to the vast majority of the population. A policy that worked in this direction would indeed constitute a 'freedom of information' act. The thought of government critics being able to race through the cyberspace of data even as it is recorded is a counterfactual that gives one pause.

Yet as a strategy of resistance it does not take into account the performative effect of the discourse of databases, their ability to constitute subjects. The implication of Lyotard's position is that 'real' subjects would recuperate the 'power' inherent in the databases, enabling them to manipulate its knowledge for their own ends, a politics different from the current conservative restrictions on the use of databases to those who can foot the bill, usually large social organizations. The thesis of the liberation of the databases presupposes the social figure of the centred, autonomous subject that the databases preclude. Postmodern culture configures multiple, dispersed subject positions whose domination no longer is effected by alienated power but by entirely new articulations of technologies of power. The cultural function of databases is not so much in the institution of dominant power structures against the individual but in restructuring the nature of the individual. Lyotard's suggestion presumes that knowledge and power are separable, that increased availability of databases equals increased knowledge equals increased power. But the viewpoint that I am proposing posits a different relation of knowledge and power, one in which knowledge itself is a form of linguistic power, the culturally formative power of subject constitution.

The process of subject formation in the discourse of databases operates very differently from the panopticon. Foucault argued that the subject constituted by the panopticon was the modern, 'interiorized' individual, the one who was conscious of his or her own self-determination. The process of subject constitution was one of 'subjectification', of producing individuals with a (false) sense of their own interiority. With the superpanopticon, on the contrary, subject constitution takes an opposing course of 'objectification', of producing individuals with dispersed identities, identities the individuals might not even be aware of. The scandal, perhaps, of the superpanopticon is its flagrant violation of the great principle of the modern individual, of its centred, 'subjectified' interiority.

A politics of databases then would respond to the cultural form of subjectification in postmodernity. Instead of developing a resistant politics of privacy to counter the alleged incursions of databases on the autonomous individual we need to understand the forms of agency appropriate to a dispersed, multiple subject and to generate strategies of resistance appropriate to that identity formation. The issue is not that the new forms of subjectification are in themselves emancipatory but that they are the new arena of contestation. A politics that circumscribes freedom around the skin of the individual, labelling everything inside private and untouchable, badly misconceives the present-day situation of digitized, electronic communications. Since our bodies are hooked into the networks, the databases, the information highways, they no longer provide a refuge from observation or a bastion around which one can draw a line of resistance. The road to greater emancipation must wend its way through the subject formations of the mode of information, not through those of an earlier era of modernity and its rapidly disappearing culture. The appeal for community, as Ernesto Laclau and Chantal Mouffe argue,[11] must take into account the forms of identity and communication in the mode of information, and resist nostalgia for the face-to-face intimacy of the ancient Greek agora. In the era of cyborgs, cyberspace, and virtual realities, the face of community is not discerned easily through the mists of history, however materialist and dialectical it may be.

NOTES

1   I shall be concerned not with all databases but only with those that have fields for individuals. Thus inventory databases, for example, are excluded from my discussion.

2   The concept of 'interpellation' entered the arena of critical theory with Althusser's essay 'Ideology and Ideological State Apparatuses' (1970, pp. 160ff), where the Marxist concept of ideology was presented as the interpellating agent. See also Kaja Silverman (1983).
3   Along similar lines, Gilles Deleuze suggests that we have changed from a disciplinary society to a society of control (1992, pp. 3–7).
4   *Time*, 11 November 1991, p. 36. I am indebted to Carol Starcevic for drawing my attention to this article.
5   See Anthony Kimery (1993, pp. 91–3, 134).
6   Rob Kling (1992, pp. 229–30).
7   David Lyon (1991) moderates the totalizing vision that is often drawn from this analysis: 'it is not so much that we are already enclosed in the cells of the electronic Panopticon, but that certain contemporary institutions display panoptic features. Panopticism is one tendency among others . . .' (p. 614).
8   'Claritas Corporation – An Overview', advertising material furnished by the company in 1991. I am grateful to Colin Fisher for providing this text.
9   The clusters have been listed in *USA Today*, 16 March 1989, p. IB.
10 Colin Hay of Lancaster University suggested this line of inquiry. See his forthcoming article.
11 See Chantal Mouffe (unpublished paper); and Ernesto Laclau (1993, pp. 277–96).

REFERENCES

Althusser, Louis 1970: Ideology and Ideological State Apparatuses. In L. Althusser, *Lenin and Philosophy and Other Essays*, London: New Left Books.
Burnham, David 1983: *The Rise of the Computer State*. New York: Random House.
Deleuze, Gilles 1992: Postscript on the Societies of Control. *October*, Winter 1992, pp. 3–7.
Frank, Manfred 1992: On Foucault's Concept of Discourse. In François Ewald (ed.), *Michel Foucault, Philosopher*, New York: Routledge.
Foucault, Michel 1966/1989: *Les Mots et les Choses*. Paris: Gallimard, translated as *The Order of Things*, London: Routledge.
Foucault, Michel 1969: *The Archaeology of Knowledge*. New York: Pantheon.
Foucault, Michel 1977: *Discipline and Punish. The Birth of the Prison*. New York: Pantheon.
Foucault, Michel 1978: *The History of Sexuality*, Vol. 1: *An Introduction*. New York: Pantheon.
Foucault, Michel 1988: An Aesthetics of Existence. In Lawrence Kritzman (ed.), *Foucault: Politics, Philosophy, Culture*, New York: Routledge.
Foucault, Michel 1991: The Question of Method. In Graham Burchell et al. (eds), *The Foucault Effect. Studies in Governmentality*, Chicago: University of Chicago Press.

Hay, Colin (forthcoming): Mobilisation through Interpellation. *Social and Legal Studies*.

Kimery, Anthony 1993: Big Brother Wants to Look into Your Bank Account (Any Time it Pleases). *Wired*, 1 (6) December.

Kling, Rob 1992: Massively Parallel Computing and Information Capitalism. In Daniel Hillis and James Bailey (eds), *New Era of Computation*, Cambridge: MIT Press.

Laclau, Ernesto 1993: Power and Representation. In Mark Poster (ed.), *Politics, Theory and Contemporary Culture*, New York: Columbia University Press.

Luke, Timothy and White, Stephen 1985: Critical Theory, the Informational Revolution, and an Ecological Path to Modernity. In John Forester (ed.), *Critical Theory and Public Life*, Cambridge: MIT Press, pp. 22–53.

Lyon, David 1991: Bentham's Panopticon: From Moral Architecture to Electronic Surveillance. *Queen's Quarterly*, 98 (3).

Lyotard, Jean-François 1984: *The Postmodern Condition*. Minneapolis: University of Minnesota Press.

Marx, Gary 1988: *Undercover: Police Surveillance in America*. Berkeley: University of California Press.

Mouffe, Chantal (unpublished paper): Democracy, Pluralism and Uncertainty.

Rule, James 1974: *Private Lives and Public Surveillance: Social Control in the Computer Age*. New York: Schocken.

Schiller, Herbert 1981: *Who Knows: Information in the Age of the Fortune*. New York: Ablex.

Silverman, Kaja 1983: *The Subject of Semiotics*. New York: Oxford University Press.

15

Authority and the Genealogy of Subjectivity

Nikolas Rose

INTRODUCTION

What kinds of human beings have we become? This question seems to have returned to the heart of social theory, embodied in a host of investigations of subjectivity, self, the body, desire, identity. It reactivates a theme that was central to sociological and anthropological thought in the early decades of the twentieth century. In different ways Durkheim, Weber, Mauss, Elias and Simmel focused upon the relations between social arrangements and the capacities, moral frameworks, cognitive organization, and emotional economy of the human being as a creature with a history and a sociology. As sociology, psychology and anthropology divided and disciplined themselves over the course of the twentieth century, these concerns were transformed in epistemological and methodological directions; the ethical and political force of this question was lost. Its re-emergence today is thus itself a phenomenon of an historical order. Indeed, at the heart of this renewed concern with the person lies an historical thesis: that something has happened in our contemporary experience that has the character of an event, and that this event concerns the kinds of persons we have come to be.

Do not some obvious changes in our culture bear this thesis out? There is the intense anxiety about personal identity that is manifested in the ways in which so many of our contemporaries frame their lives in terms of a project of self-realization, and engage in an incessant search to 'find themselves'. There is the language of lifestyle, in newspapers, television, and innumerable books and magazines, which seems to imply that persons or groups are increasingly identified not in terms of class or status, but through the ways they conduct a life for themselves: personal appearance, accoutrements, images and preferences in music and so forth. There is the way in which political argument bases itself increasingly upon the value of maximization of individual freedom and choice, and enjoins each person and family to take responsibility for the care of themselves – for their own health (diet, smoking, alcohol); passions (safe sex, contraception); procreation (abortion, genetic technology); future welfare (personal insurance for old age and sickness); security (burglar alarms, personal security systems). And there are the multitudes of 'advisors' to the self that surround us – doctors, counsellors, therapists, newspaper columnists and TV programmes – offering guidance as to how we should achieve a life of personal satisfaction, pleasure, fulfilment and self-realization, how we should cope with anxieties and uncertainties and overcome tribulations. Does not this all suggest that we inhabit a form of life that is uniquely blessed or cursed by an intensification of the value of the 'subjective'?

Perhaps it was Jacob Burckhardt, in 1860, who first popularized the thesis that the march of history had given birth to a new form of individual. Whilst in the Middle Ages man 'was conscious of himself only as a member of a race, people, party, family, or corporation – only through some general category', in the Italian Renaissance 'man became a spiritual *individual*, and recognized himself as such' (1990, p. 98). Burckhardt himself was later to lose faith in his tale of individualism, but others were to invent their history in a similar fashion. Social theorists of the nineteenth century thus utilized an image of tradition which could serve to define the distinctiveness of their own age. Marx, Weber, Durkheim and innumerable others developed different versions of this thesis that 'the individual', or 'individualism' was a modern phenomenon, one to be praised or deplored, explained in different ways, but none the less a sociological phenomenon – a consequence of the effects of changes in the social organization of collective life upon human beings.

In their diagnoses of our current condition, contemporary sociologists and social historians seek to write a postmodern sequel in which the intensification of concerns about the self is understood as the consequence, at the micro-level, of a process of 'detraditionalization' which has inaugurated the age of late modernity, postmodernity, the risk society. But, I suggest, our present 'problem of the subject' cannot usefully be understood by adding a new chapter to the historicist fable which thinkers in the nineteenth century utilized to demarcate the distinctiveness of their own age. The ways in which human beings understand themselves and act upon themselves and others do not fit into such a linear narrative, nor do they emerge as a consequence of 'more fundamental' changes elsewhere – in the conditions of production, in family forms, in 'culture'. Subjectivity has its own history, and it is a history that is more heterogeneous, more practical and more technical than these accounts suggest.

In this chapter, I argue that a critical history of 'the self' should focus directly upon the practices within which, in our own times and in the past, human beings have been *made up as subjects*: the presuppositions about human beings that have underpinned them, the languages, techniques, procedures and forms of judgement through which human beings have come to understand and act upon themselves as 'selves' of a certain type. Such a study would not try to write the history of human psychology; it would address itself to those heterogeneous authorities that have, at different times and places, problematized human conduct and developed more or less rationalized programmes and techniques for its shaping and re-shaping – authorities as diverse as leaders of religious sects, proprietors of houses of correction and asylums for the mad, sanitary reformers, philosophers, politicians, economists and sociologists. It would examine the forms of knowledge and systems of truth that underpinned such programmes, and the intellectual and practical techniques invented and deployed – ranging from fasting to behaviour modification. It would examine the practices that such programmes gave birth to, problematized, or sought to shape – the practices of criminal and civil law, of schooling, of production, of domestic service, of religious instruction, of recreation and the like. And it would consider the ways in which these developments accorded human beings various means for describing, judging, directing their own conduct, as subjects, selves, citizens, individuals, generals, lovers, teachers, labourers, wives, husbands, courtesans or other types of being. It would thus be a study of the connections between the truths by which human beings are rendered thinkable – the values attached to images, vocabularies, explanations, and so forth – and the techniques, instruments and apparatuses which presuppose human beings to be certain sorts of creatures, and act upon them in that light.

The writings of Michel Foucault are particularly suggestive here. His studies describe different facets of the ways in which, in our culture, human beings have made themselves into subjects. There were the discursive fields within which the human being had become the subject of knowledge, of regimes of explanation, classification and interpretation governed by norms of truth. There were the apparatuses within which the human being had become the subject of regulation, of practices which sought to manage the conduct of individuals, to direct them towards certain ends and to shape their conduct under diverse regimes of domination, coercion, persuasion, inducement and seduction – in prisons, schools, asylums, workhouses, factories, families and other spaces of discipline. And there were the technologies through which human beings had been made the subject of diverse 'techniques of the self', technologies that concerned the ways in which one should undertake the practical organization of one's conduct in the daily business of living, in relation to considerations as to the kind of person one should aspire to be and the kind of life one should lead.

Foucault's use of the term 'ethics' for this last set of questions sought to direct attention away from morality as a set of ideals, and towards the rather practical goals, judgements and precepts by means of which individuals relate to their own worldly conduct (Minson, 1993, provides an excellent discussion of this approach to ethics). He directed his enquiries to a domain of practical texts that offered rules, opinions and advice as to how to conduct oneself as one should; texts that were intended to be utilized as functional devices to enable individuals to question their everyday conduct and conduct themselves in their everyday lives. This was a domain of 'concern' for the self: certain ways of worrying about oneself, being troubled about oneself, anxieties about the other selves, reciprocally linked to the dissemination of certain practices of 'care' for the self, looking after oneself, being careful about oneself, making oneself the subject of techniques of solicitude and attention.

Foucault's studies were undertaken in order to unsettle the ways in which contemporary humans had come to experience themselves as the subject of a 'sexuality', with the obligation to conduct themselves by means of a kind of hermeneutics of the self in which the injunction to know oneself was to be understood in terms of a duty to explore, discover and reveal the truth of oneself in the form of one's desires (Foucault, 1986a, ch. 1). He suggested that his investigations of Greek, Roman and Early Christian ethics might form part of a genealogy of the arts of existence. An account of techniques of the self would, through a detour to antiquity, put into question the inevitability of the relations between truth, desire and inwardness that characterize our own ways of being human. It would account for this regime of the self in terms of the incorporation of certain forms of spiritual practice, first of all 'into the exercise of priestly power in early Christianity, and later, into the educative, medical and psychological types of practice' (Foucault, 1986a, p. 11).

The term *ethics* may be misleading, if one thinks of as ethical those practices that enjoin a relation to the self through the divisions of truth and falsity, permitted and forbidden, desirable and undesirable. For example, historians and anthropologists have explored the ways in which the intellect has been transformed through the inculcation of the techniques of reading, writing and calculating (Goody and Watt, 1963; Eisenstein, 1979). Others have begun to write the history of the techniques by which the body is sculpted through the inculcation of techniques of comportment, of clothing, and of expression of emotions (Elias, 1978; Bourdieu, 1979). And Foucault himself investigated the problems, practices, techniques and forms of knowledge that have sought to maximize and control the capacities of human bodies, individually and collectively, through normalization and surveillance, and so forth, inculcating a relation to the self in terms of the norms of discipline (Foucault, 1977). Techniques of the intellect, of display and of the body are frequently enjoined, utilized, deployed in the service of programmes for the moral formation and re-formation of human beings, or as means of moral display. For example, for some nineteenth-century European aesthetes, swimming – together with a valorization of a certain relation to that which was natural – was part of the formation and display of a certain romantic persona (Sprawson, 1992).

The detailed attention to the training of bodily capacities in nineteenth-century schooling – for example in relation to handwriting or posture – was part of an endeavour to produce capacities that were both useful and which embodied a certain cultivated relation to the self. The implantation of numeracy in the United States was encouraged and promoted by Republican educators, who considered that certain numerical capacities – in particular the ability to calculate provided by decimal numbers – would generate a prudent relation to the getting and spending of money, and hence to trade, to political participation and to the conduct of life itself (Cline-Cohen, 1982, pp. 148–9). A genealogy of subjectification thus needs to operate at these innumerable points of intersection between programmes for the government of others and the practical means accorded to human beings to understand and act upon themselves.

This is not a matter of a history of 'ideas' about the self, or the cultural meanings attached to personhood or identity. It is certainly possible to write a history of notions of the human being within cosmology, philosophy, aesthetics, literature, scientific thought and so forth. But it is unwise to make assumptions, based upon such evidence, about the organization and presuppositions of the mundane everyday practices that try to shape the conduct of human beings in particular sites (cf. Dean, 1994). For these practices too have their own history. Human beings neither inhabit a homogeneous domain of representations of personhood which encompasses all practices and techniques, nor do they merely internalize a certain view of themselves through their immersion in a system of meanings. Many have sought to write the history of contemporary forms of self-understanding through the history of philosophy (for example, Taylor, 1989). But philosophy has no privilege in the genealogy of subjectivity. Philosophical doctrines do not index a particular 'spirit of the age', underpin the events in other domains and practices, or spread through society because they contain ideas which seem, at a particular historical moment, to be inherently compelling. From the perspective of an analysis of the government of conduct, philosophical reflections on the nature of human beings are of interest to the extent that they are more contextual, more practical and more technical than this suggests.

James Tully (1993), writing under the rubric of 'governing conduct', has shown that philosophical and moral reflections upon the person and human conduct such as those represented by John Locke do not emerge in a disembodied realm of meditation, but are provoked by certain very specific problems such as those concerning the regulation of the labouring classes; problems of civil and religious conflict, concerns about the balance of power and the ways in which one might protect and extend commercial relations within a field of competition between states. Further, Tully suggests, Locke also sought to *embody* these reflections in various practices for governing human beings: in the 'providential apparatus' of Church and law, in 'the humanist apparatus' for the education of elites, in the apparatus for governing the poor via the Royal Navy, the houses of correction, compulsory apprenticeship and the like. Nevertheless, the grand texts of the philosophical canon have no necessary priority in an investigation of the government of conduct. Whilst philosophers may have concerned themselves with problems of government, our new understanding of ourselves emerged from a more mundane world, from the everyday philosophies of those who sought to govern the mad, the criminal, the sick, the unruly child, the hysterical woman, the childless couple, the strife-torn workplace, the dangerous town. The pertinent texts here are not those conventionally thought of as 'central' to our intellectual heritage, but those consigned to the margins: books of dream interpretation, phrenological manuals, medical pamphlets on the rearing of children, plans and programmes of sanitary reformers or proposals for new types of prison or asylum.[1] Philosophy, like other representations of human beings, is pertinent to the genealogy of conduct only to the extent that it becomes technical, connected to authorities and techniques for the shaping of life in diverse locales and practices.

Equally, one should not assign 'the self' a central role in investigations of the genealogy of subjectification. The 'self' does not form the general substrate or object of practices of 'being human' but a particular style or relation that the human being is enjoined to adopt towards itself, one that links, genealogically, certain practices in Greek, Roman, Christian with those of our own times (cf. Hadot, 1992). This caution concerning the self is not 'merely' a matter of words. Any way of describing ourselves and others – as persons, selves, individuals, personalities, characters, gendered bodies . . . – is a *resultant* of the processes under study. To speak of these processes as 'the constitution of the self' is to imply that, in some sense, these relations 'sum' into a self – a proposition that is extremely dubious.[2] Hence the sort of analysis that I am advocating does not seek to elaborate or to build upon a *theory* of the self in either psychological or fleshly guises. Rather, following Foucault's reflections on 'the relation to the self', it tries to identify and analyse the types of intellectual and practical labour that human beings have directed towards themselves and other members of their species (Deleuze, 1988, pp. 94ff). 'The self' is not that which is shaped by history, it is a particular historical plane of projection of specific projects and programmes that seek to govern humans through inciting them to reflect upon their conduct in a certain manner and act upon themselves through certain techniques.

The human being, from this perspective, is less an entity, even an entity with a history, than the site of a multiplicity of practices or labours. Its interiority is less a psychological system than a discontinuous surface, a multiplicity of spaces, cavities, relations, divisions established through a kind of in-folding of exteriority. And that which is in-folded is composed of anything which can, at a given time and place, acquire the status of *authority*: injunctions, advice, meanings, techniques, little habits of thought and emotion forming not a sphere of interiority but an array of routines of being human. The human being is that kind of creature whose ontology is *historical*; its history requires an investigation of the heterogeneous and localized intellectual and practical techniques that have comprised the 'instruments', as it were, through which being constitutes itself. (Cf. Jambet, 1992.) These have not arisen in some abstract space of thought, but always in relation to certain practices: the places and spaces, the apparatuses, relations and routines that bind human beings into complex assemblies of vision, action and judgement: whether these be those of domestic existence, sexual relations, labour, comportment in public places, or consumption. The history of our relation to ourselves should not be posed in terms of ideas, but of *technologies*: the intellectual and practical instruments and devices enjoined upon human beings to shape and guide their ways of 'being human'.

One might pursue a genealogy of subjectivity along a number of lines.[3] First, *problematizations*: where, in relation to what conditions, and by means of what images or understandings of human beings do certain aspects become the focus of concern, regulation, shaping or reformation: the will, character, desire, the unconscious, the self? Secondly, *techniques*: what means are to be used to govern the human being: the investments of values and energies in procedures for training, shaping, fashioning, mastering, monitoring particular aspects of the person – its corporeal form, its speech, comportment, manners, passions – in order to improve it; to make oneself better? Asceticism and discipline, for example, represent two of the many different modes in which work is performed upon the human being. Thirdly, *expertise*: what authority is claimed by those who have acquired the power to speak the truth about persons, to provide truthful answers to the question of how one should live, how one should direct or remake one's life? Fourthly, what are the objectives of all this work upon the human being, what *subject form* do they seek to produce: what are the images or exemplars of ideal persons promoted or assumed by these practices – wise, responsible, docile, solidaristic, independent, entrepreneurial, the active citizen or whatever? And finally, what are the goals of such practices, what *strategies* are they caught up within? In what ways are the capacities of persons related to attempts to produce certain types of family, workforce, population or society? How is the government of conduct linked up to the formation and delimitation of the political apparatus, and its differentiation from other spheres, for example those of 'personal life' or 'public opinion'?

A SOCIOLOGICAL HISTORY OF INDIVIDUALITY?

What resources do contemporary sociological approaches to the history of the self provide for such an enquiry? The sociological 'just so story' of how the human being got its individuality, as repeated once more in the notion of 'detraditionalization', is a tale in which 'the individual' or 'individualization' appears as particularly 'modern', whether this be thought of in terms of the consequences of the Enlightenment, the product of the Italian Renaissance of the fifteenth century, or the transformation to a market and commodity production from the sixteenth to the eighteenth centuries. It runs something like this. The changes associated with modernity destroyed the fixed social and cultural formations of community and kinship, which had defined the identity of subjects from outside, embedded the person within a stable order of status, within a transcendental and implacable cosmology, within a certain – even if imaginary – space and time. Such persons were not individuals in our modern sense; their personhood emerged from a collective sense of identity, their will was directed according to a traditional and unquestioned moral order, their consciousness was not of a unique individual but of the inhabitant of a given destiny. With modernity, with the move from country to town, from stability and fixity to change and fluidity, from feudalism and agriculture to capitalism, commodity production and the sale of labour on the market, the person takes on a new form: that of the unique, conscious, responsible, atomized, discrete, bounded, coherent, choosing, acting individual equipped with a personal consciousness and a personal conscience. This person is a subject simultaneously of freedom – that is to say, fated to choose, and to shape his or her own life through everyday decisions as to conduct – and of responsibility – that is to say, the locus of address of moral, spiritual and commercial obligations concerning conduct.

In our own time, it appears, a no less fundamental transformation in social relations produces a further unprecedented transformation in the human being. These transformations may be understood as the culmination of processes already present in modernity – as when Anthony Giddens speaks of 'late modernity' or Ulrich Beck of 'reflexive modernity', or they may be seen as a basic mutation in social relations, as when others adopt the language of postmodernity (Giddens, 1991; Beck, 1992; Lash and Friedman, 1992). Despite their differences, the themes that are elaborated are similar. 'Globalization', it is suggested, has eroded the remaining stabilities conferred by locale, community and tradition, thereby disrupting temporal and spatial reference points. It appears that uncertainty has been exacerbated by the amplification of risk at the personal, collective and planetary level, requiring every decision as to conduct in the present to take account of its possible future consequences. All fixed tradition and established habits seem to be questioned as never before by the breakdown of the stabilities of class and patterns of labour, the regularities of the domesticated nuclear family, the roles and divisions of men and women – those standardized forms of life promulgated by the modernization process of the nineteenth century.

This novel multiplication of possible forms of life is reinforced by the images of lifestyle circulated by the mass media, and embedded within a relentless spiral of injunctions to consume in particular ways in order to become particular sorts of people. In this new Babel, whilst a multiplicity of voices claim authority, each is questioned and doubted: none can establish its hegemony. In this account it appears that, for the first time, individuals are liberated from the constraints that previously ordained a way of life: they are required to choose a way of living in conditions of maximum uncertainty.

In these new circumstances, it is suggested, the forms of identity conferred by modernity are themselves destabilized and transformed. Identity is no longer experienced as a natural, coherent and unchanging attribute of the individual, but as the uncertain and fractured result of personal decisions and plans. Biography and identity become self-reflexive, to be constructed, worked upon, the outcome of choices – about clothes, marriage, relationships, diet – in which the individual himself or herself is the self-conscious centre of action. The contemporary proliferation of identity projects and identity politics are explicable: they simultaneously attest to the salience of identity and to its fundamentally problematic character. The burgeoning of therapy and counselling also appears to have its origins in these social and cultural shifts: individuals call upon expertise in counselling and therapy as means of planning a personal life – expert systems which reinforce, and do not violate, the requirement that life should be a personal narrative of self-determination.

The suggestion that the social and cultural relations of each age produce a particular form of personhood is common amongst historians, even when the evidence that they discuss appears to suggest something different. Take, for example, the magnificent five-volume *History of Private Life*, commenced under the general editorship of Philippe Aries and George Duby (Veyne, 1987; Duby, 1988; Chartier, 1989; Perrot, 1990; Prost and Vincent, 1991). These volumes are, in the words of one of their contributors, written against 'the heroic histories of the individual and individualism of which traditional historians have been so fond' (Ranum, 1989, p. 207) – no doubt Orest Ranum here is thinking precisely of Burckhardt and his successors. These studies are significant, it seems to me, because of the evidence that they bring to light concerning the extraordinary heterogeneity of the practices, spaces, gestures, exemplary images and representations of persons, and the ways in which these portray and instruct in appropriate forms of conduct, rituals and techniques. Unlike the grand philosophical histories of the person or self, they do not describe an historical moment in which 'the individual' was born in Western culture. Rather, they show that, from pagan Rome though Byzantium and onwards, in a multitude of different ways, the minutiae of the conduct of human beings has been attended to, described, judged, codified and instructed in relation to a whole range of practices, from those of domestic architecture to those of marital morality and sexual renunciation.

This social history of 'interiority' shows that the relation to oneself in terms of an inner space – private, unique, bounded – is itself a matter of the deployment of specific techniques within particular locales. The diversity of forms of life at different historical moments can certainly not be summed into a singular form of subject inhabiting a singular cultural configuration. Not only do we become aware of the heterogeneity of forms of person assumed in different practices – the urban dweller, the country villager, the labouring poor, the wealthy owner of capital – but we also can see the diversity of codes of conduct that orient any one human being in different fields of thought and action: erotic, spiritual, economic, aesthetic, domestic and so forth.

Such studies indicate, if evidence were needed, that our present ways of understanding and relating to ourselves are not the culmination of a unified narrative of real time – a singular linear chronicity which, despite advances and lags, moves from fixity to uncertainty, from habit to reflexivity across all domains of existence and experience. We must imagine time in ways that are more multiple than are dreamt of in the temporalities of tradition and detraditionalization. Perhaps, rather than *narrativizing* the ways of being human, we need to *spatialize* being. Such a spatialization would render being intelligible in terms of the localization of repertoires of habits, routines and images of self-understanding and self-cultivation within specific domains of thought, action and value – libraries and studies, bedrooms and bathhouses, markets and department stores, living rooms and coffee houses. Against the apparent singularity and linearity of time, and of the person within time, we might pit a multiplicity of places, planes and practices, each of which activates repertoires of conduct that are not bounded by the enclosure formed by the human skin: interiorities that are always also exteriorities, webs of tension across space that capacitate human beings through associating them with vocabularies, instruments and devices.

The work of Aries and his colleagues exposes the poverty of sociological histories of the self, because it multiplies and spatializes the histories of the relations that human beings have established with themselves. But it none the less shares something problematic with the sociological histories. No doubt it is tempting for the historian of the human subject to discover, in the forms of writing, painting, language, clothing, architectural arrangements and the like at a certain moment, the materialization of a certain 'self' consciousness.

Whilst historians of private life are usually sufficiently aware of the complexity of practices of conduct to avoid implying that a 'personality type' is produced by each historical configuration, sociological historians are less discriminating. Their interpretive schemes view cultural artifacts as indexes, expressions or origins of inwardness. They thus collapse diverse practices, organized by different concerns and through different codes addressed to different objectives, into expressions of the 'subjectivity' of the members of a culture. But, for example, depictions of the person, in literature, paintings, television programmes, films, in philosophy and aesthetics, abide by their own rules and have their own histories. Attempts to 'read off' subjectivity from such evidence embody a seductive but naïve hermeneutics. In attempting to make sense of the past in psychological terms, they inevitably project contemporary self-understandings back upon these historical traces. Only the assumed continuity of human beings as the subjects of cultural history, as subjects essentially equipped with meaning-endowing capacities, can provide the trans-historical *a priori* for such interpretive endeavours (Dean, 1994). Whatever the salience of the history of 'social representations', one should not extrapolate from such a history an account of the 'transformation of identity' across a whole society, let alone a whole epoch.

Further, it is worth insisting that changes in social arrangements do not automatically transform the nature and form of 'being human' by virtue of some 'experience' that they produce (cf. Joyce, 1994). One would be unwise to infer subjectivities from such features of social life as the consequences of urban life, new forms of communication, changes in domestic and conjugal arrangements, trading relations, the organization of labour, geographical mobility, ages at marriage or death and the like. The history of subjectification can neither be established by derivation from some other, prior domain of reality, nor disclosed by interpreting other cultural or social forms. It requires an investigation of the specific vocabularies, techniques and authorities that govern an individual's relation to himself or herself: that shape the ways in which human beings understand themselves and are understood by others, the kinds of persons they presume themselves to be or are presumed to be in the various practices that govern them. These *produce experience*, they are not *produced by* experience. Hence one needs to ask different questions. To what extent do authoritative discourses – political, religious, economic, aesthetic, erotic . . . – emphasize the unique person as the key value, as opposed to the group, the flock, the society, the volk, the state? To what extent do forms of authority, in different locales and in relation to different strata and sectors – men and women, young and old, slaves and free – attend to individual characteristics and distinctiveness, to inwardness and personality, rather than to birthplace, lineage, status and the like? What languages render human beings intelligible to themselves: the immortal spirit and the flesh of clay, the inherited constitution and the formation of character, the inborn traits and the socialized personality, the turbulent unconscious and the economy of projections and identifications? To what extent, and in what ways, are persons understood and managed, by themselves and others, in relation to values accorded to an internal self?

But are these issues not of interest precisely *because* they have psychological effects and produce different sorts of people? Norbert Elias (1978) was the most prominent of those sociologists who sought to unify and explain the histories of rules of conduct in terms of a psychology. His *History of Manners* itself provides ample evidence of the fragmentation of the history of the self into an array of problems of governing conduct in distinct practices for different sectors of society, in relation to different models, images and exemplary forms of being – the court nobility, provincial gentlefolk, young boys and girls of the wealthier classes, knights – and the complex processes by which ecclesiastical and other authorities sought to propagate these ideas and insert them into the relations that each such person should have with themselves.

Elias was not alone in attempting to understand his evidence by means of a unified psychological narrative, namely the imposition of constraints upon the expression of instincts and their internalization into a superego through socialization. This will to unify through psychology appears to grip even the most sophisticated sociological historians of the person. The paradox of all such interpretations, however, is that they themselves must rest upon a certain 'theory of the self'. They rest upon the notion – emerging only in nineteenth-century Europe – that human beings *are* characterized by something like a psychological 'personality', an interior domain within which the effects of culture are inscribed, organized and formed into a certain recognizable character. I do not draw attention to this circularity merely to make a debating point. For it is precisely the ways of understanding and practising in relation to our existence as human beings that were invented at this time – in terms of the unity of the subject grounded in a set of psychological processes; the essential interiority of subjectivity prior to its expression in thought, conduct, emotion and action; the relations to knowledge and expertise that this entails – it is precisely *this* that we need to make intelligible if we are to grasp the regimes under which we are, today, governed.

It is characteristic of our own time to try to understand who we are and what we should do by appealing to epistemology, to seek to make our experiences and our possibilities intelligible though recourse to a knowledge of the soul. But a critical history of subjectivity cannot itself rely upon such a truth. On the contrary, the aim of critical history is to make visible the conditions of emergence of this demand, the modes of its functioning, what it costs us to relate to ourselves in this way.

IS 'OUR' EXPERIENCE OF OURSELVES SO DIFFERENT?

Contemporary sociological accounts of the predicaments of the self embody a certain *style* of reflection: they constantly accentuate 'our' difference from all that has gone before. But perhaps we are not on the threshold of a new age or witnessing the close of an old one, not living in times that are so utterly late, new or post. A cursory look at some historical evidence is sufficient to suggest that the linear chronology traced out in these accounts is absurd, at least in so far as it bears upon styles that have characterized human beings' reflection upon and action upon themselves.

Examples of intense concerns with practices of self-government may be found in 'cultures' which have very different forms. Peter Brown's study *The Body and Society: Men, Women and Sexual Renunciation in Early Christianity* (1989) provides compelling evidence that there is nothing unprecedented about an intense problematization of the conduct of the self, and that the conditions under which such self-problematizations arise are heterogeneous and related to particular practices. Thus in the Rome of the first two centuries AD one can find many of the features that sociologists regard as characteristic of individualization – the problematization of people's relations with their selves in a diversity of spheres of conduct, a concern with the inward character of this relation, an emphasis upon the responsibility of the person for shaping his or her own conduct. Yet these concerns occurred within a set of social relations that were by no means 'individualized' in the sense of recognizing the coincidence of personhood with all human beings, freedom from traditional bonds and status relations, and the like. The concerns that Brown documents are neither psychological nor cultural. They are elaborated in particular doctrines concerning persons, doctrines that claim or are accorded the value of truth. They are linked to certain forms of speaking, visualizing and explaining through which individuals are enjoined to understand themselves and to problematize themselves. And they are not merely 'ideas' but are integral to certain practices – ranging from mechanisms of rule to the management of the affairs of domestic households – and to certain attempts to shape or guide the conduct of individuals engaged within these practices.

Some have suggested that the specificity of our own times lies in the pluralization of the languages of self-conduct, the need for choice amongst a diversity of spiritual guides who would teach us how to live, the personal relation between subject and mentor. But neither plurality, choice or voluntarism seems peculiar to the present. Brown emphasizes the diversity of the Christian teachers of the first and second centuries, the key role that different teachings about sexuality, marriage, continence, diet, fasting and the organization of life played in the establishment and ethical formation of the diverse Christian communities, the varied techniques of life and conscience that they taught, and which their disciples practised, and the diverse images of the person that they promulgated. He points to the way in which every well-to-do Christian of the second century 'took it for granted that their spiritual growth depended on close face-to-face consultation with beloved teachers' and to the intensity with which disciples sought prolonged intimate contact with a spiritual guide in counter-position to the insipid preaching of the clergy (p. 104). As Ian Hunter (1993) has remarked, the specific 'techniques of conscience' encouraged in such practices, which entailed the problematization of one's own conduct through self-scrutiny, and the elaboration and practice of techniques of self-control, were produced within certain specific strata and sectors of the population in relation to very particular problems of the government of conduct.

What of the argument that the contemporary predicaments of the self arise from the exacerbation of risk and uncertainty, and its psychological concomitants and consequences for life-planning by individuals? Beck (1992) has suggested that in societies structured by class, individuals did not have to make themselves the centre of their own planning and conduct of life, whereas now increasingly everyone has to choose a social identity, selecting or changing the group or subculture with which they wish to identify (p. 88). This theme, however, is by no means new: it recurs with remarkable frequency in writers deliberating about the nature of their present, from at least the twelfth century. Tradition, then as now, is always that natural mode of life which is lost, whose virtues now can only be regained by explicit acts of government and self-government. This theme has been particularly strong in discussions of urban life. There is a recurrent argument that links the changing nature of the present – all these different presents – to the ways in which urban existence sunders traditional ties and disrupts traditional certainties, forcing individuals to achieve by choice what had previously been accorded to them by fate. Studies such as those undertaken by Jacques Le Goff (1990) and his colleagues have shown how, in medieval towns, it was in relation to such anxieties that the conduct of the self in public and private places – eating, dress, speech, deportment and the like – was to be the object of elaborated rituals that were enshrined and articulated in explicit codes. Further, the conduct of life in such circumstances was held to entail all sorts of calculations about such matters as the age of marriage, the type of trade, the forms of morality: these too were subject to a welter of regulations and authorities that sought precisely to ensure that individuals *did* make themselves the centre of a life that was planned.

To take another example, in the Europe of the sixteenth and seventeenth centuries, certainly not characterized by the political doctrines of 'individualism', analogous intense and explicit stress was laid by authorities on conduct, upon the cultivation of the inner qualities of self-mastery and self-control, the development of physical, mental and spiritual qualities through a labour upon oneself, especially in those who would exercise authority over others. As Gerhard Oestreich (1982) shows, in *Neo-Stoicism and the Early Modern State*, what is involved here is neither an effect of a change in social organization nor a change in culture. Specific doctrines of self-conduct are elaborated in relation to particular problems of governing, of the authority of those who would govern, and of the changes in the forms in which political authority should be conducted in different political configurations. Conduct of certain activities is problematized from particular perspectives, in relation to particular difficulties. Battles of truth emerge over how human conduct is best to be understood. New techniques are promulgated for individuals undertaking certain tasks – military, political – to shape themselves in appropriate directions. Hence it appears that the periodic intensification of concerns with the techniques of self-conduct of the person does not accord with any logic of individualization or detraditionalization. Rather, it is a matter of tracing the ways in which explicit, authoritative languages and techniques for the government of conduct – differentiated by status, by gender, by problem area – provide the regulatory images, norms and ideals for human beings' understandings of themselves.

I suggest that these examples are sufficient to demonstrate that the whole analytic of individualization is misplaced. It is not useful to oppose 'traditional' practices which problematize human beings in terms of allegiance – to a community, a lineage or a group – and 'modern' practices which problematize them in terms of individuality and autonomy. Managing persons as individuals always entails identifying subjects in relation to the norms of particular collectivities – be they races, populations, genders or classes. Reciprocally, projects for managing individuals in the form of collectivities – whether these be for the formation of nations, armies, political parties or groups at work – have sought to specify distinctive techniques and attributes – language, dress, diet, modes of speech, manners, cognitive capacities, sexual ethics – for fashioning the self. Practices for the identification of persons always proceed through operations that are both distinguishing and locating. The injunction to be a particular sort of person is always bound up with an act of division: to be what one is, one must not be what one is not.

Brown's work is again instructive here (cf. also Gilman, 1985). To craft oneself as a male, for a young man of the privileged classes in the Roman Empire of the second century AD, was intrinsically linked to a distinction from woman and womanishness, excluding everything – in one's walk, the rhythm of one's speech, one's control over one's temper – that might represent 'softness' and 'womanishness' or threaten to produce it (Brown, 1989, p. 11). The theme of sexual renunciation was deployed both in distinguishing early Christian sects from Jews, and in the forms of identification practised by those who would be devout. To put this in the terms proposed by Michael Taussig (1993), one might say that practices for the regulation of conduct entail both alterity and mimesis – crafting oneself in the form of a copy which would be both similar to and different from those whose persons were pertinent to one (p. 129).

Even the key individualizing moment of the nineteenth century, the moment of heredity and race, preserved this dual relation. Defining individuals in terms simultaneously of their distinctiveness and their relation down a lineage, the uniqueness is not in spite of, but indeed through the fabrication of oneself as one who both copies the attributes of one's forebears (in the images that give value to one's 'make up') and distinguishes oneself from them (in the form of one's biography). This play of image, value, copy and distinction is a key technique in the folding of authority into the human being. It has a long history in the relations of exemplarity deployed in the spreading of different faiths and sects. But in the nineteenth century, this relation was secularized and governmentalized. Thus, in the manuals of advice concerning the proper conduct of the self that proliferated in the nineteenth century, to govern oneself and others appropriately was always to identify oneself as a proper wife, mother, daughter, or father, clerk, owner, day labourer. The injunction to appropriate a certain type of 'personality' – as it would come to be termed – by crafting oneself as a copy of an image with value was constituted not in a raw field of social relations, but in the calculated domains of spiritual guidance, now elaborated by doctors as much as by priests (Strathern, 1992). There is no intrinsic opposition between sculpting a *personal* identity and identification with a group, status, sector or style: the vicissitudes of identification are not ontological but historical and technical.

THE AUTHORITY OF AUTHORITY

Contemporary sociologists, in characterizing the distinctiveness of our present, often draw attention to a problem which one could term 'the authority of authority' – our uncertainty about ourselves, about morality, and about how we should feel or act in particular circumstances, is exacerbated because those who once had authority in such matters can no longer presume our obedience (cf. Giddens, 1991). In our age of heightened reflexivity, authority must continually justify itself, yet the resources that it has to do this are no longer authoritative. Of course, the thematization of our predicaments of self-conduct in terms of the decline of faith, the loss of the moral authority of religious institutions and of the political moralizing which the church supported is familiar (see, for example, Rieff, 1966).

But the question of what authorizes authority, and the self-scrutiny of authority by those who would exercise it as well as those who are subject to it, is not new. For the Greeks, it was considered particularly important that those who would exercise dominion over others could also exercise dominion over their own appetites and passions. Only those who were thus free – not a slave to themselves – would be competent to take their position of authority in the city, in the community, or in relations with others (Foucault, 1988b, pp. 6–7; cf. Minson, 1993, pp. 20–1). And, as one can see from the examples that I have already given, the moral formation of those who would exercise authority over others has been a recurrent problem. Codes of sexual deportment of the second century AD were directed to the well-born, distinguishing them from those over whom they would rule; refinement and self-control were to give an ethical basis for authority in their own eyes as much as in the eyes of their inferiors (Brown, 1989, pp. 5–32). The ideas of Roman Stoicism and the philosophy of Justus Lipsius – the humanist qualities of 'love, trust, reputation, friendly persuasion, gentle procedure, justice, development of physical, mental and spiritual qualities, powers and virtues' – were to be revived in seventeenth- and eighteenth-century Europe, in the military apparatus, amongst the political elite and in a host of locales and practices in which authority was criticized as ossified, corrupt or otherwise problematic (Oestreich, 1982, p. 87).

The nineteenth century was a period of great inventiveness in the forms of authorization of authority, with the emergence of credentialized forms in the professionalization of law, medicine and so forth – the invention of colleges and modes of training for the civil service that centred in particular upon the moral formation of those who would exercise rule: the doctor, the lawyer, the colonial civil servant. Particularly notable here, because of its transferability, was the invention of a new ethic of office in the form of bureaucracy. It is fashionable to cast scorn on the bureaucrat as a non-ethical mode of existence. '[T]he bureaucrat', writes Philip Rieff in a new Preface to *The Triumph of the Therapeutic* (1987), 'sits behind his impersonality, an expert at redistributing jargon and managing case files . . . the master organizer of our passionate indifference to the real needs of given individuals' (pp. ix–x; cf. MacIntyre, 1981). But, as Weber (1978) showed so clearly in his investigations of bureaucracy, the invention of new modes of self-reflection, self-mastery and self-control for those who would hold office in organizations of all sorts was a considerable ethical achievement, a new technology for reflecting and acting upon the person of the official, entailing a new division between the personal and the impersonal aspects of administration, and a new mode of normalizing, justifying and judging the holders of positions of significance in the machinery of public and private organizations (pp. 956–1005; cf. Hunter, 1994; and Osborne, 1994).

Placed in the context of this recurrent concern with the conduct of those competent to exercise authority, our contemporary 'crisis of authority' can no longer be viewed as a consequence of the 'reflexivity' of late modern times. It needs to be understood in terms of the ways in which problematizations of authority relate to contemporary political rationalities and ethical priorities – the bureaucratic manager is now to be problematized in relation to a perceived lack of competitiveness of industry; the expert is now to be problematized in relation to a state of dependence enjoined upon the client; the civil servant is now to be problematized because of his or her adherence to those very liberal humanist values that were once to be the answer to a problem of the exercise of official authority, and so forth. And this problematization of the authority of authority has gone hand in hand with the invention of a range of new technologies for governing those who have authority over conduct, replacing the logics of professional ethics with the invention of a new and quasi-market space of competition and regulation: accounting and budgetary discipline, outputs and targets, monitoring, evaluation and audit.

The aim of this discussion is not to replace the historicism of sociological accounts of individualization with an equally implausible doctrine of universality. But what one discovers in these historical texts about the conduct of human beings is not evidence for any general and unidirectional changes in forms of selfhood across history. Rather, one observes the ways in which, at different historical moments, in many different ways, human conduct has been governed, has been placed under the authority of different forms of truth, expert personages and more or less rationalized techniques of (re)formation. The notion of a 'detraditionalized' self is of little use because it fails to engage with the ways in which different localized practices – of domesticity and sexuality, of consumption and marketing, of production and management, of punishment and reformation, of health and illness, of security and insurance, of conflict and warfare, of management and rule – presuppose, represent and act upon human beings as if they were persons of certain sorts. A genealogy of subjectification would address the element of thought that is intrinsic to all the ways in which human beings have sought to act upon others and themselves, the authorities of thought, and the technical forms that thought has acquired in relation to human conduct.

THE POLITICS OF CONDUCT FROM THE NINETEENTH CENTURY TO OUR OWN

From this perspective, the distinctiveness of our present modes of subjectification must be understood in relation to the plethora of new rationalities and technologies for the government of conduct that have been deployed since the start of the nineteenth century. A multitude of devices were invented that would link up programmes for the amelioration of a whole variety of different problems – to do with the state of economic affairs, the level of public finances, urban order and disorder, moral degradation, lunacy, the vitality and morbidity of the population – with techniques for the regulation of the self-conduct of the individual human being. The doctrine of the liberty of the individual under the law was to go hand in hand with the infolding into that free individual of a complex of authorities that were as much secular as spiritual, and whose injunctions as to prudence, order, temperance, continence, responsibility, steadfastness, obedience and virtue were embodied in habits and in habitats – in the multitude of little practices of everyday life and in the physical organization of the spaces in which they would occur.

The great 'machines of morality' invented in the nineteenth century took a predominantly *spatial* form (Markus, 1993).[4] They operated through the spatial organization of human beings, through the instrumentalization of institutional time, through the practical collection, classification and division of persons, through materializing relations of authority in the physical relations of foreman and worker, teacher and pupil, gaoler and prisoner, asylum superintendent and inmate. As has often been pointed out, neither the architectural forms nor the organizational techniques were new – monasteries, barracks, Sunday schools, pauper schools, and a range of experiments in the colonies had all tested out such devices. But in the course of the nineteenth century these exemplars were to be widely emulated. Schools for infants and for older children were to be the site of a variety of different programmes for the shaping of character *en masse*, with the aim that the corporeal and moral habits of industriousness and obedience would be inculcated into the members of the labouring classes, to fit them 'to become good servants – good tradesmen – good fathers – good mothers, and respectable citizens'; 'the intellectually cultivated Christian mechanic is the best safeguard of our nation, and his moral worth is the very salt and leaven of civil society' (Stow, 1834, quoted in Markus, 1993, p. 84; cf. Jones and Williamson, 1979; Hunter, 1994). New regimes of the body – its purity, its hygiene, its sexual continence – were to address problems posed in terms of sexuality, disease and virtue. New regimes of the intellect – numeracy, literacy, calculation – were to install foresight, prudence and a planful relation to the future. Social danger was recast as a violation of norms of respectable citizenship and a new way was invented 'for collecting and confining those who in one way or another could introduce chaos into the social order' (Markus, 1993, p. 95), for reforming moral character by acting upon the body of the transgressor – prisons, asylums, workhouses.

Analogous spaces were invented for re-qualifying those whom disease had disqualified – hospitals, sanatoria and infirmaries – and for cleansing and purifying the soul through the medium of the body – bath-houses, wash-houses. Recreation was also to be spatially organized – no longer in the rowdy and transgressive hurly-burly of the market, the fair, the baiting of bears – but in new moral habitats – public parks, municipal swimming pools. Knowledge was to be civilized, ordered and embodied as a means of popular instruction – in zoos, botanical gardens, libraries, museums, panoramas, dioramas, exhibitions – spaces which enjoin civility and the control of the outward signs of character at the same time as they instruct in order. The space of labour itself, the manufactory, was to be problematized not only in terms of its immediate economy of wealth, but also in terms of its consequences for the habits of labour – temperance, diligence, sexual propriety. And the space of the labourer outside work was to be subject to a statistical and literary mapping that rendered the town intelligible as a spatial distribution. Figures, charts, maps, vivid descriptions of social explorers, showed how coextensive were the topographies of class, occupation, morality, criminality and disease. Thus the space of the town became intelligible in new ways, in the spatial imagination produced by all those who thought that in order to govern relations between people more effectively one had first to inscribe them. One sees, in short, a multiplication of 'laboratories of conduct' in which were performed a whole variety of ethical experiments on human beings.[5]

I have several reasons for emphasizing the spatiality of these plural routes, planes, locales, maps through which, over the course of the nineteenth century, the authoritative problematization of conduct was to be connected up to the individuals' concern for themselves. I wish to emphasize that 'moral formation' was more than a vague 'cultural' phenomenon – it was a matter of specific devices, arrangements in bricks and mortar, sewage pipes and exercise yards, maps and classifications (cf. Dean, 1994). I wish to stress, in contrast to those who see this as a work of 'the state', that the field is more complex, comprising the activities of a whole variety of authorities who translate general pronouncements about problematic features of national life into specific techniques for the shaping and re-shaping of conduct: authorities who, in many cases, urge modes of thought and action upon politicians and legislators. Further, I want to point to the ways in which this field was linked up not so much by formal connections between elements as through the circulation of a certain *language* for understanding the relations between conduct and circumstance.

In the mid-nineteenth century, the language of character established a set of mobile and productive links between political problematizations of conduct and the technical regulation of the person: the formation of a proper moral character was given a key role in strategies for the prevention of all sorts of political and economic ills. As Stefan Collini (1979) has pointed out, diverse forces argued that the development of the virtues of character – self-reliance, sobriety, independence, self-restraint, respectability, self-improvement – should be a positive function of the state: an end that statesmen should keep constantly in view in programmes of legislation and reform (pp. 29ff). Problems of human conduct were articulated as expressions of moral character, character was construed as an outcome of the interaction between constitution or stock and habits of conduct learned by example or inculcation, and good character was to be promoted though the organization of human beings in certain relations of proximity, hierarchy, visibility, and so forth. Thus new connections were established between the responsibilities of politicians and the obligations of political subjects.

As innumerable theological, physiological and educational texts spelled out, the need was for the will to exercise dominance over conduct: a matter of moral control. This was at its most intense in childhood. Education for the labouring classes was to be a means of saving them from their state of slavery to prejudice, vice and momentary passion, enhancing the possibility of control exercised by the reflective mind over bodily nature (Smith, 1992, pp. 27–65). But the struggle for control was a lifelong task: lack of this control was the explanation for all sorts of pathologies of conduct, from madness, to assaults on political order, to the woman question. New divisions and classifications of persons – by others, and by themselves – emerged here: divisions between classes of persons embodied in forms of life that both realize and produce certain forms of character; thus Charles Booth's classification of the population into eight classes, each of which was an amalgam of a mode of employment, a moral character and a form of life (Booth, 1892–7; cf. the discussion in Rose, 1985). From this moment on, the political problem of the relation between authority and its subjects was to be redefined; it was to be achieved through enmeshing subjects in practices organized on the presumption that human beings were persons of a novel sort.

This work of moral formation, the in-folding of new forms of secular authority into the subject in the form of character, was not simply a matter of 'social control' of the dangerous classes – it was as much addressed to the self-formation of the entrepreneur, the official, the bourgeois mother, as it was to the formation of the tradesperson, the labouring poor and the pauper. One sees, for example, a quite novel programme for the reform of the powers of secular authorities within the bureau and within the civil service, the creation of new regimes of self-scrutiny and self-mastery for those employed in such administrative capacities, linked to the question of the authority of both 'private' and 'public' authority in liberal polity (Weber, 1978; cf. Hunter, 1993; Minson, 1993; du Gay, 1995; Osborne, 1994). And one sees also a transformation of the modes of conduct appropriate to the bourgeois domestic space, a familialization and domestication of passions, a simultaneous eroticization of relations between husbands and wives and a policing of illicit relations within the home organized around such issues as masturbation, incest and hysteria (Foucault, 1979). This entailed new relays between political concerns across a national territory and concerns for the self organized within the space of the home, and was made possible by a novel authorization of the doctor as expert in national well-being and individual self-promotion (Donzelot, 1979).

The nineteenth century thus witnesses an outpouring of secular pedagogies for the conduct of conduct, and the secularization of clerical polemics concerning morality. Doctors, teachers and architects represent three different ways in which the government of a polity becomes dependent upon a new breed of 'engineers of the human soul' who link wisdom with technique and who keep one eye fixed on political aims whilst the other is fixed upon individual conduct – diagnosis, classification, the shaping or re-shaping of the moral order of the individual through the operation of a technique grounded in truth (Rose, 1992a). Not, of course, that one finds here any space of agreement – a plethora of voices contest for the power of truth, and many battles of jurisdiction occur – as, for example, in the disputes within the legal apparatus between doctors and lawyers as to who should have authority in relation to the criminal and under what terms should conduct be understood, judged and reformed. And against this language of prudence, obedience, diligence, foresight and character, one finds counter discourses articulated in many forms. Trades unions and parties of the left articulate an ethic of collectivity and mutuality, a mode of self-conduct embodied in a host of organizational forms and in the exemplarity of their leaders. Romantics articulate, in literature and by the making of their own lives into a work of art, an aestheticized vision of the human being and promulgate a whole regime of self-cultivation and self-display. Plurality of spaces and voices, as I have already pointed out, is not a peculiarity of our own age.

None the less, the deployment of expert authority in the sites for the formation and reformation of conduct is of particular significance, for it was out of all these encounters between public objectives and techniques of subjectification that the positive knowledges of the human being – alone and *en masse* – emerge. These positive knowledges – clinical medicine, psychiatry,

criminology, psychology, statistics, pedagogy, sociology – found their surfaces of emergence in problematizations of conduct by a diversity of political
and economic forces in different sites and in relation to different concerns
(see, respectively, Foucault, 1973; Castel, 1988; Pasquino, 1991; Rose, 1985;
Hacking, 1990; Hunter, 1988; Procacci, 1993). They produced new truths
operating according to the codes and techniques of positive knowledge –
experimentation, evidence, accumulation – and new apparatuses for accredi-
tation – laboratories, universities, scientific journals. These truths grew out
of all those diverse sites invented for the management of conduct – schools,
asylums, prisons, the reformed 'public' spaces of exhibitions, museums, parks
and gardens. And they seek to govern domains in terms of their 'internal'
laws and truths rather than in terms of external virtues: for such authorities
of conduct truth appears to teach itself in relation to the person and the ways
of managing the person. It is here that one finds the emergence of the
territory of 'the self' as a psychologically unified domain to which I have
referred earlier. As the psychological domain takes shape, with its own internal laws and processes, it becomes populated with a range of new 'personalities' – the child, the madman, the criminal, the mother, the adolescent,
the homosexual – who can be known and managed by expertise. From now
on it will be to this domain that all ethical injunctions and all hermeneutics
of the self will be directed.

Over the course of the nineteenth and twentieth centuries, these new
authorities, and the norms of positive knowledge which they elaborate, gradually colonize other practices and rationales of self-formation and self-manage-
ment, notably those to do with lawlessness, punishment, reformation, labour,
poverty, sexuality and childhood. The discourses of degeneracy, which would
culminate in the eugenic movements of the early twentieth century, were
only the most evident of the ways in which the truth of conduct was to be
articulated in the languages of science (cf. Pick, 1989). The new expertise of
human conduct entered into complex and contestatory relations with other
ethics and practices of the person, including not only the theological but
those elaborated by juridical and customary authorities (cf. Foucault, 1978a,
1978b; Smith, 1981). Whether their verdicts were accepted or not, they
none the less managed to make their presence obligatory in a whole range of
sites – thus psychiatry and criminology have become indispensable to the
pronouncing of judgment in the courts, pedagogy becomes indispensable to
teaching the young, psychology to the pastoral care offered by the priest,
clinical medicine to the moral injunctions offered by politicians concerning
promiscuity and prostitution, and so forth. Further, these modes of regulation of the person were connected up with the deliberations, strategies and

obligations of political rule and encoded in the apparatuses of citizen formation: together they traced out a new 'social' space in which the government
of a polity was intrinsically linked to the regulation of the self-government
of the responsible citizen.

As human beings at the turn of the nineteenth and twentieth centuries
came to understand themselves as inhabited by a psychological interiority
that was simultaneously unique to the individual and subject to general
processes and laws, a reciprocal 'social' territory was born. This territory was
not simply spatialized geographically, but in terms of a new topography of
collective human existence. The reactive and formalistic mechanisms of law
and rights now appeared insufficient to act upon the newly discovered social
and economic laws and processes that bound isolated individuals together or
forced them apart: a range of novel strategies sought to act defensively and
prophylactically to *produce* solidarity and thus safeguard against the collective
dangers of alienation and disruption posed by penury, ill-health, incapacity
or loss of employment. (Donzelot, 1984, 1991; Ewald, 1991; Castel, 1991.)

The social and insurantial technologies that were invented did not abandon the hope of governing individual self-conduct, but sought to achieve this
through techniques that appeared capable of tackling the large-scale, collective and systematic dangers posed by urban industrial life (cf. O'Malley,
1992). Programmes for insurance-based technologies of welfare, for example,
entailed arguments about exactly what forms of citizenship would be invoked
in individuals and their families by technical mechanisms for the collectiv-
ization of their fate.

An ethic of personal responsibility was integral to the language of democratic citizenship that took shape over the course of the twentieth century.
From Beveridge's schemes of social insurance, through Reith's view of the
vocation of a national broadcasting system, to a range of interventions into
the domestic space of the family and the productive space of the factory,
responsibility for oneself, for one's family, for one's co-workers and fellow
citizens was more than mere rhetoric. It was to be achieved through the
technical forms of regulation, folded into the person in habits of radio listening as well as in the content of broadcasts, in the little rituals of the stamp-
ing of national insurance cards, in participation in morale-raising activities
in the workplace, in the mother's newly educated ways of thinking and
acting upon her children (discussed in detail in Rose, 1989). Through establishing such a relation to its subjects, through treating them as citizens
of a democracy with obligations and freedoms, with opinions and attitudes,
whose deference would be not to status itself but to the wisdom conferred
by knowledge, and whose compliance would be assured by education and

information, authorities were to shape *themselves* according to a new democratic vocation.

These social connections between the government of others and the government of the self re-located individualized techniques for the government of the soul within the new social devices: one only has to note the swarming of all the little judges of the psyche in the schools, courtrooms, workplaces, hospitals, prisons and the other sites where the conduct of the individual remained an object of formation or reformation. And within the insurantial systems there was always another pole directed at those whose conduct, for some reason or other, was troublesome. A plurality of sites for the individualizing and diagnosing of pathological conduct took shape as nodes within the insurantial networks of welfare – from the 'availability for work' test which was always an element within insurance-based systems of unemployment benefit, job clubs and the like to avoid the demoralization of the long unemployed; child guidance clinics for the psycho-diagnosis of the troublesome and troubled child, and more (Miller, 1986; Walters, 1994). The pedagogies of citizenship here took a rather direct form: authority rested more upon its political and legal authorization than its ethical appeal to its subjects. From this point on, the relays were to multiply between the government of others and the government of oneself – a 'governmentalization' of ethics, of the resources individuals would draw upon in the understanding, planning and judgement of their everyday conduct, passions and aspirations.

A CONTEMPORARY EVENT IN THE GOVERNMENT OF SUBJECTIVITY?

Instead of seeking the distinctiveness of our own times in 'postmodern' features such as reflexivity, self-scrutiny, fragmentation and diversity, then, the question to be answered about ourselves and our present can be formulated as follows. Does the diversity of authorities of the self in our present, the pluralization of moral codes, the apparent attenuation of the links between political government and the regulation of conduct, the heterogeneity of forms of life, the valorization of choices and freedom in the shaping of a style of life, the simultaneous celebration of individuality and proliferation of techniques of group identification and segmentation – does all this signify that there has been a transformation in the ontology through which we think ourselves, in the techniques through which we conduct ourselves, in the relations of authority by means of which we divide ourselves and identify ourselves as certain kinds of person, exercise certain kinds of concern in relation to ourselves, are governed and govern ourselves as human beings of a particular sort? If new modes of subjectification have appeared today, in what practices, in relation to what problems and problematizations, within what locales, according to which codes of truth, under the aegis of what authorities, through what techniques, in what new divisions, and in relation to what general strategies of government?

Reflecting upon these questions from the point of view of our own moment, one does not, I think, observe a global transformation in forms of identity linked to transformations in the social forms of the family, of the economy or locality. For example, I do not consider that our contemporary problematics of risk have emerged out of novel existential features of our current age, but as a novel way of *reflecting upon* that experience. In seeking to make the dangers of the future calculable in the present, to master fate by making it amenable to prediction and management, these new modes of reflection simultaneously exacerbate anxiety about the consequences of each present action for our future lives (cf. Gigerenzer et al., 1989; Hacking, 1990). On the one hand, the vocabulary and techniques of risk make possible novel ways for the expert problematization of fields as diverse as waste discharge and the release of psychiatric patients into the community. A new role emerges for medical and scientific experts as advisors on risk, educators of risk and managers of risk — at the level of communities and that of individuals. On the other hand, new languages and techniques are made available for individuals to relate to themselves and their conduct, to make their future destiny appear controllable by their present lifestyle choices, to make fate manageable by choices as to eating, drinking, financial management, career decisions and sexual conduct.

Similarly the ethical valorization of certain features of the person — autonomy, freedom, choice, authenticity, enterprise, lifestyle — should be understood in terms of new rationalities of government and new technologies of the conduct of conduct (Rose, 1992b). In a whole variety of different locales — not just in sexuality, diet or the promotion of goods for consumption, but also in labour and in the construction of political subjects — the person is presumed to be an active agent, wishing to exercise informed, autonomous and secular responsibility in relation to his or her own destiny. The language of autonomy, identity, self-realization and the search for fulfilment acts as a grid of regulatory ideals, not in an amorphous cultural space, but in the doctor's consulting room, on the factory floor and in the personnel manager's office, in the training of unemployed youth and the construction of political programmes. At the same time, this language of responsible self-advancement is linked to a new perception of those outside civility — the marginalized who through wilfulness, incapacity or ignorance cannot or will not exercise such responsibility, and who are to be re-educated or 'empowered' so to do by the pedagogy of a host of new experts, deploying psychological techniques from social skills training to group relations.

These new problematizations of the human subject are intrinsically linked to new modalities for folding authority into the self. The diverse techniques of the psycho-sciences – not just those of assessment, classification and discipline, but those which produce a knowledge of social dispositions (such as attitude scales), those which deal with motivations, passions and desires – generate a whole range of techniques of therapeutic intervention upon persons and groups. They have a peculiar capacity to penetrate the calculation and actions of all those who have to act upon conduct in many different sites – priests, social workers, doctors, teachers, parents and many others (Rose, 1989; 1992a). Psychological expertise, in suggesting ways in which *those who have authority* can exercise it in relation to a knowledge of the inner nature of *those subject to authority*, accords authority a novel ethical justification as a kind of therapeutic activity. Psychology experts also provide local and practicable techniques for the government of conduct in local sites, that translate well with more general programmes for understanding and acting upon human beings as autonomous subjects.

At the same time, the habitat of the modern subject has become saturated with broadcast images of self-conduct, self-formation and self-problematization. This is not merely in the form of explicitly pedagogic television programmes and documentaries, but also in the moral predicaments portrayed and resolved in news, drama and soap opera – which presuppose certain repertoires of personhood as the *a priori* of the forms of life they display. Simultaneously, the technologies of marketing, themselves informed by the theories and techniques of the psychological sciences, propagate images of conduct in terms of new relations between the purchase of goods and services and the shaping of the self. One sees here, in the sphere of consumption, the rise of powerful new authorities and technologies for the government of conduct, the dissemination of modes, techniques and images of self-formation and self-problematization operating according to a non-geographical topography, with a guiding logic of profit rather than morality. They establish a relation to their subjects that presupposes freedom, a freedom understood in terms of the wish of individuals to conduct their own lives as projects for the minimization of risks and the maximization of quality of life. And these new modes of subjectification become available, in reverse as it were, for new techniques for the regulation of conduct, for example the use of advertising techniques in health promotion. As styles of self-display become associated, in a calculated manner, with identification and differentiation of ways of being human, the 'mirror dance' of mimesis and alterity takes new forms that are highly regulated, but exist in a complex and often contestatory relation with political, theological, medical and psychological images and norms of conduct.

These new modes in which authority is folded into the soul are connected to revised problematizations of political rule. Shifts in political rhetoric, such as that from the social citizen of discourses of welfare to the active and entrepreneurial citizen of today, and shifts in political technology, such as that from the universal provision of social insurance to a revised prudentialism in which each individual and family should provide for their own future by investment in pension schemes and health insurance, indicate that questions of security, tranquillity and national well-being are now understood in new ways. Strategies no longer seek to ensure these by acting to enhance the 'social' bonds that link one individual to another, but through activation of the self-promoting strivings of individuals themselves, in which each is to become an entrepreneur of his or her own life, running their existence as a kind of enterprise for the advancement of themselves and their family, articulating their own demands for the protection and enhancement of their own 'community'. A range of new locales, sites, devices and techniques emerge for the 'care of the self', differentially propagated amongst different ages, genders, sectors and segments of the population.

From this perspective, we have not seen the 'detraditionalization of the self' in our present, but a modification in the complex of authorities which govern the relations that different sectors of the population, in different practices, are urged to establish with themselves, and a modification in our relations with these authorities of subjectification. Analysis of these novel relations is not *critique* – no past or future moment is posited when a self, freed from the weight of political expectations and ethical obligations, could relate to itself in some unmediated manner. None the less, the government of the human being always exacts a certain cost. This is not merely in the many moments when to lapse from one's appointed forms of personhood is to risk violence – from slavery to the inquisition – or other modes of force – from sumptuary laws to psychiatry. It is also a question of the thousand petty humiliations, self-denigrations, deceptions, lies, seductions, cynicisms, bribes, hopes and disappointments, that are the price, the other side, of these 'civilizing' processes – a question of the costs of breeding an animal that could feel guilty and bear responsibility for itself and its conduct, against which it must pledge itself as guarantor (Nietzsche, 1956, p. 189). And it is also a question of the price, for any one such human animal, of an everyday life which inevitably traverses distinct and discrepant ethical domains with their competing and often irreconcilable demands.

But precisely because of the plurality, indeterminacy and heterogeneity of the languages, spaces and practices which govern us, human beings – today as in the past – inhabit a space of differentiation and choice, of moral dilemmas and ethical contestation. For our own times, then, the value of studies of authority and subjectivity might be to enable us to weigh the costs and benefits, not of being freed from government, but of governing ourselves differently.

NOTES

Earlier versions of this chapter have been presented to the Department of Sociology, Open University, 3 June 1993, and to the seminar on Identity, Modernity and Politics at the University of London School of Oriental and African Studies in December 1993. I would like to thank all those who offered comments. Particular thanks to Thomas Osborne for advice on this contribution.

1   Of course, the place of philosophical reflections in the genealogy of subjectification is variable. Jeffrey Minson, for example, makes a case for the significance of Kant's ethics in such disparate areas as the drafting of the Austrian civil code and the content of late-nineteenth-century French manuals of child pedagogy (1993).
2   While some have proposed the materiality of the body as the always changing surface upon which discourses and techniques write themselves (see, for example, Butler, 1990; Grosz, 1993; Probyn, 1993), the corporeality of the human being does not define, by right and for all time, the space within which humans have constructed an ontology for themselves. The notion of the human as, at root, embodied is itself part of a certain style of reflection and action upon the human being.
3   These questions are loosely derived from Foucault's reflections on this matter. As Mitchell Dean has recently outlined (Dean, 1994), Foucault suggested that one should differentiate 'ontology' (*what* is to be governed: pleasure, the flesh, desire), 'ascetics' (*how* it is to be governed, through what kinds of technique: prayer, confession, diary keeping), 'deontology' (the *mode of subjection*, our relation to the rules and norms in question and the reasons for this particular relation: to live a noble and beautiful life, to submit to God's law, to become a rational being, to achieve self-realization), and 'teleology' (the *aim* of these practices in terms of the creation of a certain mode of being: self-mastery through moderation, salvation through renunciation of the self, emancipation) (cf. Foucault, 1985; 1986a; and 1986b).
4   I am greatly indebted here to Thomas Markus's wonderfully rich study *Buildings and Power* (1993). Markus (p. 41) quotes Coleridge to describe these devices: 'An incomparable machine – a vast moral steam engine'. The mechanical model, as Michel Serres has shown us, is more than metaphor – if the steam engine functions as something like a weaving together of imagination, knowledge, myth and

technique in a figure of heat, water, pipes, pressures, conduits and cogs, then imagining our new technologies along the lines of the space of communication – transmission, transformation, images, flows and the like – is also more than a metaphor. It is exemplary of the multiple points of exchange between the exact sciences, the sciences of the human being, the rationalities of government and the concern for the self (Serres, 1982).

5 I owe this way of formulating the matter to Thomas Osborne.

REFERENCES

Beck, Ulrich 1992: *Risk Society: Towards a New Modernity*. London: Sage.

Booth, Charles 1892–7: *Life and Labour of the People of London*, (10 volumes). London: Macmillan.

Bourdieu, Pierre 1979: *Distinction: A Social Critique of the Judgement of Taste*. London: Routledge and Kegan Paul.

Brown, Peter 1989: *The Body and Society: Men, Women and Sexual Renunciation in Early Christianity*. London: Faber.

Burckhardt, Jacob 1990: *The Civilization of the Renaissance in Italy*. London: Penguin.

Butler, Judith 1990: *Gender Trouble: Feminism and the Subversion of Identity*. London: Routledge.

Castel, Robert 1988: *The Regulation of Madness*. Cambridge: Polity.

Castel, Robert 1991: From Dangerous to Risk. In G. Burchell, C. Gordon and P. Miller (eds), *The Foucault Effect: Studies in Governmentality*, Hemel Hempstead: Harvester Wheatsheaf, pp. 281–98.

Chartier, Roger (ed.) 1989: *A History of Private Life*, Vol. 3: *Passions of the Renaissance*. Cambridge: Harvard University Press.

Cline-Cohen, Patricia 1982: *A Calculating People: The Spread of Numeracy in Early America*. Chicago: University of Chicago Press.

Collini, Stefan 1979: *Liberalism and Sociology: L. T. Hobhouse and Political Argument in England, 1880–1914*. Cambridge: Cambridge University Press.

Dean, Mitchell 1994: 'A Social Structure of Many Souls': Moral Regulation, Government and Self-formation. *Canadian Journal of Sociology*, 19 (2), pp. 145–68.

Deleuze, Gilles 1983: *Nietzsche and Philosophy*. London: Athlone.

Deleuze, Gilles 1988: *Foucault*. Minneapolis: University of Minnesota Press.

Donzelot, Jacques 1979: *The Policing of Families*. London: Hutchinson.

Donzelot, Jacques 1984: *L'Invention du Social*. Paris: Editions de Minuit.

Donzelot, Jacques 1991: The Moblization of Society. In G. Burchell, C. Gordon and P. Miller (eds), *The Foucault Effect: Studies in Governmentality*, Hemel Hempstead: Harvester Wheatsheaf.

Duby, George (ed.) 1988: *A History of Private Life*, Vol. 2: *Revelations of the Medieval World*. Cambridge: Cambridge University Press.

du Gay, Paul (1995): Making Up Managers. In S. Hall and P. du Gay (eds), *Questions of Cultural Identity*, London: Sage.

Eisenstein, Elizabeth 1979: *The Printing Press as an Agent of Change.* Cambridge: Cambridge University Press.

Elias, Norbert 1978: *The Civilizing Process,* Vol. 1: *The History of Manners.* Oxford: Basil Blackwell.

Ewald, François 1991: Insurance and Risk. In G. Burchell, C. Gordon and P. Miller (eds), *The Foucault Effect: Studies in Governmentality,* Hemel Hempstead: Harvester Wheatsheaf, pp. 197–210.

Foucault, Michel 1973: *The Birth of the Clinic.* London: Tavistock.

Foucault, Michel 1977: *Discipline and Punish: The Birth of the Prison.* London: Allen Lane.

Foucault, Michel (ed.) 1978(a): *I, Pierre Riviere, Having Slaughtered my Mother, my Sister and my Brother.* Harmondsworth: Penguin.

Foucault, Michel 1978(b): About the Concept of the 'Dangerous Individual' in 19th Century Legal Psychiatry. *International Journal of Law and Psychiatry,* 1, pp. 1–18.

Foucault, Michel 1979: *The History of Sexuality,* Vol. 1: *The Will to Truth.* London: Allen Lane.

Foucault, Michel 1985: *The History of Sexuality, Vol. 2: The Use of Pleasure.* (trans. R. Hurley). New York: Random House.

Foucault, Michel 1986(a): *The History of Sexuality,* Vol. 3: *The Care of the Self.* New York: Pantheon.

Foucault, Michel 1986(b): On the Genealogy of Ethics: An Overview of Work in Progress. In P. Rabinow (ed.), *The Foucault Reader,* Harmondsworth: Penguin, pp. 340–71.

Foucault, Michel 1988(a): Technologies of the Self. In L. H. Martin, H. Gutman and P. H. Hutton (eds) *Technologies of the Self,* London: Tavistock, pp. 16–49.

Foucault, Michel 1988(b): The Ethic of Care for the Self as a Practice of Freedom. In J. Bernaker and D. Rusmussen (eds) *The Final Foucault,* Cambridge, MA: MIT Press.

Giddens, Anthony 1991: *Modernity and Self-Identity: Self and Society in the Late Modern Age.* Cambridge: Polity.

Gigerenzer, G. et al. 1989: *The Empire of Chance.* Cambridge: Cambridge University Press.

Gilman, Sander 1985: *Difference and Pathology: Stereotypes of Sexuality, Race and Madness.* New York: Cornell University Press.

Gilman, Sander 1988: *Disease and Representation: Images of Illness from Madness to AIDS.* New York: Cornell University Press.

Goody, Jack and Watt, Ian 1963: The Consequences of Literacy. *Comparative Studies in Society and History,* 5, pp. 000–0.

Grosz, Elizabeth 1993: Bodies and Knowledges: Feminism and the Crisis of Reason. In L. Alcoff and E. Potter (eds), *Feminist Epistemologies,* London: Routledge, pp. 000–0.

Hacking, Ian 1990: *The Taming of Chance.* Cambridge: Cambridge University Press.

Hadot, Pierre 1992: Reflections on the Notion of 'The Cultivation of the Self'. In

T. J. Armstrong (ed.), *Michel Foucault, Philosopher*, Hemel Hempstead: Harvester Wheatsheaf, pp. 225–32.

Hunter, Ian 1988: *Culture and Government: The Emergence of Literary Education*. London: Macmillan.

Hunter, Ian 1993(a): The Pastoral Bureaucracy: Towards a less Principled Understanding of State Schooling. In D. Meredyth and D. Tyler (eds), *Child and Citizen: Genealogies of Schooling and Subjectivity*, Queensland: Griffith University, Institute of Cultural Policy Studies, pp. 237–87.

Hunter, Ian 1993(b): Subjectivity and Government. *Economy and Society*, 22 (1), pp. 123–34.

Hunter, Ian 1993(c): Culture, Bureaucracy and the History of Popular Education. In D. Meredyth and D. Tyler (eds), *Child and Citzen: Genealogies of Schooling and Subjectivity*, Queensland: Griffith University, Institute of Cultural Policy Studies, pp. 11–34.

Hunter, Ian 1994: *Rethinking the School: Subjectivity, Bureaucracy, Criticism*. St Leonards, Australia: Allen and Unwin.

Jambet, Christian 1992: The Constitution of the Subject and Spiritual Practice. In T. J. Armstrong (ed.), *Michel Foucault, Philosopher*, Hemel Hempstead: Harvester Wheatsheaf, pp. 233–47.

Jones, Kevin and Williamson, Karen 1979: The Birth of the Schoolroom, *Ideology and Consciousness*, 6, pp. 58–110.

Joyce, P. 1994: *Democratic Subjects: The Self and the Social in Nineteenth Century England*. Cambridge: Cambridge University Press.

Lash, Scott and Friedman, Jonathon (eds) 1992: *Modernity and Identity*. Oxford: Blackwell.

Le Goff, Jacques (ed.) 1990: *The Medieval World*. London: Collins and Brown.

MacIntyre, Alasdair 1981: *After Virtue, A Study in Moral Theory*. London: Duckworth.

Markus, Thomas 1993: *Buildings and Power: Freedom and Control in the Origin of Modern Building Types*. London: Routledge.

Miller, Peter 1986: Psychotherapy of Work and Unemployment. In P. Miller and N. Rose (eds), *The Power of Psychiatry*, Cambridge: Polity, pp. 143–76.

Minson, Jeffrey 1993: *Questions of Conduct*. London: Macmillan.

Nietzsche, Friedrich 1956: *The Genealogy of Morals*. New York: Doubleday.

Oestreich, Gerhard 1982: *Neo-Stoicism and the Early Modern State*. Cambridge: Cambridge University Press.

O'Malley, Pat 1992: Risk, Power and Crime Prevention. *Economy and Society*, 21 (3), pp. 252–75.

Osborne, Thomas 1994: Bureaucracy as a Vocation: Liberalism, Ethics and Administrative Expertise in the Nineteenth Century. *Journal of the Historical Society*, 000.

Pasquino, Pasquale 1991: Criminology: The Birth of a Special Knowledge. In G. Burchell, C. Gordon and P. Miller (eds), *The Foucault Effect: Studies in Governmentality*, Hemel Hempstead: Harvester Wheatsheaf, pp. 235–50.

Perrot, Michelle 1990: *A History of Private Life*, Vol. 4: *From the Fires of Revolution to the Great War*. Cambridge: Cambridge University Press.

Pick, Daniel 1989: *Faces of Degeneration: A European Disorder, c.1848–c.1918*. Cambridge: Cambridge University Press.

Probyn, Elspeth 1993: *Sexing the Self: Gendered Positions in Cultural Studies*. London: Routlege.

Procacci, Giovanna 1993: *The Government of Poverty*. Paris: Editions de Minuit.

Prost, Antoine and Vincent, Gerard (eds) 1991: *A History of Private Life*, Vol. 5: *Riddles of Identity in Modern Times*. Cambridge: Belknap Press.

Ranum, Orest 1989: The Refuges of Intimacy. In R. Chartier (ed.), *A History of Private Life*, Vol. 3: *Passions of the Renaissance*, Cambridge Mass: Harvard University Press, pp. 207–63.

Rieff, Philip 1966: *The Triumph of the Therapeutic: Uses of Faith after Freud*. Chicago: Chicago University Press; 1987, with a new Preface.

Rose, Nikolas 1985: *The Psychological Complex: Psychology, Politics and Society in England, 1869–1939*. London: Routledge and Kegan Paul.

Rose, Nikolas 1989: *Governing the Soul: The Shaping of the Private Self*. London: Routledge.

Rose, Nikolas 1992a: Governing the Enterprising Self. In P. Heelas and P. Morris (eds), *The Values of the Enterprise Culture*, London: Routledge, pp. 141–64.

Rose, Nikolas 1992b: Engineering the Human Soul: Analysing Psychological Expertise. *Science in Context*, 5 (2), pp. 351–70.

Rossiaud, Jacques 1990: The City-Dweller and Life in Cities and Towns. In J. Le Goff (ed.), *The Medieval World*, London: Collins and Brown, pp. 139–80.

Serres, Michel 1982: *Hermes: Literature, Science, Philosophy*, edited by Josue Harari and David Bell. Baltimore: Johns Hopkins University Press.

Smith, Roger 1981: *Trial by Medicine: Insanity and Responsibility in Victorian Trials*. Edinburgh: Edinburgh University Press.

Smith, Roger 1992: *Inhibition: History and Meaning in the Sciences of Mind and Brain*. Berkeley: University of California Press.

Sprawson, Charles 1992: *Haunts of the Black Masseur: The Swimmer as Hero*. London: Jonathon Cape.

Strathern, Marilyn 1992: *After Nature: English Kinship in the Late Twentieth Century*. Cambridge: Cambridge University Press.

Taussig, Michael 1993: *Mimesis and Alterity: A Particular History of the Senses*. London: Routledge.

Taylor, Charles 1989: *Sources of the Self: The Making of the Modern Identity*. Cambridge: Cambridge University Press.

Tully, James 1993: Governing Conduct. In J. Tully, *An Approach to Political Philosophy: Locke in Contexts*, Cambridge: Cambridge University Press, pp. 000–0.

Veyne, Paul (ed.) 1987: *A History of Private Life*, Vol. 1: *From Pagan Rome to Byzantium*. Cambridge: Harvard University Press.

Walters, William 1994: The Discovery of Unemployment: New Forms of Social Governance. *Economy and Society*, 23 (3), pp. 000–0.

Weber, Max 1978: *Economy and Society: An Outline of Interpretative Sociology*, edited by Guenther Roth and Clauss Wittich. Berkeley: University of California Press.

Index